CW01496667

ARISTOCRACY AND ITS ENEMIES IN THE AGE OF REVOLUTION

ARISTOCRACY AND ITS ENEMIES IN THE AGE OF REVOLUTION

WILLIAM DOYLE

OXFORD
UNIVERSITY PRESS

OXFORD
UNIVERSITY PRESS

Great Clarendon Street, Oxford OX2 6DP

Oxford University Press is a department of the University of Oxford.
It furthers the University's objective of excellence in research, scholarship,
and education by publishing worldwide in

Oxford New York

Auckland Cape Town Dar es Salaam Hong Kong Karachi
Kuala Lumpur Madrid Melbourne Mexico City Nairobi
New Delhi Shanghai Taipei Toronto

With offices in

Argentina Austria Brazil Chile Czech Republic France Greece
Guatemala Hungary Italy Japan Poland Portugal Singapore
South Korea Switzerland Thailand Turkey Ukraine Vietnam

Oxford is a registered trade mark of Oxford University Press
in the UK and in certain other countries

Published in the United States
by Oxford University Press Inc., New York

British Library Cataloguing in Publication Data

Data available

Library of Congress Cataloging in Publication Data

Doyle, William, 1942–
Aristocracy and its enemies in the age of revolution / by William Doyle.
p. cm.
Includes bibliographical references and index.
ISBN 978–0–19–955985–5 (alk. paper)
1. France—History—Revolution, 1789–1799—Social aspects. 2. Aristocracy (Political
science)—France—History—18th century. 3. Nobility—France—History—18th century.
4. Aristocracy (Political science)—France—Public opinion—History—18th century.
5. Nobility—France—Public opinion—History—18th century. 6. France—Social
conditions—18th century. 7. France—Intellectual life—18th century. 8. Public
opinion—France—History—18th century. I. Title.
DC158.8.D69 2009
944.04—dc22
2008053060

Typeset by Laserwords Private Limited, Chennai, India
Printed in Great Britain
on acid-free paper by
Clays Ltd., St Ives plc

ISBN 978–0–19–955985–5

1 3 5 7 9 10 8 6 4 2

Contents

Preface

The longest chapter in this book is about the Society of the Cincinnati. As originally conceived, nearly forty years ago, it was to have been a book in itself. But there was always something else to do, and as the years slipped by it came to seem like a project that would have to wait until retirement. Then, with retirement still some way off, I was unexpectedly invited to write my 'dream book', and realized that this was the moment. Sabbatical leave was due, and I was fortunate enough to spend some of it at the Institute for Advanced Study in Princeton. There I researched the Cincinnati in depth, and wrote that chapter. I also came to recognize that there was not enough new material to merit a whole book.

The controversy over the Cincinnati, however, was always chiefly significant as an episode in a much bigger story. The challenge to aristocratic rule in the world of Europe and its colonies was a development of world-historical significance, and one seldom seriously studied for its own sake. I decided, therefore, to embed my findings on the Cincinnati in a wider study of the most fundamental part of that challenge. Thus it grew into a book about the attempt of the French revolutionaries to abolish nobility entirely, comprising both its background and its consequences. What happened in America and France does not of course exhaust the subject. The challenge transcended frontiers and resonated in every corner of the European world. But the initial example came from the revolutionaries of America and France, and that is where the main focus of the book lies.

Innumerable friends and colleagues have helped me throughout its long and unpredictable evolution. Initial interest in the Cincinnati was encouraged by the late George C. Rogers, Jr, pre-eminent historian in his day of South Carolina. The suggestion of writing the dream book came from Tony Morris, whose repeated involvement over the years in the history I have written has marked its whole course. The crucial sabbatical was engineered by Ian Wei; and Jonathan Israel and the Institute

Members at Princeton in 2004 proved a rare stimulus. The staff of the Institute Library worked wonders in procuring rare books and documents. Nor could the Cincinnati chapter have been written so easily without access to the magnificent resources of the Firestone Library at Princeton University. Earlier versions of parts of the book were tested by debate in the seminars of David Bell at Johns Hopkins, Don Sutherland at the University of Maryland, Jean-Pierre Poussou at the Sorbonne (Paris IV), the Early Modern seminars at Oxford and at the Institute of Historical Research, London, and the history research seminars at the universities of Bristol and Sussex. Ploughing a parallel furrow, Hamish Scott has also been a never-failing source of ideas, suggestions, and opportunities.

Another project, still hopefully far from completion, passes its fortieth anniversary this year. Over that time, Christine has been my frankest critic and my most unfailing support. Nothing can rob her of the most affectionate dedication yet.

WD
June 2008

Abbreviations

AAE	*Archives des Affaires étrangères*
AmHR	*American Historical Review*
AP	*Archives parlementaires de 1787 à 1860: Série I*, ed. J. Madival and E. Laurent, 90 vols. (Paris 1879-)
Bachaumont	[L.Petit de Bachaumont], *Mémoires secrèts pour servir à l'histoire de la république des lettres en France depuis MDCCLXII jusqu'à nos jours*, 36 vols. (London 1780–9)
Best.	T. Besterman (ed.), *Voltaire's Correspondence and Related Documents, Definitive Edition*, 50 vols., being vols. 85–135 of *Complete Works of Voltaire* (Geneva, Banbury, and Oxford, 1968-)
BL	British Library, London
BN	Bibliothèque Nationale, Paris
GWC	Edgar Ansell Hume (ed.), *General Washington's Correspondence concerning the Society of the Cincinnati* (Baltimore, 1941)
Jefferson Papers	Julian P. Boyd (ed.), *The Papers of Thomas Jefferson* (Princeton, 1950-)
JMH	*Journal of Modern History*
Moniteur	L. Gallois (ed.), *Réimpression de l'Ancien Moniteur*, 29 vols. (Paris, 1840–5)
SVEC	*Studies on Voltaire and the Eighteenth Century*

Introduction

Jean-Baptiste Cloots was a Baron. He liked to call himself Baron of Gnadenthal, or Val-de-Grâce in his preferred language, French. His family had been noble, he claimed, for more than 450 years, and had produced barons for five generations. Most of this was untrue.[1]

Gnadenthal was in Cleves, a tiny German principality bordering on the Dutch Republic. Since 1666 Cleves had been ruled from Berlin by the Hohenzollerns. Cloots's birth there made him a subject of Frederick the Great, King of Prussia; but his family was of Flemish extraction and, until his father bought Gnadenthal in 1748, they had all been merchants in Amsterdam. The richest of them had died unmarried in 1747, leaving his fortune to Jean-Baptiste's father, a great-nephew. He also bequeathed social ambitions.

Although, and perhaps because, the King of Spain no longer ruled Flanders, he had been prepared in 1718 to recognize the Cloots family's claims to old nobility. Five years later, Emperor Charles VI, who also had little to lose from the gesture, and plenty to gain from a new schedule of fees for the grant of titles,[2] awarded one of the family an imperial barony. When the new Baron died childless, the Emperor agreed (doubtless after the payment of further fees) to transfer the title to his elder brother, the benefactor of 1747. But that title died with him, and the acquirer of Gnadenthal had to solicit yet another from Empress Maria Theresia. It was only granted in 1756, a year before the birth of Jean-Baptiste.

---

1. Much of what follows comes from Roland Mortier, *Anacharsis Cloots, ou l'Utopie foudroyée* (Paris, 1995).
2. See Jeroen Duindam, *Vienna and Versailles: The Courts of Europe's Dynastic Rivals, 1550–1780* (Cambridge, 2003), 280.

The education of Jean-Baptiste was chosen to match the status to which his family aspired. Born a Catholic, he was sent first to a Jesuit college in Mons, and subsequently to the Collège du Plessis in the heart of academic Paris. Here he rubbed shoulders with scholarship boys, but also with nobles of authentically ancient lineage, such as Marie Joseph Paul Yves Roch Gilbert du Motier, Marquis de Lafayette. He fell in love with Paris, but as a good Prussian subject completed his education from the age of fifteen with three years at the Military Academy in Berlin, recently founded by Frederick to turn young noblemen into officers.

It did not work for Jean-Baptiste. He enjoyed the academic subjects (taught mostly in French) but he hated the military discipline. At Berlin he seems to have lost whatever religious faith he had had, and on leaving, with ample financial resources since his father's death in 1767, he returned to Gnadenthal to write tracts against revealed religion. He spent much of the 1780s frequenting the salons and lecture-societies of Paris, flaunting his irreligion, vaunting his philosophic Prussian king, and exulting in American independence. And, although he never lost an opportunity to remind his hosts of his noble credentials, the Baron of Val-de-Grâce began to show some signs of unease about how noblemen behaved. Hunting rights, he argued, were the 'passion of ignorant squireens', whose very presence in the countryside, with their gardens and game reserves, brought starvation. The military vocation of noblemen was nothing but a 'gothic prejudice', and it would be better to create a new scale of honours rewarding useful work, whose holders might walk alongside '[those] whose only titles are steeped in human blood'.[3] These remarks appeared in an eclectic collection of essays and opinions which Cloots published in 1785 under the title of *Voeux d'un Gallophile*. Gaul, he declared, was an altogether prouder name than France, which evoked its barbarian conquerors, the Franks, whom French nobles improbably (and as it proved, imprudently) liked to think of as their ancestors.[4]

Cloots' ambition was to settle in Paris, the intellectual capital, as he saw it, of the world; but not before he had made a 'two thousand league journey' across Europe and beyond to see how far the world stood in need of reform. He was far to the south when news arrived of upheavals in France. It brought him hastening back, determined to throw himself into the torrent of change now undammed by revolution in the very centre

---

3. Mortier, *Anacharsis Cloots*, 98.
4. Ibid., 101–2. On the myth of Frankish conquest, see below, pp. 45–6.

of his dreams. He first made his voice heard in March 1790, writing in the newly-founded *Chronique de Paris* and signing himself 'Le Baron de Cloots du Val-de-Grâce'. But by the time of his second article two weeks later his signature was 'Cloots du Val-de-Grâce, Baron in Germany, citizen in France'. His subject was the absurd illusions of nobles who sought to leave regenerated France to settle in America.[5] His own preference, he proclaimed, was to 'renounce my German birthplace and my gothic titles to take up the honourable quality of freeman (*bourgeois*) of Paris'.[6]

But it was not as a Parisian, or even a German, that the dubious Baron stepped onto the world historical stage. That moment came on the evening of 19 June 1790, at the National Assembly.[7] As the first anniversary of the storming of the Bastille approached, the Assembly was debating the most appropriate way of commemorating it. It was announced that a number of deputations were seeking leave to present addresses. The largest was made up, as the official record put it, 'of English, Prussians, Sicilians, Dutch, Russians, Poles, Germans, Swedes, Italians, Spaniards, Brabanters, Liegeois, Avignonese, Swiss, Genevans, Indians, Arabs, Chaldeans, etc'. Several wore colourful costumes, and they were led by the 'orator of the committee of Foreigners, M le Baron de Cloots du Val-de-Grâce, a Prussian'. The fourteenth of July, the orator declared, should not only be a French celebration, but one for the whole human race. The deputation of foreigners, many from lands where despotism still held sway, asked that they might be given a prominent place at the ceremonies being planned, to warn rulers who had usurped the people's sovereignty that the triumph of liberty and the rights of man was at hand. Frequent bursts of applause interrupted this oration. When it ended, the presiding officer of the day, Jacques-François Menou (himself a Baron), gave the Assembly's assent to the request, on condition that when they returned home the foreigners should tell their compatriots what they had seen.

Much scorn was poured on this colourful episode in the days and weeks that followed, and it has echoed ever since in histories of the French Revolution. At worst an absurd pantomime, at best an unfortunate embarrassment, it is chiefly remembered as an extreme example of the Revolution's utopian posturing, and as the debut in politics of one who was later to change his first name to the more memorable and pagan

5. For this so-called 'Scioto scheme', see below, p. 230.
6. Mortier, *Anacharsis Cloots*, 116–7.
7. *Moniteur*, vi, 657–9, 21 June 1790. See also below, pp. 233–6.

Anacharsis, and declare himself the 'Orator of the Human Race'. But Cloots was proud of his performance, particularly in the light of what happened next. Alexandre de Lameth, a noble deputy making a name for himself as a radical reformer, rose to point out that several frontier provinces represented in the Assembly had once been foreign, too, and that prone effigies of them being trampled underfoot by their conqueror Louis XIV could be found close by in the Place des Victoires. He proposed their removal. 'Those monuments of pride', he declared, 'cannot subsist under the reign of equality.' At which Joseph-Marie Lambel, a little-known commoner from a remote province, who had scarcely spoken before, stood up. 'Today', he announced, 'is the graveyard of vanity. I ask that it should be forbidden for any person to assume the qualities of Count, Baron, Marquis, etc.'[8] This intervention triggered an impassioned, if sometimes rambling, debate. Titles, observed Alexandre de Lameth's elder brother, Charles, 'are wounding to the equality which forms the base of our constitution': they were 'puerile distinctions'. Hereditary nobility was contrary to reason and harmful to true liberty. 'There is no political equality, there is no emulation for virtue where citizens have a dignity other than that which is attached to functions entrusted to them, or other glory than that which they owe to their actions.' Titles of nobility should be forbidden. Lafayette, Cloots's old schoolfellow, supported the motion 'with all my heart': it was so necessary, it scarcely needed support, he loftily pronounced. 'Do we', asked his brother-in-law and former comrade-in-arms in America, Viscount de Noailles, 'speak of Marquis Franklin, Count Washington...? These names have no need of qualification to be remembered: they are never spoken without admiration.' Count de Montmorency, from an ancient ducal family, denounced liveries and coats of arms as 'vain ostentations' and 'anti-social distinctions'; while president Le Peletier de Saint-Fargeau, scion of a long line of titled magistrates, proposed that only family names, and not those attached to landed estates, should be used in public. Strikingly, all these proposals came from noblemen. It was true that Guillaume François Charles Goupil de Préfelne, who read out a draft decree of abolition which he said had long been in his mind, sat for the Third Estate of Alençon, but his wife was noble, and he had held ennobling offices.[9] And Isaac René

---

8. The *Moniteur* records no further words, but the next speaker, Charles de Lameth, pledged his support for this and a 'second proposition', which appears to have been the abolition of hereditary nobility. This was certainly the nub of the ensuing debate.
9. Edna Hindie Lemay (ed.), *Dictionnaire des Constituants, 1789–91*, 2 vols. (Paris,1991), i, 418.

Guy Le Chapelier, an influential Third Estate deputy from Brittany who offered another draft, had been in the process of ennoblement when the Revolution had broken out. The only commoners to speak in these rather confused exchanges preferred to address the original question about the statues in the Place des Victoires. Other nobles who intervened, however, were almost inarticulate with fury. These were constitutional principles, some declared, which should only be debated at morning sessions. They were howled down. So were others who tried to dissociate themselves publicly from whatever might be decided. Seemingly they had little doubt about how any votes might go. No sustained defence of noble titles and pretensions was offered by men taken unawares by the drift of the evening. As the debate moved towards closure, with increasing calls for votes, only an Alsatian, Count Landenberg-Wagenbourg, managed to voice a coherent and principled opposition. His noble constituents, he declared, would never authorize him to accept anything contrary to their honour and their rights. He must therefore resign from the Assembly. And although his fellow nobles would doubtless submit to the Assembly's laws, 'they will know that they live with the blood with which they were born, and that nothing can prevent them from living and dying as gentlemen.' Soon afterwards, amid further shouting and posturing, a composite decree was voted.[10] Hereditary nobility, it announced, was abolished for ever. In consequence, titles might no longer be used or granted, nor liveries worn, nor coats of arms displayed. No French citizen might henceforth use other than a 'true family name'.[11]

* * *

Never one to underestimate his own influence, the former Baron Cloots was soon claiming the credit for this outcome.[12] But there was no more unalloyed truth in this than in his previous claims to generations of noble

10. Not in the *Moniteur* of 21 June, but printed in *AP*, xvi, 378 for 19 June.
11. Good secondary accounts of this session in Henri Carré, *La Noblesse de France et l'opinion publique au xviii* siècle* (Paris, 1920), 452–72; Timothy Tackett, *Becoming a Revolutionary: The Deputies of the French National Assembly and the Emergence of a Revolutionary Culture (1789–1790)* (Princeton, NJ, 1996), 292–6; Michael P. Fitzsimmons, *The Night the Old Regime Ended: August 4, 1789, and the French Revolution* (University Park, PA, 2003), 124–8.
12. *Jean-Baptiste Cloots à Charles Stanhope*, dated by Mortier, op. cit., 164, to the summer of 1790, after 14 July on internal evidence, but before the date (July 1791) when Cloots began to call himself Anacharsis.

ancestry. He had clearly not led his 'foreigners' before the Assembly with this result in mind. He was still styling himself Baron as he did so, and the group had left the floor before Lambel made his first proposal. The most that might be said was that, in the words of an American observer,[13] 'the enthusiasm of that night was brought on' by this 'kind of ambassade'. But why did it develop into an attack on nobility, and with nobles taking the lead? Why were the motions so easily carried?

These questions have not attracted much historical attention. The decree of 19 June has usually been dismissed as 'a fairly minor piece of legislation',[14] if it has been mentioned at all.[15] Alongside the political and material losses which nobles had sustained since June 1789, the suppression of titles and their symbols might indeed look like a trivial, not to say gratuitous, afterthought. But most nobles certainly thought otherwise, as the clamour which deluged the Assembly over the next few weeks was to show.[16] The abolition of hereditary titles, observed the same American onlooker, 'seems to have affected many of the Noblesse more deeply than the loss of their property'. Evidently something even more fundamental than wealth and power was at stake.

The issue was one of identity, if not race. Nobles often described themselves as a race, and this description had been used publicly by the king as recently as February.[17] The decree of 19 June was not an attempt to exterminate nobles physically, and even in the Terror there would be no intention of that. Nevertheless in noble eyes, the decree seemed nothing less than an attempt to change biology. To those who supported it, of course, it was no such thing. Its object was to demolish absurd but pernicious myths, a vindication of true biology. Either way, it was much more than a simple tying-up of loose ends. The attempt to destroy nobility was, in fact, one of the most ambitious measures ever undertaken by the French Revolutionaries. To declare hereditary distinctions abolished for ever was to attack an entire system of social identification observed by European

13. William Short to Thomas Jefferson, 25 June 1790, *Jefferson Papers*, xvi, 571.
14. William J. Murray, *The Right-Wing Press in the French Revolution, 1789–92* (Woodbridge, 1986), 105—a quotation chosen for its typicality. An important recent exception, however, is John Shovlin, 'Towards a Reinterpretation of Revolutionary Antinobilism: The Political Economy of Honor in the Old Regime', *JMH*, 72 (2000), 35–66.
15. It does not figure, for instance, in an important and up-to-date recent synthesis, Donald M. G. Sutherland, *The French Revolution and Empire: The Quest for a Civic Order* (Oxford, 2003). Abolition is mentioned in Colin Jones, *The Great Nation: France from Louis XIV to Napoleon* (London, 2002), 441, but only in passing, with no date given.
16. See below, pp. 241–2.   17. See below, p. 226.

elites since the early middle ages or indeed (some claimed) since the days
of ancient Rome. Most parts of Europe had lived for centuries under
the economic, social, and political hegemony of families that considered
themselves noble, flaunted the fact, and believed that this hereditary
quality made them fitter than others to exercise authority and command
deference. Their claims were generally accepted as proper, and true. Efforts
made by ambitious outsiders or newcomers—like the Cloots—to achieve
recognition as noble bear testimony to the prestige of noble values. If
anything, the cultural dominance of these values was intensifying as the
eighteenth century went on. The onslaught on everything noble which
began in 1788 was therefore all the more of a surprise, and 19 June 1790 was
a culmination rather than an afterthought. It was a renunciation of centuries
of history, and accordingly a traumatic shock to members of a recently
unchallengeable elite now labelled *ci-devant*, prehistoric, and incompatible
with a free and equal society.

It happened so suddenly. Or did it? The rule of nobles had never in
fact been entirely uncontested. And the intensification of noble hegemony
over the preceding century was matched by a growing volume of criticism
which even sowed doubts in the minds of those proud to be noble—such
as Baron Cloots. Nobles and their powers were widely perceived as in
need of reform. But most calls for reform sought to strengthen the nobility;
and even voices more hostile had little serious expectation that nobility
and its values might be comprehensively overthrown. In a new world
like the United States it might be possible to prevent a nobility from
appearing; but in old Europe it was far too late for that. And so the nobles
who ruled almost everywhere could happily ignore, brush aside, or even
find entertainment in talk or writings that, however hostile they sounded,
offered no serious threat.

They were fatally wrong. As in so many other spheres, the French
Revolution opened the door to the unthinkable. But the unthinkable,
by definition, was unexplored territory, and it took the revolutionaries
over a decade of turmoil and bloodshed to learn that not everything now
thinkable was doable. They soon discovered, for instance, that no amount
of legislation, no amount of state power, could extirpate religious belief and
practice. This was undoubtedly their most tragic mistake. But, at a moment
when the first blind steps on the road to dechristianization had barely been
taken, the National Assembly undertook something just as impossible in
decreeing the abolition of nobility. Landenberg-Wagenbourg's warning

was right: no legislation could prevent people from believing they were noble, or from passing on that belief to their descendants. All the state could do was deny it public recognition.

This book explores the roots and development of the conviction that nobility could and should be eliminated; and the circumstances in which it triumphed. But since that triumph proved illusory, and nobles were not eliminated, the story cannot end in June 1790. Some discussion is also needed of why and how the experiment failed. The French nobility survived, but its character was transformed by its revolutionary travails, and the state's disengagement from its affairs paradoxically set the nobility free for the first time in centuries. How nobles used that freedom would do much to determine their reputation among subsequent generations. Nor did the French state persist long in turning its back on nobility and its trappings. In 1808 the most successful of all *ci-devants*, Napoleon, created an entirely new titled hierarchy to serve his own purposes.[18] He tried to add to its lustre by incorporating men of pre-revolutionary rank, but he gave no renewed recognition to the status and titles abolished in 1790. The restored Bourbons did that; but in the Charter issued by Louis XVIII on his return, holders of Napoleonic titles, though barely six years old, were also recognized as a legitimate nobility. Neither sort of noble, on the other hand, was to enjoy any of the tangible privileges and distinctions which had marked out French nobles before 1789. Nor would post-Restoration rules and practices of recruitment, transmission, and even nomenclature, be at all the same as their pre-revolutionary counterparts. Although it had proved impossible to abolish nobility, the rulers of France had no difficulty, after the Revolution as before, in manipulating the structure of the nobility for their own purposes. If, as many nobles liked to think, nobility stood for timeless values, then perhaps its most insidious enemies were monarchs who claimed to be its friends and protectors. If, that is, as noble behaviour in the face of Revolution perhaps suggests, their most fatal enemies of all were not themselves.

18. See below, pp. 319–325.

I

Aristocracy Ascendant

The World of Eighteenth-Century Nobility

The trappings of nobility were everywhere. Every grand portal was surmounted by a crested coat of arms, while roofs and towers would be capped with proudly badged weather vanes. No private coach was complete without the arms of its owner, and coachmen usually wore their masters' livery. So did domestic servants. People with claims to nobility, or who wished to pass for nobles, also took pains to dress differently. Men carried swords, and if they held military decorations or other honours, always wore their ribbons and insignia in public. Red heels, fashionable under Louis XIV, became a synonym for courtiers. Except in times of royal mourning—observed only by those who identified with the Court, and therefore in itself a sign of pretension—nobles affected more colourful or lavishly trimmed garments. So did women, whose answer to sword-bearing was to bare more bosom than was thought modest in other ranks of society. 'The word *nobility*', reflected Montesquieu, the most influential political writer of the century, who prized his own barony, 'carries distinction with it.'[1] Everything nobles did served to accentuate, consciously or just instinctively, their distinction from the mass of other people.

In public they claimed precedence over anybody not manifestly above them in nobility's inner hierarchy. When they died they expected burial inside, not outside, their parish churches, and their grieving posterity set up monuments with wordy tributes to their virtues and (once again) their coats of arms. Even the names of 'people of condition' were different. In formal documents, noblemen always qualified themselves as Esquire (*écuyer*). Those who possessed titles invariably used them rather than their

---

1. *Mes Pensées*, 631 in *Oeuvres complètes* (Paris, 1964), 947.

family names,[2] but most French nobles were untitled. All sought, however, to be lords of manors, and then they invariably went under the names of their leading lordship, using the particle—the prefix *de*—before it. This was the most universally recognized sign of noble status. It was also the easiest to usurp. A carefully placed *de* or even apostrophe could make an ordinary name sound like a lordship (as in d'Anton or de Robespierre, both usages well attested in these future enemies of aristocracy) or permit the addition of a supposed lordship to an otherwise undistinguished patronymic (as in Goupil de Préfelne, Brissot de Warville, or Théroigne de Méricourt). Serious usurpation, however, would demand more. It required a lifestyle: 'living nobly' on landed revenues, no obvious work, and certainly no trade. In former times, that had been enough, over several generations, to allow a family to slip gradually into nobility by 'aggregation'. But in the 1660s, Louis XIV had launched widespread searches for false nobles. Documentary proof was required either of a specific act of ennoblement since the year 1560, or of public recognition of a family's nobility before that date. Hundreds of families who could produce proof of neither had seen their claims thrown out, with attendant shame and degradation. Such inquisitions ended in the 1720s, but tax collectors still required proof of noble status before granting the fiscal privileges and exemptions to which nobles were entitled. As the century went on, 'proofs' were increasingly required for the enjoyment of other benefits restricted to nobles—such as membership of elite regiments, orders, courts, chapters, monasteries, and schools. Professional genealogists made an increasingly good living, knowing full well that they were not employed to find flaws in their clients' pedigrees. But for access to the best places their concoctions still had to pass the pitiless and incorruptible scrutiny of the king's *juge d'armes*, or his genealogist, Chérin—the latter not even a nobleman himself, but among the most feared officials in the kingdom.[3]

* * *

Not all institutions required the same level of proof. Exclusivism was measured by generations, or 'degrees'; as was family prestige itself. A

---

2. The Baron de Montesquieu's family name was Secondat.
3. Louis Nicolas Hyacinthe Chérin (1762–1799) succeeded his father Bernard Chérin (d. 1785) as genealogist of the King's Orders in 1787. See below, pp. 246–7.

hereditary distinction, the very essence of nobility, was pride in ancestry. The further back an authentic line could be traced, the greater the
grounds for self-esteem among its scions. Proudest of all was immemorial
nobility, where the first traceable ancestor could be shown already to
be of gentle birth. The presumption then was that the family had always been noble. In 1759 it was stipulated that the 'Honours of the
Court', allowing presentation to the king and the right to hunt with
him, might only be granted to families with nobility traceable at least to
1400. By 1790, 462 families of stainless 'race' or 'extraction' had qualified. Their members liked to think of themselves as the only true nobles,
often citing the supposed remark of Francis I that he could create as
many noblemen as he liked, but never a gentleman (*gentilhomme*). Anyone else must have had ancestors who were demonstrably *roturiers*, not
noble. At some point the king had ennobled one of them. But all the
descendants of that person could never by these standards be more than
anoblis.

Few outside the ranks of immemorial nobles shared this extreme view-
point. After all, even around 150 of the families qualifying for the Honours
of the Court went back to a known ancestor ennobled before 1400,
while some families of technically immemorial lineage only became traceable from much later. Above all, however, *anoblis* thus defined made
up the vast majority of nobles in France. Most noble families owed
their status to a specific act of ennoblement at some moment since the
sixteenth century. It was then that kings had begun to sell public offices on a large scale, increasing their attraction by endowing them with
privileges. The most covetable privilege of all, which automatically conferred others, was nobility itself; and ennoblement by buying an office
had already become, by 1600, the classic way of entering the nobility.
Kings took care never to create too many ennobling offices. Nor did
many such offices ennoble instantaneously: most required two successive generations of twenty-year service to 'complete' a family's arrival.
At any given moment, the credentials of hundreds of upwardly-mobile
families would still be incomplete. At any moment, too, many ennobling
offices would be held by men already noble, and not therefore available
to gratify the social ambitions of newcomers. Nevertheless, that still left
nearly 3,000 offices (by the eighteenth century) whose most important
function was recognized as the ennoblement of their holders and their

families.[4] The trade in these offices ensured that between eight and ten thousand men entered the nobility between the last years of Louis XIV and the Revolution, bringing their wives and families with them. That meant that the equivalent of two commoners per day joined the French nobility over the eighteenth century, making it by far the most open in Europe. Long lineages were quite the exception. Most did not reach even as far back as the sixteenth century, and for well over a quarter of the order in 1789, the moment of ennoblement was still within living memory.

No wonder nobles of old stock felt superior. But they also felt threatened. If nobility could simply be bought, what sort of true distinction was it? Even before the end of the sixteenth century, as venality proliferated, anxieties of this sort began to be voiced, particularly among nobles whose own wealth could not match that of newcomers. Older nobles might exult in Louis XIV's drive to eliminate usurpers, but this did nothing to limit legitimate ennoblements by office purchase. During the later wars of his reign, the Sun King even sold nobility and titles directly, without any link to offices. Over the subsequent century prices for offices which ennobled most quickly, such as those of King's Secretary which required only twenty years' performance of perfunctory duties to secure the coveted hereditary status, soared to unprecedented levels. Much favoured by newly wealthy businessmen or financiers, they were universally derided as 'soap for scum' (*savonettes à vilains*), arousing the added suspicion that money made so quickly could scarcely have been made honestly. To command respect, nobility needed time: time to acquire ancestors, time to make a mark in the king's service, time to make marriage alliances with other families of distinction, time to find lands and lordships to pass down the generations, time above all to make others forget or overlook low-born ancestors. If immemorial ancestry was too much to ask of most, several degrees or generations at least could be demanded of candidates seeking admission to institutions reserved for nobles. 'No man would dispute', wrote a leading genealogist on the eve of a revolution that was to bring

---

4. The total number of ennobling offices under Louis XVI was 4,224, but over a quarter of these were normally filled by noblemen who had not needed them to acquire the status. For those already noble, indeed, these were the only sort of offices deemed appropriate. See William Doyle, *Venality: The Sale of Offices in Eighteenth-Century France* (Oxford, 1996), 79–81.

ruin to his profession, 'that today all ranks are confused; that honourable entitlements once accorded only to Gentlemen of ancient extraction, and as a reward for outstanding service, have been usurped, in the most scandalous way, by persons whose nobility is, if not quite equivocal, at least quite new'.[5] His solution was to require more rigorous proofs of nobility for entry to the most prestigious institutions. Yet this process had been going on throughout the century. The number of places reserved for nobles, mostly in schools and religious communities, rose between 1750 and 1789 by 58 per cent. Over the same period 41 per cent of them extended the number of generations of proof demanded.[6] The so-called 'Ségur ordinance' of 1781 stipulated that all candidates seeking to become army officers must prove at least four degrees or generations of nobility. Reversing a principle that since 1750 had conferred ennoblement on any officer not already noble, the Ségur ordinance marked the high point of a restrictive movement driven by the fear that impoverished nobles of old stock would be swamped by a tide of rich newcomers who valued nobility not for any traditional qualities but merely for the material advantages that the status conferred.

* * *

Nobody doubted that the tangible rewards were substantial. A noble was part of a separate order in society: the Second Estate of the realm, after the clergy. All members of the nobility enjoyed certain common privileges. They were exempt from the *taille*, the basic direct tax—except in certain provinces where it fell on land deemed noble rather than persons. They paid the capitation, a poll tax introduced in 1695, on a separate and more favourable basis from the king's other subjects. They paid no duty on the purchase of fiefs, lands held in feudal tenure. They were exempt from a variety of other burdens such as the salt monopoly (*gabelle*), forced labour on the roads (*corvée*), and the billeting of soldiers. They had the right to take their lawsuits to special chambers of the sovereign courts (*droit de committimus*), could not be subjected to corporal punishment, and, if convicted of a capital offence, were beheaded rather

5. Antoine Maugard, *Remarques sur la noblesse* (2nd edn., Paris, 1788), 3.
6. Benoît Defauconprêt, *Les Preuves de noblesse au xviiie siècle* (Paris, 1999), 47, 56.

than hanged. None of these privileges, except the last, was a noble monopoly. The network of privileges extended far beyond the noble order, and touched any part of society which the crown had found able and willing to pay for special treatment of one sort or another. But, with the exception of the clergy, no group, as a group, enjoyed such an accumulation of privilege; and it was enhanced by visible entitlements such as sword-bearing and the right to special crested coats of arms. In 1789, a privilege not exercised since 1614 would be restored: the right to participate in person in the election of noble representatives to the Estates-General, where the noble order would sit in a separate house. In this sense, the ambit of noble privilege was widening down to the very revolution that was to sweep it away; and the overthrow of this most recently revived privilege would pave the way for the destruction of all the rest.[7]

That would include privileges not strictly inherent in nobility, but which no self-respecting nobleman felt complete without: the privileges of feudal lordship. The medieval, chivalric associations of a fief lent unique authenticity to noble pretensions. A fief often brought a title, invariably the right to a particle, and entitled the holder to style himself in legal documents 'High and mighty lord'. It brought the private jurisdiction of a manorial court, dealing with a wide range of petty offences. So-called 'high' jurisdiction allowed a lord to erect gallows—although capital punishment had long been a royal monopoly. Most of the business of these private courts concerned infringements of a lord's rights and prerogatives. The latter included a monopoly of hunting, shooting and trapping; and the concomitant right to breed game for sport or even, as with pigeons, for display. Often lords also enjoyed 'banalities'—service monopolies in milling, baking, fruit-pressing, or marketing. Above all, they levied dues from all owners of land within the lordship. Feudal dues were infinitely variable. They might be payable in cash, kind, labour, or any combinations. They might be lucrative or nominal, or fall unevenly on different types of land, produce, or transaction. But because they were unearned, they were an essential ornament to lordly status, and fief-holders took care to keep the terriers in which they were recorded up to date. This was the point at which the majority of the kingdom's inhabitants who were peasants confronted the

7. See below, pp. 201–2.

domination and demands of nobles. Whether in the person of thread-bare but predatory squireens often likened to falcons (*hobereaux*), or the agents of richer but equally demanding absentees, as huntsmen rampa-ging through unfenced fields, or breeders of untouchable vermin, nobles made constant and inexorable claims on the time, patience, produce, and income of their 'vassals'—lesser landowners within their manorial jurisdictions.

The market in lordships was as brisk as that for ennobling offices. It was better to possess several than one; it was better still to be a titled lord—the owner of a barony or a marquisate. It was essential, however, once a prestigious fief was acquired, to keep it and its appurtenances in the family down the generations, as part of its ever-lengthening heritage. Titles were indivisible, and passed on to eldest sons; but otherwise there was no primogeniture in France. There was no uniform law of succession either. Property was passed on according to several hundred distinct provincial or local customs, all differing in detail. All had rules of their own, too, governing the transmission of fiefs and other property deemed noble. Yet the basic rule was that all children were entitled to a share of parental estates. It was possible, at considerable expense, to entail fiefs in the senior male line (*substitution*). Younger siblings might also be given prior claim on non-feudal patrimony. Even so, eldest sons, titled or not, could normally expect no more than the largest share of whatever parents left. The rest would be divided among all the other children of both sexes. The effect was to erode estates almost as soon as they were built up; but also to ensure that the market for land and lordships remained brisker than in countries where primogeniture, entail, or a combination of both sacrificed the claims of younger children to the stewardship of the eldest.[8]

Although nobles held lordship over most of the land in France, no more than a quarter was actually owned by them. Proportions might vary spectacularly from area to area, and many nobles owned less than richer peasants. But the largest private estates were invariably in noble hands, often including vast stretches of forest set aside for hunting. And thanks to feudal rights, noble lords received income and services from far more land than they owned. All this, peasants could see with their eyes and feel in their pockets. Less obvious, perhaps, was the fact that

---

8. Compare England: H. J. Habbakuk, *Marriage, Debt, and the Estates System: English Landowner-ship, 1650–1950* (Oxford, 1994).

much of the income of the church, deriving from perhaps one sixth of the kingdom's landed property,[9] extensive feudal revenue beyond, not to mention impropriated tithes diverted from the upkeep of the parish clergy, helped to keep the younger scions of noble houses in the relative comfort of exclusive chapters, convents, and monasteries. For whereas eldest sons would hope to compensate for the ravages of partible inheritance by finding wives with substantial dowries, the prospects for other noble children were altogether bleaker. The larger the family, the smaller their residual shares. It cost substantial sums to become an army officer or sovereign court magistrate—the only lay occupations compatible with their rank. But even a life of clerical celibacy in a respectable chapter or monastery required influence as well as proven ancestors. Daughters without adequate dowries, meanwhile, were unmarriageable; and as often as not, even nunneries expected dowries from would-be brides of Christ. Yet for children who all inherited parental nobility, there were few other occupations which did not imperil the prized status itself.

Families were well aware of these inexorable trends, and there is clear evidence that they sought to blunt their impact by limiting their own size. Over the eighteenth century the numbers in noble families fell steadily. Marriages were contracted later than in the population at large, and increasing numbers of younger sons never married at all. Fewer children were conceived, and childbearing often ended well before the onset of natural infertility. These strategies certainly served to limit the erosion of family fortunes by division between heirs, but they increased the risk that lineages might die out altogether. From the 1660s onwards, in fact, the French nobility was no longer replacing itself naturally, and overall numbers fell from 234,000 in 1700 to perhaps 140,000 in 1789. In a kingdom of rising population, nobles constituted a shrinking proportion; and one which might have shrivelled away even faster without the recruitment of perhaps 40,000 individuals over the century through venal ennoblement.[10] But the

---

9. Bernard Bodinier and Eric Teyssier, *L'événement le plus important de la Révolution: La vente des biens nationaux* (Paris, 2000), 333.

10. For diminishing noble numbers and the reasons, Michel Nassiet, 'Un chantier en cours: les effectifs de la noblesse en France et leur évolution du xvie au xviiie siècle', and Stéphane Minvielle, 'Les comportements démographiques de la noblesse française de la fin du xviie siècle à la Révolution française: une tentative de synthèse' in Jarosław Dumanowski and Michel Figeac (eds.), *Noblesse française et noblesse polonaise: Mémoire, identité, culture, xvie—xxe siècles* (Bordeaux, 2006), 19–43, 327–56. For venal recruitment, Doyle, *Venality*, 165.

concentration of so much wealth, power, and privilege in the hands of a diminishing elite, noisily seeking wherever possible to tighten its monopoly on these advantages, was a prospect scarcely calculated to spare the feelings of those with no hope of ever joining it.

It was not only inappropriate, but positively illegal for nobles to engage in retail trade, embrace base professions, farm for rent, or generally work with their hands—except to plough a small stretch of their own land or (bizarrely) to make glass. The penalty for such demeaning activities was *dérogeance*, derogation or loss of nobility. Wholesale trade had long been permitted, and there was no bar to nobles speculating in land, urban real estate, or stocks, or exploiting the mineral resources of their lands on an industrial scale. But the frequency with which royal edicts and declarations renewed the freedom to trade wholesale (the last time in 1765) was evidence of how reluctant most nobles remained to risk their reputation in any sort of trade. The principle of *dérogeance* was underpinned by deep and persistent anti-commercial prejudices. Only in Brittany was it easy to get round it. Impoverished Breton nobles could 'put their nobility to sleep' until they had restored their fortunes through trade. The father of Chateaubriand, whose gloomy, lineage-obsessed lifestyle in the crumbling castle at Combourg was memorably evoked in the son's posthumous memoirs, had done this. His nobility was immemorial, and his sons received the Honours of the Court, but he had bought Combourg in 1761 on the profits of trading out of Saint-Malo, and then, resuming a noble lifestyle, neglected it with studied care. Most poor nobles did not enjoy the luxury of such a choice. Prevented from 'regilding their arms' by fear of derogation, yet barred by penury from careers compatible with their status, they could find comfort only in the ancestry attested in their 'parchments'. Chrétien Guillaume de Lamoignon de Malesherbes, magistrate and twice a minister of Louis XVI, saw that 'Contempt is poverty's portion, and... the crime of being poor can be made up neither by birth nor by merit... a man of condition in reasonably comfortable circumstances in the world is treated very differently by the great than a man with nothing. But I say that a completely poor nobleman is not as well treated by them as a total commoner who is rich... the respect accorded to wealth is so real that everything else is nothing by comparison.'[11]

---

11. Pierre Grosclaude (ed.), *Malesherbes et son temps: Nouveaux documents inédits* (Paris, 1964), 47–51, Malesherbes to Comte de Sarsfield, 28 Nov. [1766].

Victor de Riqueti, Marquis de Mirabeau, was an improving landlord who devoted much of his life to championing the virtues of provincial nobles. But 'Without money', he admitted in 1756,[12] 'honour is nothing but a sickness.' Thanks to him, and a number of other mid-century writers,[13] the problems of the poor nobility became an increasing preoccupation of royal policy-makers.

* * *

Honour: it was the guiding principle of noble conduct, constantly on their lips, always invoked to legitimize what a noble should or should not do. Yet it was hard to define objectively. The ever-thoughtful Montesquieu believed that it was the guiding spirit of all monarchies, yet recognized that it was nothing more than a prejudice. Its nature was a constant search for distinction, and it was no mean principle that could 'oblige men to undertake all manner of difficult acts, needing determination, with no other reward than the fame of these actions'.[14] The other side of it was that nobody felt obliged to obey an order or even a law at variance with what they conceived to be their honour. 'Honour has its own laws and rules, and cannot bend … it depends on its own caprice, and not that of another.'[15] It was 'less what one owes to others, than what one owes to oneself … not so much what draws us to our fellow-citizens, as what marks us off from them'.[16]

Honour dictated respect for one's own rank: hence the horror of *dérogeance*, and avoidance of offices and appointments unworthy of one's dignity. Honour also underpinned the idea of misalliance, unequal marriage. Noblewomen especially shrank from matches with social inferiors, although impecunious gentlemen might justify marrying low-born heiresses with the thought that their money would pay for a lifestyle which they believed a distinguished ancestry demanded of them. It might be called 'restoring the fields with muck', but it was too common at every level in the nobility to be considered totally dishonourable. And as long as these sneers were not heard in public, the stigma could be borne. Public affronts to honour were another matter. Nothing short of a humiliating apology could expunge

---

12. *L'Ami des Hommes*, 3 vols. (1762 edn.), i, 123.   13. See below, pp. 53–5.
14. *De l'Esprit des Lois*, iii, chs. 6, 7.   15. Ibid., ch. 8.   16. Ibid., iv, ch. 2.

them. Otherwise any man of honour would demand the satisfaction of a duel.

Duelling was the ultimate noble conceit. 'France' wrote Count Alexandre de Tilly, who grew up at the Court of Louis XVI, 'is the homeland of duels ... nowhere else have I met with that fateful *susceptibility*, that sad disposition to believe oneself insulted ... nowhere else do they say: "honour is everything, there is nothing else in the world".'[17] Personal resolution of affairs of honour offered the chance to flaunt fighting skills, universally deemed inherent in true nobility. It demonstrated the courage without which these skills were meaningless. Duelling also showed indifference to law itself: the law of God, which forbade the taking of life, one's own as much as another's, and the king's laws, which ever since the sixteenth century had repeatedly banned the practice. Every king even swore at his coronation not to pardon any convicted duellist. After all, as well as setting a bad example of lawlessness, deaths in duels regularly deprived the kingdom of army officers, among whom the practice was most common. But the prestige of drawing the sword in matters of honour was such that even magistrates were known to flout this law. And, after declining somewhat under Louis XV, duelling became fashionable again under his grandson, with pretexts for fighting becoming increasingly trivial. In 1778 the Duke de Bourbon, a prince of the blood royal, fought with the king's brother, the Count d'Artois, to avenge a few curt phrases addressed to his wife. All royal attempts at mediation failed, although neither protagonist died. And the king's acceptance of a simple apology from his brother was scarcely calculated to discourage lesser nobles from defying his authority and his laws.

More than changes in fashion may have lain behind the reviving taste for duelling. It also made nobles feel equal. Honour was a quality which they all shared and were all committed to defending. Single combat notionally pitted like against like, and whereas any noble could refuse a challenge from a commoner, to claim rank within the nobility offered no honourable escape. Increasing numbers of colonels found themselves challenged to defend, out of uniform, indignities to which their subordinates fancied they had been subjected to in the field or the barracks. The obligations of a common code of honour fostered the illusion of equality between

17. Christian Melchior-Bonnet (ed.), *Mémoires du Comte Alexandre de Tilly* (Paris, 1986), 156–7.

gentlemen at a time when it was increasingly obvious that nothing of the sort existed.

* * *

Inequality was built into the very idea of nobility. It was by definition a social order hereditarily superior to all others. But nobility had always had clear inner hierarchies. At the head of them all came the monarch, 'first gentleman of his kingdom', inheriting his crown by feudal rules, displaying his authority by visual finery, military pomp, the royal arms everywhere, his preferred pleasure hunting the stag in his own specially reserved forests. Around him hovered his close relatives, the 'Princes of the Blood', all in line for the throne, however distantly, if royal fertility should fail. Then came the Peers of France, all of whom, apart from a handful of prelates, held the title of Duke. Dukes and Peers (for there were also a number of non-peer dukes) were generally recognized as the summit of society outside the blood royal. In 1788 their numbers, which under Louis XIV had approached fifty, were down to thirty-four laymen; and although they had no collective power and no distinctive privileges apart from the right to sit in or be judged by the Parlement of Paris, their social prestige was unchallenged. The ducal title, unlike all others, could not be bought or sold with the fief to which it was attached, and the descending hierarchy of lower titles—Marquis, Count, Viscount, Baron, Knight (*chevalier*)—meant little compared with the length of their holders' lineages. It was the latter which determined access to the Honours of the Court and the growing number of exclusive institutions. No existing ducal title, by contrast, went back beyond the sixteenth century, and many of their holders could not boast immemorial nobility. Most had reached this eminence by generations of royal service or favour, and all sustained it by great wealth. The king would not think of creating a ducal peerage without the certainty that the candidate could sustain his new dignity with appropriate revenues. Existing ducal peers, whose ambitions or improvidence had strained their resources, instinctively looked to the king to maintain their pretensions with pensions and sinecures. And these could only be obtained by assiduous attendance at Court, the centre of all significant power and patronage.

Court was where the king lived. Lavish and spectacular, it was designed to enshrine and reflect royal power and glory. Inseparable from the person of the monarch, the whole apparatus of the Court moved wherever he did. If, for most of the time since the 1680s, its main seat had been the sprawling palace of Versailles, several times a year the Court would follow the king to fresh hunting grounds at the other vast royal residences such as Fontainebleau or Compiègne around the Ile de France. Courtiers would not hesitate to follow, since proximity to the king was the purpose of their lives. It signified honour and distinction in itself, of course, for not everyone had the lineage to aspire to the Honours of the Court. But most of those who had such credentials, like Chateaubriand, could not dream of remaining courtiers after the fleeting moment of glory of their presentation. To live at Court simply cost too much for most noble pockets. Court was, above all, the ostentatious playground of a plutocratic elite. Not all of its members were of ancient stock: many families only enjoyed the Honours through dispensations of one sort or another from the strictest genealogical proofs. Their real entitlement to residence at Court was that they could afford its relentless round of display, attendance, largesse, and luxurious living. This narrow circle of perhaps 200 families lacked the official standing of the peerage, but, comprehending as it did most of the ducal families, it was perhaps a more substantive category in material terms. A long French tradition described its members collectively as grandees, *les grands*.

Possessed already of impressive accumulations of riches, patronage and power, *les grands* spent much of their time looking for more. By relentless lobbying of ministers, royal mistresses (under Louis XV), the queen (under Louis XVI), and sometimes even the king in person, they sought to capture for themselves, their relatives and their dependents the most lucrative Court offices, military commands, and ecclesiastical benefices in the royal gift. Assiduous soliciting could double already impressive incomes from the revenues of sinecures, pensions, and 'gratifications', and courtiers regarded such opportunities as their right. But it was almost impossible to be too rich at Court. All but the very wealthiest soon found that they needed whatever they could inveigle out of the king in order to maintain a lifestyle which demanded a residence and much fashionable expenditure in Paris as well as Versailles. Such insatiable needs also kept great families constantly alert to the marriage market. While the preference was always for wives of equal rank, the essential attribute was an ample dowry, and these were often to be found among the daughters of a different elite, the world of metropolitan 'Finance'. Scarcely more numerous than dukes, the great financiers whose credit kept the government afloat as receivers-general, farmers-general of taxes, or treasurers of major departments were almost all noble, even if that was usually thanks to the relatively recent purchase of an ennobling office. But the base extraction of financiers was completely eclipsed in the eyes of courtiers by the dowries they could provide for their daughters. Few *grands* were without a near ancestress whose ambitious father had paid lavishly to integrate her into the world of the Court; and if ancestry had been measured (as in Germany) by quarterings, rather than degrees of male descent, many of the most glittering pedigrees in the kingdom would have looked less immaculate. The moneyed summit of the nobility was therefore a constantly renewed blend of the oldest families and some of the newest. The ability of the moneyed interest to penetrate the genealogical defences of the Court was vividly symbolized when Mme Jeanne-Antoinette d'Etiolles, *née* Poisson, daughter and wife of Parisian financiers, and soon to acquire the title of Marquise de Pompadour, found her way in 1745 into the king's bed as Louis XV's official mistress.

Financiers themselves, essential though they were to the functioning of the king's government, could never hope for personal recognition at Court. Nor could their sons. The most they could aspire to for male offspring not destined to follow them into Finance was to buy them judicial office in a sovereign court, and to integrate them thereby into the nobility of the robe. Although for generations most of the king's ministers and closest advisers had been drawn from families which had risen through the venal magistracy, 'robins' did not normally appear at Court. Many senior magistrates, in the parlements at least, had lineages as distinguished as those of courtiers, and sometimes wealth to match. If the money was right, Parisian legal families often intermarried with courtiers. Nevertheless all magistrates were conventionally presumed to owe their nobility to venal office, and were consequently deemed inferior in rank. They for their part sniffed at the fawning snobbery of Versailles, knowing that the every-day government of the kingdom was in the hands of men like themselves, and that most ministers and senior administrators had begun their careers, however fleetingly, in the capital's parlement. But even within the 'Robe' there was a clear sense of hierarchy. Parlements outranked Courts of Aids or Chambers of Accounts, Parisian ones outshone those of great provincial capitals. Malesherbes, son of a chancellor and prime president of the Paris Court of Aids, noted that Montesquieu, a president in the Parlement of Bordeaux, 'was a man of condition, known as such in his province, but very little at Court or in Paris, where the quality of president impresses less than birth...the contradictions which he met with on this when he became known in the capital only served to irritate the desire he had to be fully recognized for what he was'. That explained, Malesherbes thought, all Montesquieu's theories about the importance of nobility.[18] But Montesquieu wrote for fame beyond his province. Most magistrates in provincial sovereign courts were content to bask in membership of what they liked to call their 'senates', knowing that their social primacy at this level was unchallenged, and had been ever since Louis XIV drained the provinces of greater families to dance attendance on him at Court. Several provincial parlements chose to emphasize their local primacy later in the century by formally excluding non-nobles from acquiring their ennobling offices—although few commoners now ever dreamed of storming these heights. For these provincial oligarchs, Paris and the Court were distant, almost fabulous worlds and, perhaps for that reason alone, always suspect, their doings largely known through second-hand gossip and scandal sheets.

All magistrates knew, besides, that their profession cut them off from other nobles, of whatever rank. When the idea of a distinct nobility of the robe first emerged around the turn of the seventeenth century, its effect was to cast all nobles of the more traditional type as a nobility of the sword (*épée*). And although a majority of noblemen probably never saw military service, the profession of arms remained the classic noble career. Even judicial dynasts, passing their offices in the parlements down the generations, sought to place younger sons as army officers. Military service evoked chivalric origins. It might be rewarded by membership of orders of chivalry. It was true that the kingdom's highest order, that of the Holy Spirit, was largely confined to courtiers of distinguished lineage and great officers of the crown. Limited to a hundred members, its blue riband became a synonym for all that was most exclusive. But the red riband of the order of Saint-Louis, created in 1693, was a reward within the reach of all serving officers, unlimited in numbers, and was earned exclusively by long service or distinction on the battlefield. Part of its appeal was that it rewarded merit alone. Everything else in the army was the result of a combination of wealth and influence. All officer ranks (and no noble would dream of serving in any other) below staff level had to be bought, although not in an open market. Colonelcies and other senior positions

---

18. Malesherbes to Sarsfield, 28 Nov. 1766 in Grosclaude, *Malesherbes et son temps...nouveaux documents,* 55. For the theories, see below, pp. 46–50.

were conferred by the king's personal decision, and therefore subject to the full range of Court solicitation. Accordingly the divide between *grands* and other nobles ran right through the army. Young courtiers might enter the service as subalterns, but they expected express promotion to command regiments in their twenties. Provincials without influence or 'protection' would languish in lower or middling ranks for the whole of their careers—assuming that they could find the money to buy a rank in the first place. At least in the navy there was no venality: navigational skill was beyond purchase. Nor did the seafaring life have the glamorous appeal, opportunity for show, and generous leave provisions of the army. It was a service for younger sons. Even so, senior naval officers tended to have attended exclusive and semi-hereditary schools (*Compagnies des Gardes de la Marine*), ensuring that even at sea there were two distinct classes of officers.

In mid-century the lack of proper training for army officers began to preoccupy the government. A military school was founded in 1751, and after the disasters of the Seven Years' War twelve provincial feeder schools were established. They were explicitly destined for the sons of officers and poor nobles, and proofs of four generations were required for entry. This was where the young Napoleon Bonaparte, from relatively poor but immemorially noble Corsican stock, received his military education on a royal scholarship. The requirement of proofs showed that the aim was not simply to improve the military preparedness of officers. It was to give preference to families which saw the army as their only true vocation, and thereby to reinforce their warrior traditions down the generations. The same trend in military thinking produced the Ségur law of 1781. By that time, too, military purchase was being phased out in the interests of professionalization. But, as the case of the navy showed, a socially exclusive service where officer recruitment and promotion did not depend on money still brought no guarantees that talent or merit would triumph. Rigorous proofs might well thwart the ambitions of the recently ennobled rich to enhance their new status with military credentials, but courtiers still expected fast-track promotion and monopoly of the highest commands. The Marquis de Ségur himself recognized that these expectations had to be accommodated, and in the late 1780s he elaborated plans to formalize the division while allowing the king more discretion to favour those with talent as well as long pedigrees. When these plans were finally adopted in 1788, however, they caused outrage. Courtiers saw increased royal discretion as an infringement of their traditional expectations, while other nobles resented being consigned explicitly to an inferior status behind what the regulations incautiously called the 'first' or 'upper' nobility, with no hope of rising to the top either by merit or length of service.[19]

Not that such hopes would ever have been realistic: what rankled was having their futility spelt out. Most nobles knew full well that they lived within narrow horizons which only undreamed-of wealth could widen. Their sincere dreams of serving the king were limited by lack of money, leaving their swords rusting over the fireplace rather than gracing a well-oiled officer's scabbard. And yet, like the *grands* of Versailles, they despised the self-styled 'senators' of the robe whose fathers or grandfathers were well remembered in the folklore of every locality as having bought their way to power and prominence. Men whose meagre resources did not match the pretensions justified by ancient lineage felt humiliated by the airs of this upstart 'robinocracy' who judged their lawsuits, bought up the best fiefs, and even tried (until prevented in 1781) to slip their sons into the army itself and so join the nobility of the sword. Perhaps half the nobility of the kingdom, living in straitened circumstances, was prey to such resentments and suspicions, clinging to ancestral pride because they had very little else to feed their self-esteem. Measures taken, largely under Louis XVI, to relieve their distress by setting aside college places, church benefices, and access to the officer corps in the army were intended to turn their pride into a source of commitment to state service by rescuing them from enforced idleness dictated by their birth. But the complaints of provincial nobles in 1789, when the convocation of the Estates-General provided the chance to voice them in the *cahiers* drawn up by electoral assemblies for the guidance of deputies, show that few of the desired effects had yet been felt.

Meanwhile all those excluded by these measures were given grounds of their own for resentment. The newly ennobled, the target of most of the exclusion, found their money had been wasted. And commoners, to whom no thought at all had been given when the exclusions were framed, were reminded that nobody without nobility counted for anything in France. 'By means of the ease with which nobility may be acquired

19. See Rafe Blaufarb, *The French Army, 1750–1820: Careers, Talent, Merit* (Manchester, 2002), ch. 1.

for money', wrote Turgot, Comptroller-general of the royal finances, to a fellow minister in 1776, 'there is no rich man who does not promptly become noble; so that the body of nobles takes in the entire body of the rich and the cause of the privileged is no longer the cause of distinguished families against commoners, but the cause of the rich against the poor.'[20] As complete outsiders, commoners scarcely understood how limited were the advantages conferred by nobility without the underpinning of wealth. Nor could they comprehend how corrosive were the inequalities within the noble order, the mutual mistrust of court and country, of sword and robe, of old stock and new, of rich and (relatively) poor. All they could see was that everybody who held any sort of public authority also enjoyed the status and privileges of nobility; and that little social esteem was enjoyed by anybody without them.

* * *

Nobles ran the king's government, and no king imagined that it might or should be any other way. Self-segregated among their courtiers, kings seldom met anybody who was not noble, apart from their valets, grooms, and huntsmen. They chose their ministers from among men they knew. Louis XIV made it a principle, and with his successors it became an instinct, to bestow nothing on anybody whom they did not know by sight. Accordingly the first concern of all courtiers was to be seen by the king. 'If they speak to you', noted the Marquis de Bombelles in his journal in 1782, 'that is called...being well treated; and when they say nothing to you or do not look at you, that is called wasting your time.'[21] Ministerial life was precarious. The most elevated servant of the crown could be dismissed at the royal whim, which usually entailed 'disgrace' and internal exile. But while in favour ministers would be showered with honours, the riband of the Holy Spirit, titles, and emoluments. Even in disgrace, they often drew substantial pensions. And they in turn used their time in power to secure patronage for their relatives, dependents, clients,

---

20. Turgot to Miromesnil, in G. Schelle (ed.), *Oeuvres de Turgot et documents le concernant*, 5 vols. (Paris, 1913–23), v, 188.
21. G. Clam-Martinic (ed.), *Marquis de Bombelles: Journal*, 4 vols. (Geneva, 1978-), i, 138, 13 Aug. 1782.

and members of pressure groups who had helped them to power. All of these would be nobles, too. Louis XIV had also made it a principle never to appoint ministers rich or powerful enough in their own right to be independent of his authority. He preferred noble families of recent extraction to dukes, peers, and scions of other great clans. The same applied to the intendants who exercised the plenitude of royal authority in the provinces. Military commands, however, remained in the hands of the cream of the sword nobility—princes and dukes—and all now took positive pride in their dependence. It was a matter of the highest distinction to serve the king, and for ancestors to have done so. Pedigrees were enhanced by the record of positions held in royal service, and deeds performed there. On the other hand, for most men in the king's service dependence was not total. The vast majority held offices, or a rank which they had paid for. Office-holders were tenured, and could only be deprived by death, resignation, forfeiture, or outright suppression. But suppression was impossible without reimbursement, and since the early seventeenth century a small annual tax (*annuel*) had exempted payers from loss on death. So offices were, in effect, hereditary and indestructible property, and the ultimate sanction of dismissal was largely beyond the king's power. Even intendants, holding revocable commissions, retained tenure in the office of Master of Requests which they normally held concurrently. Tenure therefore enabled some of the king's noble servants to defy or at least resist his will. Over the eighteenth century the parlements relied on it to buttress their increasingly vocal resistance to royal religious and fiscal policies, confident that the king was in no position to buy them out. These conflicts, and the public exchanges which they produced between the king and his judiciary, did much to educate the public in constitutional issues, and brought out implicit claims on the part of the robe nobility to an unprecedented share in the legislative process. Here was another reason for sword nobles to dislike them, even if from the outside the magistrates might appear to be spokesmen for the entire nobility and, as such, the heart of that intermediary power between ruler and ruled which Montesquieu had identified as essential to a monarchy. But in any case the limits of their judicial independence were vividly revealed in 1771, when Chancellor Maupeou dissolved the parlements and found a means of reimbursing their offices. Despite a huge outcry, only the death of Louis XV three and a half years later brought the abandonment of this experiment. The parlements and their powers were almost fully restored by Louis XVI, but the memory of Maupeou haunted his reign, and the parlements showed little unity of purpose until the final crisis of absolute monarchy in 1787–8. As Louis XIV had shown, and Louis XV too in the last years of his reign, a resolute king had nothing to fear from a magistracy which owed its entire prominence, social as much as political, to buying a share of delegated royal authority. Never united among themselves, the nobles of the robe elaborated no distinct ideology of institutional power to challenge that of their master and creator, much less a rationale for the independent authority of the nobility as a whole.

Awareness of their ultimate powerlessness, however, led increasing numbers of magistrates to dream after mid-century of a new structure of provincial power—or rather the generalization of an old one. Over perhaps a quarter of the kingdom, the monarch shared power, rather than delegated it, with Estates. Estates were representative bodies whose main function was to agree to taxation in provinces where the king had not acquired the power to impose it directly. Most *pays d'états* were small, but great provinces like Brittany, Languedoc, and Burgundy had retained this vestige of autonomy in return for raising cheaper loans on the king's behalf. No two sets of Estates were composed in the same way, but most guaranteed representation to nobles, often in a separate house. In Brittany, every noble might sit; in Burgundy, all fief-holders; elsewhere, those possessed of specific baronies, and so on. Few robe nobles sat in Estates, and in some, representation was explicitly confined to men of the sword. And usually voting was by order, allowing the body of nobles to dictate or impede any business transacted. Provincial Estates were thus the only institutions of government, apart from a handful of municipalities, to guarantee a role for nobles as nobles. But the use they made of this prerogative scarcely inspired confidence. Eating, drinking, and demagogic posturing were the hallmarks of noble behaviour in the biennial meetings of the Breton Estates, while in Burgundy only a small and diminishing number of fief-holders turned up. Vast amounts of time were spent everywhere refining and restricting admission criteria, with the same trend as in other institutions towards ever-more demanding proofs. Frustrated magistrates, largely excluded though they were from surviving Estates, might envisage their revival, in provinces where they had disappeared, as a more formidable check on governmental excesses than the parlements. Ministers knew better. They became increasingly convinced that well-designed representative institutions could expedite rather than impede the work of government. From 1778 they began to introduce provincial assemblies of property owners with tax-raising powers. Nobles were guaranteed a quarter of the seats in these assemblies, the clergy another quarter; but they did not sit in separate chambers, and voting by head ensured that the Third Estate, with half the seats, would command an effective majority. Too many sectors of noble opinion were offended by this experiment. The parlements learned that ministers saw the assemblies as vehicles for marginalizing the political role of the magistracy. Other nobles saw vote by head and deliberation in common as reducing noble representation to a powerless sham. Still others thought property a novel and dangerous basis for representation, undermining traditional distinctions of status. Attempts to generalize the assemblies in 1787 were in any case soon engulfed by the pre-revolutionary political crisis.

That crisis would bring nobles of all sorts into active political life. The Assembly of Notables with which it began in February 1787 was made up entirely of noblemen, even if some sat as prelates. They showed an unpredictable unanimity in resisting the reform proposals of the king and his ministers, and nobles throughout the kingdom rallied behind the parlements in continuing the resistance after the Assembly was dissolved. When Maupeou-like measures were taken in May 1788 to circumvent the courts, there was a generalized 'noble revolt' throughout the kingdom, in which unauthorized assemblies drafted petitions of protest and officers talked of disobeying orders. Louis XVI was deeply shocked by what he saw as the disloyalty of an order he thought he could rely on. Their mutinous gestures certainly helped to thwart these final attempts to salvage absolute monarchy, and precipitate the convocation of the Estates-General. That in turn opened up a whole new prospect. The traditional organization of the Estates General gave the Second Estate a separate, elected chamber, a guaranteed voice for the nobility as a whole in national affairs for the first time in almost two centuries. It was hardly surprising that they should fight so bitterly to hang on to this promise over the spring and summer of 1789.

Scarcely less surprising was the confidence with which the nobility initially embraced this opportunity. They saw themselves as the natural leaders of the

French nation. Not only was their social pre-eminence guaranteed by law, and constantly reinforced by the obvious desire of all the richest members of the Third Estate to buy into their ranks. They also enjoyed a cultural hegemony which made any effective challenge to their position seem inconceivable. Although they claimed to embody traditional values, with their respect for ancestry, family tradition, and divinely ordained hierarchies in church and state, nobles were also the leaders of fashion—ostentatious consumers who set the tone and style for everybody with disposable income, the main promoters of that 'luxury' which alarmed moralists and steadily undermined all sorts of traditional behaviour. The cultural life of pre-revolutionary France and its artistic production are remembered for their unequalled polish and sophistication. Much of this resulted from the patronage and involvement of members of the nobility; and if the culture of consumption was penetrating more deeply into society than ever before, often this diffusion took the form of aping tastes and behaviour pioneered by nobles.

Nobles led the great rebuilding taking place in the major cities of the kingdom from mid-century onwards. Smart Paris expanded westwards, both north and south of the river, and nobles set a trend to live upwind in spacious new *hôtels*, lavishly decorated. The land they were built on had often been sold off speculatively by other nobles fortunate enough to possess suburban estates. Similar expansion took place in prosperous provincial cities such as Bordeaux and Lyon, and many families showed little reluctance to abandon dark ancestral piles in stinking city centres for airier elegance, sometimes with gardens, in the latest style. They filled their new residences with appropriate furniture and ornaments, whose manufacture gave employment to thousands of craftsmen. They commissioned portraits of themselves to grace their drawing rooms, exhibiting them first at artistic *salons* where they crowded out other types of picture, to the despair of aesthetes.

Equally, noble tastes dominated the theatre. Nobles monopolized the best seats, and paid prices without which many theatres would have collapsed. The theatre was a place to be seen as much as to be entertained, and theatricals in which they acted themselves were a favourite pastime among courtiers and in great houses. But even when they were not acting, the portrayals they wanted to see were of characters with whom they could identify; and accordingly most successful plays were about people of high birth. The sublimities of tragedy could only be conveyed, it was thought, in exalted language that only exalted people used. And wit, the soul of comedy, was presumed to be beyond characters of low education and habits. It was true that, as the century went on, increasing numbers of playwrights experimented with what they called 'dramas' which purported to depict the everyday problems of ordinary people, but this trend remained controversial, and its successes were uneven. More popular in the provinces and on peripheral metropolitan stages less frequented by nobles, dramas were often denounced by leading critics as boring and unworthy of the great privileged companies of players. Their runs at the French or Italian comedies tended to be short, as the aristocratic patrons who kept theatrical finances afloat stayed away.

Theatrical tastes owed much to education. All nobles were steeped in the classics from earliest youth, and many had taken regular part in school plays on classical themes. The best education was very expensive, and disproportionate numbers of noblemen whose parents could afford it went to a handful of colleges in or around Paris. At the Jesuit colleges of Clermont or Harcourt, or the Oratorian college of Juilly, sons of courtiers mingled with future magistrates and children of financiers and other rising professional men. Most provincial capitals harboured Jesuit colleges where elites of more local ambition followed the same basic classical curriculum. And although the expulsion of the Jesuits in the 1760s opened the way to wider variety in education, the weight of tradition served to stifle radical innovations in successor schools. In any case, only a minority of nobles could afford to educate their sons in such colleges, and the military academies established in the 1770s, expressly designed to cater for poorer ones, never provided remotely enough subsidized places. Noble women were even less well provided for. Daughters of great or rich families or heiresses deemed likely to find husbands among *les grands* would be sent to exclusive convents where they would receive instruction appropriate for the circles to which they were destined. They emerged far more polished and cultivated than many noble men. Most noble daughters, however, if sent out to school at all, imbibed little more than piety and domestic arts from the provincial nuns to whom they were entrusted. Levels of education, therefore, closely reflecting those of wealth, were yet another source of division within the nobility, and largely determined how far its members engaged with the advanced culture of the century.

Noble writers were relatively few, although their numbers grew after mid-century. But if they accounted for only 14 per cent of published authors under Louis XVI, well over a third of authors of importance were drawn from the nobility. Hardly any of the latter represented the world of the Court or *les grands*, and spokesmen for provincial landlords like the Marquis de Mirabeau, were almost as rare. Exceptional scientific talent could emerge from anywhere: *anoblis* like the naturalist Buffon or the chemist Lavoisier, or old sword stock such as the mathematician Condorcet. Most important noble authors, however, came from the nobility of the robe, where writing and argument were professional requisites. The best known was undoubtedly Montesquieu, who made his name in 1721 with the social satire of the *Persian Letters*, and laid out the parameters for half a century of political theorizing with *The Spirit of the Laws* in 1748. After giving up his presidential office in Bordeaux and devoting himself to letters full-time he was elected to the forty-man French Academy, the summit of literary success. But there he, and subsequent newcomers like the *anobli* Voltaire, found plenty of great lords with few or even no literary accomplishments, a fitting symbol of the way birth could always usurp places notionally reserved for talent.

Without noblemen, on the other hand, most of the provincial academies which proliferated over the century might not have come into being at all. Urban phenomena, they owed their foundation to learned local notables with the influence to persuade the crown to charter them; and that meant men who enjoyed nobility, relatively recent though it might be. Membership of an academy lent additional social cachet, both because of what it said about one's interests and means of pursuing them, and because of who the other members were. This was enough to make learned and leisured non-nobles seek membership, and over the century they came slightly to outnumber their social superiors. The latter, however, played the dominant role in organizing the readings, concerts, and above all the essay competitions by which the provincial academies had their main impact on cultural life.

Academies were a world of men. Scarcely half a dozen women secured election to them over the entire century—and all were noble. Their role, however, cannot have been more than peripheral compared with that of the *salonnières,* intellectual hostesses in whose rooms writers and men of cultivation met to discuss the latest ideas and artistic productions of the day. They too, were not numerous, although to the eight great *salons* which flourished in Paris over the century could be added a number of similar gatherings in the greater provincial cities. Their role is hard to measure but impossible to deny in promoting new ideas, sampling and tasting the latest writings, facilitating literary contacts, and forging links between high thinkers and high society. And most of their hostesses were noble women, using their status to give currency to what was discussed by inviting influential people to participate and recount what they had heard to a wider fashionable world. *Salons* were inconceivable without this context. They would have no function to perform if *les grands* and the values which emanated from them had not dominated cultural life. Writers and artists needed noble patronage, as well as whatever intrinsic merit their work had, if they were to have any hope of making a significant public impact. Even Jean-Jacques Rousseau, who spurned the implied condescension of such contacts, drifted in and out of their embrace, and died in 1778 as the rent-free trophy tenant of a Marquis.

Yet persons of condition who accepted invitations to *salons* were also conceding a sort of equality to the non-noble intellectuals they met there. They did not come simply to inspect the work of mere craftsmen. In another context, indeed, many nobles were prepared to see themselves as craftsmen—symbolically at least—as they flocked to join masonic lodges. French freemansonry was largely the creation of nobles, courtiers intrigued by the mysteries dangled before them by Jacobite exiles from Scotland. It offered the attractions of robes (or at least aprons), rituals, secrets, and exclusivism—all second nature to noblemen—combined with the autonomy denied them by the jealous suspicions of absolute monarchy. The spread of freemasonry over the middle decades of the century was perhaps the last triumph of the Court as the originator of fashion. And although the explosive growth of the movement in later decades was driven by commoners anxious to share in the 'secret', at least 3,000 nobles were known to have joined lodges, and the two great networks which took shape in the 1770s were headed by princes and courtiers. A fundamental tenet of freemasonry was the equality of all brother masons; but each lodge had an inner hierarchy, and there were different levels or degrees of masonic initiation. In lodges where nobles and commoners mingled, nobles tended to win easier if not automatic election to offices of honour. In cities where several lodges existed, hierarchies of prestige soon emerged, and nobles tended to concentrate in certain lodges and avoid others. Masonic equality was thus relative, if not largely notional. Joining a lodge was just another fashionable thing to do, another way, even, of flaunting social superiority. Nevertheless, for nobles to commit themselves in such numbers to a movement that was autonomous, elective, and overtly egalitarian seemed at variance with some of the most fundamental principles of nobility. It would come in retrospect, when masonic plotting was blamed for the Revolution, to seem like reckless blindness to their own best interests. It might equally be interpreted as a sign of loss of faith in traditional values. Or perhaps it demonstrated a complete (if misplaced) confidence that nothing could shake the dominance which nobles enjoyed in most spheres of national life.

✻ ✻ ✻

It was a confidence only reinforced by the knowledge that a similar dominance was found almost everywhere else in Europe. Every nobility had its own individual characteristics, and there were wide disparities in their privileges and powers. The French nobility enjoyed no collective political power like the Polish *Szlachta*, who even elected the king. French peers had no House of Lords as their British counterparts did, and the nobility as a whole had no representative house in a functioning legislature, as it did in Sweden. French nobles owned hardly any serfs, unlike those of much of Germany and nearly all of Eastern Europe. Nor were their great estates kept together down the generations by primogeniture and/or entail, as they were in Great Britain, Spain, much of Italy, or southern Germany. Unlike most other nobilities, they measured their ancestry by degrees, not quarterings; and, thanks to the unique institution of ennobling venal offices, their ranks were open to moneyed outsiders as nowhere else.

Taken together, such differences gave the nobility of France a distinctive character. Even so they scarcely outweighed all that it had in common with other nobilities. The conviction that all nobles were fundamentally equal was widespread, yet everywhere the different quality of nobility was measured by ancestors and alliances. Everywhere status was displayed by armorial bearings, liveries, and sword-bearing. Lordship of land was the quintessential source of noble incomes, hunting—that training-ground for mounted warfare—the classic pastime. Not all nobles spurned trade, but most preferred, if they felt the need for an occupation at all beyond the idle glory of 'living nobly', to serve their king. The eighteenth century gave them unprecedented opportunities for doing so. The proliferation of standing armies created a need for professional officers: the Prussian model of a nobility committed to the army as an escape from impoverished idleness was widely influential after the mid-century victories of Frederick the Great. The administrative structures required to underpin the ambitions of such states also offered expanding scope for noble energies. As in France, therefore, the public life of almost every European state was conducted and managed by nobles in ways which they could all instinctively recognize and feel entitled to share. Only in a few—Poland, Sweden, Great Britain, Württemberg—did they wield their power collectively through parliamentary institutions. But everywhere the individual levers of power were worked by hands unscarred by toil, unstained by commerce, but ornamented by gold signet rings.

Over the century the richer nobility became increasingly cosmopolitan. Noble credentials from one country were readily accepted in others—some said too readily, so that the easiest way to usurp the status was to assume it abroad. Ease of passage between countries was helped by knowledge and use of the French language. Its acceptance throughout European polite society was one of the more enduring triumphs of Louis XIV's determined promotion of his kingdom's power and prestige. 'French authors', wrote Frederick the Great, 'have made their language universal; it has replaced Latin: it is the language of scholars, of politicians, of courtiers, of women, and in a word is understood everywhere ... at present anyone who knows French can travel all over Europe without needing an interpreter.'[22] And those who spoke the language of France so readily were naturally particularly interested in what went on there. Paris was as much their cultural capital as that of the French themselves. French language gazettes, usually published outside the kingdom but well supplied with authentic copy, kept them amply informed. Crowned heads and a handful of magnates also subscribed to the *Correspondance littéraire*, a fortnightly gossip sheet privately distributed from Paris by the German entrepreneur Frédéric Melchior Grimm. (Eventually it won him ennoblement as an imperial Baron—whereupon he abandoned literary journalism for diplomacy.) The doings of the French Court also riveted the nobility of the rest of Europe. They had their own Courts, but they knew them mostly to be conscious imitations of the archetype established by Louis XIV and still functioning at Versailles. Their interest in what went on there was insatiable. When, in

22. Quoted in Louis Réau, *L'Europe française au siècle des lumières* (Paris, 1951), 22–3.

1776, Turgot fell spectacularly from power, a courtier-priest at Versailles was struck by the level of interest abroad. 'Paris', he reflected, 'is still the capital through the curiosity which our events inspire throughout Europe. Our pamphlets, our legal briefs, our internal quarrels, our political discussions are followed with interest. I do not see Parisian circles having the same interest in the daily events of Vienna, Petersburg, Naples and Stockholm ... '.[23]

Such onlookers learned little, and probably had no great desire to learn, about France and its nobility beyond Paris and Versailles. So when they thought of their French counterparts they thought of red-heeled spendthrift courtiers, intrigue around the throne for patronage and pensions, luxurious metropolitan lifestyles, reckless gambling, and sexual licence. The unglamorous world of the provinces scarcely figured, except as an object of ridicule. Nor were such distant observers really aware of the jealousies and antagonisms which robbed the French nobility of any inner unity. The nobility they saw, and felt a sympathetic identity with, was a glittering façade, more fragile than anybody knew. Its high profile made it an easy target for critics, but its unity was largely the invention of those who would later bring it down.

23. Jehan de Witte (ed.), *Journal de l'Abbé de Véri*, 2 vols. (Paris, 1933), i, 462, 16 June 1776.

2

Ideologies of Inequality

F ew nobles felt the need to define nobility. Their hereditary superiority was self-evident from their ancestry, or would become so in
their posterity. But, if called upon to rationalize their identity, they could
invoke a range of explanations and justifications: mystical, historical, functional—often a blend of all three. Some were very old, and rooted in
Christian and chivalric tradition. Others were much more recent, elaborated in response to perceived challenges. All would prove vulnerable to
rational criticism in the eighteenth century.

* * *

Fundamental, in a Christian society, was divine sanction for the social
hierarchy. God had ordained that in human affairs some should be set in
authority over others. Some were made to command, most to obey. And,
as in the divine order itself, authority passed down from father to son.
Rulers and their sycophants in the pulpit were fond of quoting St Paul
(Romans, xiii, 1–2): 'The powers that be are ordained of God. Whosoever
therefore resisteth the power resisteth the ordinance of God: and they that
resist shall receive unto themselves damnation.' The injunction could be
extended from political to social authority, and fashionable preachers were
as willing to tell *les grands*, as much as kings, what they wanted to hear. 'It is
not accident', proclaimed Jean Baptiste Massillon, Bishop of Clermont and
author of much-reprinted sermons, 'that has caused you to be born great
and powerful. God, from the beginning of time, has destined this temporal
glory for you, marked with the seal of his splendour, and separated from

the crowd by the lustre of titles and human honours.'[1] He was echoing the even more anthologized Bishop of Meaux, Jacques-Bénigne Bossuet, who proclaimed to a Court audience in 1683 that 'I do not need to tell you that it is God who grants great birth, great marriages, children, posterity... God has prepared in his eternal counsel the great families which are the fount of nations.'[2]

At parish level, priests in their weekly homilies to the faithful laid regular emphasis on the overwhelming duty of obedience to whoever enjoyed legitimate authority. Legitimacy was compromised, however—though never negated—if those whom God had raised up failed to fulfil the duties incumbent on their station. Those born to greatness were constantly reminded from the pulpit and in the confessional that their position in the world brought obligations. Nobility, their priests warned, meant setting a Christian example of virtuous behaviour, respecting the sacraments, dispensing charity, and eschewing the sin of pride to which nobles were especially prone. No evidence suggests that a majority of the nobility were not routine observers of the requirements of piety, and of course men of noble birth controlled the ecclesiastical hierarchy and monopolized all its best benefices. No wonder they accepted that superiority of extraction like theirs was the will of God. But the flagrant debauchery and extravagance of Court life, the luxury in which all nobles of means lived, the vanity which obliged them to do so, and the disdain they showed for the majority of their fellow Christians, reflected poorly on God's choice of instruments. Some of them, like the philosophic Baron d'Holbach, devoted much of their lives to promoting atheism—although always in the privacy of his own house or through writing anonymously. God's sanction for noble pretensions could also be cast into doubt by the open contempt for moral conventions of certain notorious figures, such as the Marquis de Sade, who spent the years from 1778 to 1790 imprisoned without trial, as a threat to women in general, at the request of his wife's family. Or there was the Count de Mirabeau, younger son of the physiocratic Marquis, who was also imprisoned at his father's request to terminate sexual scandal, and

---

1. Quoted in Bernard Groethuysen, *The Bourgeois: Catholicism vs Capitalism in Eighteenth Century France* (1927; Eng. trans., New York, 1968), 132.
2. 'Oraison funèbre de Marie-Thérèse d'Autriche, Infante d'Espagne, reine de France et de Navarre', 1683, in R. Doumic (ed.), *J. -B. Bossuet, Oraisons funèbres* (Paris, no date), 87–8.

who in 1784 would launch the first overt attack on the very principle of nobility.[3]

* * *

However much the failings of individual nobles might cast doubt on their order's part in the divine plan, claims to God's sanction for noble pre-eminence rested on more than biblical authority and priestly precept. All of recorded history seemed to show that the multitude was destined to be ruled by a superior minority. 'There have been *nobles* in all nations', declared that great compendium of eighteenth-century knowledge, the *Encyclopédie*, in 1765, '…there is scarcely a well-ordered nation which has not had some idea of nobility'.[4] The first example it offered was from Deuteronomy. Others were drawn from ancient Greece, Mexico, Peru, Japan, and modern Europe. But by far the lengthiest discussion was of the various forms of nobility in ancient Rome.[5]

They would have been instantly familiar to a readership which had learnt Latin at school largely through the medium of Roman history. The very word 'noble' was Roman in origin. It described people 'known' for distinguished ancestry and entitled to display portraits of great forebears. The most obvious Roman parallel with later nobilities, however, was the patrician order, a hereditary caste said to be descended from the original counsellors chosen by Romulus when he founded the city. Patricians had originally monopolized all the offices of state, and the long-term decline of the republic could be perceived in terms of advances made by inferior plebeians at their expense. Yet the patricians were always disproportionately well represented in public affairs, and long dominated the leading deliberative body in the state, the Senate. The Senate was not a hereditary body, being made up in principle of former magistrates, but those who achieved membership without a background of previous

3. See below, pp. 122–8.
4. Vol. xi, 165, 167. The two articles from which these quotations come were by the jurist Antoine-Gaspard Boucher d'Argis (1708–91), ennobled in 1753 by office in the Parlement of Dombes.
5. See Renato Galliani, *Rousseau, le luxe et l'idéologie nobiliaire: Etude socio-historique SVEC* 268 (Oxford, 1989), ch. 8.

office-holding in their families were forever stigmatized as newcomers, *novi homines*. That included members of a secondary hereditary group, better known to history for their wealth than their skills in mounted warfare, but called the equestrian order. If Caesar, who finally brought about the destruction of the republic, was a patrician, Cicero, who strove to preserve it, was an equestrian. The writings of both were staples of classical education. Cicero's dream was that the traditional order of things might yet be saved by joint action of the various elites—patricians, senators, equestrians—who together by this time had come to be known (in opposition to demagogic *populares*) as *optimates*, the best people. It was the implicit lament of most of the Roman historians who told this story that they had failed to unite. But from Livy, Plutarch, and Cicero himself (all providing texts regularly studied in colleges where nobles were educated) students could learn what the qualities that made the best people were. These writers praised sobriety, courage, honour, respect for these values in ancestors, and above all, virtue—that commitment to the common good without which no collectively ruled state, no republic, could flourish.

The notion of *optimates* undoubtedly derived, in the mind of the well-educated Cicero, from a Greek rather than a Roman concept: aristocracy. But the Greek idea of aristocracy did not, except implicitly, connote a group of people. Aristocracy originally meant a form of government. It was government by the best people. In the classic formulation of Aristotle,[6] governmental types were threefold: the one, the few, and the many. All three had good or bad forms. Aristocracy was the good form of government by the few. The bad form was oligarchy. Accordingly, nobles tended to see themselves as the sort of people who ruled in aristocracies. They did not like to think of themselves as vulgar oligarchs, without moral legitimacy. In practical everyday terms, however, the distinction was hard to draw. In the eighteenth century the two words tended to be used interchangeably to mean government by a self-perpetuating few, whether good or bad. *Oligarchy*, in fact, came to be used less and less; and when observers sought to characterize any government where power was vested in a minority, they usually called it an aristocracy. By the 1770s the word was also beginning to be used to describe the social group exercising such power, though seldom with approval. A decade later, first in the Dutch patriot movement, then among French revolutionaries, the word *aristocrat* was coined.[7] It began as

6. *Politics*, iii, 6–7; iv, 7.   7. See below, pp. 157–8.

political abuse, but like many such descriptions, it was soon embraced by the abused as a badge of honour. Already in October 1789, Catherine the Great was informing the departing French ambassador that whatever he did back in Paris, she would remain an aristocrat: 'that is what I do'.[8]

* * *

What nobles did, or were presumed to do, was the basis of yet another frequently cited rationale for their powers and privileges. A medieval tradition divided the community into those who prayed (the clergy), those who fought (the nobility), and those who worked (everybody else). These were the three Estates of the medieval realm.[9] The classification was accurate enough with respect to the First and Third Estates, but it seems unlikely that there had ever been a time when all nobles performed military service. By the sixteenth century, with the first great surge of venal ennoblement, the idea of the nobility as an exclusive caste of warriors was already manifestly absurd.[10] Many, perhaps most, renaissance noblemen certainly still saw warfare as their destiny, but too many other functions now conferred the privileges of nobility, even if less than full peer-recognition.

Paradoxically these non-military functions and privileges helped to perpetuate commitment to a separate noble order. The market value to the crown of selling membership of such a group, and of blackmailing those desperate to retain and pass on its advantages, made it unthinkable to diminish its mythical status in any way. The myth of a functional order dedicated to defending the kingdom was also treasured by authentic chivalric families (or those who thought they were) as a yardstick with which to impugn the credentials of newcomers. And it had more severely practical implications. The most widely recognized criterion of French nobility was exemption from the *taille*, the basic direct tax. The original justification for this exemption was that nobles already paid the 'blood tax'. Contributing to the defence of the realm with their persons, they should not be expected to contribute from their pockets as well. Every nobleman

8. Comte de Ségur, *Mémoires ou souvenirs et anecdotes*, 3 vols. (Paris, 1826), iii, 531: 'moi je resterai aristocrate, c'est mon métier'.
9. See Georges Duby, *The Three Orders: Feudal Society Imagined* (Chicago, IL, 1980).
10. Ellery Schalk, *From Valor to Pedigree: Ideas of Nobility in France in the Sixteenth and Seventeenth Centuries* (Princeton, NJ, 1986).

who became an army officer in centuries long after the disappearance
of chivalry could invoke this justification of his order's most treasured
privilege, emphasizing his own social utility as he did so. But how it
justified the exemption of that majority of the noble order who never
served the king in arms was far from self-evident.

A majority of the noble order found themselves similarly excluded in
practice from a variant often added to the argument from function: nobles
served the king with their advice. The king had always been expected
to take counsel before reaching any important decision, and nobles saw
themselves as the most appropriate people to give it. Non-noble ministers
or counsellors were seen as a grotesque and dangerous aberration, and
kings acknowledged as much by invariably ennobling the rare examples,
or by promoting any who were lowly placed in the noble hierarchy. And,
whereas great nobles of the Renaissance disdained the routine drudgery of
ministerial office, they believed that the king should consult them regularly.
At times of royal minorities, princes and other great officers of the crown and
Court felt entitled to share the responsibility of government with whoever
was regent of the kingdom. Ignoring such expectations could result in open
revolt.[11] Louis XIV brought those days masterfully to an end. The honour of
serving him, he made clear, was nobody's birthright—although in practice
he never dreamed of delegating his authority to any but noblemen. And
the limitations of granting *les grands* a say in everyday government were
highlighted under the Regency which followed his death by the short-lived
fiasco of multi-conciliar rule, the so-called Polysynody. After that it was left
to the parlements, with their right of remonstrance, to maintain the claim
to proffer advice—but they did so as jurists rather than as the nobles they
incidentally were. And there was an obvious objection both to judicial and
conciliar arguments that nobles were the monarch's natural advisors. The
vast majority of nobles lived outside the institutions or networks where
such counsel might be found, and never had the opportunity to advise their
king. They were understandably ambivalent about the claims of privileged
minorities to the exercise of these functions.

But nobles at large never forgot that there was one forum where
their collective say in the affairs of the kingdom was guaranteed, even
though it had lain dormant since 1614. The noble order, along with the

---

11. See Arlette Jouanna, *Le devoir de révolte: la noblesse française et la gestation de l'Etat moderne,
    1559–1661* (Paris, 1989).

clergy and the Third Estate, was entitled to separate representation in the Estates-General of the kingdom. In 1614, indeed, noble representatives had been drawn exclusively from men of the sword: ennobled magistrates had sat with the Third Estate. It was an ambiguous precedent, which might have proved contentious if the Estates had actually met on any of the three occasions when convocation was contemplated over the subsequent century. But nobles were confident enough of their entitlement to separate representation and voting in the Estates to lead calls for their convocation at moments of crisis or emergency. They saw the Estates-General as a natural vehicle for their own aspirations, and expected to play the leading role when they met. In no other circumstances could they appear more obviously to be part of the very constitution of the kingdom. Nowhere would their hegemony be more apparent. It was an assumption that they took fatefully for granted in 1789.

The medieval functionalist view of society was carried to its greatest elaboration in the early seventeenth century by Charles Loyseau, a minor office-holder (and not a noble) whose *Treatise of Orders and Plain Dignities* (1610) declared orders to be the work of nature herself. Defining order or estate as 'dignity with aptitude for public power', Loyseau declared that 'nobility is an order which ... gives to him who is noble an aptitude for many fine offices and lordships assigned to nobles ... office follows order and is conferred on him who is of the order to which it is assigned'.[12] As the author of other vast treatises on lordships and on offices, Loyseau remained well known, to jurists at least, throughout the two centuries after he wrote, and he was cited with approval as late as 1776 by the Parlement of Paris in its remonstrances against commutation of forced labour on the roads (*corvée*) into a universal tax.[13] The magistrates' argument was that since nobody exempt from the *taille* was subject to the *corvée*, the nobility should not pay the new tax. But they generalized their argument into a defence of all social gradation. 'To establish an equality of duties between men, and to destroy those distinctions necessary in a well-ordered monarchy, would soon lead to disorder (the inevitable result of absolute equality). The result would be the overthrow of civil society, the harmony of which is maintained only by the hierarchy of powers, authorities, pre-eminences, and distinctions

---

12. Howell A. Lloyd (ed.), *A Treatise of Orders and Plain Dignities* (Cambridge, 1994), 9.
13. English text in Keith Michael Baker (ed.), *The Old Regime and the French Revolution* (Chicago, IL, 1987), 119–22.

which keeps each man in his place and protects all Estates from confusion.' Loyseau had said so. The magistrates also reminded the king that the social order had its origin in divine law, that it was not formed by chance, and that time could not change it. And they appealed directly to the medieval past in asserting that 'the personal service of the clergy is to fulfil all the functions related to education and religious observance and to contribute to the relief of the unfortunate through its alms. The noble dedicates his blood to the defence of the state and assists the sovereign with his counsel. The last class of the nation, which cannot render such distinguished service to the state, fulfils its obligation through taxes, industry and physical labour.' It was ironic that these judicial defenders of the nobleman's military vocation, noble to a man, should be regarded still by many army officers as not true nobles at all.

✳ ✳ ✳

If anything, Loyseau devoted more of his treatise on orders to discussion of ancient Rome than of France. Rome, on the other hand, had ruled the territories that were to become France for close on half a millennium, so the histories of the two were intertwined. Indeed, the story of how Gaul had become France produced one of the most influential explanations of the origins of noble power, and one which everybody who sought to justify nobility in historical terms had to confront. This was the idea that nobles were descended from the warlike Franks who had overrun Gaul under their leader Clovis as the western empire collapsed, subjugating the supine and romanized Gauls. The descendants of the Franks were therefore racially superior, and enjoyed their privileges and prerogatives by ultimate right of conquest.

Similar ideas were to be found, perhaps with more justification, among the nobilities of eastern Europe. Hungarian nobles claimed descent from conquering Magyars, the Polish *Szhlacta* from fabulous 'Sarmatians', and both used the exploits of these supposed heroic ancestors to justify their monopoly of political rights and exemption from taxation in their re-spective countries. Conquest was the basis of their 'golden' freedoms, and a vindication of the serfdom to which their peasants were subjected. It was an ideology directed as much against the power of kings as towards the subjugation of the rest of society; and the French version of it first became influential when royal authority seemed incapable of maintaining order in the kingdom in the sixteenth century.[14] It was reinvigorated in the form best known to the eighteenth century in reaction to the domestication of the greater nobility by Louis XIV. Its most notorious advocate was Count Henri de Boulainvilliers (1658–1722), not himself a great nobleman, but indisputably of old stock.[15] Boulainvilliers believed, unoriginally enough, that the only true nobility was immemorial, and that it went back to 'a sort of aristocracy' of Frankish conquerors whose credentials were older than the monarchy and owed nothing to the action of kings. Renowned for his antiquarian knowledge, he was recruited by disaffected *grands* who dreamed of a share in political authority when the Sun King's reign was over. Later he worked for the Regent Philippe d'Orléans, in whom he saw the best hope for a genuine revival of independent noble power. But hardly any of his writings were published in his lifetime, and even the editions which appeared during the decade after his death came out abroad. His endless laments at the debasement and adulteration of the old nobility, and his virulent denunciation of venality[16] were scarcely calculated to appeal to that ever-growing majority of nobles who owed their status to money. Boulainvilliers' fame, which is well attested right down to 1789,[17] owed as much to those who took issue with him as to any appeal that his historical ideas might have had to the nobility as a whole. But there was a vivid simplicity about nobility going back to Frankish conquerors, and the uncritical acceptance accorded to the idea by the *Encyclopédie* suggested that by the 1760s it had become accepted wisdom.

Yet arguably there was more for *anoblis* of whatever vintage to relish in the writings of Boulainvilliers' most celebrated opponent, the *abbé* Jean Baptiste Dubos (1670?–1742). In his *Histoire critique de l'establissement de la monarchie française* (1734), Dubos roundly rejected the idea of a conquering race of Franks. They came into Gaul as allies of the Romans, helped to protect Gaul against the inroads of genuine barbarians like the Goths or Vandals, and mingled with the Gallo-Romans on a basis of equality. Clovis was not, as

14. See William F. Church, *Constitutional Thought in Sixteenth Century France* (Cambridge, MA, 1941).

15. See Harold A. Ellis, *Boulainvilliers and the French Monarchy: Aristocratic Politics in Early Eighteenth Century France* (Ithaca, NY, 1988); Lionel Gossman, *Medievalism and the Ideologies of the Enlightenment: The World of La Curne de Sainte-Palaye* (Baltimore, MD, 1968), 276; Galliani, *Rousseau, le luxe et l'idéologie nobiliaire*, 151–8.

16. See in particular *Essais sur la Noblesse de France, contenans une dissertation sur son origine et abaissement* (Amsterdam, 1732), 230–300.

17. See André Devyver, *Le Sang épuré: Les préjugés de race chez les gentilshommes français de l'Ancien Régime (1560–1700)* (Brussels, 1973), 404–14.

Boulainvilliers had implied, the elected leader of a band of noble equals. His authority was conferred on him by Roman emperors, that of his successors as rulers of France could be traced back to the same source, and derived in no way from their subjects. It followed that nobility was either a creation of monarchy, or, as the beneficiary of feudal claims and institutions, a form of usurpation. A work so favourable to monarchical pretensions encountered no problems in publication, and was frequently reprinted over the century. And although its main purpose was to vaunt absolute monarchy rather than to decry nobility, opponents of noble claims would appeal to it during the pamphlet wars of the Revolution.[18] In the meantime, however, Dubos may be said to have lost the argument—not to the dead Boulainvilliers, but to the count's far more influential admirer: Montesquieu.

✻ ✻ ✻

Montesquieu was a nobleman of old stock. He did not owe his status to the judicial offices in the Parlement of Bordeaux which he and his more immediate ancestors owned and occupied. He was a classic exemplar of how the realities of noble identity defied easy categorization. He loved the 'gothic' moated and pinnacled castle of La Brède which he inherited from the even more distinguished family of his mother. There he wrote most of De l'Esprit des Lois, a vast, sprawling treatise which transformed European understanding of political institutions, and not least the role of nobility.

He was already famous when it appeared in 1748. He made his name in 1721 with the satirical Persian Letters which lampooned French society as it emerged from the shadow of Louis XIV. Among his targets were the absurdities of Court life under the old king, and the petty snobberies which riddled the high society of Paris. Also clear in these Letters, however, fifteen years before Boulainvilliers set his posthumous stamp on it, was Montesquieu's sympathy for the idea of ancient Gaul overrun by freedom-loving and king-suspecting Franks.[19] He returned to it in 1748, explicitly rejecting the obedient integrationism of Dubos.[20] The later books of De l'Esprit des Lois showed that Montesquieu was fascinated by the early history of feudalism in France. But his true contribution to the defence

---

18. See below, pp. 178–87.   19. Letter 131.
20. De l'Esprit des Lois, xxvii, chs. 1–4; xxx, chs. 23–5.

of noble claims was less historical than functional. Nobles for him were not, as Boulainvilliers had seemed to imply, anterior to kings; nor, as Dubos argued, entirely beholden to them, in strength or weakness, for whatever authority they wielded. In Montesquieu's scheme, kings and nobles, and the fate of both, were completely inseparable.

The idea sprang from a radical re-categorization of the Aristotelian taxonomy of states. In place of the rule of one, of the few, and of the many, Montesquieu proposed despotisms, monarchies, and republics.[21] Despotism and monarchy were both the rule of one, but monarchs ruled according to law, despots by will alone. Republics were the rule of more than one, although they could be subdivided into democracies, where the whole body of citizens ruled, and aristocracies, where power was in minority hands. The minority might or might not be made up of nobles, but when it became hereditary Montesquieu called the state an oligarchy.[22] The true place for nobles, however, was in monarchies; for all types of government had a tendency to degenerate, and the besetting threat to the rule of one according to law was that it might slip into rule by will alone. What prevented this in monarchies was the existence of intermediary bodies, whose power underpinned the rule of law. 'The most natural subordinate intermediary power is that of the nobility. It enters in some way into the essence of monarchy, whose fundamental maxim is: *no monarch, no nobility: no nobility, no monarch.* Then you have a despot.'[23]

The political thought of the next forty years would amount in many ways to little more than a discussion of Montesquieu, but few of his claims were to echo more loudly than this one. It made the nobility the watchdog of the constitution, the protector of the people against the caprices of the king, and the king's saviour from his own worst instincts. Could any role be nobler? It was reinforced by Montesquieu's assigning a guiding spirit to each of his types of government. Without laws, despots ruled by fear. But the principle animating monarchies was that quintessentially noble value, honour. 'Monarchical government entails ... pre-eminences, ranks, and even an original nobility. The nature of *honour* is to desire preferences and distinctions; and so it belongs, of itself, to this government.'[24] Within the wider intermediary role assigned to the nobility, finally, Montesquieu

21. Ibid., ii, *passim.*
22. But he only uses this term once, in a footnote to a chapter on the corruption of the aristocratic principle: ibid., viii, ch. 5.
23. Ibid., ii, ch. 4.   24. Ibid., iii, ch.7.

laid particular importance on the 'depository of the laws', by which he clearly meant the parlements. As a former president in a parlement himself, he knew that they often described themselves in this way, and he was happy to single out the nobility of the robe as the most reliable custodians of the fundamental laws which kept the kingdom free of despotism.[25]

But in doing so he did not shrink from disparaging other nobles. A depository of laws was necessary because of 'the ignorance natural to the nobility, its inattention, its contempt for civil government'.[26] And no stricture was too harsh for the courtiers who surrounded monarchs: 'Ambition in idleness, lowness in pride, the desire to grow rich without work, aversion to truth, flattery, treason, perfidy, abandonment of all commitments, contempt for the duties of a citizen, fear of the prince's virtue, hopes for his weaknesses, and more than all that, the perpetual ridicule thrown at virtue, make up, I believe, the character of most courtiers, present in all places and at all times.'[27] Even honour, that noble mainspring of monarchies, was 'philosophically speaking ... false'.[28] Its justification was simply that it made monarchies work, taking the place of the virtue which animated democracies, and which also suffused the moderation which was the mainspring of aristocracies. Even in the latter, virtue was 'not so absolutely required'[29]: the nobles who ran most aristocracies and 'repressed' the people in their own interests, were only virtuous, and therefore moderate, out of self-preservation.

To divorce nobility so consistently from virtue was radical and shocking. Ever since the sixteenth century, nobles had liked to define themselves as especially virtuous. Virtue had many meanings, of course,[30] but they all included the idea of selflessness. The supreme noble virtue was taken to be courage in battle, to the point of willingness to sacrifice life itself; but it also included qualities such as loyalty, honesty, and other forms of upright conduct.[31] The problem with defining nobles in these terms had always been that virtue could not convincingly be shown to be hereditary. Boulainvilliers still clung to the idea in the generation before Montesquieu, but saw it more in terms of family tradition than true

---

25. Book xx, ch. 22 contains a lengthy encomium of 'that profession (*état*) in which there is no way to distinction except by competence (*suffisance*) and by virtue'.
26. Ibid., ii, ch. 4.   27. Ibid., iii, ch. 5.   28. Ibid., iii, ch. 7.
29. Ibid., iii, ch. 4.
30. See Marisa Linton, *The Politics of Virtue in Enlightenment France* (Basingstoke, 2001), 22–50.
31. Schalk, *From Valor to Pedigree*, ch. 2.

heredity.[32] Montesquieu did not even make the attempt. 'I speak here', he declared, 'of political virtue, which is moral virtue in the sense that it directs itself to the general good.'[33] It was fostered by a range of historical and environmental conditions, but innate in nobody. And it was very unlikely to be found in monarchies, where 'The State subsists independently of love of country, desire for true glory, self-renunciation, sacrifice of one's most cherished interests, and of all those heroic virtues that we find in the ancients, and which we have only heard about.'[34]

Montesquieu loved a paradox. He was also unafraid to contradict himself at different points in this vast compendium of maxims and observations, and indeed he was often torn between admiration for contradictory things. Thus, with Boulainvilliers, he admired the 'fine spectacle' of feudal laws, 'which produced regulation with a leaning towards anarchy, and anarchy with a tendency to order and harmony'.[35] Yet, with all the ancient writers, he sang the praises again and again of republican virtue, with its equality, frugality, and simplicity. Apart from his obvious sympathy for the parlements and, by implication, the noble magistrates like himself who sat in them, all his favourable remarks about nobles and their values were back-handed. Even honour, their paramount quality and the mainspring of monarchies, was repeatedly depicted as a form of selfishness which could only have beneficial results under a monarchy, and even then only to prevent it from becoming something worse.

There was therefore plenty to outrage nobles in Montesquieu, and re-publicans could feel reassured by him that there was no true place for a nobility outside monarchical states. On the other hand France *was* a monarchy, with no prospect of becoming anything else, and the president (who was also a Baron) was at his most unequivocal in declaring, in rare italics, that monarchy and nobility were inseparable. He also assigned nobles a clear constitutional role in keeping monarchy true to itself. There were echoes in this of the tradition of nobles as the king's natural advisors, but they were faint. Montesquieu's nobles enjoyed no natural right to their constitutional role. It was merely their function so long as a king sat on the throne; a justi-fication but not an entitlement. In that sense it was conditional, a functional argument for nobility framed for an age which increasingly questioned any claims based upon prescription, custom or habit, and expected everything

32. Ellis, *Boulainvilliers*, 19–20, 166, 199–200.
33. *De l'Esprit des Lois*, footnote to iii, ch. 5.   34. Ibid.   35. Ibid., xxx, ch. 1.

to be rationally demonstrable. It was to prove the first, and most durable, of several attempts to endow nobility with a utilitarian justification.

* * *

Several books of De l'Esprit des Lois were devoted to discussing trade, but Montesquieu believed that 'great commercial enterprises are not for monarchies, but for the government of more than one'.[36] Accordingly, trade was not for nobilities either. 'People struck by what is done in some States, think that in France there should be laws which encourage nobles to trade. That would be a way of destroying nobility there, without any benefit to trade. The practice of that country is very wise: merchants are not noble, but they can become so. They have the hope of obtaining nobility, without the actual inconvenience of it.'[37]

This was to reject a much-discussed panacea for the problems of that majority of the nobility who were in poor or straitened circumstances. The crown itself had a long record of trying to encourage nobles into wholesale trade at least.[38] Even Boulainvilliers had argued for this.[39] Voltaire in his best-selling Philosophical Letters of 1734 had praised the way younger sons of British peers openly went into trade, and castigated the French nobility's contempt for commerce.[40] Everybody, complained the Marquis de Lassay two years later, was saying that the French nobility should follow the English example. He disagreed. The function of the nobility, he insisted, and its glory, was to fight. Lassay was an obscure if self-important author, there was nothing remotely original about his ideas on the nobility, and it was eighteen years before his reflections were posthumously made public.[41] But then they proved the occasion for a full-blown statement of the case for nobles trading, the abbé Gabriel François Coyer's La Noblesse commerçante (1756).

Coyer, a polymathic essayist, was not really interested in defending any sort of nobility. The entire language of his pamphlet was suffused with scorn for nobles and their way of life, from the opulent spendthrifts of the Court down to the indigent hobereaux whose plight ostensibly concerned

---

36. De l'Esprit des Lois, xx, ch. 4.   37. Ibid., xx, ch. 22.
38. See above, p. 17. Also Guy Richard, Noblesse d'affaires au xviiie siècle (Paris, 1974), 31–48.
39. Etat de la France, iii, 506.   40. Deuxième Lettre. Sur le Commerce.
41. See Leonard Adams, Coyer and the Enlightenment (SVEC 123, Oxford, 1974), 62–4; and Nick Childs, A Political Academy in Paris, 1724–1731: The Entresol and its Members (SVEC, 10, Oxford, 2000), 25–8, 118–9.

him. Strictures first comprehensively voiced by Coyer would be widely echoed in the anti-noble rhetoric of 1789 and beyond.[42] He believed that all forms of trade, wholesale and retail alike, should be open to nobles, and that *dérogeance*, 'that singular gothic law', should be abolished. Nobles would then be free to escape poverty, to which the laws condemned them, by going into business. But Coyer was unmistakably indifferent to whether nobility survived or not. His main concern was the prosperity of France as a whole, and his fundamental targets were idleness and waste. A flourishing commerce, unimpeded by artificial restrictions which had kept some citizens unproductive, would do more for the power of the kingdom than the strongest armies. In any case, there were more than enough noblemen for the army's needs, whilst poverty prevented most even from dreaming of the military career for which they were supposedly made. They would do better to enrich themselves in business, and plough their profits into cultivating lands now neglected for lack of capital investment:

> I will not examine whether new men, raising themselves up by labour, are not more estimable than old Nobles fallen low through doing nothing. However that may be, to prevent the downfall of the Nobility, let us give it Commerce to support it, it will there find preservation and improvement for its lands, extension of its possessions, strength for its rights, security for its privileges, consideration from its vassals, education and establishment for its children. What is required for all this? Riches. Commerce provides them.[43]

Starting with a refutation of Lassay, Coyer went on to reject Montesquieu on this subject.[44] But the effect of his polemic, within months, was to provoke an even more uncompromising reply.

Royal blood ran in the veins of the Chevalier d'Arc, author of *La Noblesse Militaire ou le patriote françois*. He was the illegitimate son of Louis XIV's illegitimate son, the Count de Toulouse. This alone was enough to win him a hearing; but in any case he was articulating what many nobles wanted to hear. The French monarchy, proclaimed d'Arc, was military. It had achieved its greatest glory, and would continue to do so, by force of arms. The nobility was central to this achievement, driven on by its guiding prejudice, a love of glory and honour. Much of this was clearly derived

---

42. See Jay M. Smith, 'Social Categories, the Language of Patriotism, and the Origins of the French Revolution: The Debate over *noblesse commerçante*', *JMH*, 72 (2000), 339–74: more recently, the same author's *Nobility Reimagined: The Patriotic Nation in Eighteenth Century France* (Ithaca, NY, 2005), 111–120.

43. G. F. Coyer, *La Noblesse commerçante. Nouvelle edition* (London, 1756), 40–41.

44. Ibid., 144.

from Montesquieu, but d'Arc's conclusions were altogether more extreme. Whereas Montesquieu had argued that a taste for luxury was appropriate in monarchies, d'Arc saw luxury and the power of money as corrupting the martial spirit. Commerce and nobility were entirely incompatible. True wealth lay in shunning luxury. To live nobly was 'to serve the State in military or other charges' whereas all trade was 'a degradation, through the sort of cupidity attached to it'.[45] D'Arc's monarchy sounded in some ways more like one of Montesquieu's republics, and his martial values were obviously derived from a model much quarried by Montesquieu in discussing them: Sparta. D'Arc offered a classically-inspired refurbishment of the medieval ideal of an order of warriors.

Since nobles were born to fight, all army officers should be recruited from their ranks. If, as Coyer claimed, there were not enough places in the army to match the number of nobles, the complement should be expanded. Regiments could be shadowed by all-noble companies of volunteers. All forms of military venality should be eliminated. With that, men of wealth would shun the austerities of a military career, whilst the poor nobility would flock to join the colours. No noblemen who had not served by the age of thirty would be deemed worthy of the status, and would be stripped of it. But common soldiers who had demonstrated officer-like qualities of honour, courage, and patriotism, could be promoted and granted nobility for life. Large noble families, meanwhile, should be supported by the king with pensions and privileges. 'It is important that [nobility] should have assured means, in order to multiply the country's defenders by itself multiplying.'[46] Meanwhile, officers should be encouraged to appear at Court in uniform as a recognition of their supreme social value.

Many of these themes would recur in discussions of army reform after the disasters of the Seven Years' War that was just beginning as d'Arc wrote. The ideal of an all-noble officer corps had already begun to take shape in 1750 with the introduction of ennoblement for all non-noble officers after a certain length of service.[47] D'Arc reinforced the trend with his new variant on the old warrior ideal. His noblemen would be austerely dedicated to service, which would be largely its own reward.

---

45. *La Noblesse militaire ou le patriote françois* (Paris, 1756), 85. See also Smith, *Nobility Reimagined*, 120–31.
46. Smith, *Nobility Reimagined*, 90–1.
47. Emile G. Léonard, *L'Armée et ses problèmes au xviiie siècle* (Paris, 1958), chs. 9, 12, 14 ; Blaufarb, *French Army*, chs. 1, 2.

They would serve their country (*patrie*) as much as their king. And in return they would be guaranteed their position at the head of the social hierarchy, immune from the corrupting influence of wealth and luxury.

* * *

The debate between Coyer and d'Arc echoed on throughout the later 1750s, with a large number of other pamphleteers joining in.[48] Whereas most of the literary journals which tracked the controversy sympathized with Coyer, a majority of the lesser pamphleteers who published their own reflections supported, not to say parroted, d'Arc. One participant, however, supported neither, since neither of their prescriptions accorded with his own view of how nobles could be most useful to society.

The Marquis de Mirabeau published *L'Ami des Hommes* in 1757. It was subtitled 'a treatise on population', but it was actually a paean to social stability. A nobleman of immemorial stock, Mirabeau believed as much as Boulainvilliers or d'Arc in the traditional orders of society. Like them, he thought that proper values had been corrupted by the corrosive power of wealth and luxury. 'My whole art in general,' he wrote, 'is to put gold back in its place.'[49] He scorned Coyer's faith in commercialism, as likely to make a bad situation worse. And although he called the noble order military, implying that the magistrates of the parlements, though fully the intermediary power defined by Montesquieu, were nevertheless little more than bourgeois, he showed no interest in elevating the military vocation of the nobility in the manner of d'Arc. He had himself resigned from the army in disgust when his ambitions were blocked. He took solace in tending and expanding his estates, and this was the course he now recommended to the nobility as a whole. He was every bit as contemptuous of the Court and *les grands* as Montesquieu and the long tradition of anti-curial polemic which the president had drawn upon. But he was equally hostile to Paris, a bottomless pit of waste and extravagance, where nobles were tempted

---

48. For full surveys, see Elie Carcassonne, *Montesquieu et le problème de la constitution française au xviiie siècle* (Paris, 1927), 225–32; J. Q. C. Mackrell, *The Attack on 'Feudalism' in Eighteenth Century France* (London, 1973), 85–100; Smith, *Nobility Reimagined*, 129–42.

49. *L'Ami des Hommes ou traité de la population*, 2 vols. (Hamburg, 1758), i, 442. See also Galliani, *Rousseau, le luxe et l'idéologie nobiliaire*, 175–8; Smith, *Nobility Reimagined*, 90–9.

to squander their finest assets on the worthless trivia of fashion. Mirabeau urged the spendthrift denizens of Court and capital back to the land, which was the ultimate source of their wealth.

Mirabeau scarcely disputed Coyer's bleak picture of the neglected state of noble lands, although he deplored the *abbé*'s sarcastic tone. But since there was no other source of true wealth (a conviction which made the Marquis an easy convert to the new ideology of physiocracy in 1758),[50] the way to regenerate the nobility, morally as much as economically, was for them to devote all their energies to agricultural improvement. Absentees should return. Waste should be brought under cultivation. Landlords should look after the peasants with paternal care, firmly but justly. The problems of agriculture, and of taxing it, should be regularly ventilated in provincial Estates, which should be restored in provinces where they had disappeared. Not only would all this boost the economy of the kingdom, it would restore the nobility to the natural authority to which they were born.

Mirabeau made no attempt to hide the inspiration he derived from an imagined feudal arcadia in the middle ages. While ignoring and eliding the careful distinctions which Montesquieu had drawn between honour and virtue, his debt to the president's historical researches was clear.[51] But the distinctive role which he assigned to the nobility was one which Montesquieu had scarcely touched upon—even if he took much personal pride in his record as an improving landlord. For Mirabeau, the nobleman who resided on his lands and cultivated them to the full extent of their capacity was the custodian of the kingdom's prosperity, the true friend of mankind. Mirabeau affected to disdain utility: 'if one accustoms men to calculate all rights only according to their utility ... what dangerous progress could not that cause in men's minds'.[52] Nevertheless, what he was proposing was another way in which nobles could claim to be useful, and thereby justify their separate and superior status. He ignored the fact that most of the land in France was not owned by nobles, and that they had yet to set any sort of example of good husbandry. But it implicitly acknowledged, like d'Arc's dream of a Spartan caste of ascetic professional officers, that claims to social superiority

50. See Elizabeth Fox-Genovese, *The Origins of Physiocracy: Economic Revolution and Social Order in Eighteenth Century France* (Ithaca, NY, 1976), ch. 4.
51. See Carcassonne, *Montesquieu et le problème*, 235–9.
52. Quoted in Fox-Genovese, *Origins of Physiocracy*, 142.

needed to be justifiable in functional terms appropriate to the modern world.

* * *

No new or even refurbished rationales for the pre-eminence of the existing nobility were formulated over the remaining three decades of the old order. Yet there were moves to systematize a principle never entirely absent from the idea of nobility, although never fully formulated in explicit terms. Virtue, and merit in the service of the king, had traditionally been seen as natural attributes of nobility. They were also seen to qualify commoners for ennoblement. 'It is most reasonable', Loyseau had written, 'that the sovereign prince should honour with the title of nobility someone whom he sees to be endowed with a distinct virtue, and thereby reward his particular merit and stimulate virtue in every one.'[53] This argument was all the more persuasive for the contrast it presented with the normal way of achieving noble status. Purchase of an ennobling office was a practice which few found defensible in any terms, and most found embarrassing, throughout its history.[54] Nor had nobles proud of their warlike vocation ever objected seriously to the idea of ennobling commoners who had proved their valour in the field. Even d'Arc thought this legitimate. Six years before he wrote, in fact, an edict of 1750 effectively acknowledged that outstanding military achievement by *roturier* officers should automatically be rewarded by admission to the nobility.

How far distinction in other vocations deserved the same reward remained more ambiguous. Louis XIV had set an example by ennobling certain writers and artists, but any idea of systematic gratuitous ennoblement for any group was opposed by genealogical diehards, not to mention administrators who knew the fiscal value of selling offices and the disadvantages of multiplying privileges and exemptions. Eventually, in 1767, it was decreed that outstanding services to commerce and industry should be recognized by ennobling two businessmen every year. Others were promised recognition as 'living nobly' and granted certain honorific privileges.[55] Both before and after this a number of other men of commerce

---

53. *Treatise of Orders*, 96.   54. See Doyle, *Venality*, ch. 8.
55. Marcel Reinhard, 'Elite et noblesse dans la seconde moitié du xviiie siècle', *Revue d'histoire moderne et contemporaine*, iii (1956), 14–15.

were randomly elevated, along with a range of advocates, medical men, administrative officials, and a handful of writers and artists. Altogether there were perhaps a thousand non-venal ennoblements over the century.[56]

The grounds upon which they were honoured were set out in the official letters of ennoblement which they received. A few referred, disingenuously, to restoring a nobility inexplicably lost, thus preserving the myth of hereditary qualities. Most, however, frankly recognized that ennoblement came as a reward for merit. There had never been any perceived incompatibility between merit and other noble values.[57] To excel in war, and more generally in the service of the king, was to achieve the glory and virtue to which all true nobles were expected to aspire, and this was merit indeed. As the debate over Coyer's *Noblesse commerçante* shows, by the eighteenth century many were prepared to see equal merit in a more general social utility, which included the enrichment of the state and society through successful commercial activity. The decisions to ennoble *roturier* officers in 1750 and certain businessmen in 1767, show the crown moving towards the idea of ennoblement as a standard recognition for meritorious service. Nobility had always been more or less freely available to anyone who was financially successful, and few in that position ever resisted its allurements for long. But in experiments with ennoblement on grounds of merit and utility alone can be seen the dim outlines of something different: a nobility of reward rather than purchase or inheritance, recruiting the best rather than providing them in advance. It was the principle that would be enshrined, after revolutionary upheavals, in the Legion of Honour and the Napoleonic hierarchy of titles.[58]

* * *

The ultimate justification for nobility was that it needed none. Its value was self-evident in the minds of those who possessed it, sought it, recognized it in others, and transmitted it down the generations. Whether immemorial, or acquired from the only authority entitled to confer it, the king, it was

56. Guy Chaussinand-Nogaret, *La Noblesse au xviiie siècle* (Paris, 1976), 55.
57. See Jay M. Smith, *The Culture of Merit: Nobility, Royal Service, and the Making of Absolute Monarchy in France, 1600–1789* (Ann Arbor, MI, 1996). On an emerging perception of medieval chivalry as a form of meritocracy, see Gossman, *Medievalism and the Ideologies of the Enlightenment*, 282–8.
58. See below, pp. 315–325.

a quality inherent in persons and their progeny, and inalienable except in clearly defined circumstances of forfeiture. It was a genetic trait inherited at birth, and extinguished only with life itself.

This argument, however, was seldom voiced before the French Revolution, and strictly speaking it was not an argument at all. It was a belief, a matter of faith and prejudice, and not susceptible of refutation. In that sense it was also indestructible, beyond rational challenge. What could never be beyond rational challenge was the right of people possessed of this self-defined quality to exercise power and command prestige and deference. This was why arguments from divine will, the historical record, and the functional needs of society had been formulated, and were periodically restated or reformulated. Yet by the eighteenth century only functional arguments retained their persuasive power, recast into the language of utility. Neither God's intentions, nor how things had been done in former times, any longer in themselves offered much credible justification for an existing order of things. But Montesquieu's intermediary powers and custodians of the laws, d'Arc's Spartan order of officers, or Mirabeau's class of improving landlords, incorporating though they all did elements of previous noble ideals, offered a fresh range of roles in which nobles could justify their distinctive character to the rational temper of the century. More challengingly, so did Coyer's invitation to embrace commerce.

And yet, these utilitarian rationales offered ideal types of nobility rather than images of the order as it actually was. They offered little support if the nobility failed to live up to them. Coyer's urgings into commerce and Mirabeau's call back to the land fell on completely deaf ears. The defeats of the Seven Years' War cast serious doubt on the martial qualities of French officers so vaunted by d'Arc, yet they resisted the quarter-century of reforms which followed every step of the way. Attempts to create an army which the chevalier would have approved left many officers resentful and demoralized. And Montesquieu's prized depositaries of the laws, the parlements, were swept aside by Chancellor Maupeou in 1771, seemingly unable to prevent the monarchy from degenerating into despotism. They remained in disarray even after Louis XVI restored them. In all these instances nobles failed in the exalted functions mapped out for them by their rational defenders. It left them all the more open to rational attack.

3

Ageless Antagonisms

The Limits of Discontent

No order so dominant could hope to escape criticism. Nor could the everyday exercise of noble power expect to go entirely uncontested. But before the eighteenth century neither criticism nor contestation were systematic or sustained, and neither produced a coherent challenge to the legitimacy of noble hegemony itself. Nobles, individually or collectively, might fall short of the standards or behaviour expected of them. Such lapses offered grounds for complaint. Or nobles might exceed the powers or authority which those subject to them thought legitimate or just. This could provoke defiance, sometimes with violence. But seldom, in either case, was the principle of nobility, or the legitimate entitlement of nobles to power or respect, called into question. After all, there was no alternative. In an agricultural world, the lords of the land seemed destined to constitute the social elite. And the evidence of those fleeting moments when noble power had been successfully defied, whether in classical, medieval, or more recent history, suggested that the result would be disorder and bloody chaos. Peasant rebels or urban mobs who butchered persons of condition and sacked and looted their dwellings spread terror far beyond the ranks of their lordly victims. Incapable of exercising power themselves, they were a threat to everybody with anything to lose, and promised only anarchy. For every John Ball, inciting English peasants to rebel in 1381 with:

> When Adam delved, and Eve span,
> Who was then the gentleman?

There were thousands to echo Shakespeare's Ulysses:[1]

---

1. *Troilus and Cressida*, Act I, Scene iii.

Take but degree away, untune that string,
And, hark, what discord follows!

* * *

In French memory, the equivalent of the Peasants' Revolt had come a generation earlier, with the *Jacquerie* of 1358. As much as anything, these rebels were protesting at the failure of lords to protect their vassals against wartime marauders. But their revolt, which brought the brutal slaughter of many lords, was remembered as an orgy of social revenge, and when the word *jacquerie* passed into the French language as a term for any peasant revolt, it carried these connotations with it. In less remote times, when order broke down in the countryside, the dues demanded by lords were frequently denounced, and insurgents vowed that they would no longer pay. Occasionally, intransigent lords in remote places were killed before order was restored; and then, retribution was invariably more proportionate to the fears aroused than to the damage done. But what is remarkable about the great epidemic of popular disorders which swept France between the 1540s and 1675 was the relative lack of social animosity unleashed. Peasants were provoked into rebellion by the depredations of the soldiery in the wars of religion or the struggle against the Habsburgs from the 1630s onwards. Rebels affected by Protestantism sought to throw off tithes levied by the Catholic church. Above all, these were rebellions against taxes, and those who sought to levy them. The latter were seldom noblemen—or not of a sort which other nobles would readily recognize. They were petty officials or private contractors (*traitants, partisans*) whom the rebels suspected of traducing or exceeding the king's intentions in order to line their own pockets. And nobles were often sympathetic to peasant grievances. They disliked the rival authority of royal agents, whom they were at one with their peasants in regarding as social upstarts. At the same time, they envied them their obvious wealth. Subjected themselves to rising levels of indirect taxation, nobles found that royal claims on the incomes of their vassals made rents and dues harder to collect. Gentlemen would even sometimes be found at the head of popular resistance, often by popular demand. And when disturbances were over, bodies of nobles in authority (like the Parlements of Bordeaux or Rennes in 1675), found themselves punished by a suspicious king for allowing disorder, perhaps deliberately, to get out of hand.[2]

These solidarities did not survive into the eighteenth century. The Protestant peasants who defied Louis XIV's persecutions in the *Camisard* rebellion of 1702–8 enjoyed no noble support. Nor did the hungry rustic price-fixers whose lawlessness terrified Parisians in the 'Flour War' of 1775. These were the only two popular outbreaks before 1789 comparable in scale to those of the previous century. Neither articulated any challenge to the social hierarchy, and nor did most of the lesser, local disturbances which were endemic throughout the century but scarcely noticed beyond their own localities. Over 8,500 incidents have been counted between 1661 and 1789. Only twelve of these (or 0.15 per cent) were motivated by clear hostility to nobles or their privileges.[3]

On the other hand, 512 violent episodes challenged the exactions of feudalism and lordship, three-fifths occurring after 1760.[4] A parallel trend, below the level of violent confrontation, witnessed peasant communities increasingly prepared to challenge their lords in the royal courts over what they claimed were new or uncustomary practices or demands.[5] The tradition was not new. Peasants could be found suing their lords for breach of feudal obligations as far back as the twelfth century. But by the eighteenth century the self-confidence of village syndics, encouraged by the receptivity of royal courts and officials to their claims, was unprecedented. And although not all lords were nobles, feudal rights were generally recognized as essential appurtenances of authentic nobility. At their fullest, they allowed lords to adjudicate in their own cause through manorial courts. Litigation in the king's courts was an implicit rejection of this jurisdiction. Some nobles at least perceived it as a challenge to all lordly authority. It proceeded, lamented the procurator-general of the Parlement of Paris in 1747, from 'chimerical ideas of natural and primitive liberty, so contrary to the establishment of estates and of monarchies, to the right of conquest and to historical facts vouchsafed to us by the oldest

2. See Pierre Deyon, 'A propos des rapports entre la noblesse française et la monarchie absolue pendant la première moitié du xviiᵉ siècle', *Revue historique*, xxxviii (1964), 341–56.
3. Jean Nicolas, *La Rébellion française: Mouvements populaires et conscience sociale, 1661–1789* (Paris, 2002), 29–36.
4. Ibid., 216.
5. See Hilton L. Root, *Peasant and King in Burgundy: Agrarian Foundations of Absolutism* (Berkeley, CA, 1987), ch. 5.

monuments.'[6] Forty years later, such ideas were to prove anything but chimerical, and they would sweep away all other claims to legitimacy. The abolition of the entire apparatus of 'feudalism' on the night of 4 August 1789 would be an essential precondition for the abolition of nobility ten months later. Before that happened, however, episodic eighteenth-century resistance to the operation of feudalism, even if rising in volume, offered little evidence that nobility itself was yet being called into question.

* * *

Nor did the literary heritage prized by the eighteenth century furnish many fundamental criticisms of the traditional organization of society. It was true that the classical authors were full of instances of patricians, senators, or others roughly identifiable as nobles, behaving in ways detrimental to the welfare of the body politic. Aristotle, Cicero, Livy, and Plutarch all offered stories of republics brought down by the selfishness of elites who ought to have known better. Cicero memorably despaired that, while Pompey and Caesar were tearing the Republic apart, effete senators were more interested in pondfuls of tame fish.[7] But these familiar lamentations concerned the failings of men rather than fundamental flaws in social organization. If men were virtuous, Aristotle had declared, the best would rule, and that would be an aristocracy.[8] Mere wealth produced oligarchy, but ancient wealth and virtue together produced good birth, and the combination was unbeatable. Those who thought their birth good could feel reassured by an authority as eminent as Aristotle; but his corollary was that if claimants to nobility and its advantages lacked virtue, they were more likely to endanger the state than to lend it strength. And this was certainly the lesson drawn, both from their study of the classics and their own experience, by the political writers of later medieval Italy. Most were forgotten by the eighteenth century, but two remained famous and much read, even if their remarks on nobility were scarcely central to their celebrity.

One was Dante. Many men of noble birth were consigned by him to the tortures of the Inferno, but he discussed the whole idea of nobility in

---

6. Quoted in Nicolas, *Rébellion française*, 217–8. The reference to 'conquest' suggests a ready acceptance by this noble magistrate of Boulainvilliers' version of the origins of nobility.
7. Letter to Atticus, June, 60 BC, in L. P. Wilkinson, *Letters of Cicero* (2nd edn, London, 1959), 48.
8. *Politics*, iv, 8.

the fourth book of his unfinished *Banquet* (*Convivio*, 1304–8).[9] Cast out of his native Florence by the triumph of an aristocratic faction, the poet saw the ambitions of nobles as dangerous to a republican state. He also disputed definitions of nobility that were clearly already widely accepted. It was not ancient wealth, for riches of any sort were inherently base. Nor was it hereditary distinction, since nothing guaranteed that a man of nobility would beget descendants to match him. Some might not even try to measure up to their ancestors, and these were the lowest of the low. The only true nobility, Dante therefore concluded, was virtue, a personal quality that had nothing to do with families. That virtue was not necessarily inherited was to be a central plank in all critiques of noble pretensions. It was certainly a conviction shared by Dante's fellow Florentine, Machiavelli. But for Machiavelli the very presence of a nobility was barely compatible with the civic selflessness which he meant by virtue. In his *Discourses on the first ten books of Titus Livy* (1514–19), a meditation on what made city republics viable and able to achieve greatness, he concluded that 'where the gentry are numerous, no one who proposes to set up a republic can succeed unless he first gets rid of them all'. Gentlemanly ways led straight to corruption. 'The term "gentry" is used', he explained, 'of those who live in idleness on the abundant revenue derived from their estates, without having anything to do either with their cultivation or with other forms of labour essential to life. Such men are vermin in any republic and in any province; but still more pernicious are those who, in addition to the aforesaid revenues, have castles under their command and subjects who are under their obedience ... men born in such conditions are inimical to any form of civic government.' Only a monarchy could keep such forces of corruption in check.[10] In *The Prince* (1513, first printed 1532), Machiavelli approached the subject from a ruler's point of view, and here again there was little comfort for nobles. Their constant desire, he asserted, was to rule and oppress the people. They could not be satisfied without doing injury to others, they always harboured rebellious tendencies, and always put their own interests first.[11] Although these warnings were primarily addressed to a prince newly raised

---

9. See Quentin Skinner, *The Foundations of Modern Political Thought*, 2 vols. (Cambridge, 1978), i, 45–6.

10. *Discourses*, i, 55. Perhaps significantly, the *Discourses* was one of the books that Napoleon insisted should be part of his portable travel library: Maximilien Vox (ed.), *Correspondance de Napoléon: Six cents lettres de travail (1806–1810)* (Paris, 1943), 216. Napoléon to Louis Barbier, 17 July 1808.

11. *The Prince*, ch. 9, 'Concerning a civic principality'.

up by his fellow-citizens, it was clear that Machiavelli thought such noble behaviour congenital. Except as a force to play off against the populace, nobles seemed no more useful to princely states than to republics. It was perhaps fortunate for Europe's nobilities, therefore, that almost from the start the cold amorality which Machiavelli recommended to princes brought universal execration to his name. Although his insights and analyses were to prove hugely influential among writers on politics over the next two centuries and beyond, he was repeatedly denounced, and few dared admit themselves in any way his disciples. In these circumstances his undisguised contempt for nobilities of any sort could be dismissed as part of an indefensible system of thought, if indeed it was noticed at all amid the chorus denouncing his more central tenets of statecraft.[12]

Even more radical than Machiavelli was a tract being written in England at the same time as *The Prince*. Thomas More's *Utopia* (1516) depicted an imaginary country where nobility did not exist. In this dream island there was no money, no private property, and everyone was equal. The only distinction prized by the Utopians was virtue, but More's clear implication was that, so far from being an attribute of nobility, virtue was least likely to be found among those who considered themselves noble. *Utopia* was a sustained polemic against pride, luxury, and idleness, vices typical of 'all rich men, chiefly those who have estates in land, who are called noblemen and gentlemen, together with their families, made up of idle persons, that are kept more for show than use'.[13] Their nobility was a 'conceit—that they are descended from ancestors who have been held for some successions rich, and who have had great possessions; for this is all that makes nobility at present'.[14] Even hunting, that favourite sport of gentlemen, was condemned as a false pleasure: 'the desire of bloodshed, even of beasts', was 'a mark of a mind that is already corrupted with cruelty'.[15]

First published in Antwerp, within a generation *Utopia* had been translated into French, a rare distinction for an English work before the eighteenth century.[16] But its very title, which gave a new word to European languages, could only blunt its impact as a call to action. Utopia

12. See Sydney Anglo, *Machiavelli—The First Century: Studies in Enthusiasm, Hostility and Irrelevance* (Oxford, 2006).
13. Sir Thomas More, *Utopia* (London, 1892 edn), 84.   14. Ibid., 117.
15. Ibid., 120.
16. See Terence Cave (ed.), *Thomas More's Utopia in Early Modern Europe: Paratexts and Contexts* (Manchester, 2008).

meant nowhere, a reproach perhaps to established ways, but almost by definition a world that could never exist.[17] Most sixteenth-century writers preferred to deal with the world as it was rather than as it could never be. Accordingly, the existence of a noble elite continued to be taken for granted. There was broad agreement that true nobility lay in virtue, and a rather more furtive concession that nobles who lacked it did not deserve their status. But it was also widely asserted that nobles were by far the most likely people to be virtuous, whether as a result of family tradition or of the high level of education which the sons of noblemen increasingly sought over this century.[18] Many writers on nobility warned, especially during the disturbed decades of the wars of religion, that if the nobility as a whole fell short of these high ideals, its social predominance might be at risk.[19] But most of them saw this danger coming from adulteration of the order by upstarts rather than the overthrow of hierarchy itself; and the outright hostility of Machiavelli and More found few echoes over the rest of the century in which they wrote.[20]

The identity and functions of nobilities, however, remained a vexed subject. Many sought reassurance in a mythical past of chivalric values. Jousting was never more popular than in a century when firearms were making knightly combat obsolete. There was also a vogue for romances set in former times when knights-errant set out to fight monsters, protect the weak against evil, and brave unimaginable dangers as the selfless champions of unattainable ladies. The purpose of Cervantes' *History of Don Quixote de la Mancha* (1605–15) was to parody these tales in the story of a provincial gentleman who drove himself mad with reading them. The effect was to pour scorn and ridicule on a whole range of supposedly noble attitudes and reflexes. Don Quixote equips himself with rusty armour, a half-cardboard helmet and rides forth on a broken-down horse to seek knightly adventures which he can dedicate to his lady Dulcinea. Squired by Sancho Panza, an illiterate peasant who volubly pinpoints the absurdity of his master's obsessions, the self-styled knight undergoes a series of humiliations born of his own

---

17. But it could still be invoked as a warning against egalitarianism. See *Lettres d'un Sicilien à un de ses amis* (1714), cited in Galliani, *Rousseau, le luxe et l'idéologie nobiliaire*, 130.
18. Skinner, *Foundations*, i, 236–43; Schalk, *From Valor to Pedigree*, ch.3.
19. Schalk, *From Valor to Pedigree*, ch. 4.
20. Certain Parisian pamphlets at the time of the League in the 1590s came close to attacking the whole principle of nobility, and were perceived as doing so. But they were not numerous, and gave rise to no tradition after the crisis of Henry IV's coming to power in 1594: Schalk, *From Valor to Pedigree*, 100–7.

deluded imagination. Everything he aspires to becomes a subject of ridicule. Among his tormentors are a series of heartless noblemen and women who show themselves contemptuous of the high ideals which he professes.

Don Quixote was translated into French almost as soon as it was published. It appeared in other languages shortly afterwards, and by the eighteenth century could be read in every major European tongue. There were no fewer than fifty-nine editions in French alone down to 1782.[21] No reader could overlook Cervantes' contempt for chivalric values, and not smile at the way he caricatured them. The Jesuit Father René Rapin (1621–87), an influential literary critic under Louis XIV, believed that Cervantes had written the book as a deliberate attack on the Spanish nobility after a lifetime of slights from grandees.[22] This opinion was widespread in the early eighteenth century, although it would be hard, even in such a vast and sprawling text, to find criticisms of nobility as direct as those of Machiavelli or More. But for such a widely read work to depict knighthood, chivalry, honour, and the mindless aggressiveness that went with them as the obsessions of a madman, more risible than reasonable, could scarcely fail to provoke critical reflections on values that many noblemen still found, or claimed to find, inspiring.

The seventeenth century, however, produced nothing else to disturb the confidence of nobilities. It was true that the civil war in England led to the abolition of the House of Lords and unleashed some egalitarian-sounding rhetoric from Levellers and other dreamers in the New Model Army. But, apart from a few echoes in Bordeaux,[23] events in Protestant England evoked no sympathy in France, merely horror at republicans executing a king. In any case, the English Republic was run by and for landed gentlemen, no attempt was made to persecute men of title unless they were active royalists, and its rapid failure after the death of Cromwell reassured all friends of order and hierarchy.

Under Louis XIV writers preferred to concentrate on the blessings of social stability. While Molière ridiculed the ignorant pretensions of Monsieur Jourdan in *Le Bourgeois Gentilhomme* (1670), La Bruyère in *Les Caractères ou les moeurs de ce siècle* (1688–96) satirized not so much the principle of nobility as its everyday corruption. If only high society were not debased by the ambitions of dubiously-enriched financiers and the blandishments

21. Maurice Bardon, '*Don Quichotte' en France, 1605–1815*, 2 vols. (Paris, 1931), ii, 846–51.
22. *Réflexions sur la poétique* (1674); Bardon, '*Don Quichotte*', i, 275.
23. Sal Alexander Westrich, *The Ormée of Bordeaux: A Revolution during the Fronde* (Baltimore, MD, 1972), 48–59.

of the Court, he seemed to say, then all would be well even in a world dominated by nobles. 'The nobility risks its life for the safety of the State and for the sovereign's glory; the magistrate frees the prince of part of the care of judging his people: both are most sublime functions and of marvellous utility; men are scarce capable of greater things, and I know not from whence robe and sword have found their contempt for one another.'[24] And although 'men of outstanding virtue have neither ancestors nor descendants: alone they make up their entire line',[25] they were so rare as scarcely to Count in normal life. Yet social distinction was hardly justifiable without some assumption of virtue or merit, and La Bruyère's clear intention was to remind his readers of this. So was that of the poet Boileau Despréaux, historiographer-royal, who devoted the fifth of his *Satires* (1665) to the subject of nobility. He dedicated it to the proud and officious Marquis de Dangeau, a courtier later lampooned by La Bruyère under the pseudonym of *Pamphile*, but now flattered as the opposite of all the vices criticized by the poet. Nobility, Boileau declared, was not an empty dream (*chimère*), but neither the glory of chivalric ancestors nor 'worm-spared parchments' were enough to justify noble pretensions. Virtue alone was the true mark of a noble heart, and that meant imitating famous ancestors, pursuing honour, eschewing vice, respecting the laws and avoiding injustice. It meant tirelessly seeking glory on the battlefield. Without all these, heroic ancestors were so many reflections on their descendants' shame—if indeed their line had avoided periodic adulteration by unfaithful wives. In primitive times, Boileau observed, merit alone attracted nobility, and the titles, arms, and appeals to ancestry which came to be called its marks were the fruit of debasing honour and ennobling vice. A taste for luxury and display followed, and then bad debts, redeemable only by unworthy marriages:

> For if blood be not rais'd by the glitter of gold
> Pride of rank is but vain, be it never so old.[26]

Many traditional criticisms of noble behaviour were brought together in this satire, but it ended in a eulogy of the established order. Noblemen had only to imitate the selfless example of a hardworking young king to be all that they should be.

---

24. *Les Caractères*, 'Des Grands', 40.   25. Ibid., 'Du mérite personnel', 22.
26. Car, si l'éclat de l'or ne relève le sang
      En vain l'on fait briller la splendeur de son rang.

Serve so noble a master; and show that today
Your prince rules over subjects deserving his sway.[27]

The reign of Louis XIV, in fact, offers only one unequivocal example of opposition to nobility, and it came from a person of no consequence in his own lifetime. Jean Meslier (1664–1729) was a country priest in the French Ardennes.[28] From 1689 until his death he was the incumbent of Etrépigny, a village of less than 200 inhabitants a few miles from where he had been born. Until 1716 his ministry there gave his superiors no qualms or cause for dissatisfaction, and his compassion for his parishioners is well attested. But in that year he fell out with a local lord, whom he accused from the pulpit of trampling the poor and maltreating village orphans. And when he died he left hundreds of pages of violent 'Memoirs' addressed to his parishioners in which he confessed himself an atheist and an enemy to all established forms of authority. Most of this manuscript was devoted to a detailed demolition of Christian teaching, but one reason adduced by Meslier for its falsity was that 'a religion which suffers, which approves and which even authorizes the tyranny of the Great, to the damage of peoples, cannot be true, nor truly be of divine institution'.[29] 'All men', Meslier affirmed, 'are equal by nature, they all have equally the right to live and walk upon the earth, equally to enjoy there their natural liberty and to share in the goods of the earth, each and every one working usefully to have things useful and necessary to life.'[30] It was true that all societies needed some sort of hierarchy, but they ought to be 'just and well-proportion'd' raising none so high above others that the latter had nothing, or that pleasures and pains were not shared. The first ancestors, he declared:

of those who make so much noise and so much ado of their nobility, were bloody and cruel people, oppressors, tyrants, traitors, violators of public Faith, robbers, parricides, and in a word the oldest Nobility was nothing but wickedness sustain'd by power, and impiety bolster'd by dignity. What has been done till now by making nobility successive, or hereditary, or elective, or otherwise, but to perpetuate exorbitant power and honour, acquir'd and

27. Sers un si noble maître; et fais voir qu'aujourd'hui
Ton prince a des sujets qui sont dignes de lui.
28. For his life, ideas, and influence, see Maurice Dommanget, *Le Curé Meslier. Athée, communiste et révolutionnaire sous Louis XIV* (Paris, 1956).
29. Rudolf Charles (ed.), *Le Testament de Jean Meslier*, 3 vols. (Amsterdam, 1864), ii, 168.
30. Ibid., 170.

swell'd by the most enormous vices, by practices unworthy of men and of which their very authors have in all times been asham'd. So it has come about that the most unjust outrages and the most violent usurpations have been cover'd and are cover'd still today with the specious pretext of justice and of virtue, when at bottom 'tis nothing but true brigandage. These unjust and cruel usurpers feign to uphold the liberties and rights of peoples, their Religion and their laws, when at bottom they are the greatest tyrants in the world, rascally hypocrites, atheists, reprobates.[31]

French peasants were little more than the slaves of nobles:

For truly every day we see the vexations, the violence, the injustices and the ill-treatment which they commit on poor people. Not content to have everywhere the finest houses, the finest lands and the finest patrimonies, they must also try by cleverness and subtlety or by violence to get what others have, they must have themselves paid dues, exact forc'd labour, and command services not due to them. They are not even content if they are not granted all they ask for and do not see everyone else crawl to them. The least upstarts and the slightest village lords make themselves fear'd and obey'd by the people, exacting injustices that are public burdens from them, always attempting to usurp something from one or another and grabbing whatever they can. These people are rightly compared to vermin, for just as vermin cause only upset and continually eat and pick at the body of those they infest, so these people do nothing but trouble, torment, eat and pick at poor people. They would be fortunate, these poor people, if they were not disturbed by these wicked vermin, but it is certain that they will always be unhappy so long as they do not rid themselves of them.[32]

And while priests set out to terrify their flocks with fear of devils, the true 'Devils and Devilesses' were 'all those fine gentry the Great and the Noble … all those fine Ladies … whom you see so well dressed, so finely arrayed, so well comb'd, so well powder'd, so well scented, and glittering so with gold, silver and such precious stones … these are your greatest enemies and the ones who do you the most evil.'[33]

Meslier knew *Don Quixote*, and had read La Bruyère, whose satire on *Les Grands* he cited with approval. He drew on the main classical authors, and above all on Christian polemicists and the Bible itself.[34] But his attacks on the social order were not central to his true target, which was the falsity of religion. The iniquities of the social system which it countenanced were

31. *Le Testament* Charles, 173–4.   32. Ibid., 179–80.   33. Ibid., 180–1.
34. On his sources, Dommanget, *Le Curé Meslier*, 119–20, and ch. III, *passim*.

merely adduced as further proof that religion could not be the creation of a benevolent God. Nor were any of Meslier's fulminations widely known before the 1760s. As many as thirty-five copies of his manuscript may have been in circulation by 1750,[35] and one of them reached Voltaire in 1735. Twenty-seven years later the Sage of Ferney published a series of extracts under the title it has since enjoyed: *Testament de Jean Meslier*. They were chosen for their criticism of religion, not of society, and represented only a fraction of Meslier's full text. Only the story of his quarrels with the local lord, related by Voltaire by way of introduction, hinted at the priest's hostility to nobility. But the priest who had died asking God's pardon for a lifetime preaching the lies of religion became a hero to atheistic freethinkers in the later eighteenth century; and the context of his unbelief no doubt encouraged one of his most enthusiastic promoters, Holbach, in his denunciations of the evils of nobility.[36]

✳ ✳ ✳

Meslier, who outlived the Sun King's reign by fifteen years, forms a symbolic bridge from ages when noble hegemony could only be challenged fleetingly and fruitlessly, when even hostile thinkers saw no hope of practical change, to a time of more coherent and sustained criticism, when new bases for social power came to seem possible. As the rector of Etrépigny was secretly propounding the natural equality of all men in the silence of his presbytery, across the English Channel the same doctrine was being openly proclaimed in more philosophical terms. John Locke's ideas on equality, translated into French as early as 1700, would form the foundation of all advanced eighteenth-century thinking about human affairs.

Locke proclaimed unequivocally that all men are born equal, and that they bring nothing into the world with them except their cognitive capacities. They inherit no original sin, much less (by implication) any other qualities such as nobility. And although Locke recognized that men could not remain equal, and had a right to accumulate private property, he was not far from Meslier in condemning its disproportionate distribution. For Locke and his disciples, men were made what they were by their experiences.

---

35. Jonathan I. Israel, *Radical Enlightenment: Philosophy and the Making of Modernity, 1650–1750* (Oxford, 2001), 690.
36. See below, pp. 140–2. On Meslier and Holbach, see Dommanget, *Le Curé Meslier*, 423–8.

Conservative conclusions, it was true, could be derived from this: for Montesquieu, the important experiences were the result of forces beyond human control, such as geography, climate, and historical circumstances and legacies. But Locke himself suggested more radical possibilities in pointing to the potential of education. Human affairs could be moulded by human action, and nothing in how they were arranged or operated was inevitable or pre-ordained. Accordingly, institutions or social structures might have no eternal legitimacy. Their claims could be subjected to the tests of justice and utility, and if found wanting by those criteria, they might be changed, improved. Locke himself, who came from gentlemanly stock and owed much in his life to the protection of noblemen, drew no social inferences from his arguments, and those who acknowledged his ideas most overtly, such as Voltaire, the Encyclopedists, and other French materialist philosophers, largely used them to attack the claims of revealed religion. But any acceptance of Lockean premises left the way open to challenging claims of other sorts, including those of hereditary authority.

These seeds bore little enough fruit before the 1750s. Despite translation, Locke remained little known in France before the outlines of his ideas were presented by Voltaire's *Lettres Philosophiques* of 1734. And although the sojourn in England of 1726–8 which led Voltaire to write this introduction to English culture was occasioned by a violent clash with a brutish and arrogant nobleman of ancient family, Voltaire did not use this publication to denounce the breed—merely suggesting that contempt for trade was unworthy of nobles, and that merchants had more right to the gratitude of mankind than courtiers.[37] He mocked the nobility of Germany where 'up to thirty Highnesses of the same name possess nothing but coats of arms and pride'. It was a stereotype which he would evoke again a quarter of a century later in the family of Baron Thunder-ten-Tronckh, whose sister, the reputed mother of the eponymous *Candide* (1759), refused to marry the father because, though a nobleman, his escutcheon could only prove seventy-one quarterings. But Arouet the poet, who had given himself a cognomen with a particle, who spent his life in the company of or correspondence with some of the grandest of *les grands*, the flatterer of kings and courtiers, voiced no principled objection to a society run by men of condition. Although in 1734 he urged French nobles to follow the younger sons of English peers by embracing trade, by 1766 he was pouring ridicule

37. *Lettres Philosophiques*, letter X.

on the *abbé* Coyer as the man who 'wanted to make Montmorencies and Chatillons into shopkeepers'.[38]

In the 1730s, meanwhile, the most pointed criticisms of the nobility came from voices firmly within the order. Their impact then was limited. One was that of the Marquis d'Argenson (1694–1757), an old school friend of Voltaire, and destined briefly to be foreign secretary in the 1740s. Between 1733 and 1737 he produced a long manuscript, *Considérations sur le gouvernement ancien et présent de la France*.[39] Unpublished until 1764, seven years after its author's death, it was nevertheless well known in the literary world of the capital. A firm believer in a strong monarchy, d'Argenson thought that the king should rally his ordinary subjects to him by instituting a limited form of local democracy. In this context, he saw the nobility as the greatest enemies of both king and people. D'Argenson's initial stimulus to write seems to have been Boulainvilliers' contention (first printed in this decade)[40] that the nobility were the descendants of conquering Franks. While not disputing this, he differed from Boulainvilliers in thinking the results a disaster. The conquerors had enslaved the people, and their descendants had constantly striven to restrict the king's authority. Under the democratic administrative monarchy now proposed, the Marquis advocated equality of taxation, the redemption of feudal rights and dues, abolition of the sale of offices and open competition for all appointments, with no privileged access for nobles. Nor should those bodies of noble magistrates, the parlements, enjoy any powers beyond their judicial functions. 'Under my system', he wrote, 'the true and essential function of the monarchy would be to preserve equality and prevent the formation of a hereditary aristocracy.'[41] Meanwhile, 'Never will the kingdom of France be happy until our monarch loves commoners instead of loving the nobility. This latter order is good for warfare; yet it is worth no more than the common order of soldiers today ... the nobility seem very like the drones in the hive, who eat honey without working.' 'What more cruel,' he concluded, 'than to be pushed aside by people who have no other talents than being noble and rich?' But d'Argenson offered no ideas as to how these radical aims

38. Best., 9386, Voltaire to Joseph-Michel-Antoine Servan, 13 April 1766.
39. The most accessible recent account of his thought is in Childs, *A Political Academy in Paris*, 185–90 and *passim*. See also Guy Chaussinand-Nogaret, 'Un aspect de la pensée nobiliaire au xviiiᵉ siècle: l'antinobilisme', *Revue d'Histoire moderne et contemporaine*, xxix (1982), 443–9; Galliani, *Rousseau, le luxe et l'idéologie nobiliaire*, 172–5.
40. See above, pp. 44–5.
41. Quoted in Chaussinand-Nogaret, 'Un aspect de la pensée', 446, 447.

might be achieved, and in the famous private journal which he kept in the 1740s and 50s, his often caustic observations on public affairs revealed an everyday mind much less radical than that of the thwarted careerist of the 1730s. His unpublished writings also display ambiguities about the value of nobility, suggesting that his true preference was to reform rather than to abolish it.[42]

Despite the similarity of their names, the Marquis d'Argens (1701–71) came not from the metropolitan administrative elite but from the robe nobility of Provence. Reluctant to follow family traditions, he travelled widely before joining the army. Invalided out in 1734, he turned to literature, writing against religion, and he settled first in the tolerant world of the Dutch Republic, a major centre for French-language publishing.[43] Later he found a congenial niche at the court of Berlin, where he became a cultural arbiter under the Francophile rule of Frederick. Initially he wrote about the situation in the France he had just left, adopting the pose of the bemused foreigner reporting home on the strange ways of the country he was visiting. This by now well-established way of criticizing French manners had been perfected (though not originated) by Montesquieu's *Lettres Persanes* of 1721. In *Lettres juives, ou correspondance philosophique, historique et critique* (1738), d'Argens adopted the guise of a Sephardic Jew from the Levant. Most of the text was devoted to the absurdities of doctrinal disputes among Christians, but the social and institutional hegemony of nobles was witheringly condemned. It was based not on virtue or talent, but on money. The whole merit of many nobles, he observed, consisted of 'hunting, hitting peasants, impregnating their farmers' daughters, going to law against their village priests for a few honorific rights, and getting drunk with their stewards on Sundays'.[44] And in public affairs:

> Every day honours are accorded to a noble fool, son of a noble fool, grandson of a noble fool, great-grandson of a noble fool. Just because a man can Count a long run of ignorant and ridiculous ancestors whose example he perfectly follows, he has the right to exemption from a number of taxes and enjoys divers privileges that raise him above the rest of his fellow citizens. What is it to me that one of a man's forefathers was a captain of horse at the time of

---

42. See N. Johnson, 'L'idéologie politique du Marquis d'Argenson, d'après ses œuvres inédits', in *Etudes sur le xviiiᵉ siècle*, ii, *Idéologies de la noblesse* (Brussels, 1984), 21–8.

43. See Israel, *Radical Enlightenment*, 586–600.

44. *Lettres juives*, vi, 15–16, quoted in John Lough, *The Philosophes and Post-Revolutionary France* (Oxford, 1982), 59.

the Crusades? What! Must I honour an imbecile because one of his ancestors was killed by a Saracen or went off to the Holy Land?[45]

Few of the Prussian *Junkers* among whom d'Argens spent his last thirty years could make such claims. But, expected by their king to serve him with professionalism as army officers and administrators, they offered a striking contrast to many of their French counterparts. It was thrown into relief by their successful performance alongside, and then in the field against, the French in the wars of the 1740s and 50s. Their example, as Frederick the Great never tired of saying, was a persuasive argument for the qualities of noblemen; but not of the sort that so many had become in France. So long as French arms continued successful, as they broadly did until after the victory of Fontenoy in 1745, the kingdom's nobility could feel satisfied with itself, and could brush aside the gibes of men like Voltaire, d'Argenson, or d'Argens, who all enjoyed the benefits and attractions of the status even as they criticized it. When, in the subsequent decade, France's rivals seemed to be pulling ahead, more serious questions began to be raised about the nobility's claims to be the natural leaders of the nation.

✳ ✳ ✳

The initial stimulus to debate in the 1750s came from Montesquieu's ostensible defence of the role of nobles in monarchies in *De l'Esprit des Lois* of 1748.[46] The 'quarrel' about Montesquieu's formulations rumbled on until his death in 1755, and one of its central elements concerned his thinly disguised depiction of Great Britain as an ideal political model. Between 1743 and 1748, for the first time in over three decades, France had been at war with the island state, and the struggle had taken place as much in North America and India as in Europe. Fears were now widespread that the 'Modern Carthage' would use the commercial wealth derived from worldwide trade to destroy France's traditional, not to say natural, European hegemony. Coyer's *La Noblesse commerçante*, published as undeclared war continued to rage on the North American frontier, was based upon the premise that France could only remain competitive if she committed herself as wholeheartedly as her rival to commerce. The question in this context was how the energies and values of the

---

45. Quoted ibid., 58.   46. See above, pp. 46–50.

nobility might be harnessed and redirected to this end. Yet the corollary of suggesting that nobles take to trade was that their traditional disdain for it was outdated and indefensible; and Coyer lost no opportunity to condemn the way nobles behaved in general. The effect of d'Arcq's response to him was to provoke ripostes in which he was even more explicit—ranking soldiers, magistrates, and great lords with beggars in the category of idlers producing no wealth.[47] It also drew other critics of nobility into the argument. Gentlemen were never likely to adapt successfully to trade, one argued.[48] It would be better to make merchants noble than to make nobles merchants. Another, aware of how easily the supposedly inbred qualities of nobility could be bought, suggested that those possessing it sell or lease it out to commoners and use the proceeds to pay their debts. True nobility, he concluded, resurrecting a classic theme, resided only in courage and virtue.[49] The noble-sounding Rochon de Chabannes agreed, but concluded that for that reason nobility could never be other than personal. Hereditary nobility merely promoted and sustained idleness.[50] The controversy was widely reported in the French language press,[51] with Coyer and his supporters receiving a broadly more sympathetic hearing than those siding with d'Arcq. It even found its echo among ministers. The comptroller-general of finances, Jean Moreau de Séchelles, thought this would be a good moment to renew the edict of 1701 permitting nobles to enter wholesale trade without derogation; with the additional inducement that those who did so would be spared the indignity of registering with commercial courts.[52] And when he circularized all the parlements and intendants about the proposal, the forty-seven responses were largely favourable. Only four parlements and five intendants thought trade and nobility incompatible, although several other respondents foresaw hostility from merchants afraid of competition. The minister, however, had fallen by the time these reactions came in, and fierce opposition from the Parisian guilds dissuaded his successors from issuing a new edict. Evidently some

47. *La Noblesse militaire et commerçante; en réponse aux objections faites par l'auteur de La Noblesse militaire* (Amsterdam, 1756): and *Développement et défense du système de la Noblesse commerçante* (Amsterdam and Paris, 1757). See also Smith, 'Social categories', 348.
48. Séras, *Le Commerce ennobli* (Brussels, 1756).
49. The appropriately named J. H. Marchand, *La Noblesse commerçable ou ubiquiste* (Amsterdam, 1756). See also Shovlin, 'Towards a reinterpretation of revolutionary antinobilism', 49.
50. M. A. J. Rochon de Chabannes, *La Noblesse oisive* (1756)
51. See Mackrell, *Attack on 'Feudalism'*, 92–9.   52. Richard, *Noblesse d'Affaires*, 62–4.

influential non-nobles thought their superiors were best left to vegetate in the isolation of their own prejudices.

The 1750s were also the decade in which Jean-Jacques Rousseau first made a literary stir. In neither of the two *Discourses* for which he was known before the three great works of 1761–2 (*La nouvelle Héloïse, Du Contrat Social, Emile*) did he address the question of nobility directly; but his central themes—virtue, luxury, inequality—were inseparable from all discussion of nobility and its impact on society. Readers of Rousseau could readily conclude that the virtue habitually claimed for nobility by its defenders had little to do with the more generalized republican quality exalted by him; that noble values were responsible for much of the pernicious spread of luxury that he condemned; and that the most glaring of human inequalities were those claimed by the traditional rulers of society.[53] The Second Discourse, on the *Origins of Inequality* (1755) came closer to explicit condemnation. The natural moral equality of primitive mankind, Rousseau argued, had been destroyed by the lust for property, dominion and distinction—but there was no legitimacy in any of it. 'Adroit usurpation was made into irrevocable law, and for the profit of the ambitious few the Human Race was henceforth subjected to labour, to servitude and to misery.' Endless conflict was the result, 'and all those horrible prejudices which place in the rank of virtues the honour of shedding human blood'. But also social distinctions, with 'descendants rising ever higher the further off they got...; the more distant and uncertain the cause, the greater the effect; and the more idlers a family could number, the more illustrious it became'. The discourse concluded that it was against the Law of Nature, however defined, 'that a child should command an old man, that an imbecile should lead a wise man, and that a handful of people should wallow in superfluities, whilst the hungry multitude lacks necessities.' Two generations later, this incendiary language would help to make Rousseau a hero to revolutionaries, and no doubt it contributed to the tide which would sweep nobility away.[54] In the 1750s, however, when the strengths and weaknesses of the noble order were being discussed by others in very specific terms, Rousseau's approach

53. Renato Galliano has argued, however, in *Rousseau, le luxe et l'idéologie nobiliaire*, 304–5, 333–4, 365–74, that Rousseau's muted condemnation sprang from his fundamental acceptance of noble-inspired ideologies elevating virtue and deploring luxury as the corrosive consequence of increasing non-noble wealth.

54. For an example of revolutionary citation from the Second Discourse in criticism of the nobility, see Carré, *Noblesse de France et l'opinion publique*, 230.

was too general and theoretical, and his renown not yet well-enough established, for him to influence opinion much. Notoriously, the Academy of Dijon declined to honour the Second Discourse as it had the first.

For all the debate over *La Noblesse commerçante*, in fact, the greatest blow sustained by the nobility in the 1750s did not come from the criticism of pamphleteers. It came from the performance of nobles in the field they claimed as peculiarly their own: warfare. The Seven Years' War was a disaster for French arms both on land and sea. The qualities of leadership, courage, and commitment attributed by d'Arcq and a host of predecessors to the nobility had failed to prevent a naval defeat by the commercial is-landers,[55] and even more humiliation at the hands of Frederick the Great and his modern Spartans on the battlefields of Germany.[56] A military superiority that the French had taken for granted since the time of Louis XIV had been shown to be hollow. Even where French officers had fought with courage, they had all too often lacked discipline, not to say basic military competence.

Out of this shameful showing would arise, in the two subsequent decades, a reform movement aimed at making the French armed forces a match for the rivals who had worsted them. The smashed navy was resolutely rebuilt, to the point where, in the American War of Independence, it would briefly capture control of the North Atlantic and make possible the decisive Franco-American victory of Yorktown.[57] This was achieved without much change in the social background of naval officers. Most of the permanent complement remained noblemen, even if largely younger sons; and an attempt to set up a more meritocratic naval training academy was abandoned after a few years. Traditional structures seemed vindicated by ultimate success. Nor was noble dominance in the army challenged, despite far more extensive restructuring. Quite the reverse: the drive to make French armies a match for the Prussians involved copying them, and to that extent making French officers if anything more aristocratic than before. The professed aim was to make them more professional and to stimulate their vocational commitment.[58] And if that involved the

55. See James Pritchard, *Louis XV's Navy, 1748–1752: A Study in Organization and Administration* (Kingston and Montreal, 1987), 55–70.
56. Léonard, *L'Armée et ses problèmes*, 195–202; Lee Kennett, *The French Army in the Seven Years' War: A Study in Military Organization and Administration* (Durham, NC, 1967), 54–71.
57. Jonathan R. Dull, *The French Navy and American Independence: A Study of Arms and Diplomacy, 1774–1787* (Princeton, NJ, 1975).
58. David D. Bien, 'The Army in the French Enlightenment: Reform, Reaction and Revolution' Past and Present, 85 (1979), 68–98; Blaufarb, *French Army* 16–37.

tacit abandonment of the belief that military qualities were hereditary, it was replaced by the equally exclusivist and explicit conviction that they were best fostered by generations of family tradition. Purchase was progressively abandoned, which helped to eliminate the recently ennobled rich, but did nothing to dent the expectations of courtier playboys that they would continue to receive the best colonelcies and ranks above. And if military education was now to be fostered by a network of specialist schools, they recruited exclusively among provincial noble families and often with a substantial element of metropolitan patronage. No wonder later revolutionaries thought that the aristocratic grip on the officer corps was strengthening in the generation before 1789.

Nevertheless many nobles felt aggrieved. There were still not enough places in military schools, or regimental postings to satisfy all who felt entitled to them. And the systematic paring down of the prestigious but militarily marginal parade regiments of the Royal Household outraged the courtiers who customarily staffed them. The irony was that such policies were the work of ministers increasingly drawn (after 1758) from the Court nobility itself. At least they could disclaim responsibility for what many saw as an even greater humiliation than military defeat: the Austrian alliance which had sucked France into European engagement in the first place. That could be plausibly attributed to the upstart Madame de Pompadour and her circle of clients. But the Duke de Choiseul, who actually owed his rise to her support, maintained this alliance after the war, and it stood in many eyes as evidence of the folly of entrusting high policy to frivolous and irresponsible Court factions.

✳ ✳ ✳

These reactions formed part of a much wider inquest into the significance for the kingdom of the war's disasters. The whole decade of the 1760s was marked by intense national introspection, positively encouraged in many ways by the government. Not until the Revolution was the press as wide-ranging and free as it was down to 1770.[59] Works long considered too dangerous to publish, such as Meslier's *Testament* and d'Argenson's

---

59. Jack R. Censer, *The French Press in the Age of Enlightenment* (London and New York, 1994), 164–8. See also Joël Félix, *Finances et politique au siècle des lumières: Le ministère L'Averdy, 1763–1768* (Paris, 1999), 23–5.

Considérations, now appeared in print for the first time. Rousseau, it is true, did not escape unscathed when in 1762 he excoriated the artificiality of modern high society in *Emile*, and questioned the legitimacy of all existing political order in the *Social Contract*; but his tribulations gave his work an international resonance. In the *Social Contract* he brushed hereditary aristocracy aside as the worst of all forms of government,[60] and declared that the basic flaw in the Roman republic had been its failure to abolish the patrician order at its outset.[61] And over the decade he fell out with most of the aristocratic friends and patrons who had expedited his earlier career. In 1771 he had harsh words to say about noble power in Poland, in a characteristically trenchant formulation perhaps copied later by Sieyès: 'The Polish nation is made up of three orders: the nobles, who are everything, the burghers, who are nothing, and the peasants who are less than nothing.'[62] Polish nobles would never be happy and free, he declared, so long as they held their brothers in chains. But these remarks were not published until 1782, six years after their author died, as the privileged guest of the Marquis de Girardin.

Meanwhile the debate over the historical origins of the nobility rumbled on. In the 1750s it had been given renewed contemporary relevance by the claims of the parlements to be the spokesmen for and defenders of the 'fundamental laws' of the monarchy. Their most extreme apologist, the Jansenistic jurist Louis-Adrien Le Paige, had claimed in 1753 that France enjoyed immutable fundamental laws constraining the freedom of the monarch, and had done so ever since the time of Clovis.[63] This proposition outraged Gabriel Bonnot de Mably, who had made a name earlier in the century with lavish praise for the providential development of absolute monarchy. Naturally he had then found the arguments of Dubos congenial.[64] By the 1760s, however, years of patient historical research had changed Mably's mind, and destroyed his admiration for absolutism. In *Observations sur l'histoire de France*, which he offered to the public in 1765 in response to what he saw as a more open post-war atmosphere,[65] he rejected

60. Bk. III, ch. 5.   61. Bk. III, ch.10, fn.

62. *Considérations sur le gouvernement de Pologne*, ch.vi. See also below, p. 178.

63. *Lettres historiques sur les fonctions essentielles du parlement, sur le droit des pairs, et sur les loix fondamentales de la monarchie.*

64. *Parallèle des Romains et des Français, par rapport au gouvernement* (Paris, 1740). For Dubos, see above, pp. 45–6.

65. Johnson Kent Wright, *A Classical Republican in Eighteenth Century France: The Political Thought of Mably* (Stanford, CA, 1997), 142–53.

all the leading recent interpretations of early French history—whether of Boulainvilliers, Dubos, Montesquieu, or Le Paige. There had been no nobility among the Franks, and they had come to Gaul not as conquerors but as liberators. Yet they had established no enduring institutions either, neither a monarchy of clear legitimacy, nor bodies with the power to constrain it. The early history of France had been a process of constant flux, and only after the breakup of Charlemagne's empire did a feudal nobility begin to establish itself by usurping property rights over lands and vassals originally enjoyed only conditionally. In return for royal recognition of this power, they had thrown in their lot with the monarchy to smother any relics of earlier liberty. Nor were Le Paige's heroes, the nobility of the robe, spared. Not only were their vaunted fundamental laws a myth: they had no interest in establishing or restoring institutions (such as the Estates-General) which might protect the liberties of the nation at large. And, as Mably was putting the finishing touches to a further volume of *Observations* in 1771, the attack of Maupeou on the parlements showed that they did not have the power, either.[66]

Nobles emerged from Mably's analysis as the villains of French history: by turns greedy, ambitious, and craven, their claims based upon self-serving myths and lies. If they had ever been of service to the nation, it had been by accident, and the only possible further service that he foresaw (in a work written in 1758 but not published until 1789)[67] was likely to come about by accident too: forcing a bankrupt king to convoke the Estates-General. After the ease with which Maupeou smashed the parlements, Mably did not expect that to happen either. The *Observations* therefore offended everybody, as their author often tartly foresaw in the text of his voluminous footnotes. For that reason alone, the work was extremely successful, running into ten editions before Mably's death occasioned a collection of his published works in 1785. By then the *Observations* were widely regarded as a definitive refutation of claims to hegemony based on distant history. When, in the debate on the abolition of nobility on 19 June 1790, the *abbé* Maury claimed that nobility existed two centuries before fiefs, he was met with cries of 'Read Mably!'[68]

66. See below, pp. 83–4.
67. *Des Droits et des devoirs du citoyen*. For a full discussion of its significance, see Keith Michael Baker, 'A Script for the French Revolution: The Political Consciousness of the *abbé* Mably', in his *Inventing the French Revolution* (Cambridge, 1990), 86–106.
68. *Moniteur*, iv, 678. See also below, p. 235.

In the mid-1760s the government returned to the question of the nobility and commerce. As part of a far-reaching series of economic initiatives launched by the comptroller-general L'Averdy, a renewal, mooted a decade previously, of the declaration of 1701 permitting nobles to trade wholesale was at last issued in March 1765.[69] More innovative was a corollary, proclaimed in an *arrêt* of the king's council in 1767. Every year two businessmen were to be ennobled for their services to commerce, whilst wholesale merchants in general were to be considered as 'living nobly' and allowed to carry swords.[70] It was timid enough, and down to 1787 scarcely forty men of business found themselves ennobled for their services to commerce. Even so it was controversial. The physiocrats, at the height of their influence in promoting the paramountcy of agriculture in all economic development, were afraid that an attempt to dignify and recognize the value of commerce would ultimately seduce its most successful practitioners into noble disengagement and waste. Coyer, after a decade of occasional writings on other topics, returned to criticizing social habits in his satire against trade guilds *Chinki: Histoire cochin-chinoise qui peut servir à d'autres pays* (1768) and once more took the opportunity to condemn the idleness inherent in the noble outlook.[71] More radical still was Pierre Jaubert, a country priest from near Bordeaux, whose unsigned *Eloge de la roture* (1766) argued that nobles who inherited their privileges had done nothing to deserve them. Jaubert welcomed the edict of March 1765, although he was afraid that trading nobles might enjoy an unfair advantage through superior credit.[72] On the other hand he clearly believed that all the nobility's advantages were unfair. After ritual disclaimers that his strictures did not apply to every nobleman, he roundly denounced all claims to hereditary distinction. Nobility was an 'accidental' or 'chance' quality. However old it was, *roture* was older. It went back to Adam himself, none of whose sons ever claimed nobility. Nobility could never, and should never, be more than personal.[73] Its heredity had been established by violence, by forgetting that all men were originally brothers, and through the weakness of kings in the face of ambition. Distinction should only be accorded to

69. Richard, *Noblesse d'affaires*, 46–7; Félix, *Ministère l'Averdy*, 426–7.
70. Reinhard, 'Elite et noblesse', 14–15.
71. Bachaumont, iv, 88, 22 Aug. 1768. See also Adams, *Coyer and the Enlightenment*, 38–9.
72. *Eloge de la roture. Dédié aux roturiers* (London, 1766), 23. See also Smith, *Nobility Reimagined*, 132–4, 140–1.
73. Smith, *Nobility Reimagined*, 12–19.

merit, and 'it is not people of merit who are lacking in a State, but often places and employments are lacking for people of merit'.[74] Commoners constituted the most considerable of all political bodies. In fact, 'the people essentially constitutes the State', and 'any titled person who has no merit in his own account, is one of the heaviest burdens that the earth bears'.[75] Nobles were then denounced for their extravagance and slavery to fashion, the heartlessness of their dynastic marriages, the greed with which they looked forward to their parents' death, their constant search for privileges to evade taxation, and their contempt for agriculture. By contrast, though shamefully despised by most nobles, la roture was the most necessary and most useful body in the state. Most of Jaubert's themes were far from new, and had been thoroughly rehearsed in the controversies of the previous decade. His originality was to bring them together not as a mirror for noble reform, but to suggest that the true distinction was not to be noble at all. His language would not have been out of place a quarter of a century later. All that was lacking in 1766 was the sense that anything could be done to increase the 'regard' which Jaubert thought the merits of the Third Estate deserved.[76]

The merits of the Third Estate as the industrious and virtuous part of society became a fashionable theme in the 1760s. The paintings of Greuze and the later Chardin idealized the lives of ordinary people and gave them, as critics noted, a 'noble' quality. Engraved prints of Greuze's best-known works sold by the thousand.[77] In the theatre, Diderot argued for the merits of the *drame*, a genre that was neither tragedy nor comedy, but whose characters were ordinary people leading ordinary lives, and not speaking in verse. Beaumarchais' first published views on the theatre argued a similar case in 1767,[78] and his second play *Les Deux Amis ou le Négociant de Lyon* (1770) was dedicated to the Third Estate. Yet this, and other attempts at *drames* by him and Diderot, failed when performed. The greatest success was achieved by plays which moved theatrical norms on more gently. The sensation of the decade was Belloy's *Le Siège de Calais* (1765) which, in evoking a heroic episode from the Hundred Years' War, stoked patriotic

---

74. Ibid., 28.   75. Ibid., 42–3.

76. See the discussion in Shovlin, 'Political Economy of Honor', 55–6.

77. Thomas E. Crow, *Painters and Public Life in Eighteenth Century Paris* (New Haven, CT, and London, 1985), 141–2; Warren Roberts, *Morality and Social Class in Eighteenth Century French Literature and Painting* (Toronto, 1974), 129–30.

78. *Essai sur le genre dramatique sérieux* (Paris, 1767).

resentment against the English but had bourgeois heroes and a noble—if ultimately repentant—villain. The highly successful plays of Sedaine also satirized noble values by setting them against upright conduct on the part of commoners. And yet the hero of the best known, *Le Philosophe sans le savoir* (1765), though a businessman whose son is made to undergo the torments of a duel, emerges in the end as a nobleman who has renounced his status. Towards 1770 a less ambiguous critical tone began to be heard. In *Le Marchand de Smyrne*, the second comedy of the 29-year-old Sébastien Nicolas Roch Chamfort, a Turkish slave trader attempts to sell his stock of western captives by discovering what they can do. Among them are a genealogist, whose skills are characterized as useless, an unsaleable German Baron, and a haughty Spanish gentleman who when asked 'What do you do?' replies 'Nothing'. Years later, accused of the revolutionary crime of 'aristocracy', Chamfort would offer this play as evidence of long-standing egalitarian convictions.[79]

Another enthusiastic advocate of the *drame* was Louis-Sébastien Mercier, despite the early lack of success of his own plays. He sought to cushion theatrical disappointment with other writings, and achieved striking success with a utopian satire *L'An 2440, rêve s'il en fut jamais* (1771).[80] Like More's prototype, this utopia was a critique of current times, comparing them to a better world six centuries into the future. In that world there would be no hereditary or venal nobility—or at least not one officially recognized:[81]

> Among us … is no longer known that class of men who, under the title of nobility (which, height of ridicule, could be bought) would press to crawl around the throne, wished only to follow the calling of arms or of the Court, living in idleness, gorging their pride on old parchments and presenting the deplorable spectacle of a vanity equal to their misery. Your grenadiers shed their blood with as much intrepidity as the noblest among them and did not set so high a price on it. Besides, in our Republic such a denomination would have offended the other orders of the State. Citizens are equal: the only distinction is that which virtue, genius and work make between men.[82]

79. P. R. Auguis (ed.), *Oeuvres complètes de Chamfort*, 5 vols. (Paris, 1825), v, 322–3, Chamfort au citoyen Laveau, 8 Sept. 1793.
80. It proved a best-seller. See Robert Darnton, *The Forbidden Best Sellers of Eighteenth Century France* (London, 1996), 115–36.
81. Ch. vi, 'Embroidered Hats', which sets out Mercier's system of distinction, speaks of 'princes and dukes who enjoy their wealth unrecognized since they have not earned the right to marks of distinction'.
82. Ch. xxxvi, 'Form of the Government'.

The latter, however, would be recognized by the right to wear embroidered hats, and free access to the king's council: 'Policy and reason alike allow this distinction: it is only injurious for those who feel themselves forever incapable of higher things.' Princes would exist in this future world, and would even display coats of arms, but they would be innkeepers, maintain open table for the poor, and not pursue the 'ignoble or low' pastime of hunting.[83]

Sedaine, Beaumarchais, Chamfort, and Mercier were of a generation that would live to see the attempt to abolish nobility completely. But whatever their criticisms, none of them could have thought what was to happen twenty years later at all likely, or even perhaps desirable. Beaumarchais had added a particle to his name and bought an ennobling office. Chamfort would soon find himself living on the largesse of a princely household. Mercier seems not to have envisaged the complete disappearance of nobility even in his twenty-fifth-century utopia. And the early 1770s, meanwhile, would bring a vivid demonstration of the perils of weakening aristocratic institutions. In 1771 Chancellor Maupeou ruthlessly remodelled the parlements, dispossessed half the noble magistracy, and emasculated their power to resist the royal will. At the same time the relative freedom of public discussion and publication that had marked the 1760s came to an end,[84] while many of the king's debts were renounced and a whole programme of new taxes was pushed through. Despotism had struck, and nothing in France seemed to have the power to resist it.[85] Quite opposite conclusions about the role of the nobility could be drawn from this. The most obvious was to underline the doctrine of Montesquieu that there was no true monarchy without noble intermediary powers to restrain it, making sure that the laws were observed. Widely adopted by the stricken parlements and their supporters, its logic was that France needed nobles and aristocratic institutions even more strongly entrenched than before. More disquieting was the perception that all the institutions of aristocratic power had failed to prevent Maupeou from overturning the kingdom's whole constitutional fabric. Having failed militarily, the nobility had now failed politically too. The fate of the parlements, the main target

---

83. Ch. xxiv, 'The Innkeeper Prince'.
84. See Jeremy D. Popkin, *News and Politics in the Age of Revolution: Jean Luzac's* Gazette de Leyde (Ithaca, NY, 1989), 139–40; Censer, *French Press in the Age of Enlightenment*, 168–74.
85. See Durand Echeverria, *The Maupeou Revolution: A Study in the History of Libertarianism, France, 1770–1774* (Baton Rouge, LA, 1985), 81–3; Carcassonne, *Montesquieu et le problème*, ch. ix.

of Maupeou's attack, was particularly abject. Montesquieu's 'depositary of the laws' had been almost effortlessly overridden. The view of Mably, who published the concluding sections of his *Observations* on French history as Maupeou was carrying through his *coup*,[86] was that the magistracy had sold out to the forces of despotism like the feudal nobility before them. Nor did their history give grounds for expecting anything else. It was with their supine and venal collusion, after all, that the monarchy had dispensed with the only body truly capable of resisting its ambitions, the Estates-General.

Belatedly, however, they now began to call for this ultimate national assembly. Mably had once thought that this was how France might yet be rescued from its history, and only a few years after his death in 1785 that hope would be vindicated. In 1771 he had lost all hope of that. Did the magistrates and noblemen who now followed Malesherbes[87] in begging Louis XV to consult the nation really expect him to listen either? They certainly gave little enough thought to the problems that would arise when his successor yielded to such demands seventeen years later, problems that would only be resolved by a full-scale attack on the powers and pre-eminence of nobility itself. The call for the Estates in 1771 was largely rhetorical and abstract, and, if they thought about it at all, those espousing it presumably expected that nobles would continue to enjoy the dominant role in the assembly's proceedings as they had at its last meeting in 1614.[88]

In any case these voices were soon silenced. And the demand was forgotten when, less than four years later, Louis XV died and, within a matter of months, Maupeou and his ministerial allies were dismissed. The parlements were restored with their powers almost intact, amid scenes of popular jubilation. In the euphoria of a new reign, with a young king who seemed responsive to public opinion, the apparent need for the Estates vanished, and optimism about the monarchy's capacity for benevolent reform revived. All nobles might legitimately imagine that they would play a full part in that, and until 1787 Louis XVI would never dream of acting

86. Wright, *A Classical Republican*, 154–8.
87. In the remonstrances which he wrote for that court in February 1771. See Pierre Grosclaude, *Malesherbes, témoin et interprète de son temps* (Paris, 1961), 237–41; Echeverria, *Maupeou Revolution*, 86.
88. If indeed they knew anything about that somewhat futile occasion. See J. Michael Hayden, *France and the Estates-General of 1614* (Cambridge, 1974).

without their collusion. Long before then, however, it had become clear that no reform in the state was possible that did not threaten the interests of one part or another of the nobility. And that was even true of the policy which at last restored its martial self-esteem, the alliance with the United States of America.

4

Aristocracy Avoided

America and the Cincinnati

No nobility had ever been established in America. Nobody who had freely braved the rigours and perils of a North Atlantic crossing since the early seventeenth century had done so in order to replicate or find replicated the institutions or hierarchies of the old world. Much of the allure of America was precisely that European constraints—religious, political, or social—held no sway there. Long before they dreamed of independence, British subjects in the thirteen colonies were taking pride in their freedom from hereditary hegemonies, and in their own lack of deference. As early as 1722,[1] young Benjamin Franklin was entertaining Bostonians with mockery of titles of honour:

> In old Time it was no disrespect for Men and Women to be call'd by their own Names: *Adam* was never called *Master* Adam; we never read of Noah *Esquire*, Lot *Knight* and *Baronet*, nor the *Right Honorable* Abraham, *Viscount* Mesopotamia, *Barron* of Carran;[2] no, no, they were plain Men, honest Country Grasiers, that took Care of their Families and their Flocks.

Two decades later, this time in Philadelphia, and now with first-hand experience of British social hierarchies, Franklin used his most famous mouthpiece *Poor Richard* to pour more pointed scorn on hereditary pretension.[3] A nobleman claiming pure ancestry back as far as the Norman conquest, he observed, would derive it mathematically from 1,048,576 noble ancestors; and 300 years further back would need to find more ancestors than there had been people in the world, which 'shows the Impossibility of preserving Blood free from … Mixtures, and

---

1. *The New England Courant*, 18 Feb. 1722/3, reprinted in J. A. Leo Lemay (ed.), *Benjamin Franklin: Writings* (New York, 1987), 49–50.
2. *sic*: but is this a misprint for Canaan?   3. Reprinted ibid., 1269.

that the Pretension of such Purity of Blood in ancient Families is a mere Joke'.

Satirical asides of this sort were intended as much to confirm prejudices as to change minds—although Franklin's opinions on the subject never changed, and would prove unexpectedly influential decades later on another continent.[4] But much of his success as a young journalist was rooted in saying things that appealed to his colonial readers' instinctive common sense and idea of themselves. By the 1770s, freedom from European hierarchies had become a commonplace of American identity. 'What is an American?' asked one chapter of Hector St John de Crèvecoeur's *Letters from an American Farmer* (1782), one of the first books to present an authentic (if perhaps over-idyllic) picture of life in colonial America to a European audience. The answer offered by this French immigrant was complex, but a consistent strand was the egalitarianism of Americans. American society 'is not composed, as in Europe, of great lords who possess every thing, and of a herd of people who have nothing. Here are no aristocratical families, no courts, no kings, no bishops.'[5] 'Mighty lords' did not cream off the surplus of industrious farmers to embellish their castles. 'Strangers to the honours of monarchy', Americans did not aspire to the possession of affluent fortunes, with which to purchase founding titles, and frivolous names'.[6] This picture was transmitted to France when Crèvecoeur's *Letters* were published there in 1784. It was kept before French eyes throughout the later 1780s by Jacques-Pierre Brissot, future revolutionary, who (without as yet having been there) used it to rebut a more critical account of conditions in the new republic by the philosophical soldier the Marquis de Chastellux.[7]

Whether Americans really were as egalitarian as they liked to think was another matter. Their ambivalences were well exemplified by Abigail Adams, the formidable wife of the future second president, himself a vocal critic of nobility. Touring England in 1787, she noted that her mother's family name, Quincy, had once been held by the earls of Winchester.[8] 'Titles' and 'Genioligy', she wrote, 'have heitherto been of so little consideration in America that scarcely any person traces their descent

4. See below, pp. 121–3.
5. *Letters from an American Farmer*, ed. Susan Manning (Oxford, 1997), 40.   6. Ibid., 132.
7. See Leonore Loft, *Passion, Politics and Philosophie. Rediscovering J.-P. Brissot* (Westport, CT, 2002), 14. On Chastellux, see also below, p. 87.
8. Lyman H. Butterfield (ed.), *The Adams Papers. Diary and Autobiography of John Adams*, 4 vols. (Cambridge, MA, 1961–2) iii, 204. Diary of Abigail Adams, 21 July 1787, and letter to Mrs. Cranch, 15 Sept. 1787.

beyond the third Generation.' But 'can it be wondered at', she reflected later in the year, 'that I should ever wish to Trace an Ancestor amongst the Signers of Magna Carta.'

There might have been no established nobility in America, but nobles and men of title were not unknown. Generals or admirals commanding British forces in the colonies were seldom without titles or membership of orders of chivalry. Occasionally a colonial-born governor or other servant of the crown would be rewarded with a knighthood or baronetcy. The entire province of Maryland was notionally the 'property' of Lord Baltimore, whose ancestors had received it by charter from the crown. Admittedly he was an absentee proprietor; but in Virginia the largest single resident landowner was Thomas, Lord Fairfax, whose 5 million acres dominated the province's northern reaches.[9] In that province, indeed, observed that Swedish connoisseur of noble ways, Count Hans Axel von Fersen, in 1782, 'each proprietor wishes to be a lord...All of those who engage in commerce here are regarded as inferior to the others: they say they are not gentlemen and they do not wish to live in the same society with them.'[10] Europeans were often surprised to encounter such reflexes in the new world, when there was no ultimate ennoblement to aspire to. But gentility—the work-free style and polite attributes which were merely a prerequisite for nobility in Europe—was an ideal widely pursued throughout the American colonies for its own sake. Just as in Europe, most successful men of commerce sooner or later sought to invest their profits in land, leisure, and ostentation, to assume the style of gentlemen. Franklin himself sold up his printing business to embrace a life of cultivated leisure as soon as his accumulated fortune permitted;[11] and up and down the tidewater, from Savannah to Boston, the self-made merchants of the Atlantic seaports relentlessly poured their profits into hiding their origins, living high, putting on airs, building grand houses, and accumulating real estate. Admittedly this was harder to achieve in New England than in Virginia or South Carolina. Land was still relatively plentiful in the southern colonies, and the cultivation of sub-tropical crops

---

9. Jackson Turner Main, *The Sovereign States, 1775–83* (New York, 1973), 302, 307. See also J. Franklin Jameson, *The American Revolution Considered as a Social Movement* (2nd edn; Princeton, NJ, 1967), 33–5.

10. Quoted in H. Arnold Barton, *Count Hans Axel von Fersen: Aristocrat in an Age of Revolution* (Boston, MA, 1975), 35.

11. See Gordon S. Wood, *The Radicalism of the American Revolution* (New York, 1991), 38, 85–6.

on large plantations worked by slaves made it easy for landed elites to imitate European ideals of noble living. But Massachusetts, Rhode Island, and Connecticut were densely settled, plots were small, and a credible gentleman's identity was much more difficult to establish. That did not deter successful families such as the Hutchinsons or Hancocks of Boston from displaying their superiority through lavish town houses and country retreats.

American gentlemen were no less determined to pass on their superior standing to their children, and to perpetuate their names. In the southern colonies, property was transmitted by the English law of primogeniture. Testamentary freedom could circumvent its operation; but many testators, so far from taking advantage of this to share out their property between heirs, sought (as in England[12]) to reinforce the effects of primogeniture by establishing entails to keep key blocks of property intact down the generations, under the control of a single and preferably male heir. Further north, inheritance was partible and entail rare, but gentlemanly dynasties could still be maintained, like noble ones in Europe, by carefully arranged marriages linking families of equal status or aspiration. Cultural hegemony could also be consolidated through education. By mid-century, most of the colonies had a well-established college where gentlemen could buy their sons superior attainments. At Harvard, Yale, or the colleges at Princeton, New York, or Williamsburg men destined for future provincial prominence would imbibe that extensive knowledge of the classics which would enable them, for the rest of their lives, to lard their conversation with classical allusions or tags in Latin or Greek and so mark themselves out as men of cultural accomplishment on either side of the Atlantic.[13] This classical training in its turn would provide ancient models with which to identify. They could recognize themselves as patricians, with a hereditary aptitude for leading their fellow citizens, as in ancient Rome. And they could naturally think themselves best equipped for government of their thirteen little polities—all, in Aristotelian terminology, aristocracies.

The levers of local power were certainly in their hands. From their ranks were appointed most colonial governors, who in turn nominated their friends and clients to crown offices, and seats on the governors' councils

12. See Habakkuk, *Marriage, Debt, and the Estate System*.
13. See Carl J. Richard, *The Founders and the Classics: Greece, Rome, and the American Enlightenment* (Cambridge, MA, 1994), ch. 1.

which constituted the upper houses of colonial legislatures. They also largely controlled who was elected to the lower houses by manipulating property qualifications, electoral districts, and the processes of election itself. This was the apparatus of the established order, and it gave those who made it work a strong identification with the ultimate authority in that order, the crown of Great Britain. In colonial terms, if not strictly classical ones, monarchy and aristocracy went together. They provided the same sort of mutual support as Montesquieu described between kings and nobilities.[14]

* * *

Among the mainsprings of the American Revolution was the breakdown of this relationship. When the king in parliament sought to impose taxes and commercial restrictions without consulting the institutions of colonial representation, the threat to the power of colonial aristocracies was stark. They reacted by standing aside when rioters attacked the bearers of royal authority in Boston, New York, Philadelphia, and Charleston. But it soon became clear that many of the rioters were hostile to all sorts of authority, and that defiance of the king threatened to develop into defiance of hierarchy in general. In some colonies insurrectionists in the under-represented back country even looked to the crown for protection against the indifference of tidewater oligarchs. Either way, the revolutionary struggle unlocked the instinctive egalitarianism of most of the American population, and demonstrated the fragility of 'aristocratic' power. By the mid-1770s popular defiance had made the thirteen colonies virtually ungovernable. Men of wealth and property were now seriously alarmed, and probably more than were prepared to admit it longed for some way of restoring harmony with the British crown. The delegates to the first Continental Congress in the autumn of 1774 were all drawn from the traditional elites, but they were not chosen for their conservatism, and were sent to Congress by assemblies without legal standing, acting under popular pressure. Their mandate was less to seek conciliation than to organize resistance. They claimed legitimacy in the name of the people as a whole.[15] So did the second Congress, which they summoned for

14. See above, p. 47.
15. See Richard B. Morris, *The Forging of the Union, 1781–1789* (New York, 1987), 55–8.

May 1775 with the stipulation that it should be elected without reference to traditional authorities or procedures. By the time it met, fighting had begun, and Congress soon found itself raising an army, and revenues to pay for it. Talk of separation from Great Britain, whether enthusiastic or apprehensive, was everywhere. Residual loyalism was eventually swamped by the tide of approval that met Tom Paine's *Common Sense* over the first months of 1776.

Common Sense was an attack on monarchy. It was time, Paine argued, for the colonies to assert their own maturity, throw off the patriarchal authority of George III, and proclaim an independent republic. Monarchical power was a usurpation, an affront to the natural equality of mankind. But:

> To the evil of monarchy we have added that of hereditary succession; and as the first is a degradation and lessening of ourselves, so the second, claimed as a matter of right, is an insult and an imposition on posterity. For all men being originally equals, no *one* by *birth* could have a right to set up his own family in perpetual preference to all others for ever, and though himself might deserve *some* decent degree of honour of his contemporaries, yet his descendants might be far too unworthy to inherit them ... Most wise men, in their private sentiments, have ever treated hereditary right with contempt; yet it is one of those evils, which when once established is not easily removed; many submit from fear, others from superstition, and the more powerful part shares with the king the plunder of the rest.[16]

So one of the central features of aristocracy stood condemned by the same arguments that rejected monarchy. If, therefore, there was to be a republic, could there be any place for hereditary distinctions in the new nation?

The Declaration of Independence, when it was adopted seven months later, implied not. It proclaimed as a self-evident truth that all men are created equal. The Declaration was written by Thomas Jefferson, a Virginia planter who, at thirty-three, had already one of the most widely read and best educated minds in the colonies. It was endorsed by a drafting committee of five, which also included Benjamin Franklin and John Adams, the intellectual leader of New England-resistance to British claims. Whatever their differences, now and later, about how the new republic should function and evolve, Jefferson, Franklin, and Adams were at one in believing there was no place in it for nobility of any kind.

16. *Common Sense* in Eric Foner (ed.), *Thomas Paine: Collected Writings* (New York, 1995), 16.

Nor were they alone in this, or conspicuously in advance of their compatriots. Over the spring of 1776, as the break with monarchy inexorably approached, Congress authorized and urged the thirteen colonies to constitute themselves into free and independent states. It was the signal for bitter power struggles in most of them, as opposed interest groups sought to ground advantage or protection in constitutional law. Many of the debates in constitutional conventions, and in press discussions of their proceedings, revolved around the powers and make-up of upper houses—or indeed (in some states) whether they were desirable at all.[17] The argument against them, which triumphed in Pennsylvania, was that they could only obstruct the popular will and must, however constituted, be a bulwark of aristocracy.[18] Yet even there, unicameralism owed much of its success to the fact that no upper house had existed even before 1776. Elsewhere, apart from Georgia, the traditional English rationale of checks and balances prevailed, with upper houses retained broadly to represent property, and lower, persons. Nowhere was a senate limited to the wealthy more firmly established than in Maryland;[19] but the framers of the state's new constitution went to great trouble to disguise the idea that this meant aristocratic rule. In the declaration of rights with which the constitution was prefaced, they stipulated that 'no title of nobility or hereditary honours, ought to be granted in this state'.

Maryland was not the first state to adopt a declaration of rights, but it was the first to include this specific provision. The Virginia Declaration of Rights, drafted by George Mason and adopted in June 1776, preceded that of Maryland by five months, but the furthest it went against aristocracy was to declare that 'no man, or set of men, are entitled to exclusive or separate emoluments or privileges from the community but in consideration of public services, which not being descendible, neither ought the offices of magistrate, legislator or judge to be hereditary'.[20]

This provision was directed at tendencies visible in office-holding in a number of the pre-revolutionary colonies and it was echoed in the declaration of rights drafted by John Adams for Massachusetts and adopted

17. See Gordon S. Wood, *The Creation of the American Republic, 1776–1783* (Chapel Hill, NC, 1969), ch. vi.
18. See J. R. Pole, *Political Representation in England and the Origins of the American Republic* (London, 1966), 251–80.
19. Main, *Sovereign States*, 161–5.
20. Text in R. R. Palmer, *The Age of the Democratic Revolution*, vol. i, *The Challenge* (Princeton, NJ, 1959), 518.

in 1780. Long before that, in December 1776, the new constitution of North Carolina proclaimed that 'no hereditary emoluments, privileges or honors ought to be granted or conferred in this state'.[21] And by that time steps were being taken to generalize the ban on titles and heredity to all of the United States. In the summer of 1776, immediately after independence had been declared, a congressional committee was set up to draft ground rules for the union and relations between its constituent states. They were to be termed Articles of Confederation. A first draft, by John Dickinson, hitherto the most eloquent opponent of independence in Congress, stipulated (Article iv) that nobody in the service of the United States, or what he still called colonies, should accept any gift or emolument from the British king or any other foreign state, 'nor shall the United States assembled, or any Colony grant any title of Nobility'.[22] Over the next sixteen months, Dickinson's draft was much amended in the committee; and although laid before Congress on 15 November 1777, the Articles of Confederation did not become operative until March 1781 owing to disputes between various states which repeatedly postponed their ratification. But the attack on nobility was now even clearer than in Dickinson's draft. No person, it was now stated (Art. vi) 'holding any office of profit or trust under the United States, or any of them [shall] accept of any present, emolument, office or title, of any kind whatever, from any king, prince, or foreign state; nor shall the United States, in Congress assembled, or any of them, grant any title of nobility'.[23]

* * *

The new nation therefore explicitly rejected old Europe's governing principle of social authority. In the summer of 1778, Benjamin Franklin, by now the representative of Congress in Paris, received a mysterious letter which he believed came with the approval of George III. It suggested, as a basis for reconciliation with the rebel colonies, that America might be governed in the king's name by a House of 200 American peers, including

21. Main, *Sovereign States*, 170.
22. Merrill Jensen, *The Articles of Confederation* (Madison, WI, 1940), 255. Although Jensen declares, on Dickinson's authority, that 'every article was bitterly fought over' (127), he devotes no discussion to this question, leaving us to presume that it was at least less contentious than many others.
23. Ibid., Appendix, 264–5.

Franklin himself and John Adams, who had recently arrived from America to reinforce him. Hard to authenticate, the letter was not taken seriously. 'An Aristocracy of American Peers!' snorted Adams when he recalled the episode, 'hereditary Peers I suppose were meant, but whether hereditary or for Life, nothing could be more abhorrent to the general Sense of America at that time, which was for making every Magistrate & every Legislator eligible & that annually at least...We thought the whole subject so futile that I think We never transmitted any Account of it to Congress.'[24]

Peers and nobles were one thing, and the young republic might already appear safe from them. But they were not the same thing as aristocracy; and it may be that, in Maryland or Virginia, public rejection of a titled elite was designed to mask the continued power of an untitled one. Thomas Jefferson was certainly convinced that more positive measures were necessary to ensure the purity of the Commonwealth of Virginia.[25] He resigned his seat in Congress in order to promote them at home in the House of Delegates. Nearest his heart was a bill to prohibit entails. 'The transmission of...property from generation to generation in the same name', he later recalled, 'raised up a distinct set of families who, being privileged by law in the perpetuation of their wealth were thus formed into a Patrician order, distinguished by the splendor and luxury of their establishments...to annul this privilege, and instead of an aristocracy of wealth, of more harm and danger, than benefit, to society, to make an opening for the aristocracy of virtue and talent, which nature has wisely provided for the direction of the interests of society, & scattered with equal hand through all it's [sic] conditions, was deemed essential to a well ordered republic.'[26] Entails were less common in Virginia than Jefferson supposed,[27] and perhaps that was why the bill passed with relatively little opposition by the end of 1776. A complementary measure took longer. Primogeniture, in Jefferson's view, was a 'feudal and unnatural distinction which made one member of every family rich, and all the rest poor'.[28] In his determination to eradicate 'every fibre...of antient or future aristocracy', he introduced a bill to establish partible inheritance, 'the best of all Agrarian laws'. But he left the legislature in order to become governor before he could guide this

24. Butterfield, *Adams Papers, Diaries*, iv, 151–3.
25. See Dumas Malone, *Jefferson the Virginian* (Boston, MA, 1948), 250–7.
26. *Autobiography* (1821) in Merrill D. Petersen (ed.), *Thomas Jefferson: Writings* (New York, 1984), 32.
27. Wood, *Radicalism of the American Revolution*, 47.   28. *Autobiography*, 44.

law through, and it was not enacted until 1785, when he was far away in France. By then, however, both entail and primogeniture were well on the way to disappearance throughout the new nation. Both had entirely gone by 1792, so effectively had the future president 'laid the axe to the root of Pseudo-aristocracy'.[29]

Yet his anti-aristocratic programme for Virginia in 1776 had aimed at more. Part and parcel of it had been the disestablishment of the Anglican Church, which 'relieved the people from taxation for the support of a religion not theirs; for the establishment was truly of the religion of the rich, the dissenting sects being entirely composed of the less wealthy people'.[30] And perhaps most fundamental of all was a lavish provision, which did not pass because of its cost, for universal republican education. Its object was to qualify all the commonwealth's people 'to understand their rights, to maintain them, and to exercise with intelligence their parts in self-government'. Republicans must be educated to cherish their institutions, to make them work, and to recognize what threatened them. The system would also aim to identify and bring on the ablest students, the future leaders of the Commonwealth, true or 'natural', the aristocrats of each generation. It was essential, in Jefferson's view, to act soon and decisively while the republic was in its infancy. 'It can never be too often repeated', he wrote in 1781, 'that the time for fixing every essential right on a legal basis is when our rulers are honest, and ourselves united. From the conclusion of this war we shall be going down hill. It will not then be necessary to resort every moment to the people for support. They will be forgotten, therefore, and their rights disregarded … The shackles, therefore, which shall not be knocked off at the conclusion of this war, will remain on us long, will be made heavier and heavier, till our rights shall revive or expire in a convulsion.'[31]

* * *

How easily, imperceptibly, and perhaps unconsciously, backsliding habits could become established was prefigured early in October 1776. The high command of the newly established Continental Army of the United States

---

29. Petersen, *Writings*, 1308, Jefferson to John Adams, 28 Oct. 1813.   30. *Autobiography*, 44.
31. *Notes on the State of Virginia*, in Petersen, *Writings*, 287.

was apprehensively observing the landing of British troops near New York. George Washington, the commander-in-chief, was there, and so was John Adams, inspecting the state of the army on his way from Philadelphia to Massachusetts. Among Washington's entourage was Henry Knox, a Bostonian bookseller whom Adams knew. Knox, enjoying the rank of colonel and soon to be promoted brigadier-general, was exhilarated by his transformation into a military man. Bookish both, he and Adams compared the armed struggle now beginning to the republican conflicts of ancient Rome. Knox hoped it would prove just as memorable, and 'said he should wish for some ribbon to wear in his hat, or in his button hole, to be transmitted to his descendants as a badge and a proof that he had fought in defence of their liberties'. Adams, who recalled this conversation to Thomas Jefferson twelve years later,[32] noted that 'He spoke of it in such precise terms, as showed he had revolved it in his mind before.' By 1788 this was an important recollection, as both Adams and Jefferson knew, for Knox's dreams of perpetuating military glory seemed to have been the origin of what they both saw as the most determined attempt to create an American order of nobility.

Seven years passed before Knox sought to give substance to his idea. During that interval he had been in the thick of much of the fighting, and he was present, and active, at the final scenes of victory in 1781 when the British surrendered at Yorktown. The army they surrendered to was commanded by George Washington; but most of the troops who invested the little coastal town, and all the warships cruising offshore preventing its relief, were French. Whether the Americans could have won the war for their independence without the help of the French will always be debatable; but they could certainly never have achieved it so quickly and decisively without the presence of thousands of French regular troops and the flower of the French navy. The irony was lost on nobody. A republic committed from its foundation to civil and political equality, and bound by its own Articles of Confederation to spurn titles of nobility, made its first international alliance with a kingdom governed by nobles. If anything, the hegemony of nobles within France was intensifying,[33] and nowhere more obviously

---

32. Julian P. Boyd (ed.), *The Papers of Thomas Jefferson* (Princeton, NJ, 1950–) [hereafter *Jefferson Papers*], xiii, 11, 'Memorandums on a Tour from Paris to Amsterdam, Strasburg, and back to Paris', 16 March 1788. See also North Callahan, *Henry Knox, General Washington's General* (New York, 1958), 210.

33. See above, pp. 13, 25–6.

than in the very army now employed to help these rebels against a king and an aristocratic parliament. Almost to a man, the French officers[34] were noblemen. Those among them who were decorated veterans of the Seven Years' War always, in the French way, wore their insignia. Franklin, who as American minister in Paris was surrounded by such display, was concerned that his countrymen might 'have been too much struck with the Ribbands and Crosses they have seen among them hanging to the Buttonholes of Foreign Officers'.[35] Titles were always punctiliously used, even among volunteers who served under American rather than French command. The most celebrated was Lafayette, who was always known to his American comrades in arms as 'the Marquis'. To Americans he would dismiss this as a 'chance rank',[36] and swear that 'Nobility is But an insignificant kind of people for Revolutions. They have no notions of Equality between men, they want to govern, they have too much to looze.'[37] But it is hard to believe that his meteoric rise to general rank in the American army would have occurred if he had been a penniless nobody; and he never hesitated to flaunt his birth among fellow Frenchman.[38] At least it was authentic; but that of another successful European volunteer was more dubious. Friedrich Wilhelm Augustus Heinrich Ferdinand, Baron von Steuben, had seen seventeen years' service as an officer in the army of Frederick the Great, but he really was a penniless adventurer when he arrived in America in 1777.[39] His experience in Europe's most successful and well-drilled army was the key to his rise in a rebel force made up at first largely of undisciplined militia and volunteers. Always wearing his Prussian medals, he liked to be known as a Baron, but the particle *von* had been assumed by his grandfather. And Steuben himself added the final 'n' to his name in order to validate a false genealogy reaching back to the sixteenth century. In this, like Baron Cloots,[40] he was a more typical European nobleman than many liked to think—although it was easier to usurp the status among Americans who took a pride in not understanding its intricacies.

34. The most reliable list is Gilbert Bodinier, *Dictionnaire des officiers de l'armée royale qui ont combattu aux Etats Unis pendant la guerre d'indépendance, 1776–1783* (Vincennes, 1983).
35. Franklin to Sarah Bache, 26 Jan. 1784, in Petersen, *Writings*, 1084.
36. Stanley J. Idzerda (ed.), *Lafayette in the Age of Revolution: Selected Letters and Papers, 1776–1790*, 5 vols. (Ithaca, NY, 1977–83), ii, 326, Lafayette to Franklin, 11 Oct. 1779.
37. Ibid., 335, Lafayette to Franklin, 2 Nov. 1779.
38. See Louis Gottschalk, *Lafayette Joins the American Army* (Chicago, IL, 1937); Lloyd Kramer, *Lafayette in Two Worlds* (Chapel Hill, NC, 1996), 24.
39. J. M. Palmer, *General von Steuben* (New Haven, CT, 1937), 14–16.
40. See above, p. 1.

After Yorktown the British rapidly opened peace negotiations, and the French withdrew their forces from North America. Even Lafayette returned to France to help expedite peace negotiations, and bask in the adulation of his compatriots.[41] The American army, however, remained mobilized until the last British troops prepared to leave, its morale crumbling as Congress failed to find means for paying it off. By the spring of 1783 there was widespread talk of mutiny in the camp at Newburgh, New York.[42] Senior generals were said to be implicated, including possibly Knox and his friend Steuben. Fears of mutiny were being talked up in Philadelphia, where Congress was sitting and many leading figures were dissatisfied with the weak and decentralized structure of authority under the Articles of Confederation. It took a dramatic and unusually passionate intervention from Washington himself to dissuade the Newburgh 'conspirators' from making more overt threats against Congress. As a result, a relieved legislature hurriedly made enough financial promises to enable the disbandment of the army to begin in May. Henry Knox saw this as the moment to realize his long-pondered dreams of commemorating the armed struggle for independence.

The idea was not his alone. Several groups of officers, at Newburgh and elsewhere, appear to have been discussing ways to keep in touch after demobilization, perhaps with thoughts of further action in case Congress should default on its promises.[43] But nobody was better placed than Knox, with the bulk of the army still gathered around him, to turn such plans into a reality. Early in April, before peace had yet formally to be announced, he began to draft proposals. The proclamation came on 19th, and at once Knox and a group of associates called a meeting for 8 May 'for the purpose of considering the expediency of the officers of the army forming themselves into a military society'.[44] It

41. Louis Gottschalk, *Lafayette and the Close of the American Revolution* (Chicago, IL, 1942), 329–86.

42. See Richard H. Kohn, 'The Inside History of the Newburgh Conspiracy: America and the *coup d'état*', *William and Mary Quarterly*, 3rd series, 27 (1970), 187–220.

43. Asked in October to join the organization which Knox and his friends had by then set up, Brigadier-General Jethro Sumner wrote from North Carolina that 'Before any intimation of what had been done ... the Officers of this line had it in contemplation to form themselves into a society.' Curtis Carroll Davis, *Revolution's Godchild: The Birth, Death and Regeneration of the Society of the Cincinnati in North Carolina* (Chapel Hill, NC, 1976), 5. Sumner to William Heath, 28 Oct. 1783.

44. Minor Myers, Jr, *Liberty without Anarchy: A History of the Society of the Cincinnati* (Charlottesville, VA, 1983), 24. See also Markus Hünermörder, *The Society of the Cincinnati: Conspiracy and Distrust in Early America* (New York and Oxford, 2006), 15–19.

finally took place on 10 May, under the chairmanship of Steuben, the senior general present. The delegates discussed Knox's draft set of rules for the Society, the so-called *Institution,* appointed a committee to produce a final version, and reconvened on 13th at Steuben's headquarters in Fishkill. Here they set themselves up as founders of the Society of the Cincinnati.

* * *

The Cincinnati, declared the *Institution*,[45] were to be a 'society of friends' dedicated to perpetuating the memory of the struggle for American independence. Its basis was to be in the 'immutable principles' of preserving 'inviolate those exalted rights and liberties of human nature for which they have fought and bled'; promoting and cherishing 'union and national honor between the respective States … of the American empire'; and 'extending acts of beneficence, according to the ability of the Society, towards those officers and their families, who unfortunately may be under the necessity of receiving it'. To the latter end, members were required to pay a membership fee of one month's pay, and invited to make further donations to the Society's funds.

There were echoes in this of the discontents voiced earlier in the year at Newburgh: the charitable mission of the Society suggested that it expected Congress might not meet its commitments towards 'deranged' (ie retired) officers. Such echoes would arouse fears, which lasted for more than a generation, that this, the first body other than Congress to enjoy representation from every state, might harbour politically dangerous ambitions.[46] Perhaps it was to dispel such worries in advance that the founders adopted their name. Lucius Quinctius Cincinnatus was familiar to all Latinate men who had studied Roman history through Livy.[47] A poor farmer, he had been called from the plough and given dictatorial powers by the Senate, in order to save the republic from its enemies the Aequi. The powers were granted for six months, but Cincinnatus routed the enemy within six weeks, resigned the dictatorship and returned to the

---

45. Frequently reprinted, the most accessible recent text is the appendix to Myers, *Liberty without Anarchy*.
46. See Merrill Jensen, *The New Nation: A History of the United States during the Confederation, 1781–1789* (New York, 1950), 262–5.
47. Livy, III, xxxvi–xxix. See also Richard, *The Founders and the Classics*, 55–6.

plough. All this made him an ideal model of patriotic, republican virtue, and the founders of the Society declared themselves 'resolved to follow his example, by returning to their citizenship'.

Yet republican citizenship was scarcely compatible with some of their other intentions. Membership of the Society was open to 'all the officers of the American army, as well as those who have resigned with honor, after three years' service in the capacity of officers, or who have been deranged by the resolution of Congress'. But the Society was also intended 'to endure as long as they shall endure, or any of their eldest male posterity, and, in failure thereof, the collateral branches who may be judged worthy of becoming its supporters and Members...and as a testimony of affection to the memory of the off-spring of such officers as have died in the service, their eldest male branches shall have the same right of becoming members, as the children of the actual members of the Society'. Although provision was also made for a limited number of honorary members 'eminent for their abilities and patriotism, whose views may be directed to the same laudable objects' it was perfectly clear that this was to be a closed caste of former warriors, transmitting membership down the generations by primogeniture: a sort of American nobility.

There was worse. Now was the moment for Knox to introduce his beloved ribbons. 'The Society shall have an Order, by which its members shall be known and distinguished, which shall be a medal of gold, of a proper size to receive the emblems, and suspended by a deep blue riband two inches wide, edged with white, descriptive of the union of France and America.' The medal would depict Cincinnatus with his plough, with the motto *Omnia relinquit servare rempublicam* ('He relinquished all to save the republic'). Members would presumably be able to flaunt it in civil life, just as European nobles wore their orders and stars. Some European nobles, indeed, would be able to add this one to their others: a final provision of the institution was that membership should be extended to the generals and colonels of the French army in token of 'the generous assistance this country has received from France'. If this was the germ of an American nobility, it was to be one closely associated with the most glittering European example. And this intention began to influence its conduct almost at once. On 20 May Steuben wrote to Major Pierre Charles L'Enfant, a Frenchman in the American service with a reputation for draughtsmanship, asking him to suggest designs for the medal. L'Enfant replied:

A medal ... is considered in the different states of Europe, only as the reward of the laborer or the artist, or as a sign of a manufacturing community ... in an Institution of this sort, the main design should be to render it respectable to everybody, and that it is only in appealing to the senses that you can engage the attention of the common people who have certain habitual prejudices which cannot be destroyed. A gentleman already invested with any European Order would be unwilling to carry a medal [but] ... a new and particular form will be adding a recommendation to its real value, and engage those invested with it to wear it in the same manner, as their other Military Order, which is the surest means of putting it at once upon a footing with them.[48]

He enclosed designs for insignia incorporating a bald eagle, 'which is peculiar to this continent', and offered to go to Paris, where there were 'persons ... capable of executing it to perfection', to have his designs made up. At a meeting on 19 June L'Enfant's designs and offers were accepted.

Meanwhile the Society announced itself and its intentions to the world. The plan envisaged a branch in every state, and ranking commanders were written to with a request to take charge of establishing them. Steuben also wrote to Anne-César de La Luzerne, French minister in Philadelphia, and the leading French commanders in the war, inviting them to be founding members. Finally a deputation waited on George Washington, requesting him as commander-in-chief of the army to be the Society's first president-general. Seemingly without hesitation, he accepted. His signature was added to the 'parchment roll' establishing the Society at the head of thirty-five other founder members. Preoccupied with the disbandment of a still restive army, Washington had more pressing matters on his mind than the details of a veterans' club. It was in any case not due to convene for its first plenary meeting until all the state societies had been established; and ample time, until May 1784, was left for that. Neither he, nor Knox, nor any of his co-founders foresaw that those months would see their society become the first subject of serious public controversy in the world's newest republic.

✳ ✳ ✳

Only late in September was Washington able to turn his mind to the Society over which he had agreed to preside. 'I shall be obliged to you',

---

48. Text in Edgar Erskine Hume (ed.), *General Washington's Correspondence Concerning the Society of the Cincinnati* (Baltimore, MD, 1941) [Hereafter *GWC*], 11–13, L'Enfant to Steuben, 10 June 1783.

he wrote to Knox,[49] 'for pointing out *in precise terms* what is expected from the President of the Cincinnati previous to the General Meeting in May next. As I never was present at any of your Meetings, and have never seen the proceedings of the last, I may, for want of information of the part I am to act, neglect some essential duty which might not only be injurious to the Society, but Mortifying to myself.' Knox, now officially Secretary of the Society, sent him the *Institution,* and appears to have asked him to write as president to the senior army officer in each state where a Society was not yet known to be forming, and also to the senior French officers named in the *Institution.* The general further agreed to write to Lafayette asking him to coordinate enrolments and take subscriptions in France, and to give letters of credence to L'Enfant for the mission to Paris to procure insignia or 'eagles' as they were now being called.[50] At the same time he announced to Knox a donation of $500 to the Society's funds. No doubt he was already contemplating the even greater compliment to the ideals of the Society which he implicitly made when, on 23 December, he came before Congress sitting at Annapolis, and resigned his command, his mission completed.[51] This was how republican soldiers ought to behave. The example created a sensation throughout Europe and America.

By then, however, the Cincinnati ideal, as espoused by the Society at least, was under mounting attack throughout the republic.[52] Its most redoubtable foe was Judge Aedanus Burke, of South Carolina.[53] Born in Galway and educated by the Jesuits at Saint-Omer in France, Burke had come to America in the 1760s. He was settled in South Carolina by the time of the war, and established as a judge before it was over. He knew everybody of importance in Charleston—including Major-General William Moultrie, who, as the senior army officer in the state, was asked to organize its branch of the Cincinnati. It took shape at the end of August 1783, but already Burke had heard about it and was determined to oppose it.[54] Some later said (though Burke called them liars) that his motive was jealousy at not being eligible for membership. He seems genuinely to have disliked the whole idea of aristocracy. Among his favourite books was

---

49. *GWC*, 19. 23 Sept. 1783.   50. Ibid., 22. 16 Oct. 1783.
51. See Garry Wills, *Cincinnatus: George Washington and the Enlightenment* (Garden City, NY, 1984), 10–16.
52. Hünemörder, *Society of the Cincinnati*, 25–8, 81–8, 135–53.
53. John C. Meleney, *The Public Life of Aedanus Burke: Revolutionary Republican in Post-Revolutionary South Carolina* (Columbia, SC, 1989).
54. Meleney, *The Public Life of Aedanus Burke*, 84–5.

Don Quixote, that sustained lampoon of knightly ideas.[55] Nor would an Irish Catholic be likely to think kindly of the Protestant Ascendancy who monopolized power in the land of his birth.[56] And he was certainly deeply suspicious of the way big landowners in South Carolina had used the opportunities of the war to buttress their own wealth and power further at the expense of conveniently presumed 'loyalists' who had prospered while the British controlled Charleston and the tidewater. His first printed work, signed *Cassius* and published in January 1783, was *An Address to the Freemen of South Carolina* which protested at the fines and confiscations imposed on loyalists by a dubiously elected state assembly.[57] A fair proportion of the more famous pamphlet which followed ten months later was devoted to the same local issue.[58]

Considerations on the Society or Order of Cincinnati, also signed *Cassius*, was published in Charleston in the third week in October.[59] The author clearly had a copy of the Society's *Institution* in his hands, since he quoted liberally from it. From it he deduced (erroneously) that the moving spirit behind the Society was Steuben, a European nobleman. 'But I have the honor to tell Baron Steuben, that though an order of peerage may do very well under the petty princes of Germany, yet in America it is incompatible with our freedom.' (p 11) For an incipient order of peerage was what Burke considered the Cincinnati to be. 'It is in reality, and will turn out to be, *an hereditary peerage*; a nobility to them and their male issue.' (p 7) It was 'self-created, and an infringement of a general law of the Union'—article six of the Confederation. But:

> though the order cannot, at present, be sanctified by legal authority...if they but keep up with firmness and perseverance against opposition...; if they have but patience, subtilty and address to cloak their design under a pious name of raising a charitable fund; so as to make it go down only for a few years; even if they are obliged from policy to lay aside the *badge and blue ribbon*:...the next generation will drink as deep of noble blood, and a hereditary passage be as firmly settled in each potent family, and riveted in our government, as any order of nobility is in the monarchies of Europe. This Order is planted in a fiery, hot ambition and thirst for power, and its branches will end in tyranny. The Cincinnati will soon be corrupted and,...in less

---

55. Ibid., 20. See above, pp. 64–5.
56. He speaks in *Considerations*, 23, of the newly founded Order of St Patrick as 'only a link in the chain which ties[the Irish] down'.
57. Meleney, *Public Life of Aedanus Burke*, 76–83.   58. pp. 25–9, out of 32.
59. Edgar Erskine Hume, 'Early Opposition to the Cincinnati' *Americana*, xxx (1936), 599–600.

than a century it will occasion such an inequality in the condition of our inhabitants, that the country will be composed only of two ranks of men; the patricians or nobles and the rabble. (pp. 7–8)

The history of ancient Rome was invoked as an awful warning: the ambition of the Patrician order was blamed for all the misfortunes of the republic. Burke excoriated the *'pride and insolence* on the one hand, and oppression and cringing habits on the other' that Sallust had marked out as *'the common disease of a nobility'* (p 11). Montesquieu (though uncited) had clearly taught him that a distinct order of patricians or nobility 'however thought necessary to support the throne of a prince, or form a barrier between him and his people, is a bane and a curse to a republick' (p. 9); while from Robertson's *Charles V* he took the assurance that 'the modern nobility of Europe … was formed out of the rude, barbarian Generals and field officers of the Goth and Vandal army', many of its titles being self-created (p. 23). Blackstone was ridiculed for calling peers, who were 'actually tools and rivets for driving and clenching poverty, meanness and abasement of the people', pillars for supporting the crown (p. 24). Generals whose true glory had been the establishment of the republic, apparently set this at nothing 'unless they have a quaint title stuck upon their family, and a badge or bawble dangling at the button-hole' (p. 25). To thwart them, Burke urged, 'Let the Legislature immediately enter into spirited Resolutions' against 'a dangerous insult to the rights and liberties of the people, and a fatal stab to that principle of equality, which forms the basis of our government' (p. 30).

'The more I reflect on this institution, and the political consequences it will involve', Burke declared at the start of his argument (p. 5), 'the more I am filled with astonishment … that it should be so little to have been attended to, that it is not even the subject of private conversation.' His achievement was to change all that. The identity of 'Cassius' was an open secret from the start, and within weeks of its publication had been reprinted in Philadelphia with the epigraph *Blow ye the Trumpet in Zion*. It was serialized in a Boston newspaper early in 1784, and in Connecticut later in the spring.[60] Replies began to appear in Philadelphia before 1783 was out. A self-proclaimed 'Obscure Individual', in a wordy, not very cogent or clearly argued pamphlet, printed extensive extracts from

60. Myers, *Liberty without Anarchy*, 66, n. 6; Wallace Evan Davies, 'The Society of the Cincinnati in New England, 1783–1800', *William and Mary Quarterly*, 3rd series, v (1948), 5–12.

the Society's *Institution,* and pointed to the example of Washington, the Society's president-general, who 'having restored the Goddess Liberty to her country and built her a permanent habitation there, he quietly retires to the rural shade, the glory and wonder of the age'.[61] In December an anonymous 'Member of the Society' in Maryland offered a point-by-point rebuttal of Cassius's 'bugbears, to frighten children, [rather] than serious cautions addressed to reasonable men'.[62] The Cincinnati, he pointed out, were a private society with no charter or privileges, and in no sense an order. They did not need congressional authorization, and they had no ambitions either to become a peerage, or a 'bond of political union' (p. 12). Besides, 'the consequences of our institution are yet in futurity; they will admit of no proof from parallels so distant as those you have attempted to draw, and can only be guessed at from present circumstances' (p. 16). But this uncertain 'futurity' was precisely the source of all the controversy, which swept through the newspapers of most of the states over that winter, and intensified as the date of the Society's first general meeting approached in May 1784. Town meetings anxiously discussed the new society in Connecticut and Massachusetts, and in February the commonwealth's senate established a committee 'to consider what measures are necessary to be taken in order to prevent the ill consequences of any combinations that are, or may hereafter be formed, to promote undue distinction among the citizens of this free State, & tending to establish a hereditary nobility, contrary to the federation of the U. States, & the Spirit of the Constitution of this Com'th'.[63] The lower house endorsed the move, and on 22 March they jointly resolved that the Cincinnati was an 'unjustifiable' society and 'dangerous to the peace, liberty and safety of the United States in general, and this Commonwealth in particular'.[64] Rhode Island, meanwhile, was widely (though inaccurately) rumoured to be about to disfranchise known members of the new Society. New England sentiment was well summed up by Samuel Adams, organizer of the Boston 'Sons of Liberty' during the struggle for independence. It was a plan, he wrote, 'disgustful to common feeling... This country must be

61. *Observations on a late Pamphlet, entitled 'Considerations upon the Society or Order of the Cincinnati'* (Philadephia, PA, 1783), 19. Hume, 'Early Opposition', 599, suggests that the author was Brigadier-General Stephen Moylan.
62. *A Reply to a Pamphlet, entitled, Considerations on the Society or order of Cincinnati, etc., published in South Carolina* (Annapolis, MD, 1783), 8.
63. Quoted in Davies, 'Society of the Cincinnati in New England', 12.
64. Quoted ibid., 13.

to a great degree humiliated and debased before they will patiently bear to see individuals stalking with their assumed honorary badges, and proudly boasting, "These are the distinctions of *our* blood" ... the Cincinnati are very unpopular here.'[65] Even the admission of foreigners, proven friends of the new republic as most of those eligible were, was viewed with suspicion, since most of them were, as Adams put it, 'the subjects of different nations, (and those nations widely differing in their principles of government) ... Are we sure that these two nations will never have separate views, and very national and interested ones too ... ?'[66]

At the turn of the year, Washington wrote to the state societies to tell them that he had fixed the first general meeting of the Cincinnati at Philadelphia for the first Monday in May.[67] The responses he received showed that some members were disturbed at the growing clamour, and were reluctant to commit themselves to attending such a controversial event. Even Knox was worried. 'The Cincinnati appears (however groundlessly)', he wrote from his native Boston on 21 February, 'to be an object of jealousy. The idea is, that it has been created by a foreign influence in order to change our form of government ... Burke's pamphlet has had its full operation. The cool, dispassionate men seem to approve of the institution generally, but dislike descent.'[68] He reported the disquiet of the Massachusetts legislature, in the light of which the state's society had deemed it prudent not to offer any honorary memberships for the moment. By the time this letter arrived, however, almost a month later,[69] Washington had received even more disturbing news from France.

* * *

Even before the formation of the Cincinnati, rumours were circulating in Europe that the American struggle for independence was to be commemorated by some form of chivalric order. A French newspaper published in Germany carried a report in March 1783, dated 1 January in Philadelphia,

---

65. James T. Austin, *The Life of Elbridge Gerry, with Contemporary Letters* (Boston, MA, 1828), 422, Adams to Gerry, 19 April 1784.
66. Ibid., 426, Adams to Gerry, 23 Apr. 1784.
67. Letters of convocation in *GWC*, 42–3, 46–9.
68. Ibid., 95–6. See also Callahan, *Knox*, 213–4.
69. Ibid., 122, Washington to Knox, 20 March 1784, where he says 'Your letter of the 21st ulto. Did not reach my hand until yesterday.'

that a body of twenty-four 'Knights of Liberty' was to be established, with Benjamin Franklin (of all people) as its chancellor.[70] The first news of the Cincinnati's establishment, however, probably reached France with one of its founding members, Colonel Jean-Baptiste Gouvion, a French engineer officer who had volunteered for service in America at the same time as Lafayette, and who set off home to France in June 1783. Knox, in a letter to Lafayette,[71] said Gouvion would give him full details. Perhaps other rumours originating with Gouvion led to Washington being approached later in the summer from Warsaw by a group calling itself the Order of Divine Providence.[72] It offered to make thirty-six senior American officers knights of the order, with suitable insignia to wear, on payment of a subscription. This 'Order' was in fact as self-created as the Cincinnati, and shared the purpose of accumulating funds to relieve its poorer members. The ever-cautious Washington referred the offer to Congress, where it met with a hostile reception and was eventually rejected, with considerable publicity, at the height of the press furore over the Cincinnati in January 1784. And by then, a somewhat different furore had broken out in France.[73]

Official news of the formation of the Cincinnati came with the arrival of L'Enfant at Le Havre on 8 December. The major had spent the months after the acceptance of his offer to procure 'eagles' in organizing his voyage. By mid-October he was ready to leave. Washington gave him letters of credence for transacting business on behalf of the Society, and individual letters of invitation to join for Lafayette and the senior officers named in the Society's *Institution*.[74] The general had previously agreed with Knox that 'the Marquis de Lafayette would be the most proper person in France to interest in our affairs',[75] and accordingly the Marquis was requested, in the letter to him conveyed by L'Enfant, to receive signatures and subscriptions from 'any of the Foreign Officers who are qualified by serving three years in our Army'.[76]

70. Myers, *Liberty without Anarchy*, 16–17, 21–2. A photocopy of a MS extract from this issue (12 March 1783), p. 184 is in the file 'Cincinnati, opposition to' in the library of Anderson House, Washington, DC.
71. Idzerda, *Lafayette*, v, 137, Knox to Lafayette, 16 June 1783.
72. See Myers, *Liberty without Anarchy*, 53, referring to Washington Papers, Library of Congress, 443, xi, Heintz to Washington, 13 May 1783.
73. Hünemörder, *Society of the Cincinnati*, 125–131.   74. *GWC*, 20–1, 23–4, 26–7, 30–1.
75. Ibid., 28, Washington to Knox, 29 Oct. 1783.
76. Ibid., 29, Washington to Lafayette, 30 Oct. 1783.

It was the sort of opportunity that Lafayette loved. 'His foible', as Jefferson later remarked, 'is a canine appetite for popularity',[77] and he always tried to appear at the centre of things. The moment L'Enfant delivered Washington's letter he made contact with the foreign secretary, Vergennes, whom he had perhaps warned in advance about the existence of the Society after the arrival of Gouvion.[78] He now asked Vergennes to seek the king's permission for his subjects who had served in the American army to join the Society. He expressed hopes, too, that the same permission would be extended to officers who had served under the French flag. Finally he enclosed a draft announcement of the Society's establishment, objectives, and inclusion of French members for the official *Gazette de France*. It duly appeared on 23 December,[79] but, doubtless to Lafayette's annoyance, it was less a reflection of his activity than that of others to whom Washington had written. General Rochambeau had already written two days earlier to the Marquis de Ségur, minister of war, on behalf of his own officers. D'Estaing, the senior admiral, had contacted the navy minister, the Marquis de Castries. Rochambeau even enclosed his own translation of Washington's letter for the king's eyes.[80] As a result, the royal council had already discussed the subject by the time Lafayette wrote, and the two ministers informed their respective correspondents that permission had been given for them and their officers to join the Society. Even more important (as it proved), the king had consented to his officers wearing the insignia of the Cincinnati alongside their French decorations, a privilege only extended previously to the highly prestigious and exclusive order of the Golden Fleece. Nothing could have marked it out more clearly, in European eyes, as an order of chivalry of the first rank.

It was now the talk of Paris, and would remain so throughout the winter. American veterans were soon clamouring for admission to the Society and the right to wear its precious riband and bald eagle. 'Our badge' Lafayette reported to Washington,[81] 'is highly wished and warmly contended for by all those who hope they have some claim to it. The Nation have been very

77. *Jefferson Papers*, xi, 95, Jefferson to Madison, 30 Jan. 1787.
78. Idzerda, *Lafayette*, v, 388–9, Lafayette to Vergennes, 16 Dec. 1783. 'You know the regulations' of the Cincinnati, he noted.
79. Text in Baron Ludovic de Contenson, *La Société des Cincinnati de France et la Guerre d'Amérique, 1778–1783* (Paris, 1934), 28; translation in *GWC*, 34–5.
80. Contenson, *La Société des Cincinnati*, 24.
81. L. Gottschalk (ed.), *The Letters of Lafayette to Washington* (Philadelphia, PA, 1976) 273, Lafayette to Washington, 25 Dec. 1783. Also in Idzerda, *Lafayette*, v, 179–80.

much pleased with the attention our Society has paid to the Alliance.' But this sunny report might have been phrased another way: 'warm contention' could equally have been described as an undignified stampede to establish membership. 'All that mattered to us', reminisced Count de Ségur, son of the war minister and later elected secretary of the French Society, 'was the pleasure of showing this warriors' palm on our chests, and to draw the gaze in public places of a crowd of idlers attracted and assembled by the least novelty.'[82] At least young Ségur's claim to membership was unimpeachable. But so diverse were the solicitations of others that Lafayette, Rochambeau, and soon enough Washington himself found themselves applied to like heralds or *juges d'armes* to assess the credentials of suppliants. Matters were not helped by the vagueness of the rules for membership, not to mention issues which their framers had not thought of in the camp at Newburgh. Any American officer with three years' proven service might join, but the *Institution* only spoke of French colonels and ranks above. Four French admirals were named, but others forgotten, and nothing at all was said of captains in the fleet which had made the victory at Yorktown possible. What of officers who had served in the Americas, but not on the mainland? What of those prevented from serving for three years by wounds, or others who had been longer in American or French service together but not three full years in either? Officers who had fought honorably in the war, but by chance not in the American theatre, also felt their efforts belittled by the distinction. As early as 24 December, Louis Antoine, Count de Bougainville, the celebrated circumnavigator of the globe, wrote to Washington to complain of his exclusion, despite having commanded ships of the line in American waters throughout the war.[83] The next day d'Estaing, though himself named a member in the *Institution*, wrote on behalf of 'the gallant officers whom I conducted twice into North America', who were 'mortified' at what they believed was the 'mistake' of excluding ships' captains.[84] Two weeks later Charles de Lameth, though not promoted colonel until after he left America wounded in both legs, following several years' service, complained that he was excluded, whilst colonels with less than two months' service before hostilities ended got in.[85] Meanwhile there was much amusement at the illiteracy of officers clamouring to wear 'the cross of Saint Signatus', thinking this a new decoration under Christian

82. *Mémoires ou souvenirs et anecdotes*, 3 vols. (Paris, 1826), ii, 43–4.   83. *GWC*, 35–6.
84. Ibid., 39–41.   85. Ibid., 49–51.

rather than classical tutelage.[86] 'The Cincinnatus riband', a caustic French observer reported from Versailles at the end of May, 'is furiously prostituted here and in Paris. We scorn the red ribands which so many contemptible folk dishonour, but in truth American blue ribands are straining our eyes.'[87]

There was also tension between the French founders. 'I need not telling you', Lafayette reported to Washington, 'old Rochambeau wants to be as conspicuous as he can … as you know he does in every other affair.'[88] D'Estaing, meanwhile, as the senior French officer eligible for the Society, was critical of Lafayette's influence in complicating L'Enfant's mission.[89] All were anxious that the public should learn of their activities, and the press was well informed of ceremonies held on 19 January to inaugurate the French branch of the Society.[90] They ended with a grand banquet at which toasts were drunk to Washington and the American army, but began with separate meetings. Fifteen officers in the American service met first at Lafayette's, where the Marquis distributed the eagles which L'Enfant had by now manufactured. Only then did they proceed to Rochambeau's house, where a body of qualifying officers from the French auxiliary army were invested by their former general. D'Estaing, meanwhile, was planning to ensure that his former captains were all admitted. Having learnt that Washington had asked L'Enfant to order a more elaborate eagle set with diamonds for him to wear on ceremonial occasions, the admiral intervened with the jeweller to have it made more elaborate still, and inscribed as a gift to Washington from French sailors. He paid for it himself, but hoped for reimbursement from the captains once they had been admitted to the Society.[91] The publicity given to the new order brought a fresh wave of applications to join. L'Enfant reported to Steuben that it was more coveted than the cross of St Louis,[92] and Lafayette was worried from the start that

86. Horace Walpole had heard a version of this story as early as December 1783: Myers, *Liberty without Anarchy*, 147. See also Ségur, *Mémoires*, i, 45–6. Washington received at least one letter asking for the decoration in these terms: *GWC*, 219–20, Alexandre de Gubain to Washington, 13 June 1785.

87. [Métra] *Correspondance secrète, politique et littéraire,* 17 vols. (London, 1788–9) xvi, 213, 28 May 1784. The 'red riband' refers to the order of Saint Louis, ostensibly a reward for military merit. See above, p. 23.

88. Gottschalk, *Letters*, 274. 10 January 1784.

89. *GWC*, 81–3, Hume's translation of d'Estaing to La Luzerne, 18 Feb. 1784.

90. Bachaumont, xxv, 70–1, 27 Jan. 1784; 102, 9 Feb. 1784. Louis Gottschalk, *Lafayette between the American and the French Revolution (1783–1789)* (Chicago, IL, 1950), 59–60.

91. *GWC*, 81–3, Hume's translation of d'Estaing to La Luzerne, 18 Feb. 1784.

92. Gottschalk, *Lafayette between*, 58–9.

it could be devalued: 'In case the Badge is multiplied, it will loose its price in Europe.'[93] He turned down some dubious applications, although he forwarded them all to Washington, with the comment that 'if such were admitted, the pretensions would be numberless, and come from very disagreeable persons'.[94] Among those he did admit, however, was Baron Frédéric de Kalb, son of a volunteer who had come to America with him in 1777 and who, by then a major-general in the American service, had been killed in action in 1780.[95] Almost from the start, therefore, the French branch of the Cincinnati was admitting hereditary members.

Yet heredity, as in America, was its greatest problem. Complaints about it were being heard within weeks of L'Enfant's arrival.[96] Particularly vocal were Americans resident in Paris, who were now receiving belated news of the controversies in America from newspapers sent over from home. John Jay, about to return to America from his service as a peace commissioner, wrote that the order 'does not, in the opinion of the wisest men whom I have heard speak on the subject, either do credit to those who formed and patronized or to those who suffered it'.[97] He was open in his own disapproval, fearing that 'it would eventually divide us into two mighty factions. The permission of the king of France for his officers to be of that order was asked, but the like compliment was not paid to our own sovereign.'[98] Franklin said little in public, but when his daughter sent him American papers, he replied at length with scornful amusement.[99] 'I only wonder' he wrote, 'that, when the united Wisdom of our Nation had, in the Articles of Confederation, manifested their Dislike of establishing Ranks of Nobility, by Authority either of the Congress or of any particular State, a Number of private persons should think proper to distinguish themselves and their Posterity, from their fellow Citizens, and form an Order of *hereditary Knights*, in direct Opposition to the solemnly declared Sense of their Country.' Honours, he said, should pass backwards to ancestors,

93. Lafayette to Washington, 10 Jan. 1784 in Gottschalk, *Letters*, 274.
94. Ibid., 279, 9 March 1784.   95. *GWC*, 104, Kalb to Washington, 3 March 1784.
96. Idzerda, *Lafayette*, v, 185, Lafayette to James McHenry, 26 Dec. 1783; Gottschalk, *Letters*, 389, Lafayette to Washington, 25 Dec. 1783.
97. Henry P. Johnson (ed.), *The Correspondence and Public Papers of John Jay*, 4 vols. (New York, 1891), iii, 111–2, Jay to Gouverneur Morris, 10 Feb. 1784.
98. Austin, *Life of Gerry*, 425, Jay to Gerry, 19 Feb. 1784. Jay declared openly, reported Gouvion to Knox in March, 'that if it did take well in the States he would not care whether the Revolution had succeeded or not.' Francis S. Drake, *Memorials of the Society of the Cincinnati of Massachusetts* (Boston, MA, 1873), 30.
99. Petersen, *Writings*, 1084, Franklin to Sarah Bache, 26 Jan. 1784.

in the Chinese manner. 'But the *descending Honour*, to Posterity who could have no share in obtaining it, is not only groundless and absurd, but often hurtful to that Posterity, since it is apt to make them proud, disdaining to be employ'd in useful Arts, and thence falling into Poverty, and all the Meanness, Servility and wretchedness attending it; which is the present case with much of what is called the *Noblesse* in Europe.' He offered a modified version of *Poor Richard*'s calculation of 1751[100] to show how little of an original Cincinnatus's blood would remain in the veins of a ninth-generation descendant. He then went on to ridicule the badge, its bald eagle looking more like a turkey (though none the worse for that), and the poor Latin of the motto.[101] The Doctor was so pleased with these reflections that he considered casting them into an anonymous pamphlet. He soon realized how dangerous this course might be for an accredited diplomat, and only later did he find a more indirect means of broadcasting his views.[102] John Adams, now American minister in the Dutch Republic, had no such inhibitions. He freely declared in public that the Cincinnati were 'a *French blessing*' dreamed up by Lafayette and his posturing compatriots. Soon enough the Marquis heard about this, and wrote to Adams to protest.[103] The idea had not been his, he asserted, truly enough. Less plausible was his assurance that 'Orders, titles, and Such other foolish tokens of Vanity, Are Not More Valued in France, Not Even So Much, As they are in Germany, Russia, Spain, & Great Britain.' And if the Cincinnati were dangerous, entirely or in part, they should be dissolved or amended, and 'I Heartily Would Consent to the destruction.' Adams expressed no regret or reassurance in his reply.[104] 'It is not my intention to discuss the question', he tersely rejoined:

> It is too ample a field. But it is not done by the Sovereigns of our Country. What would be said, in any Nation of Europe, if a new order, was instituted by private Gentlemen, without consulting the Sovereign? It is against our Confederation and against the Constitution of Several States as it appears to me. It is against the Spirit of our Governments and the Genius of our people ... It has and will unavoidably introduce Contests and Dissentions,

100. See above, p. 86.
101. The British *chargé d'affaires*, in his dispatch of 23 Jan. 1784, also sneered at 'words, for which a boy of ten years old would have been flogged at Eton or Westminster'.: Oscar Browning (ed.), *Despatches from Paris 1784–1790 (1784–1787), Camden Third Series,* xvi (London, 1909), 1.
102. See below, p. 122.
103. Idzerda, *Lafayette in the Age*, v, 201–3, Lafayette to John Adams, 8 Mar. 1784.
104. Ibid., 211–2, 28 Mar. 1784.

than which nothing is more injurious to Republican States, especially new ones. I sincerely hope our officers...will voluntarily, after a little reflection lay it aside.

But Lafayette's claim that he was ready for that to happen seems to have been sincere enough. By March he was beginning to see the whole enterprise as a quagmire. 'Most of the Americans here', he wrote to Washington on 9th, 'are violent against our Association. You easily guess I am not remiss in opposing them; and, however, if it be found that the hereditary right endangers the true principles of democracy, I am as ready as any man to renounce it. You will be my compass, my dear general... *To you alone* I would say so much.'[105] This letter, and another giving full details of all the contentious cases which had arisen, was entrusted to L'Enfant, who sailed for America on 16 March with a set of eagles and plates for printing diplomas of membership, together with an offer from the French Cincinnati to donate 60,000 *livres* to the Society's funds. His aim was to present these at the first general meeting scheduled for May. He arrived in New York on 29 April.[106]

✲ ✲ ✲

It was early in March that news of the Society's establishment in France reached Washington.[107] From Lafayette he learnt that Louis XVI had given permission for his subjects to join, and wear the eagle; but also that 'the hereditary part of the *Institution* has its comments'—just as in America. This seems to have convinced the general that the May meeting must take some action, and be fully attended to give authority to whatever was done. 'I think, not only the whole number chosen should attend, but the abilities of them should be coolly, deliberately, and wisely employed, when met, to obviate the prejudices and remove the jealousies, which are already imbibed.' 'A thin meeting', he told another correspondent, 'will bring the Society into contempt.'[108] Washington's concern was reported

---

105. *GWC*, 109.   106. Ibid., 146, L'Enfant to Washington, 29 Apr. 1784.

107. *GWC*, 122, Washington to Knox, 20 Mar. 1784, where he speaks of 'the official letter which I have lately received from the Marq. De Lafayette.' This would appear to be the latter's letter of 10 Jan., enclosing a further one about the Society: Gottschalk, *Letters*, 274. The enclosure seems to have been the letter of 25 Dec. 1783.

108. Ibid., 124, Washington to Benjamin Walker, 24 Mar. 1784.

to the French foreign secretary by La Luzerne, the French minister in Philadelphia, who stayed with him at Mount Vernon early in April.[109] La Luzerne was himself a Cincinnatus; but one who was not, never having fought in the war, was Washington's fellow Virginian, Thomas Jefferson. The general now sought a detached opinion from this cool observer of the public scene, currently a member of Congress, as to how inflamed their compatriots were, how justifiably, what congressional opinion was, and what ought to be done.[110]

Jefferson appears to have been bursting to give Washington his views for some time.[111] He had always regretted, he replied, that one who commanded such universal respect had become involved with a body of such contentious potential. The desire of the Society's founders to commemorate their wartime comradeship he thought natural, '& I have no suspicion that they foresaw, much less intended, those mischiefs, which exist perhaps in the forebodings of politicians only'. But those apprehended 'mischiefs' were complex, and widespread. As well as heredity, there were fears about foreign influence, about the perpetuation of military ways, about any organization not authorized by Congress, and about what the Society might do when Washington's own guiding influence was removed. Congress, Jefferson thought, 'as a body if left to themselves, will in my opinion say nothing on the subject', but if pressed from outside he thought they might act against the Society, since no member he had spoken to was in favour of it, and Burke's pamphlet had been very influential. As to what should be done, he did not advise the general directly, but if the Society were to choose to amend its rules 'so as to render it unobjectionable, I think this would not be effected without such a modification as would amount almost to annihilation; for such would it be to part with it's inheritability, it's organization, & it's assemblies'. Yet, if it were to go this far, the neatest and least painful way might be to seek the endorsement of Congress, and be met with certain dissolution from that body. The tone was restrained and respectful, and it may be that Jefferson was not yet as deeply hostile to the Cincinnati as he was later to become.[112] But Washington could scarcely fail to see that he was being advised to find a way of closing the Society down.

109. AAE, Correspondance politique, Etats-Unis, 27, f. 282. An English translation in *GWC*, 133–4.
110. *Jefferson Papers*, vii, 88, Washington to Jefferson, 8 Apr. 1784. Also in *GWC*, 130–1.
111. *Jefferson Papers*, vii, 105–8, 16 Apr. 1784. Also in *GWC*, 135–7.
112. See below, p. 136.

The first general meeting of the Cincinnati was arranged for 4 May. On his way to Philadelphia, Jefferson recalled, Washington 'called on me at Annapolis. It was a little after candle-light, and he sat with me till after midnight, conversing, almost exclusively, on that subject... and when I expressed an idea that if the hereditary quality were suppressed, the institution might perhaps be indulged during the lives of the officers now living, and who had actually served, "no," he said, "not a fibre of it ought to be left, to be an eye-sore to the public, a ground of dissatisfaction, and a line of separation between them and their country"; and he left me with a determination to use all his influence for its entire suppression.'[113]

No such determination is immediately evident from the notes which Washington made as a guide to action on 4 May.[114] They seem to imply that the Society might survive if its *Institution* was changed so as to:

Strike out every word, sentence and clause which has a political tendency.

Discontinue the hereditary part in all its connections, *absolutely*, without any substitution which can be construed into concealment...

Admit no more honorary Members into the Society.

Reject subscriptions, or donations from every person who is not a citizen of the United States.

Place the funds upon such a footing as to remove the jealousies which are entertained on that score.

On the other hand, a further suggestion, apparently innocent, that it would be 'magnanimous' to entrust funds already accumulated to 'the Legislatures', would be to invite these bodies to act as Jefferson had predicted Congress would.[115] A proposal to allow the French Cincinnati to adjudicate on their own affairs and membership also seemed calculated to separate the fate of the two wings of the Society, while a suggestion that there should be no more general meetings was tantamount to letting the whole body wither away. But 'No alteration short of what is here enumerated will, in my opinion, reconcile the Society to the Community, whether these will do it, is questionable.' The public, finally, would need to be persuaded why 'this order... is a feather we cannot consent to pluck from *ourselves*, tho'

---

113. Andrew E. Lipscomb and Albert Ellery Bergh (eds.), *The Writings of Thomas Jefferson*, 20 vols. (Washington, DC, 1903), xvi, 63, Jefferson to Martin Van Buren, 29 June 1824.
114. *GWC*, 152–4.
115. And some of the wording of this memorandum (not all quoted here) was a verbatim transcription from Jefferson's letter of 16 April.

we have taken it from our descendants'. But 'If we assign the reasons, we might I presume as well discontinue the order.'

A close reading of the general's thoughts on 4 May, therefore, seems to confirm Jefferson's recollection of forty years later. Washington had intended to use the Philadelphia meeting to wind the Society up. Yet by the time he reached Philadelphia, events had overtaken him. Major L'Enfant had arrived, bringing news of the Society's success in France, and of its endorsement by Louis XVI.[116] He also brought plates for printing membership diplomas, and 'a bundle of eagles' to dazzle the eyes of the assembled delegates. These circumstances made it impossible for Washington to propose dissolution directly when over forty delegates from twelve states[117] convened on the morning of 5 May.[118]

Perhaps he still hoped to promote it indirectly. Certainly he was determined to change the Society's more controversial features, and he opened the meeting by inviting each delegation in turn to report on how the Cincinnati had been received in its home state. Seven reported opposition, especially to 'the hereditary part'. The General observed that this showed the need for fundamental changes, and that, 'was it not for the connection we stood in with the very distinguished Foreigners in this Institution, he would propose to the Society to make one great sacrifice more to the world, and abolish the Order altogether'.[119] Congress, he revealed, (having heard it from Jefferson) in making provision for the creating of new states, had just stipulated that nobody who held a noble or hereditary title was to be allowed public office in them.[120] His final revelation was one of the

116. Jefferson's recollection was that Washington told him, on the way back from Philadelphia, that L'Enfant had arrived in the middle of the meeting, and that this had swung it against self-abolition. But only three years after the event the General wrote to him that he distinctly remembered L'Enfant arriving *before* the meeting: GWC, 312, Washington to Jefferson, 30 May 1787. Either way, the essence of the matter was explained by Washington to Alexander Hamilton on 11 Dec. 1785 (GWC, 241): 'Had it not been for the predicament we stood in with respect to the foreign officers and the charitable part of the Institution' he would have argued for 'abolishing the Society at once'. This is the interpretation of events passed on to the public in 1788 by Filippo Mazzei, *Recherches sur les Etats-Unis*: Constance D. Sherman [ed. and trans as] *Philip Mazzei, Researches on the United States* (Charlottesville, VA, 1976) 337.

117. Not every delegate elected was present, e.g. Nathaniel Greene of Rhode Island, who excused himself with suspicious prolixity: GWC, 164–5, Greene to Washington, 6 May 1784.

118. The fullest contemporary account of the meeting is Winthrop Sargent (ed.), 'Journal of the General Meeting of the Cincinnati in 1784', *Memoirs of the Historical Society of Pennsylvania*, vi (Philadelphia, PA, 1858), 71–75.

119. Ibid., 82.   120. See also Hünemörder, *Society of the Cincinnati*, 40.

letters sent him by Lafayette on 9 March, in which the Marquis declared himself happy to give up heredity if it should be found in conflict with 'those sacred republican principles for which we have fought, bled, & conquered'.[121]

Even Knox was prepared to go that far. L'Enfant had brought him a letter from the Marquis de Chastellux, a well known philosophic author and a qualifying veteran of the war.[122] Chastellux condemned the hereditary aspects of the Society, and Knox revealed his views to the meeting.[123] Washington then renewed the attack. 'In a very long speech, & with much warmth and agitation' he declared that, if heredity were not given up, he would feel obliged to resign from the Society. That left them little choice. Repudiation by the Father of his Country would completely ruin the Society's reputation. There was some isolated protest at this moral blackmail, and it took over a week and several redrafts before the *Institution* was satisfactorily amended.[124] Further determined oratory secured some lesser concessions. Thus the French Society was authorized to conduct its own affairs, after a formal vote that the naval captains and a number of individual petitioners should be admitted. Meanwhile the French offer of 60,000 *livres* was politely refused, and all future foreign donations renounced. General meetings were not completely abandoned, but were only to be triennial. No new honorary members were to be admitted, and accumulated funds were to be offered to state legislatures. Additionally, it was informally agreed that eagles should not be worn in public, in the European manner.[125] All these changes were explicitly subjected to the final approval of the several state societies; and together they were enough to persuade Washington to accept re-election for three years as president-general. But there was no disguising that his victories at Philadelphia were in reality a series of rearguard actions.

A revised and much compressed *Institution* was printed, together with a circular letter to all the state societies explaining the changes. Both were also made publicly available, and widely reported, at least in the New

121. Gottschalk, *Letters*, 277.
122. Author of *De la Félicité publique* (1772), and soon to publish an account of his travels in America in the early 1780s, *Voyages dans l'Amérique septentrionale dans les années 1780, 1781, 1782* (Paris, 1786). This was the work denounced by Brissot on the evidence of Crèvecoeur's *Letters of an American Farmer*. See above p. 87.
123. Sargent, 'Journal', 84.   124. The amended *Institution* in *GWC*, 160–3.
125. Sargent, 'Journal', 115.

England press.[126] Not so much remarked on was the reaction of the various state societies. Most took their time in responding, and other news had in the meantime diverted the press's attention. The circular letter[127] urged them to accept the abandonment of heredity, and to seek charters from their legislatures that would lend their future activities more legitimacy. None of them fell into the latter snare, crafted for Washington by Jefferson, and no branch was ever chartered.[128] But most accepted that heredity could not be maintained. Virginia meekly followed the general's lead, and the Massachusetts branch, in one of the fiercest centres of opposition, could scarcely be expected not to do the same, especially with Knox himself reconciled to the loss. Rhode Island, Pennsylvania, Maryland, both the Carolinas, and Georgia also accepted the changes in the course of the next few months. But New York, New Hampshire, Delaware, and New Jersey postponed their decisions; and when, several years later, they considered the new *Institution*, all but New Jersey among these refused to ratify it on the explicit grounds that heredity was desirable. This fundamental change, therefore, was never ratified by the Society as a whole, and later most state branches which had at first accepted the new *Institution* rescinded their decision. Consequently, a hereditary Society of the Cincinnati exists to this day. But the public abandonment of heredity in May 1784 certainly calmed the storm which had raged since the end of the previous year. By July, Knox already thought opposition 'dead'.[129] He was not quite right, but never again was it so formidable, widespread, or sustained. It was ironic that the Society probably owed its survival to French officers who valued the eagle as a new hereditary badge of chivalry. In this sense John Adams was vindicated in calling it a 'French blessing'. As the secretary of the New York society put it, 'It seems, therefore, that our allies alone have saved the society.'[130] A former *aide-de-camp* to Washington, he was too reverential to add: saved it from destruction at the hands of the modern Cincinnatus himself.

Much of the general meeting in May 1784 had been taken up with translating letters and petitions from France, and adjudicating on different

---

126. Myers, *Liberty without Anarchy*, 64, 69 n. 57.   127. *GWC*, 170–4.
128. At least, not in the eighteenth century. Some achieved incorporation in the different conditions of the nineteenth: *GWC*, 211 fn.
129. *GWC*, 201, Knox to Jefferson, 26 July 1784.
130. Lieutenant-Colonel Benjamin Walker, quoted in Friedrich Kapp, *The Life of Frederick William von Steuben* (New York, 1859), 568. Also in Myers, *Liberty without Anarchy*, 65.

issues which had arisen there—particularly the case of the naval captains. And a special letter was sent to France to explain the change in the *Institution*.[131] Lafayette received this, and other news of the meeting, while he was waiting in Lorient in late June for a ship to America.[132] He could not resist writing triumphantly to Adams, who had criticized his proposed voyage as a pointless piece of vainglory and distraction for the new republic. 'My principles', he declared, 'have ever been against heredity, & while I was in Europe disputing about it with a few friends, my letters to the assembly, & still more particularly to the president, made them sensible of my opinion upon that matter. Until heredity was given up, I forbore mentioning in Europe what sense I had expressed ... Whatever has been thought offensive, you see the Cincinnati has given it up.'[133] Characteristically, the Marquis was taking the credit for that. But in fact, one decision which he had urged upon Washington in March had not been taken at Philadelphia. He had wanted the French Cincinnati to have separate chapters for American officers (like himself) and those in the king's service. The two might then have gone separate ways on the question of heredity. Now, as he prepared to leave the country, he was unable to prevent leadership of the French Cincinnati from falling entirely into the hands of Rochambeau and d'Estaing, the ranks of their likely supporters vastly swelled by the potential admission of around 160 naval captains.[134] By the time the French Society formally met on 4 July to receive the news from Philadelphia, he was on the high seas and unable to influence their proceedings for several months.[135]

In his absence, the two senior officers, Rochambeau for the army and d'Estaing for the navy, acted with enthusiastic vigour. First they relayed the decisions about French members, collective and individual, taken at Philadelphia, to the king. The permission he had given the previous December for his subjects to join the society had been conditional on lists being kept, and approved by him. As early as March 1784 Rochambeau had warned Washington that 'a considerable addition would perhaps not

---

131. Sargent, 'Journal', 111–2.   132. Gottschalk, *Lafayette between*, 81.

133. Charles Francis Adams (ed.), *The Works of John Adams*, 10 vols. (Boston, MA, 1850–6), viii, 205, Lafayette to Adams, 25 June 1784.

134. See Gottschalk, *Letters*, 280. The rough calculation from names qualifying in 1784 in Contenson, *Cincinnati de France*, 128–280. Christian de Jonquière, *Officiers de Marine aux Cincinnati: Annuaire* (Toulouse, 1988) cites 124 founding members, but admits that his calculations are approximate.

135. He arrived back in France on 20 Jan. 1785: Gottschalk, *Lafayette between*, 151.

be So Well received';[136] and this proved to be the case. In August Ségur notified him that although the king approved the admission of the special cases considered at Philadelphia 'his majesty' (as Rochambeau translated this for Washington[137]) 'thinking not convenient that the association be perpetuated in the Kingdom he gives me order to prevent [*prévenir* = warn] You he Will permit no more for the future that any of his subjects be yet admitted in it'. The addition of the naval captains, notified to Castries independently by d'Estaing,[138] had certainly almost doubled the numbers of potential French Cincinnati; and d'Estaing had yet other ideas for making the Society more visible, such as allowing wives and daughters to wear their menfolk's insignia—significantly on the grounds that this was the practice in the genealogically exclusive Order of Malta.[139] June 1784 also saw the arrival in Paris of Gustav III of Sweden, travelling under the transparent incognito of the Count de Haga. He was accompanied by Hans Axel von Fersen, who had fought in America as colonel in the Royal Deux Ponts regiment. As soon as he heard of the Cincinnati, Fersen asserted his right to join and display the eagle, but ran into fierce opposition from his king. 'As far as the American order is concerned, I remain adamant in my position', wrote the monarch. 'This mark is intended to commemorate a rebellion which, although crowned with success, is still criminal in the eyes of a king. It is not for the sake of the king of England that I will not allow my subjects to wear it; it is for my own sake, for that of all kings, whose cause this is.'[140] Told of this opposition by Rochambeau, Washington commented drily that 'Considering how recently the K-g of S-ed-n has changed the form of the Constitution of that Country, it is not much to be wondered at that his *fears* should get the better of his *liberallity* at any thing which might have the semblance of republicanism.'[141] Louis XVI, perhaps, felt that monarchical solidarity was called for at this juncture. Perhaps, too, he was disconcerted at the way the Society's general meeting had changed the rules to which he had consented for his own subjects the previous December. There was no disguising that heredity had been abandoned because of its incompatibility

---

136. *GWC*, 101.   137. Ibid., 207, Ségur to Rochambeau, 28 Aug. 1784.
138. Contenson, *Cincinnati de France*, 68, Estaing to Castries, 19 Aug. 1784.
139. Anderson House Library, 'Idées sur l'Association des Cincinnati', signed Estaing, 13 July 1784. See also Contenson, *Cincinnati de France*, 62; Myers, *Liberty without Anarchy*, 156.
140. Barton, *Fersen*, 45.
141. *GWC*, 203, Washington to Rochambeau, 20 Aug. 1784. The reference is to the coup of 1772, in which Gustav III asserted royal power at the expense of the Swedish parliament.

with republicanism. Yet the French Society at its 4 July meeting accepted the revised *Institution*.[142] It is true that it also recommended that children of French members ought to be allowed to wear their parents' eagles, and that descendants of Lafayette should wear them for ever, but this only added to the general confusion.[143] The king and his military ministers must have wondered if they had stepped into a situation beyond their control.

And if so, they were right. The issue had first become controversial because in America there existed something not allowed in France: a free press. Washington and his fellow delegates in Philadelphia had consciously bent to the force of public opinion. But even in France the king's control of public debate was uncertain, and growing more so. The American controversy over the Cincinnati was about to wash into Europe, and nothing Louis XVI's ministers could do was able to prevent it.

* * *

The link was Franklin, whose hostility to hereditary rank was of long standing.[144] It had not been dimmed, seemingly, by eight years of being lionized by the cream of Parisian society. It came pouring out in the letter to his daughter which he wrote on receiving news of the uproar in America.[145] Ever since 1777, the former printer had entertained himself in exile by producing ephemera on a private press at his house in Passy,[146] and as time went by his output became more substantial. When news of the Cincinnati controversy arrived he was engaged in setting up *Information to those who would remove to America*, in which he warned prospective emigrants to the new republic that it was not 'advisable for a Person to go thither who has no other Quality to recommend him but his Birth. In Europe it has indeed its Value, but it is a Commodity that cannot be carried to a worse Market than to that of America ... a mere Man of Quality, who on that account wants to live upon the Public, by some Office or Salary, will be despis'd or disregarded.'[147] Distributed simultaneously in French

---

142. See Asa Bird Gardiner, *The Order of the Cincinnati in France* (Newport, RI, 1905), 36 n.; Myers, *Liberty without Anarchy*, 157.

143. Estaing, 'Idées', cited above, n. 131; Contenson, *Cincinnati de France*, 48.

144. See above, p. 86.   145. See above, pp. 111–2.

146. Carl Van Doren, *Benjamin Franklin* (New York, 1938), 661–4; Alfred Owen Aldridge, *Franklin and his French Contemporaries* (New York, 1957), 80–4.

147. *Writings*, 976–7.

and English, this tract was an immediate success; and Franklin considered following it up by printing a version of his letter to his daughter. He even had it translated into French in readiness. But the *abbé* Morellet, the well-connected man of letters who did the work for him, advised that such an outright condemnation of the principle of hereditary nobility would never receive permission to be published, much less if written by the American minister to the French Court.[148] Franklin recognized the truth of this but, reluctant to let the idea go, he turned to a less respectable but already notorious man of letters, the Count de Mirabeau. Pursued by debts and sexual scandal, Mirabeau was attempting to live by his pen. He was constantly at bitter odds with his father, who a quarter of a century beforehand had praised the virtues of provincial noblemen in *L'Ami des Hommes*. The father had been obliging to Franklin on his first visit to France in 1767, and the doctor felt he could reciprocate by helping the son.[149] He gave him Burke's pamphlet on the Cincinnati, and his own letter to his daughter, suggesting that Mirabeau write something on the subject. The count's own younger brother had fought in America, and his claim to join the Cincinnati had been accepted (though Mirabeau could not yet know this) by the Philadelphia assembly.[150] The Mirabeaus were of old noble stock in Provence. But Mirabeau's closest friend and collaborator at this time was the playwright and essayist Chamfort, who would chiefly be remembered as the author of a posthumously published set of maxims and anecdotes showing sardonic disenchantment with the high society of his time. This did not prevent him from living off aristocratic largesse, and calling himself Dechamfort to imply noble birth—but clearly he enjoyed the prospect of biting the hand that fed him. Besides, his English was better than Mirabeau's. They set out to translate and recast Burke together.[151] On 13 July they visited Franklin and read the result, 'which they have much enlarg'd', the doctor noted in his journal, 'intending it as a Cover'd Satyr against Noblesse in general. It is well done. There are also Remarks on the last Letter of Gen Washington on that Subject. They say Gen. W. miss'd

148. Van Doren, *Franklin*, 709. See Dorothy Medlin, Jean-Claude David, and Paul Leclerc (eds.), *Lettres d'André Morellet*, 3 vols. (Oxford, 1991), i, 510, Morellet to Franklin, 16 Mar. 1784.
149. Van Doren, *Franklin*, 371; Albert Henry Smyth (ed.), *The Writings of Benjamin Franklin*, 10 vols. (New York, 1907), ix, 271, Franklin to William Temple Franklin, 8 Sep. 1784.
150. *GWC*, 208, Rochambeau to Washington, 9 Sep. 1784.
151. Mirabeau's letters to Chamfort make it clear that the latter translated Burke's text for him: Auguis, *Oeuvres*, v, 367, Mirabeau to Chamfort, 22 June 1784; 385, undated.

a beau Moment, when he accepted that Decoration. [Declaration?] The same of the M de la Fayette.'[152] The problem now was to find a publisher beyond the surveillance of the French government. It was decided to seek one in England, where Mirabeau went late in August. Franklin provided him with letters of introduction to Benjamin Vaughan, whose contacts in the world of English publishing had secured the first English edition of his own works,[153] and Dr Richard Price, Unitarian minister and vocal Welsh apologist of American independence.[154] He told them both that 'the best judges' thought the tract Mirabeau brought with him on hereditary nobility was clear, forceful, elegant, and deserving of a publisher which he hoped they would help him find. This was not done without difficulty. English printers were reluctant to print for an uncertain French market, and only the promise of an English translation, undertaken by a radical but rich young Francophile, Samuel Romilly, seems to have secured an outlet.[155] *Considérations sur l'Ordre de Cincinnatus*, signed openly by Mirabeau (complete with his title of Count), and dated 20 September, finally appeared in November.

Aedanus Burke was not flattered by what Mirabeau and Chamfort had done with his pamphlet. He got hold of a copy in 1785, and in an open letter to Mirabeau published in the *South Carolina Gazette and Public Advertiser* he denounced the way the Count had stripped 'this offspring of mine' and quoted verbatim 'whole pages, paragraphs and sentences' without acknowledgement.[156] It was true that Mirabeau had not given chapter and verse for all his obvious borrowings. But he made clear on the title page of the first French edition that this was an 'imitation of an Anglo-American pamphlet', and in his preface cited the Philadelphia edition (doubtless the one obtained from Franklin) which named Burke as the true identity of 'Cassius'. Whole swathes of the text were indeed lifted from the original, but a great deal else, including most of the material on South Carolina, was omitted. The entire production in any case was

152. Library of Congress, Franklin's Journal, 13 July 1784. I am grateful to Professor Ellen R. Cohn, editor of *The Papers of Benjamin Franklin*, for a photocopy of this entry.
153. Smyth, *Writings*, ix, 269–70, Franklin to Vaughan, 7 Sep. 1784.
154. E. E. Hale and E. E. Hale, Jr, *Franklin in France*, 2 vols. (Boston, MA, 1887), ii, 388, Franklin to Price, 7 Sep. 1784.
155. Auguis, *Oeuvres de Chamfort*, v, 419, Mirabeau to Chamfort, 10 Nov. 1784; 428, undated. See also *Memoirs of the Life of Sir Samuel Romilly Written by Himself, with a Selection of his Correspondence, Edited by his Sons*, 3 vols. (London, 1840), i, 79.
156. Meleney, *Aedanus Burke*, 91.

much longer, incorporating important portions of Franklin's letter, as well as many extra points and rhetorical flourishes by Mirabeau or Chamfort.[157] It included as an appendix a letter of 1778 from Turgot to Richard Price on the principles of new American state constitutions; together with extracts from Price's own *Observations on the Importance of the American Revolution*, published in July 1784, embellished by late contributions from Guy Jean-Baptiste Target, a leading member of the Paris bar then spending time in London.[158] All this made it a compendium of every argument currently available against the principle of hereditary nobility.

* * *

Mirabeau was aware, he declared at the outset, that the Cincinnati had already abandoned heredity with the adoption of the revised *Institution*. But he did not believe (correctly as it proved) that this would make it disappear, at least 'in opinion, which is the true seat of nobility' (p. v).[159] Accordingly the burden of the argument was unaffected. With Washington at its head, this entirely unauthorized society was seeking recruits and support in all the monarchies of Europe. How could the general have failed to realize that this 'guilty, dangerous and vulgar' organization would compromise his august reputation?[160] For in reality it was an attempt to create 'an actual patriciate ... a military nobility, which will, ere long, become a civil nobility and an aristocracy the more dangerous because, being hereditary, it will perpetually increase in the course of time, and will gather strength from the very prejudices, which it will engender' (pp. 8–9). In the end it would undermine the republic itself. Roman history was invoked, as in Burke, to demonstrate how hereditary elites originated and behaved. As for the nobility of modern Europe, its origins were well known to lie in barbarian marauders who, even as they assumed vainglorious titles, 'laid

---

157. During the Revolution, assailed by accusations of 'aristocracy', Chamfort defended himself by claiming to have written 'les morceaux les plus vigoureux' of this anti-aristocratic pamphlet (Auguis, *Oeuvres de Chamfort*, v, 325, 'Lettre à ses Concitoyens'). This scarcely justifies the claim of Emile Dousset, *Chamfort et son Temps* (Clermont-Ferrand, 1974), 113, that he wrote the most important parts of it, but certainly some of the more epigrammatic statements echo his *Maximes et Pensées*.

158. Auguis, *Oeuvres de Chamfort*, v, 422, Mirabeau to Chamfort, 30 1784.

159. Quotations in English are from Romilly's English version, *Considerations on the Order of Cincinnatus ... translated from the French of the Count de Mirabeau* (London, 1785).

160. None of these reflections on Washington appeared in Burke's original.

the foundations of that barbarous feudal system, which for ages debased all human kind, converted whole nations to herds of slaves, and a few individuals into broods of tyrants' (p. 12). And meanwhile this nobility 'composed originally of a troop of robbers and assassins', had gone on to be 'recruited from time to time with public defaulters, and plunderers of the people' (pp. 15–16)—a plain allusion, reinforced by an extensive footnote, to how the French nobility had been changed by the sale of offices. Several pages were then devoted to denouncing the outward signs flaunted by nobles; appropriate enough, perhaps, under monarchy, where ranks were essential to its eternal quest of enslaving mankind, but otiose in a republic, where virtue alone was needed among equal citizens. This point was buttressed with extensive quotations from the constitutions of the various states, and the Declaration of Independence, all available in French since a translated collection had appeared in 1783.[161] The conclusion: 'Natural equality: political equality: civil equality. Such is the doctrine of the legislators of America.' (pp. 31–2)

But Mirabeau's main quarry was not the Cincinnati in America. It was, as Franklin saw and applauded, 'noblesse in general'. The first of all human rights was equality, and any attempt to divide mankind into patricians and plebeians was an affront to that right. And the idea that honour could or should be transmitted down the generations to the children of a few was an insult to all the other inhabitants of any country. At this point Franklin's letter of 1784 was drawn upon to praise the Chinese for ennobling ancestors rather than descendants: 'Retrospective honour is, besides, beneficial to the state; it encourages parents to give a virtuous education to their offspring, and thus actually make true nobility, the nobility of the soul, hereditary.' (p. 61) Honour by succession, in contrast, was absurd and ridiculous, and a footnote introduced the doctor's calculation that nine generations reduced descendants' share of the original progenitor's blood to $1/512$. All that was incalculable and incommensurable was the vanity of those prizing this sort of ancestral distinction. It was in fact positively harmful to them:

> because they find it more convenient to enjoy a conventional, than to deserve a personal dignity; because it renders them haughty and indolent; because it leaves them no prospect of advancement, but in the trade of a soldier, which requires neither abilities nor industry; because it founds upon hereditary pride

161. The translation was by the Duke de La Rochefoucauld d'Enville, assisted by Franklin. Van Doren, *Benjamin Franklin*, 656.

an inequality of fortune, which is as prejudicial to particular families, as it is to the state. Such is the perennial source of vanity and beggary, of meanness and pride, of slavery and tyranny, which pours over countries infected with this lineal nobility all kinds of public and private evils. (p. 62)

Meanwhile, the Cincinnati were warned that the 'factitious' nobility they were attempting to become would not impress the nobles of Europe.

Carry among Europeans your paltry decoration, and the distinction which you would fain transmit to your posterity. See how they will be despised. See how high the titled slaves of despots, who carefully preserve for ages the monuments of their servitude, will imagine themselves placed above you. See what a superiority they will affect over men, who were only heros [*sic*]; and then judge of a conventional nobility; since, beaming with virtues and with glory, you are yet, in the eyes of European noblemen, but plebeians. (p. 78)

Mirabeau ended by detailing measures reported to have been taken against the Cincinnati by the various states, and by an account of the amendment of the original *Institution* in 1784.[162] Both that and the amended version were quoted in full, together with Washington's circular letter introducing the latter. A series of critical footnotes denounced the reasoning of the letter and argued that the only safe way to amend the Society was to dissolve it, and send its eagles to be melted at the mint. There should, one footnote pregnantly observed, be only one society within the state, above all in matters of public affairs, and that should be the republic itself, made up of all sane and mature male citizens.[163] Beyond that, there should only be individuals and families. Any formal association was a usurpation of the republic's rights, and likely to introduce inequality among its members. A final peroration implored Washington to disentangle himself from the whole enterprise. Little did Mirabeau realize how much the general would have liked to.

Mirabeau had brought together or flagged up all the most important documents available to Europeans in the mid-1780s on American public affairs. Whilst the appendix carried Turgot's letter of 1778 criticizing the balance of powers incorporated in most of the new state constitutions, several pages of text drew attention to La Rochefoucauld's translation of those constitutions, with extensive quotation. A footnote also mentioned

162. Picking up the widely reported exclusion of Cincinnati from public life in Rhode Island. But this was a groundless report: Myers, *Liberty without Anarchy*, 52.
163. Prefiguring the revolutionaries' hostility to any sort of corporation.

the anti-aristocratic warnings of Mably, whose four letters to John Adams, *Observations sur le Gouvernement des Etats-Unis d'Amérique* had been published in the same year (1783). Finally Mirabeau brought Richard Price to French readers, not simply as the recipient of Turgot's letter, but also as the author of the newly published *Observations on the Importance of the American Revolution*, with their explicit warnings against granting hereditary honours, titles of nobility, and primogeniture.[164]

Here were all the materials for an informed debate, assembled in incendiary language. Chamfort later claimed, admittedly when it was in his vital interests to do so, that the pamphlet delivered 'the harshest blows to the French aristocracy, in public opinion.'[165] Yet it did not trigger a debate in the way Burke's original had in America. Later writers were keen to refute various of its claims, particularly its aspersions against Washington,[166] but there were no sustained replies. Printed in England, it was difficult to obtain in Paris.[167] Several periodicals reviewed it, noncommittally enough,[168] but perhaps the disreputable reputation of the author, and the speed with which he moved on to find other targets, compromised public acceptance of the seriousness of his arguments. Perhaps, indeed, of the several authors, Chamfort exercised the most enduring influence against aristocracy, not so much by the barbs which he contributed to the text, as by the advice he gave to Emmanuel-Joseph Sieyès, author four years later of the most devastating of all polemics against the French nobility.[169] But by the early summer of 1785 the Cincinnati were becoming old news in Paris, and there were fresh distractions to engage the public's fleeting attention—the controversy over Mesmerism, the publication in January of Necker's best-selling book on the administration of finances, a series of alleged miscarriages of justice, and, soon enough, the diamond necklace affair. It would take a political crisis to forge the anti-noble arguments collected in the *Considérations* into a practical ideology for the destruction of noble power. But when it did,

164. Richard Price, *Observations on the Importance of the American Revolution, and the Means of Making it a Benefit to the World* (London, 1785) (New Haven edn 1785), 59–61.
165. 'Lettre à ses concitoyens', cited above, n. 157.   166. See below, p. 133.
167. Medlin, David, Leclerc, *Lettres de Morellet*, i, 556, Morellet to Lansdowne, Apr. 1785. Bachaumont reported, xxix, 102, 23 June 1785, that copies were only now belatedly appearing.
168. e.g. Grimm, *Correspondance Littéraire*, May 1785, but this was a private newsletter distributed to foreign courts.
169. He claimed, for example, to have thought up the title and echoing opening lines of Sieyès's *Qu'est-ce que le Tiers Etat?*: Dousset, *Chamfort et son temps*, 121. Paul Bastid, *Sieyès et sa pensée* (new edn, Paris, 1970), 56, 349–50, reports the fact, but is sceptical of its likelihood.

at least none of them were in any way unfamiliar, and that was in some measure thanks to Franklin, Chamfort, and Mirabeau.

* * *

Mirabeau's *Considérations* reached the United States late in 1785. An American edition of Romilly's translation was published in Philadelphia in 1786; but by then the American controversy was cooling, too. A copy of the English edition, sent to Washington in November 1785 remained unread for weeks. 'I thought', the general wrote, with a hint of irritation, 'as most others seemed to think, that all the exceptionable parts of the institution had been done away with at the last general meeting; but, with those who are disposed to cavil, or who have the itch of writing strongly upon them, nothing can be made to suit their palates. The best way, therefore, to disconcert and defeat them, is to take no notice of their publications. All else is but food for declamation.'[170]

Yet declamation sporadically continued.[171] A bill was introduced in the North Carolina legislature to exclude Cincinnati from sitting in either house—although it was never passed.[172] Suspicion remained so rooted in Massachusetts that Knox kept postponing an application to the Common-wealth legislature for a charter; and membership of the Society was invoked against General Benjamin Lincoln when he ran for lieutenant-governor. John Adams, now ambassador in London, remained unimpressed by the changes the Society had made; perhaps he had read Mirabeau on the subject. 'I have been asked,' he wrote to Elbridge Gerry, who had inflamed the Massachusetts legislature against the Society, 'why I have not written against it? Can it be necessary for me to write on such a thing?'[173] It was 'the deepest piece of cunning yet attempted. It is sowing the seeds of all that European courts wish to grow up among us, viz. of vanity, ambition, corruption, discord and sedition. Are we so dim-sighted as not to see, that the taking away the hereditary descent of it will not prevent its baneful influence? Who will think of preventing the son from wearing a ribbon and a bit of gold that his father wore?' He worried that the

---

170. *GWC*, 239, Washington to Samuel Vaughan, 30 Nov. 1785; 242, Washington to Knox, 11 Dec. 1785.
171. Hünemörder, *Society of the Cincinnati*, ch. 3.   172. Myers, *Liberty without Anarchy*, 71.
173. Austin, *Life of Gerry*, 427–30, 25 April 1785.

virtue essential to all successful republics was already in decay across the Atlantic.

As the next date for a general meeting approached, again in Philadelphia—May 1787—Washington began to put forward a somewhat desperate series of excuses for not being there.[174] By the end of October he had gone further, declaring that he did not even wish to be re-elected president-general.[175] By then, however, threats to the republic were coming from other directions, and were now more real than imaginary. Shays's rebellion in Massachusetts in 1786 was the most widespread organized defiance of constituted authority since independence. It shook confidence in the stability of the republic and served to reinforce a growing call for the Articles of Confederation to be revised so as to strengthen federal power against the caprices of the states. After months of uncertainty and lobbying, in February 1787 Congress formally approved a convention to draft revisions to the Articles of Confederation. It was set to meet in Philadelphia in May, and Virginia insisted that its delegation should be headed by Washington. Quite apart from the risk to his much-treasured reputation should the Convention fail, the general could scarcely be in Philadelphia in May and not be at the Cincinnati meeting. At first he professed reluctance to attend either occasion,[176] but he was soon persuaded that the Convention was too important in national terms for him not to appear. He therefore reluctantly agreed to go to the Cincinnati meeting as well, despite apprehensions arising from the failure of several state societies to accept the revised *Institution*.[177]

What happened at this meeting is poorly documented.[178] It appears that Washington did not take the chair, although he accepted re-election as president-general. It also appears that many delegates came mandated to abandon the revised *Institution* but that once again Washington's likely refusal to serve with the original *Institution* made the assembly postpone the issue until an extraordinary general meeting the next year—which in the

---

174. The first hints of reluctance come in a letter responding to Washington from David Humphreys, 24 Sept. 1786 in *GWC*, 254.
175. Ibid., 264–5, Washington to Horatio Gates, 31 Oct. 1786.
176. *GWC*, 276, Washington to David Stuart, 19 Nov. 1786; 280–2, Washington to James Madison, 16 Dec. 1786.
177. Ibid., 299–300, Washington to Knox, 2 Apr. 1787.
178. Myers, *Liberty without Anarchy*, 98, speaks of a deliberate 'news blackout'. Estaing's 'Idées' on the French Society were certainly tabled, as an endorsement on the copy in Anderson House makes clear, but no upshot is recorded.

event proved inquorate.[179] The fact is that the constitutional Convention eclipsed everything else happening that summer in Philadelphia. No fewer than twenty-one of the fifty-five drafters of the Constitution were members of the Society, and fears that they might act together to promote military interests and a strong executive, if not a monarchy, haunted the minds of many onlookers.[180] Most of the Society's members certainly seem to have seen themselves as bastions of order in potentially anarchical times. But there is no evidence of their acting in concert during the Convention to secure pre-agreed results.[181] Washington was outraged at the very imputation, but by September 1788 he conceded that 'Indeed, the phantom now seems to be pretty well laid.'[182] The Constitution itself, as produced by the Convention, was evidence enough. It incorporated the prohibition of titles of nobility found in the Articles of Confederation. As a clause, noted James Madison in the *Federalist*, the most celebrated defence of the Convention's work,[183] it 'needs no comment'. Nor did he or his collaborators in this series devote any space to a provision whose importance they thought self-evident. Only towards the end of the series, and almost as an afterthought, did Alexander Hamilton, a zealous Cincinnatus from New York and open defender of heredity in the Society, give the issue passing notice, and then he was unequivocal. 'Nothing', he wrote, 'need be said to illustrate the importance of the prohibition of titles of nobility. This may truly be denominated the corner stone of republican government.'[184]

✱ ✱ ✱

Apart from the re-election of Washington, the only positive achievement of the 1787 general meeting of the Cincinnati was to admit to honorary membership the Marquis de Bouillé, who had commanded French forces in the West Indies during the war, but never served on the continent.[185] This admission was an exception to the rule operated since 1784 which made the French Society the arbiter of French admissions. It had not prevented

179. Myers, *Liberty without Anarchy*, 96.
180. Davies, 'Society of the Cincinnati in New England', 22–3.
181. Hünemörder, *Society of the Cincinnati*, 114–7.
182. *GWC*, 338, Washington to Col. William Barton, 7 Sep. 1788.
183. *The Federalist*, no. 44, 25 Jan. 1788.   184. Ibid., no. 84, 28 May 1788.
185. *GWC*, 313–14, Washington to d'Estaing, 1 June 1787; Contenson, *Cincinnati de France*, 70–1, 257.

many French officers from applying to Washington for recognition of their eligibility. Some even wrote to Congress on the dangerously misguided assumption that the Cincinnati was an order of chivalry instituted by the new Republic. None went to the length of the Marquis du Bouchet, who crossed the Atlantic in 1784 to secure his acceptance, declaring that 'Disapointment [sic] Would Be a Stain upon my honour, Wich could never Be Blotted out.'[186] He was accepted, but others were referred back to France. Lafayette had now returned there, and he, d'Estaing, and Rochambeau continued to adjudicate on requests for the eagle. Louis XVI, for his part, appears to have relented on his previous decision to allow no more admissions. He was even prepared to recognize officers promoted to colonel or ship's captain after their service in America as deserving honorary membership. Lists of such candidates continued to be forwarded to him into the Revolution, and the last twenty-seven names were approved as late as 3 February 1792.[187] This was long after the abolition of nobility and orders of chivalry,[188] which shows that both the king and (implicitly) the National Assembly regarded the eagle as a military decoration rather than an attribute of nobility. No doubt the formal, if reluctant, adherence of the French Society to the revised *Institution* made this easier. Baron de Kalb, admitted for his father's services before its adoption, remained the only second-generation member in France. When the distinguished admiral the Count de Grasse died in 1788, his only son failed to secure admission.[189] Much of the activity of the French Society between 1785 and 1788, in fact, was a matter of carefully reviewing marginal cases for admission, a tedious and sometimes disagreeable process. Well might Lafayette confide in February 1786 to an American correspondent: 'You ask my opinion respecting the Cincinnati. I wish it had not been thought of.'[190]

In all, 237 French officers became members of the Society between 1784 and 1792, 115 by special dispensation as honorary members.[191] The numbers

---

186. *GWC*, 183, Du Bouchet to Washington, 17 May 1784.
187. Contenson, *Cincinnati de France*, 71.
188. See below, pp. 257–8. 189. Myers, *Liberty without Anarchy*, 158.
190. Connecticut State Library, Hartford. Governor Joseph Trumbull Collection. Military General Correspondence, 1760–1867. Vol. ii, doc. 185b, Lafayette to Jeremiah Wadsworth, 10 Feb. 1786. Also quoted in Myers, *Liberty without Anarchy*, 157. In his 'Idées' of 1784, d'Estaing had suggested that Lafayette be named president for life of the French Society. But this proposal seemed to be subject to the approval of the General Assembly, and as such cannot have been considered until 1787. Even then the outcome is unknown.
191. Contenson, *Cincinnati de France*, 51, 72, accepts Gardiner's figure (*Order of the Cincinnati in France*) of 370, but speaks of 'bien des oublis' discovered in the course of his own researches.

were relatively small, but, as senior officers, their profile was high. Nor were the issues stirred up by Franklin and Mirabeau forgotten when the former returned to America, and the latter went off to seek new journalistic copy in Berlin. Franklin's successor, Jefferson, arrived in Paris just before Mirabeau left for England with his manuscript. Already suspicious of the Cincinnati in America, he followed European discussion of them closely. After two years in the French capital, he reported to Washington that: 'I never heard a person in Europe, learned or unlearned, express his thoughts on this institution, who did not consider it dishonourable & destructive to our governments ... every writing which has come out since my arrival here, in which it is mentioned, considers it, even as now reformed, as the germ whose developments is one day to destroy the fabric we have reared. I did not apprehend that while I had American ideas only. But I confess that what I have seen in Europe has brought me over to that opinion.'[192] He was certain that sooner or later 'this institution will produce an hereditary aristocracy which will change the form of our governments from the best to the worst in the world. To know the mass of evil which flows from this fatal source, a person must be in France, he must see the finest soil, the finest climate, the most compact state, the most benevolent character of people, & every earthly advantage combined, insufficient to prevent this scourge from rendering existence a curse to 24 out of 25 parts of the inhabitants of this country.'

Even so, as a good diplomat, Jefferson felt obliged to defend his compatriots in public. This letter to Washington contained the text of an article on the United States in the *Encyclopédie méthodique*, a vast compendium attempting to build on the earlier success of Diderot's *Encyclopédie*.[193] The article's author, Jean-Nicolas Demeunier, had, like most French writers on America during these years, never been there, but he had the good sense to submit his text to Jefferson before publication. 'I found it', the latter said, 'a tissue of errors, for in truth they know nothing about us here.'[194] He found a lengthy section on the Cincinnati particularly ill-informed, and practically rewrote it to emphasize the misguided good faith of the

---

Myers, however, (123) reduces this number to 237, out of 413 eligible. The usual care of Myers's scholarship makes this figure seem more credible.

192. *Jefferson Papers*, x, 531–3, 14 Nov. 1786. Also in *GWC*, 270–1.
193. See Robert Darnton, *The Business of Enlightenment: A Publishing History of the* Encyclopédie, *1775–1800* (Cambridge, MA, 1979)
194. Loc. cit., n. 183.

Society's founders. But the author did not accept all Jefferson's suggestions, and Washington found a number of further errors.[195] Nevertheless this account of the Society and other American matters was more accurate than anything else available in Europe,[196] and made perfectly clear that fear of a new nobility was the prime source of apprehension about the Cincinnati. The account given by Filippo Mazzei in his *Researches on the United States* (1788) was also carefully vetted by Jefferson in the light of his own, and perhaps Washington's, personal knowledge.[197] Originally written in Italian, the translation into French of the book's chapters on the Cincinnati was undertaken by the Marquis de Condorcet and his wife to ensure the strictest accuracy, and here Mazzei took particular care to vindicate Washington and Lafayette from the strictures of Mirabeau. Although the founding of the Society, he somewhat fancifully acknowledged, 'frightened all friends of liberty... In Europe, where the evils of aristocracy are omnipresent, it made more of an impression than in America... and if the Americans were not afraid, it was because the character of almost all the members were opposed to the spirit of aristocracy.'[198]

By this time, however, the whole significance of aristocracy was about to be galvanized into new urgency by the collapse of the old regime in France. As surely as excitement about the Convention and the new Constitution eclipsed other controversies in America, the agony of absolute monarchy that began with the Assembly of Notables in February 1787 monopolized public attention in France. Arguments about aristocracy were about to be given a new context.

✳ ✳ ✳

It was at this moment that John Adams chose to publish his *Defence of the Constitutions of Government of the United States of America*.[199] It was

195. *Jefferson Papers,* xi, 388–9, Washington to Jefferson, 30 May 1787. Also in *GWC*, 311–13.
196. See Durand Echeverria, *Mirage in the West: A History of the French Image of American Society to 1815* (Princeton, NJ, 1957), 123–4.
197. Mazzei's account of the 1784 general meeting seems to reflect what Washington told Jefferson in his letter of 30 May 1787. He certainly sought to exonerate Washington and Lafayette from accusations of seeking to establish an American nobility, but in attempting this, of course, he could not fail to raise the basic issues. See Mazzei (ed. Sherman) *Researches,* 336–43.
198. Ibid., 336.
199. For useful discussions, see Palmer, *Age,* i, 271–6; Pole, *Political Representation,* 216–23; Wood, *Creation,* 567–92.

ostensibly a response to Turgot's letter to Price of 1778 which Mirabeau had printed as an appendix to his *Considérations*. As such it was the last substantial contribution to the debate occasioned by the Cincinnati. There were signs in his letter to Gerry about the Cincinnati in 1785[200] of the thinking that Adams now set out at length, but the book never mentioned the Society explicitly. His aim was broader: to refute Turgot's objections to the balance of powers incorporated in most of the state constitutions in blind imitation (as the Frenchman saw it) of a flawed British model. Adams, in long and wearisome historical detail, argued that no republic had ever prospered for long without a balance in its constitution between the powers of one, the few, and the many. The true enemy of republics was aristocracy, the few, whose greed and ambition sought constantly to subvert republican equality, either by corrupting the people or by conniving with tyranny. Aristocracy, however, could not be eliminated. It would arise naturally from the unequal distribution in nature of merit, abilities, and property. All republican constitutions could do, therefore, was to contain it by a guaranteed but clearly circumscribed role in a separate upper house or Senate. Only in England (which Adams called a 'regal republic') had this been successfully accomplished, before the establishment of the United States.

Adams's contempt for 'hereditary titles, honours, offices, or distinctions', and his pride in their absence from America, was as explicit in his book as ever.[201] But his evident admiration, not to say reverence, for the British constitution left many of his compatriots incredulous and suspicious. Nor could his timing have been less happy. He was defending existing state constitutions, and his work had no influence on the Convention which in the same year produced the federal one; but it was soon taken as an encomium of the Convention's work, to the dismay of all who had thought British ways and patterns thoroughly shaken off. And his constant harping on the 'different orders of men' into which all societies would inevitably divide ran against all that the French would seek to achieve in and after 1789. It is true that, although Jefferson promised to seek a translator in 1788,[202] the *Defence* did not appear in French, and then abridged, until 1792. But Adams's most influential American opponent found translators, and eminent ones, too, three years earlier. *Observations*

---

200. See above, p. 128.   201. *Works*, iv, 382.
202. *Jefferson Papers*, xi, 177, Jefferson to Adams, 23 Feb. 1787.

on government, including some animadversions on Mr Adams' Defence of the Constitutions ... By a Farmer of New Jersey, appeared in New York before 1787 was out. It was believed to be by Governor William Livingston, but was actually by John Stevens. Adams hit the same raw nerve in Stevens as the Cincinnati had in Aedanus Burke. The New Englander (absent in Europe, after all, for the best part of a decade) had failed to realize not only that America harboured no 'orders, ranks or nobility',[203] but also that its laws against primogeniture, and its commercial freedom, made it unlikely that an overweening aristocracy could ever develop. In America, Stevens argued, the people alone were sovereign, and no separate share of power was vouchsafed to any distinct order of men. This was as far from the shared British sovereignty of king, lords, and commons as it was possible to get, despite any superficial similarities in the new constitution. French friends of America were delighted to hear the message. They wanted no slavish imitation of Great Britain in the constitution they were hoping to forge for themselves in the spring of 1789. Condorcet, Mazzei, and others seized on this pamphlet much as Franklin and Mirabeau had seized on Burke's five years earlier, and produced a 'translation' which was more like a complete recast.[204] In this form it fed influentially into political debates during the elections to the Estates-General, including that on the nobility and its pretensions.[205]

✳ ✳ ✳

French fascination with all things American did not fade with the on-set of the Revolution. The French retained a paternal and proprietary interest in the republic they had helped into being, and its distinctive pattern of society, until their own revolutionary consensus fell apart.[206] America's lack of a hereditary nobility was now axiomatic to French thinking, but after 1789 the Cincinnati were scarcely mentioned. The French Society itself became defunct, with the monarchy which had sanc-tioned it, in 1792, although the eagle appeared from time to time in

203. Quoted in Wood, *Creation*, 583.
204. *Examen du gouvernement d'Angleterre comparé aux constitutions des Etats-Unis* (Paris, 1789). See L. Rosenthal, *America and France: The Influence of the United States in France in the xviiith Century* (New York, 1882), 160–2.
205. See below, p. 223.
206. Echeverria, *Mirage*, 161–74; Rosenthal, *America in France*, 166–271.

the buttonholes of survivors until the last, Théodore de Lameth, died in 1854.[207]

The American Society did not disappear. Its 2,166 original members[208]—almost half of those eligible to join from their war service—comprised some of the most prominent figures in public life, and none made a secret of their membership. If they did not wear their eagles in public, some had themselves painted wearing them. Above all, heredity prevailed.[209] Only three state societies adopted the amended *Institution* and stood by their acceptance, thereby renouncing heredity. Three others had rejected the new rules from the start, and the rest had adopted them either reluctantly or conditionally, and often mandated their representatives at general meetings to press for a return to the original principles of 1783. Gradually Washington's demands of 1784 were forgotten; and the general himself, now President of the United States, played no further active role in the Society, though regularly re-elected president-general until his death. Jefferson, radicalized by the French Revolution and appalled by the anti-democratic tone of its American critics, many of whom were members, remained suspicious of this 'self-created [society], carving out for itself hereditary distinctions, lowering over our Constitution eternally, meeting together in all parts of the Union, periodically, with closed doors, accumulating a capital in their separate treasury, corresponding secretly and regularly',[210] but his suspicions were never borne out. Swamped in numbers by an expanding nation (they never came near the 10,000 estimated by Aedanus Burke), and passing on their status by strict primogeniture, their destiny was to become a tiny self-regarding caste, with no collective or institutional power. If anything resembling an American aristocracy did grow up, it was not from this seed.

Nevertheless the controversy surrounding their birth had been an essential step in discrediting noble claims and ideals. Americans were forced to confront ambiguous and half-conscious assumptions about the nature of their society, and how it was affected by the establishment of a republic. For the first time since antiquity, a polity had been created where nobles by definition had no role, and were widely regarded as a dangerous alien

---

207. See Myers, *Liberty without Anary*, 164–71. It was revived in 1922 as a hereditary society. See ibid., 239–42, and Contenson, *Cincinnati de France*, 103–16.
208. Calculated, minus the French, from Myers, *Liberty without Anarchy*, 123.
209. Hünemörder, *Society of the Cincinnati*, 94–100.
210. *Jefferson Papers*, xxviii, 228, Jefferson to James Madison, 28 Dec. 1794.

species. Discussion of the Cincinnati during the republic's formative years, however wild and alarmist,[211] helped to ensure that it would remain that way. And this in turn showed the European world beyond America that a society without nobles was possible, and could work.

The controversy also produced, in Mirabeau's adaptation of Burke's pamphlet, the first overt and direct attack on the principle of nobility in Europe itself. Criticism was nothing new. Nor was debate about the nature and function of nobility. Asides and unspoken implications in these exchanges had often come close to questioning the entire range of noble claims, habits and entrenched hegemonies. But nobody before Mirabeau and his collaborators had devoted an entire polemic to a comprehensive onslaught on nobles and all they stood for. Three years before recourse to the Estates-General opened up the whole issue of nobility in France, French echoes of the Cincinnati controversy laid out the full repertoire of arguments against the claims of hereditary distinction. All of them would be deployed in the electoral struggles of 1788, 1789, and beyond.

211. Hünemörder, *Society of the Cincinnati*, ch. 8.

5

Straws in the Wind

The Breakdown of the Old Order

Even before the challenge from America, disturbing tremors were beginning to shake the nobilities of Europe. Between 1772 and 1775 Russia was wracked by the greatest popular uprising of the century, led by the Cossack Pugachev. In June 1774, as the courtiers of Versailles sought to take the measure of their new monarch, serfs along the faraway Volga were massacring lords by the thousand. Rumours of these disturbances helped to trigger an uprising further west, in Bohemia, the following year. It was less bloody, but marked by widespread refusals to pay seigneurial dues and perform labour services. Ultimately, both outbreaks were put down with military force, but the rulers of the two great eastern empires drew opposite conclusions from them. Catherine II decided that the Russian nobility must be supported more positively and integrated more firmly into the fabric of regional government. A series of new benefits were conferred on the most socially dominant aristocracy in Europe, culminating in the Charter of Nobility of 1785 which endowed them with a range of privileges that many of their counterparts further west might well envy.[1] The Habsburgs, however, saw excessive noble prerogatives as a provocation to their humbler subjects, as well as a threat to their own revenues. The Empress Maria Theresia accelerated measures to limit the exactions of lords, while her restless son and co-ruler from 1765, Joseph II, chafed at her timidity and dreamed of breaking landlord power entirely.[2]

He could take encouragement from Gustav III of Sweden. The crown prince was in France when he acceded to the throne in 1771, and he

---

1. Paul Dukes, *Catherine the Great and the Russian Nobility* (Cambridge, 1967), 222–9; Isabel de Madariaga, *Russia under Catherine the Great* (London, 1981), 296–9.
2. Derek Beales, *Joseph II: In the Shadow of Maria Theresa, 1741–1780* (Cambridge, 1985), i 98–100.

returned to his northern inheritance inspired by Maupeou's decisive action against aristocratic bodies constraining royal power. The next year he overthrew the independence of the Swedish diet, through which rival factions had governed the kingdom, unconstrained by the crown, since 1720. Turning his back on half a century of aristocratic constitutionalism,[3] he reasserted the executive authority of the monarchy, to the dismay of great lords who had hitherto governed in the interests of their order. To win support for his actions the king portrayed noble rule in Sweden as anarchical and corrupt. He and his supporters compared it to the unpatriotic anarchy of Poland,[4] where the 'golden freedom' so vaunted by the *Szlachta* had reduced the commonwealth to such paralytic impotence that its three neighbours were at this very moment annexing its outlying provinces without meeting any serious resistance.[5]

With even the much-admired British parliament floundering towards disaster in its dealings with America, the ability of aristocracies to manage the affairs of nations looked increasingly questionable. New theoretical criticisms of the legal and economic basis of noble power were also being raised. 1770 and 1773–4 saw the first French translations of Adam Smith's *Theory of Moral Sentiments* (1759). Smith was steeped in French literature and history, and had spent the mid-1760s in Paris frequenting the leading centres of intellectual debate, including the regular philosophic assemblies at the house of Baron d'Holbach. He did so as the paid tutor of a Scottish Duke, who continued to provide him with a handsome pension for the rest of his life. He was not deterred from accepting this position by his own analyses of the worthlessness of the great. Being born to greatness, he had argued, positively discouraged men from aspiring to knowledge, industry, patience, self-denial, or virtue of any kind.[6] All such men cared about was cutting a figure in order to retain the deference with which others treated them.

> The man of rank or distinction ... whose whole glory consists in the propriety of his ordinary behaviour, who is contented with the humble renown which this can afford him, and has no talents to acquire any other, is unwilling to embarrass himself with what can be attended either with difficulty or distress.

3. See Michael Roberts, 'On Aristocratic Constitutionalism in Swedish History' in his *Essays in Swedish History* (London, 1967), 14–55.
4. A. Geffroy, *Gustav III et la Cour de France*, 2 vols. 2nd edn, (Paris, 1867), i, 154–5.
5. Herbert H. Kaplan, *The First Partition of Poland* (New York, 1962).
6. *Theory of Moral Sentiments*, ii, section iv.

To figure at a ball is his great triumph, and to succeed in an intrigue of gallantry, his highest exploit. He has an aversion to all public confusions, not from the love of mankind, for the great never look upon their inferiors as their fellow-creatures ... but from a consciousness that he possesses none of the virtues that are required in such situations, and that the public attention will certainly be drawn away from him by others.[7]

In the *Inquiry into the Nature and Causes of the Wealth of Nations* (1776) Smith went on to question the economic value of spending on display and services; of royal courts and other 'great corporations'; of cultivation by serf labour; and of the accumulation of great estates by primogeniture and entail. The latter, he declared, 'are thought necessary for maintaining this exclusive privilege of the nobility to the great offices and honours of their country; and that order having usurped one unjust advantage over the rest of their fellow citizens, lest their poverty should render it ridiculous, it is thought reasonable that they should have another'.[8] Within two years, *Wealth of Nations* had been translated into French, and extracts from it were soon also readily available. By the 1780s Smith's general ideas were widely familiar to French economic thinkers, contributing to the emergence of ideas of commercial republicanism which regarded nobilities and their values as obstacles to socio-economic progress.[9]

It is harder to judge the anti-noble influence of the Scotsman's most notorious host in the 1760s, Holbach. The Baron was a *parvenu,* his German title and the bases of his immense fortune inherited from an uncle naturalized as a French subject in 1749. He was unsure enough of his social standing to invest extensive capital in an office of King's Secretary, with its attribute of full transmissible nobility. He also bought his son an office in the Paris parlement and saw his daughters safely married to noblemen of impressive old stock. Apart from hosting regular gatherings of fashionable thinkers at his lavish house in the rue royale, he devoted much of his time to publishing anonymous tracts against religion.[10] He was appalled by the return to strict censorship under Maupeou, and he welcomed the new dawn promised by the accession of Louis XVI, especially as it brought to power an old *habitué* of the rue royale, the

7. *Theory of Moral Sentiments*, ii, section v.   8. *Wealth of Nations*, Bk ii, ch.2.

9. Richard Whatmore, *Republicanism and the French Revolution: An Intellectual History of Jean-Baptiste Say's Political Economy* (Oxford, 2000), 6–10.

10. See Alan Charles Kors, *D'Holbach's Coterie: An Enlightenment in Paris* (Princeton, NJ, 1976).

physiocratic intendant Turgot. In *Ethocratie* (1776) Holbach sketched out a programme of reform for the state, with a fulsome dedication to a virtuous young king. Fourteen chapters offered 'moral laws' for every group in society. Aristocratic government, he held, was most likely to end in usurpation and tyranny, and he explicitly rejected Montesquieu's separation of honour and virtue. Without the latter, there could be no true honour, or true glory, or permanent happiness for any nation.[11] The world of the Court was denounced at length, in well-worn terms, as a corrupt centre of greed, ambition and intrigue. A whole chapter was devoted to the nobility. Heredity, the Baron argued, should probably be abolished: 'Should titles, superannuated parchments preserved in gothic castles, entitle those who have inherited them to the right to aspire to the highest dignities of the church, the court, the robe or the sword, without having besides any of the talents necessary to fill them worthily? Because warrior Noblemen were once able, at the risk of their lives, to contribute to the conquest of a kingdom or the pillage of provinces, must their descendants still think themselves, after so many centuries, entitled to ill-treat their vassals, oppress the tillers of the soil, exact from them harmful rights, cruel servitudes, and indeed throw onto laborious indigence taxes that wealth alone should bear?'[12] Feudal government, whose relics were everywhere still, was denounced as 'systematic brigandage'.[13] In their own interests, kings should force their nobles to 'give up the countless injustices which by long possession have come to be seen as rights'. These 'supposed rights enjoyed by their ancestors, and to which they themselves are so strongly attached through vanity, ignorance and prejudice, are manifestly against their own interests, laying Nobility open to the hatred of citizens, harming society, aggrieving the cultivator, hampering trade, discouraging industry, setting obstacles to plenty and to general happiness, and diminishing the revenues, comfort and wellbeing of Nobles.'[14] Holbach called for 'an administration more just for nations, and less partial to Nobles', which would force them to give up tax-exemptions justified by a military service no longer exclusively performed by them, and which now meant that it was always the rich who contributed least to the state's needs.[15] Government should 'stifle to its very seeds' hereditary pride, and force nobles 'to instruct themselves and to be useful in order to obtain distinctions, rewards

11. *Ethocratie ou le gouvernement fondé sur la morale* (Amsterdam, 1776), 12.
12. Ibid., 43–4.   13. Ibid., 46.   14. Ibid., 49.   15. Ibid., 51–2, fn 20.

and honours'. Yet what was happening was the opposite, and these days (as the author well knew!) 'any man can ennoble himself with his money'.[16]

> And so, by the unwisdom and avarice of Princes, nobility has become a frivolous and ridiculous distinction which, presupposing neither talent nor personal merit in whoever buys or obtains it, serves only to swell the number of useless, idle and bad citizens... According to the common ideas of so many vulgar Noblemen, to live nobly is to know nothing and do nothing; occasionally to go to war; wholehearted commitment to vegetating, intriguing, caballing at court; appearing in public with magnificent clothes, coaches, servants and horses; ruination at play or with fallen women; drowning in debts and spurning creditors; robbery and deception. By a strange reversal of ideas, it would seem that a man of quality should only make himself known by lofty contempt for every useful talent and for every virtue necessary to any good citizen.[17]

So one of the greatest problems facing governments was how to make nobles useful and virtuous. Holbach's solution was to deprive them of harmful privileges, shrink the Court, make honours the reward of personal merit alone, send nobles back to the land,[18] while at the same time preventing the accumulation of overlarge estates by prohibiting entails and primogeniture.[19] He stopped short of advocating the entire abolition of the order. But any nobility reformed along the lines he suggested would scarcely be recognizable.

Like most of Holbach's works, *Ethocratie* was printed in Holland and its distribution in France was not officially authorized. Anonymous, it seems unlikely to have ridden on the backs of its author's best-selling tracts against religion.[20] But a copy was certainly in the possession of, and used by, Sieyès, who was to become the most influential foe of the nobility in 1789.[21] In 1776 it seems to have been offered as a programme for Turgot to follow. Taking as a warning the peasant uprising in Bohemia, Holbach recommended a recent tract against seigneurial exactions, Boncerf's *Les Inconvénients des droits féodaux*.[22] This was a work also produced to support

16. *Ethocratie ou le gouvernement fondé sur la morale* (Amsterdam, 1776), 53.   17. Ibid., 55.
18. Ibid., 57.   19. Ibid., 57.
20. Robert Darnton, *Edition et sédition: L'univers de la littérature clandestine au xviiiᵉ siècle* (Paris, 1991), 169–70; id., *Forbidden Best-Sellers*, 65.
21. Murray Forsyth, *Reason and Revolution: The Political Thought of the Abbé Sieyès* (Leicester, 1987), 64, 206.
22. *Ethocratie*, 50, n.20.

the work of Turgot, although the minister deplored it.[23] Boncerf was a minor official in financial administration, and an enthusiast for the physiocratic principle of removing burdens on agriculture. His pamphlet argued that many feudal dues were complex, difficult, and expensive to collect, and he recommended a scheme to buy them out. The proposals were modest, but they came at a moment when other reforms introduced by Turgot were being portrayed as a threat to the kingdom's entire social hierarchy. The magistrates of the Parlement of Paris, confronted by edicts designed (among other things) to destroy the productive monopolies of the Paris trade guilds and commute forced-labour services on public highways (*corvée*) into a tax, reinforced a campaign of judicial resistance with a clampdown on pamphleteers defending the minister. Boncerf's tract was condemned to be publicly burnt. The intention was to embarrass Turgot, but as always a public condemnation made everyone anxious to read the subversive work. Turgot felt obliged to extend royal protection to the author, but it was soon being alleged that peasants were refusing to pay dues to their lords with Boncerf in their hands.[24] Meanwhile, the parlement denounced the edict on the *corvées* in formal remonstrances.[25] Turgot's proposal was to replace forced labour, to which nobles were not subject, with a tax to which they were. According to the magistrates, this was a fundamental challenge to the privileges of the nobility, since the *corvée* went with the *taille* as a badge of *roture*. They defended these claims with the traditional argument that the kingdom's born defenders paid their taxes in blood. It was the last great restatement of the oldest (and by now least credible) justification for noble power before the Revolution swept it away.[26]

Speaking for his minister, the king rejected the magistrates' fears. 'My intention is not to confuse degrees (*conditions*) or to deprive the nobility of my kingdom of the distinctions which it has acquired by its services, which it has always enjoyed under the protection of kings, and which I shall always uphold.'[27] He compelled the parlement to register all the 'six edicts' comprising Turgot's full reform programme. But the ferocity of

23. Douglas Dakin, *Turgot and the Ancien Regime in France* (London, 1939), 247–8; Mackrell, *Attack on 'Feudalism'*, 164–168.

24. Mackrell, *Attack on 'Feudalism'* 166–7.

25. Jules Flammermont (ed.), *Les Remontrances du Parlement de Paris au xviiie siècle*, 3 vols. (Paris, 1888–98), iii, 590–600.

26. See above, pp. 43–4.

27. Jehan de Witte (ed.), *Journal de l'Abbé de Véri*, 2 vols. (Paris, 1933), i, 419.

the crisis had dented the young monarch's faith in his comptroller-general, and in the weeks that followed the sustained hostility of the Court and even his fellow ministers continued to erode his royal support. Within two months, it had entirely gone, and on 12 May 1776 Turgot was dismissed. Most of his legislative programme, including *corvée* commutation, was promptly abandoned. Turgot's downfall was a triumph for defenders of privilege of all sorts, and the undisguised rejoicing among courtiers and magistrates left no doubt that noblemen believed an insidious enemy had been vanquished.

The order as a whole faced no other public challenge for the next ten years. The fact that the finances were run between 1776 and 1781 by a non-noble Protestant foreigner meant little beside the fact that Necker paid for a major war without new taxation, and thereby largely shelved the question of what taxes nobles should or should not pay. To be sure, some of his policies were unpopular with certain sections of the nobility, but on this account alone they gratified others. Courtiers disliked his determined attempts to rein in expenditure on sinecures, but everybody excluded from Versailles applauded. Sovereign court magistrates were alarmed by his proposals to entrust tax distribution to provincial assemblies;[28] but country gentlemen could welcome a guaranteed quota of seats to be allotted in these bodies to noble landowners. Sword nobles in general viewed the marginalization of the proud 'robinocracy' with happy anticipation. Necker deplored waste at Court, but he loved a great lord. He happily connived at the capture of the secretaryships of state for war and the navy by two Marquis, Ségur and Castries respectively.[29] They in turn were able to take credit for military successes in America under the leadership in the field and on the seas of noble officers. Meanwhile Ségur's famous (or infamous) ordinance of 1781 safeguarded the grip of the old nobles of the Court on the military hierarchy.[30] Magistrates and *anoblis* might fume at an exclusion directed more at their families than at those of commoners. Necker was unsympathetic. In the treatise on the *Administration of Finances*, a best-seller which he published three years after leaving the government,[31] he denounced ennoblement through venal offices as adulterating true nobility even as it seduced otherwise productive citizens and investors into

---

28. Jean Egret, *Necker, Ministre de Louis XVI* (Paris, 1975), 126–33.
29. See John Hardman, *French Politics 1774–1789: From the Accession of Louis XVI to the Fall of the Bastille* (London, 1995), 56–9.
30. See above, p. 24.   31. Necker, *Administration of Finances*, 3 vols. (Lausanne, 1784).

untaxed idleness. He called for the college of King's Secretaries, the most straightforward gateway into the nobility, to be bought out.[32] Nobles of old stock could only welcome this, and only bourgeois with ambitions and wealth beyond their breeding could object. He neglected to mention that he had himself purchased the Swiss barony of Coppet; but in any case any damage done to the nobility at large by his writings was not immediate. Insofar as his ideas and policy initiatives stoked traditional rivalries within the order, they helped to fan the disunity that proved so fatal in and after 1789.[33] But when the revolutionaries came to abolish nobility and its outward signs in 1790, Necker would not hesitate to denounce what he saw as a vindictive and dangerous measure of social revenge.[34]

* * *

Buoyed by Turgot's downfall and the abandonment of his programme, nobles throughout the kingdom flaunted their indifference to what the lower orders might think. The parlements, having basked in public adulation as they confronted the despotism of Maupeou in the name of the laws and liberties of the nation, now threw away their upright reputation with scarcely a thought. Several of them spent years after 1774 in undignified squabbles between 'remainers' who had cooperated with the chancellor, and intransigent 'returners' from the exile into which he had sent them. Justice came to a standstill for long periods in cities like Bordeaux and Grenoble as the king's magistrates preferred to spend their time in recrimination and mutual persecution.[35] The Bordeaux magistrates compounded their image of self-absorption in 1780 by joining the trend set by Grenoble and Aix over the previous generation to formally debar non-nobles from acquiring offices in their company which ennobled by definition. The decision was the culmination of several years' refusal to admit the grandson of an *anobli* from La Rochelle to the presidential bench, a spectacle of obstruction which attracted much adverse comment, both in Bordeaux and

32. Ibid., iii, 148–57. See also Henri Grange, *Les Idées de Necker* (Paris, 1974), 125–8.
33. See below, pp. 188–9.   34. See below, pp. 240–1.
35. Jean Egret, *Le Parlement de Grenoble et les affaires publiques dans la deuxième moitié du xviii*e *siècle*, 2 vols. (Grenoble, 1942), ii, ch. 1; William Doyle, *The Parlement of Bordeaux and the End of the Old Regime, 1771–1790* (London, 1974), chs. 11 and 12.

the capital.[36] The Parlement of Paris, meanwhile, having unambiguously embraced the cause of privilege in opposing Turgot, relapsed for the best part of a decade into supine acquiescence in whatever the government proposed.[37]

At Court, the instinctive extravagance of an empty-headed young queen set an example which it became good form to follow. Men had their own example in the person of the king's youngest brother, the Count d'Artois, who ran up vast debts which the king wrote off, and built a small house in 64 days for a bet, naming it after the trifle he thought it: Bagatelle. In 1782 the demands of courtly extravagance finally caught up with a branch of the illustrious house of Rohan, that of the Grand Chamberlain of France, the Prince de Guéméné. He was forced to declare bankruptcy. Hundreds of creditors were ruined. 'You cannot take a step in the capital,' noted a close observer of Court affairs, 'without hearing the name of M de Guéménée loaded with blame and fury'.[38] He was reputed to owe 28 millions, and had kept on borrowing to maintain his credit. This, it was said, was bordering on fraud, and it was grimly noted that another fraudulent bankrupt had recently been hanged for bad debts of a mere 6,000l. The affair completely eclipsed in public attention a different example of noble arrogance from the previous spring.[39] At the opening performance in the new French Theatre, attended by the queen and a glittering selection of *les grands*, the young Count de Moreton-Chabrillan, son of a well-placed courtier, ordered an attorney to give up his balcony seat. When the attorney refused, Chabrillan accused him of theft and called the guardians, who dragged him by the hair out of the auditorium. The attorney at once lodged a judicial complaint against a nobleman 'of the sort who used their rank or their quality against a bourgeois'.[40] Thirty onlookers offered him unsolicited witness statements of support. He refused an out-of-court settlement from the count's embarrassed father, and government-inspired mediation by senior magistrates. The case was

---

36. Doyle, *Parlement of Bordeaux*, 18; also William Doyle, 'Dupaty 1744–1788: A Career in the Late Enlightenment', *SVEC*, 230 (Oxford, 1985), 35–46.
37. William Doyle, *Officers, Nobles, and Revolutionaries* (London, 1995), 30–3.
38. Bombelles, *Journal*, i, 156. 5 Oct. 1782.
39. Noted in the MS Journal of the bookseller Hardy, 'Mes Loisirs': BN MSS fr. 6684, ff. 140, 144, 155, 203; and in Bachaumont, xxi, 173–4 (10 Apr. 1784), 193 (19 Apr.), 239 (10 May); xxi, 36 (28 July), 59–60 (17 Aug.), 62–3 (18 Aug.), 70–1 (24 Aug.), 78 (26 Aug.). See also Sarah Maza, *Private Lives and Public Affairs: The Causes Célèbres of Pre-Revolutionary France* (Berkeley and Los Angeles, CA, 1993), 149–50.
40. Bachaumont, xxi, 38 (29 July 1782).

carried as far as the parlement, where despite prolonged attempts by some magistrates to defer to Chabrillan's rank, he was eventually condemned to apologize, acknowledge the plaintiff as a man of honour, and donate 6,000*l*. to various charities. The verdict was popular, although some complained that it was a cheap price that any fool might pay for the freedom to insult honest citizens.

* * *

Such incidents were evidence that the behaviour of noblemen in life was every bit as outrageous and despicable as that of literary stereotypes now being offered to a rapidly expanding reading public. The Europe-wide literary sensation of the mid-1770s was Goethe's *The Sorrows of Young Werther* (1774). It had been translated into French three times by the end of 1775.[41] Among the many tribulations which help to drive the brooding young hero to suicide is the way he, a commoner, is treated by the polite society of the small principality in which he lives. Although individual nobles meet him on equal terms in private, they become cold and embarrassed when their fellows object to Werther's presence at an aristocratic gathering. Later they apologize, but by then the upstart's ostracism is the talk of the town, and he abandons a promising career there in humiliation and despair.

Even the fiercest French critics of noble arrogance were always convinced that matters were worse in Germany; but if any felt that their noble compatriots were likely to be less cruel and heartless, a best-selling French novel would soon suggest otherwise. *Les Liaisons dangéreuses* by Choderlos de Laclos was published, with instant success, in March 1782, at the very moment when the Moreton-Chabrillant affair was gripping the gossip of Paris. Laclos, himself a nobleman, was an army officer who had taken to writing to while away the boredom of life in remote provincial garrisons. His novel was a story of cold-hearted seduction and pitiless revenge, told in a series of letters between former lovers, a Viscount and a Marquise. Their victims are women of lesser standing, whose innate virtue is not proof against the smooth wiles of polished libertines. And although the perpetrators are both punished in the end by fate—the Viscount killed

---

41. Nicholas Boyle, *Goethe: The Poet and the Age, i, The Poetry of Desire* (Oxford, 1992), 175.

by a fellow nobleman in a duel—the book achieved instant notoriety as a black celebration of immorality. Everyone was convinced, too, that the main characters were drawn from life, and there was much speculation as to who they might be. The scandal was such that steps were taken to restrict the book's sale, and Laclos was ordered by the minister of war to leave Paris and rejoin his regiment.[42] Epistolary novels describing the tribulations of heroines pursued by predatory gentlemen had been fashionable ever since Richardson's *Pamela* (1740–1) and *Clarissa* (1748–9), with which several critics compared *Les Liaisons*. And Laclos explicitly invited comparison with Rousseau's *Nouvelle Héloïse* on the title page, with an epigraph drawn from that novel. But in the depiction of sexual predation as a game played by ruthless nobles to amuse themselves and ward off the boredom of otherwise pointless lives, readers could easily recognize the hedonistic world of the Court and the capital and learn that it was even more depraved than they thought. It was, reminisced Tilly,[43] who later took pains to meet the author, 'one of those disastrous meteors which fell from a flaming sky at the end of the eighteenth century'.

Yet, like him, every noble was desperate to read it. The queen herself was said to have had a copy bound with no title on the spine to hide the shame of possessing it.[44] When it was banned, the rush only increased. It should never have been allowed, reflected a conservative courtier—on completing it.[45] 'M Choderlos de Laclos... has judged his age, and above all what is called the high society of Paris. A work that should have destroyed his reputation has made him fashionable, because all we want is wit.'

Meanwhile, an even more sensational *succès de scandale* was brewing. In 1775, with *The Barber of Seville*, Beaumarchais achieved the dramatic triumph that had eluded him in the previous decade. Abandoning the sentimental *drames* of everyday life which he had vainly tried to popularize, he produced a comedy in a well-established tradition. Figaro, a servant who lives on his wits, helps his aristocratic master Count Almaviva steal

---

42. Hardy, 'Mes Loisirs', BN MSS fr. 6684, ff. 154–5, 18 May 1782; Bachaumont, xx, 211 (29 Apr. 1782), 250 (14 May), 271–2 (29 May); xxi, 299–300 (13 June).
43. *Mémoires*, 249.
44. Maurice Allem (ed.), *Choderlos de Laclos: Oeuvres complètes* (Paris, 1951), introduction, 9.
45. Bombelles, *Journal*, i, 145, 14 Sept. 1782.

his beloved from a doltish bourgeois guardian. The play ran for twenty-seven performances in Paris, and 24,000 people paid to see it.[46] It was also performed the next year at Court. Buoyed by this, the ever-resourceful Beaumarchais began work on a sequel in 1778. By 1781 it was ready, and the author made sure that its existence was well known. Almost as soon as *La Folle Journée, ou le Mariage de Figaro* was read and accepted by the actors of the *Comédie française*, the news had spread across Europe.[47] The play won the grudging approval of an official censor and was soon being read in private gatherings throughout the fashionable world of Paris and the Court. Eventually the king demanded to read it, too. But, outraged by Figaro's criticisms of government and censorship, he declared that it would never be performed. Nobody took him seriously. In fact, a group of courtiers, encouraged by the king's own feckless brother the Count d'Artois, arranged a first performance by invitation at a minor Parisian theatre. On 13 June 1783 half the audience had already taken their seats and aristocratic carriages were jamming the streets outside, when a royal order arrived to cancel the production. The king had only learnt of it that morning, and acted promptly. A mixture of astonishment and outrage greeted his intervention, and people spoke of oppression and tyranny.[48] It was the talk of Versailles and the capital. What, people asked, was in the play that the monarch found so dangerous and offensive?

Beaumarchais and his courtly backers were therefore undeterred. And with the promise that offending passages would be removed, the king was persuaded by the queen to allow at least a private performance at the country house of one of her intimates, before an audience of princes, peers, their ladies, and other prominent courtiers. It took place, in the author's absence abroad, on 27 September 1783. On returning, he sensed that a full public performance could probably not now be prevented indefinitely, and he bombarded ministers and the king himself, with requests for a new censor (by now a fifth) to purge the text finally of objectionable passages.[49]

46. John Lough, *Paris Theatre Audiences* in the Seventeenth and Eighteenth Centuries (London, 1957), 182.
47. Gunnar and Mavis von Proschwitz, *Beaumarchais et Le Courrier de l'Europe: Documents inédits ou peu connus*, SVEC 274 (oxford 1990) 673. Daubcourt to Beaumarchais, 5 Nov. 1781.
48. Mme Campan, *Mémoires sur la vie de Marie-Antoinette, Reine de France et de Navarre* (Nelson edn, Paris and Edinburgh, undated), 189–93.
49. Proschwitz, *Beaumarchais*, ii, 768–9, Beaumarchais to Lenoir, 27 Nov. 1783; 774, Beaumarchais to same, 17 Jan. 1784; 775–84, Beaumarchais to Breteuil, 17 Jan. 1784; 802–3, Beaumarchais to Louis XVI, March 1784.

He was himself, he claimed, swamped with enquiries as to what was happening. Finally, Baron de Breteuil, minister for the Royal Household, agreed to assemble a panel of men of letters (which included Chamfort) to discuss the play line by line. In their presence, Beaumarchais argued that his play was in a mainstream comic tradition, and that if all the criticisms of previous censors were accepted, sixty other classic comedies would need to be proscribed for similar reasons. He sent a list of them to the king. Whether it was on account of this, or the constant pressure of the royal family and all he heard about the public mood, the king finally gave way. Performance at the *Comédie française* was authorized, and the opening took place on 27 April 1784.

Once again the cream of high society was there, including the king's more sober brother, the Count de Provence. People fought for admission, and some were trampled in the crush. The passages to which the king had objected were scarcely changed, and the opening scene described Count Almaviva's threat to revive the most notorious (though least well authenticated[50]) of feudal rights, the *droit de seigneur* or *cuissage,* under which a lord could enjoy a vassal's newly-wed wife on the first night of the marriage. Neglecting his countess, Almaviva lusts after her maid, now engaged to his servant Figaro. The main plot sees Figaro repeatedly thwart his master's designs and in the final act, when it appears he might yet fail, he exclaims bitterly against the Count:

> Because you are a great lord, you think yourself a great genius! ...
> Nobility, wealth, rank, positions, all this makes you so proud!
> What have you done for so much? You gave yourself the
> trouble of being born, that's all. Otherwise, you're pretty ordinary.[51]

He goes on to inveigh against press censorship, arbitrary imprisonment, and favouritism, before the intrigues resume and all is resolved with Figaro wedding his unsullied bride and the Count begging his wife's forgiveness.

The play was a runaway success. It had a quite unprecedented initial run of seventy-three performances and was seen during that time by over 97,000 people.[52] When it was printed, with a preface by the author, a

---

50. See the discussion in M. Garaud, *Histoire générale du droit privé français: la révolution et la propriété foncière* (Paris, 1959), 102–9.
51. Act V, sc. iii.   52. Lough, *Paris Theatre Audiences*, 182.

year later, 6,000 copies were said to have been sold in six days.[53] And the rush to see it was led by nobles of all sorts. 'Everyone speaks ill of it, and everyone wants to see it', wrote an Alsatian noblewoman returning to Paris from a tour in Germany.[54] 'Great lords, it seems to me, were tactless and immoderate in applauding it so; they were slapping themselves in the face; they laughed at their own expense, and what is worse, made others laugh too. They will regret it later…Beaumarchais has shown them their own caricature, and they have responded: That's it, we are just like that.' Yet Beaumarchais, who had paid good money to ennoble himself, denied any intention of insulting the noble order. All he wished to do, he claimed in the preface he wrote in reply to his critics,[55] was to lampoon abuses; and he quoted earlier writings of his own in which he declared nobility an essential intermediary power between a monarch and his subjects. Descent from distinguished ancestors could not be held against any man; and surely no great lord could object to the count's libertinism being thwarted? At least 'I had the generous respect not to endow him with any of the vices of the people.'[56] Some nobles, it is true, were shocked at the portrayal of a Spanish grandee in such an unflattering light.[57] But French grandees continued to revel in the wit of Beaumarchais. In August 1785, *The Barber of Seville* was revived at Versailles, with the queen herself playing the as-yet un-won countess and the Count d'Artois, Figaro.

Sallies against the nobility, in fact, were perhaps the least of the reasons why *The Marriage of Figaro* was such a sensation. Its intrinsic qualities as a play, a piece of comic writing, and a successful sequel, made it likely to do well in any circumstances. Add to this its long and very public gestation, the prohibition by the king himself, and Beaumarchais' talent as a self-publicist, all fanning public curiosity: it could scarcely fail. The importance of Figaro's final tirade lay much more in its denunciation of censorship and the arbitrary powers of government than in his scorn for Almaviva's high birth. Figaro's fleeting despair, and the count's belated return to his duty, added a fashionably serious note to what was otherwise

---

53. Hardy, 'Mes Loisirs', BN MSS fr. 6685, f. 92, 6 Apr. 1785.
54. Suzanne Burkard (ed.), *Mémoires de la Baronne d'Oberkirch sur la cour de Louis XVI et la société française avant 1789* (Paris, 1982), 304.
55. Maurice Rat (ed.), *Théâtre de Beaumarchais* (Paris, 1956), 166–7.   56. Ibid., 158.
57. Anne Vassal and Christine Rambaud (eds.), *Nicolas Ruault: Gazette d'un Parisien sous la Révolution* (Paris, 1976), 42–3, 10 May 1784.

a farce, gratifying Beaumarchais' never-abandoned longing to write moral drama.[58] When, two years later, Mozart and Da Ponte set the play to music in Vienna, the character of the Count could scarcely be changed: but Figaro's rant against him was omitted. Joseph II, like his brother-in-law, had refused permission for a German translation of Beaumarchais to be performed. It was, he said, too 'freely written'[59] for the usual Viennese audience. But he allowed the text to be published, and agreed to a musical version, in Italian, when Da Ponte promised to leave out anything that might 'offend the delicacy and decency of a performance at which his sovereign Majesty presided'. On these terms, the Holy Roman Emperor himself endorsed *Figaro* publicly, authorizing its first performance by the Court opera company. An unflattering picture of a great nobleman, after all, accorded well enough with the monarch's own hostility to overmighty subjects.[60]

✳ ✳ ✳

Only with hindsight, therefore, can the greatest theatrical sensation of the 1780s be seen as more than a satirical pinprick in the thick hide of nobility. But it was not the only one. While the irresponsible antics of Court life inspired a swelling stream of contemptuous rumour and pornographic innuendo, all reflecting badly on nobles enjoying the highest public profile, everyday aspects of noble behaviour which any inhabitant of the French capital might encounter were highlighted throughout the decade in the sketches of Louis Sébastien Mercier's *Tableau de Paris* (12 vols, 1781–88). Mercier's aim, to some extent fulfilled, was to repeat the success of his best-selling *L'An 2240*,[61] and the fact that the first two volumes were briefly banned gave it a successful launch. Within the first few pages the author was denouncing hunting rights, and the desertion of the countryside by nobles seduced by the luxuries of the capital and the

58. *La Mère coupable*, first performed in 1792, was a further sequel: a story of intrigue with no comic element at all. It failed, just as Beaumarchais's first dramatic efforts had.
59. Lorenzo Da Ponte, *Memorie* (edn. Garanzi: Milan, 1976), 105–6.
60. Volkmar Braunbehrens, *Mozart in Vienna, 1781–1791* (London, 1990), 212–15. See also Derek Beales, *Mozart and the Habsburgs* (Reading, 1993); and T. C. W. Blanning, *The Culture of Power and the Power of Culture: Old Regime Europe, 1660–1789* (Oxford, 2002), 440.
61. See above, pp. 82–3.

Court.[62] Later, in a chapter ostensibly condemning the usurpation of titles,[63] he concluded that 'of all the prejudices which render us stupid, the most unreasonable and the most insolent is that of nobility ... it is fair to pour ridicule on that crowd of men who would wish to separate themselves, in the name of ancestors real or false, from their fellow citizens, more honest, more useful and more commendable than these nobles, gentlemen and gentry, whatever name they take, or usurp, or have received by the chance of birth'. 'Men of letters', he confessed in the second volume[64] (appearing at the same time as the first), 'are making every effort today to bring down the vanity of titles to its true emptiness, and to set up in their place the useful and commendable works of famous men of all sorts ... And so open war is declared between men of letters and the Great; but the latter, for certain, will lose the battle.' Contempt for *les grands* was one of the things, declared a fellow scribbler and future revolutionary, Jacques-Pierre Brissot, that he loved about Mercier[65]—even as he flaunted a usurped 'de Warville' added to his own name. Many of Mercier's targets in noble behaviour were traditional butts of literary scorn traceable as far back at least as La Bruyère: the crawling courtier, greedy for patronage, who disdains the less well born; impoverished grandees who marry new money while begging their ancestors' forgiveness; king's secretaries buying instant hereditary nobility with their offices; the cascade of snobbery marking every degree of rank. But they conveyed the message of how little the structures of power and esteem had changed since the days of Louis XIV. 'The outward repulsion has gone, but at bottom it is all the same.'[66] Only the freedom of writers to voice such criticism had improved; and indeed later volumes in the series were published and distributed without the intervention of the literary police. Mercier took advantage by attacking the vanity of displaying coats of arms and inventing ancestors: 'Of all the pettiness of which the human mind is capable, this seems to me the most miserable and the most ridiculous.'[67] In volume viii (1783) he denounced the presumptuous mendicancy of poor nobles, who laid claim to public appointments in order to sustain their idleness: 'A poor

62. Vol I, ch. iv, 'Physionomie de la grande ville', and vi, 'Où est le gouvernement féodal?'.
63. Vol. I, ch. lxxviii, 'Les aigrefins'.   64. Vol. II, ch. xxxvii, 'Auteurs'.
65. Brissot to the Société typographique de Neuchâtel, 14 March 1782, quoted in Jean-Claude Bonnet (ed.), *Tableau de Paris*, 2 vols. (Paris, 1994), i, introduction, cxxxvii.
66. Vol. V, ch. cdxxxv, 'Financières'.   67. Vol. VI, ch. Cdlxviii, 'Cachets'.

noble does not ask for something to get bread, but to get servants.'[68] In this volume, too, a whole chapter was explicitly devoted to the nobility and its supposed justifications.[69] Provoked by a tract recently brought out in Neuchâtel by his own publisher,[70] Mercier laid out in a few pages many of the arguments that would be revolutionary commonplaces only six years later. 'Nobility,' he observed, 'in its origin, stood between king and people. It would be difficult today to say exactly what it is in the State.' Deprived of political power, nobles still retained both their social authority and their insatiable greed. They never allowed commoners any promotion or reward, whatever their talents or services rendered to the country. And if it was true that they shed their blood to defend it, so did the commoners who filled the ranks. The spread of education and enlightenment had made men more alike, whereas noble power in previous centuries had flourished on the weakness and ignorance of others: 'Man more than ever is the noble son of his own works. Races which only have sterile pride on their side should fall back into the crowd, until they have shown virtues that are living rather than dead.' All should be equal under the king, and distinctions of pride and prejudice were 'injurious to the body of the nation, and unwise for the service of the country'.

Only the absence of reverential capitals in words like *nation* and *patrie* marked the polemic of this chapter out as written before the Revolution. By the time Mercier's eleventh and twelfth volumes (1788) appeared, that revolution was imminent, and he returned confidently to the charge, excoriating orders of chivalry and genealogists,[71] and nobles in general as 'the greatest enemies of our national manners'. Nobility now was a 'ridiculous prejudice', and the nation had no need of men whose only claim to distinction was their birth.[72] Those who aspired to join such an order were ridiculed afresh:[73] 'Ways of becoming noble have so multiplied that a commoner with his own name is coming to be a rare being... Let us hope', he concluded, 'that a day will come when it will be an honour to be a commoner, or useful to the country, which means much the same thing.'

68. Vol. VIII, ch. dcxxx, 'Distribution des aumônes'.   69. Vol. VIII, ch. dcl, 'Noblesse'.
70. M. Barthès, *Nouveaux essais sur la noblesse, où, après avoir recherché l'origine et l'état civil de l'homme noble chez les peuples connus, on se propose de le guider dans différents âges et emplois de la vie* (Neuchâtel, 1781).
71. Vol. XI, ch. cmxxii, 'Quartiers de noblesse'.
72. Vol. XI, ch. cmxliv, 'Titres de noblesse'.
73. Vol. XI, ch. mmxxviii, 'Les deux noblesses'.

Whether, even as late as 1788, Mercier seriously expected such a day seems improbable.[74] Hoping, at the end of the next decade, to repeat his earlier success by describing the post-revolutionary capital, in 1799 he published *Le Nouveau Paris*. He now had little enough to say about the nobility, but before the Revolution, he recalled in an early chapter,[75] France was governed by 'the oldest, cleverest and most enterprising aristocracy that ever existed', and the most astonishing thing was that 'this revolution which changed the face of France and must occupy all of Europe, should have come about at the moment when aristocracy seemed to have perfected its system of insolence'.

At least Mercier, unlike so many others who wrote about nobility or professed to despise it, made no attempt to acquire or even feign the status himself. Few resisted that temptation, and certainly not the author of another popular part-work of the 1780s, Jacques-Henri Bernardin de Saint-Pierre.[76] Bernardin was to be chiefly remembered as the author of one of the earliest truly romantic novels in French, *Paul et Virginie* (1788). Originally, however, this was not a free-standing work but the last part of a sequence of writings begun in 1773 with the direct encouragement of Jean-Jacques Rousseau. They began to be published in 1784 under the title *Etudes de la Nature*.[77] Intended to demonstrate the benevolent abundance and variety of creation, they appealed to a public intoxicated with the wonders of science and nature,[78] as well as to churchmen anxious to find new proofs of the divine plan. And, emboldened by the success of his observations on nature, in his later editions Bernardin moved on to reflect on society. His thirteenth study (1787) considered the nobility. His thinking on this was as confused as critics tended to find his reflections on the natural world. Nobility was originally granted, he thought, to reward virtue, but this function was closed off when it became hereditary, because it denied 'other citizens the roads to distinction' (*illustration*).[79] Making nobility 'the apanage of a certain number of families' also discouraged industry by promoting

74. On his pre-revolutionary attitudes, see Norman Hampson, *Will and Circumstance: Montesquieu, Rousseau, and the French Revolution* (London, 1983), 76–83.
75. *Le Nouveau Paris*, ch. viii, 'Les quatre tourbillons'.
76. Fernand Maury, *Etude sur la vie et les oeuvres de Bernardin de Saint-Pierre* (Paris, 1892), i, 144.
77. Maury, *Etude sur la vie*, 139–49.
78. See also Robert Darnton, *Mesmerism and the End of the Enlightenment in France* (Cambridge, MA, 1968), 10–45.
79. L. Aimé-Martin (ed.), *Oeuvres de Jacques-Henri Bernardin de Saint-Pierre* (Paris, 1833), 448–9.

'a fatal lethargy', and tended to establish two nations within one, which destroyed patriotism and opened the way to subjugation by foreigners. He instanced the fate of Poland. On the other hand, Bernardin was also opposed to recruiting new nobles by venality. A much better system was to imitate the Romans, recruiting meritorious commoners into the nobility by adoption. The right to adopt would be a new noble privilege, but it would reconcile the orders. 'Thus, for example, a poor gentleman would solicit virtue among the people, and a virtuous man of the people would look for a well-endowed patron among nobles. These political bonds seem to me more powerful and honourable than those of financial marriages, which, bringing together two citizens of different classes, often alienate their families.' Yet heredity was still a problem, and not one solved by opening nobility to trade, where nobles might have neither the aptitude nor the capital. It would be better to make nobles of good husbandmen: but that would create too many. Perhaps the king should acquire the monopoly of buying up lordships, which could then be redistributed not to men whose only merit was their wealth. Bernardin's favoured solution, however, was only to ennoble citizens of distinction posthumously, because 'death alone assures reputations'. Citizens deemed worthy of it would be accorded perpetual recognition in a public 'Elysium'—a more democratic version of the Pantheon established a few years later, when nobility had at last been abolished.

None of these utopian daydreams seemed to envisage abolition of the existing nobility—merely its purification. They would later be invoked by pamphleteers more unequivocally hostile,[80] and Bernardin himself would offer a refined version of them to the revolutionaries of 1789.[81] But in the years preceding the breakdown of absolute monarchy nothing more than limited reforms were seriously thought of. Even the consistently bitter jibes of Mercier conveyed no sense that the way of the world could soon be changed. It was no coincidence that his ideal world of 2440 was situated seven centuries into the future. And so the only unambiguous denunciation of nobles and their power in these years, underpinned by practical experience across the Atlantic, was Mirabeau's tract against the Cincinnati.

80. e.g., the satirical tract *Lettre de M. le Marquis de M***, Gentilhomme Breton à Monseigneur l'Evêque de ***; sur les Débats entre le Tiers et la Noblesse* [1789], 26, fn.
81. *Voeux d'un Solitaire* in *Oeuvres*, 682–6. See also below, p. 182.

Elsewhere in Europe, it is true, practical attacks were beginning to materialize. The Emperor Joseph II who had been brooding incautiously on how to 'attack the nobles' in his hereditary dominions since shortly before the imperial crown came to him in 1765,[82] spent the first few years after his assumption of sole power in 1780 setting up a cadastral survey of landholding in preparation for an attempt to abolish serfdom. He would launch it in 1789, to the horror of nobles throughout his realms, in the form of a 'physiocratic urbarium' clearly designed to force them to break up estates dependent on forced labour. In Sweden Gustav III, no enemy to nobles in principle, found his plans to make war on his northern neighbours obstructed in 1786 by the House of Nobles in the four-chamber diet. He responded by fanning traditional grievances among the other orders against noble pretensions, and used the passions thus aroused to force the passage in 1789 of an Act of Union and Security further increasing royal power at parliamentary (and aristocratic) expense.

Both these challenges to noble authority came from monarchs, neither of whom, in daily life, dreamed of surrounding themselves with anyone other than princes or other great magnates. Both would learn, too late, the lesson of Montesquieu that kings and nobilities must stand or fall together. The self-styled 'Patriots' of the Dutch Republic never doubted it; and in their struggle to curb the authority of the Stadholder William V they produced a new term for people with noble or oligarchical pretensions. The idea of aristocracy was as old as ancient Athens, but nobody seems to have used the term *aristocrat* to define a political actor until Joan Derk van der Capellen tot den Pol.[83] He, too, was a noble—another Baron—although as so often not one with unambiguous or uncontested credentials. And nobody while he lived knew him to be the author of an anonymous and incendiary pamphlet freely distributed in Amsterdam in 1781, *To the Netherlands People*. It called upon all Dutch patriots to unite against William V and the privileged 'aristocrats' who ruled the republic. The author's hope was to sweep the country into an alliance with the fledgling United States and France to weaken the power of the British, who he thought had held the republic and its established authorities in thrall for too long. He had his wish, although he did not live to see its less-than-triumphant results.[84] For six years after his intervention the politics of the republic grew ever-more polarized between parties who referred contemptuously to one another as democrats or aristocrats. Their confrontations were fully reported to French readers by the most widely-read of newspapers produced abroad, the Dutch-based *Gazette de Leyde*,[85] and Louis XVI and his ministers lent open support to the democratic Patriots. Until the death of Frederick the Great in August 1786 their progress seemed unstoppable. The new Prussian king, however, was brother to the Stadholder's wife. With British support, he marched his army into the republic in September 1787, and France made clear that she could not intervene on the Patriots' side. William V's power was saved, the aristocrats triumphed, and many Patriots became refugees in the towns of French Flanders. They arrived in time to witness the political categories which they had pioneered widely adopted among their hosts.

* * *

Nobody foresaw it. While courtiers, magistrates, and army officers capered and postured in complete indifference to public perceptions, moneyed men scrambled more energetically than ever to join their privileged ranks. Prices for ennobling offices soared well beyond the rate of inflation, and were accelerating.[86] Genealogists agonized about the scale of usurpations, and proposed elaborate schemes to eliminate them.[87] And while the number of institutions requiring ever more vigorous proofs of nobility continued to expand,[88] manuals of genealogy, collections of laws and customs relating to nobility and the offices conferring it, and ever more erudite entries in works of reference, all proliferated.[89] On the eve of its abolition,

---

84. He died in 1784.
85. Jeremy Popkin, *News and Politics in the Age of Revolution* (Ithaca, NY, 1989), 167–187.
86. Doyle, *Venality*, 217–23, 234–8.
87. Maugard, *Remarques sur la Noblesse* (2nd edn, Paris, 1788), 3–5.
88. Defauconprêt, *Les preuves de noblesse au xviii* siècle, 44–50, 55–60, 78–82.
89. In addition to Maugard's *Remarques*, see L. N. H. Chérin, *Abrégé chronologique d'édits...concernant la Noblesse* (Paris, 1788, reprinted 1974); P. G. Guyot, *Traité des droits, fonctions, franchises, exemptions, prérogatives et privilèges annexes à chaque dignité, à chaque office, et à chaque état, soit civil, soit militaire, soit ecclésiastique*, 4 vols. (Paris, 1786–8). Noteworthy too are various entries in *Encyclopédie Méthodique: Finances*, 3 vols. (Paris, 1787) and *Jurisprudence*, 3 vols. (Paris, 1783). On competition between genealogists, see Maugard, *Lettre à M. Chérin...sur son Abrégé chronologique d'Edits concernant le fait de la Noblesse* (Paris, 1788) (BL FR 127 (92))

nobility in France was being refined, defined, and categorized as never before.

And when, confronted by a financial crisis which he saw no means of resolving by conventional measures, the comptroller-general Charles Alexandre de Calonne persuaded Louis XVI in 1786 to convoke an Assembly of Notables to endorse a plan of reform, this handpicked body was made up entirely of noblemen.[90] Only they, it was assumed, would carry the weight and public respect which the minister hoped would promote widespread acceptance of his ambitious proposals. Lafayette, who was appointed to the assembly on account of his transatlantic exploits, told George Washington that 'The Assembly was very properly chosen both for honesty, abilities and personal consequence',[91] and few outside observers seemed to have questioned the credentials of the 144 princes, bishops, courtiers, administrators, magistrates, and provincial officials who convened at Versailles on 22 February 1787.

No part of the kingdom's institutional or social structure would have been left untouched by the proposals which Calonne, initially in the strictest secrecy, laid before them. No vested interest would have survived unscathed. And if the greatest loser from his schemes would have been the church, a number of the basic prerogatives of the nobility would also have been threatened. While exemption from the *taille*, that crucial touchstone of noble status, would have remained, the proposal of 1776 to transform the *corvée* into a universal tax now resurfaced. A minority of members accepted that nobles should pay the tax, but most did not.[92] Calonne hoped to soften the impact of this and other perceived losses by proposing that henceforth the nobility should be exempted from the capitation, which they already paid on a separate basis. The idea was rejected with indignation for the transparent bribe it was.[93] The Notables were practically unanimous in accepting that all should be equally subject, and on the same basis, to whatever new taxes were introduced—even if many were hostile to the land tax in kind that Calonne favoured. Another

---

and *Lettre de M. Chérin ... à M.* *** *à l'occasion d'une Brochure et d'un Prospectus ayant tous deux pour titre Lettre à M. Chérin* (Paris, 1789) (BL FR 127 (3)).

90. It is true that a handful of mayors convoked enjoyed nobility that was recent or incomplete, but none were unambiguously *roturiers*.

91. Gottschalk (ed.), *The Letters of Lafayette to Washington*, 322, no. 196, 5 May 1787.

92. Pierre Chevallier (ed.), *Journal de l'Assemblée des Notables de 1787* (Paris, 1960), 29: Jean Egret, *La Pré-révolution française, 1787–1788* (Paris, 1962), 29.

93. Egret, *Pré-révolution*, 30.

of his central proposals was to entrust the assessment and collection of taxes to provincial assemblies. Launched in two generalities by Necker in 1778, these bodies were generally thought to have worked well. Calonne proposed to generalize them, with elected rather than nominated members. But although he proposed, like Necker, to guarantee a quota of seats for the clergy and the nobility, the village assemblies who would do the electing would be made up of the richest taxpayers irrespective of status. Several Notables found this a dangerous departure from traditional respect for the established social hierarchy.

Yet the concerns of the Notables as noblemen were of relatively minor importance compared with confusion about the true state of the finances, mistrust of Calonne, and a whole range of more technical reservations, in leading the Assembly's proceedings to deadlock within a matter of weeks. Calonne's response to this unexpected opposition, seemingly with the king's backing,[94] was to offer his hitherto secret proposals for general public discussion. On the last day of March, under the title *Avertissement,* a summary of them was widely distributed around Versailles and the capital, and copies were sent to parish priests to read from the pulpit. The proposals were presented as measures of universal benefit. They were being obstructed, implied the *Avertissement,* by the selfish greed of the privileged, who were more concerned to protect their own material advantages than to bring relief to the people. The language was deliberately inflammatory:

> What difficulties could weigh against such advantages? What could be the pretexts for concern?
> We will pay more! ... No doubt, but who?
> Only those who did not pay enough; they will pay what they owe in just proportion, and nobody will be burdened.
> Privileges will be sacrificed! ... Yes: as justice requires, and needs demand. Would it be better to overload yet further the non-privileged, the people?
> There will be a great outcry! ... That was to be expected.
> Can one do general good without harming a few particular interests? Can there be reforms without complaints?[95]

Patriotism, and the honour so dear to French hearts, however, would triumph in the end. Already the 'first Orders of the State' had accepted

---

94. Hardman, *French Politics*, 86, 237–8; Chevallier, *Journal*, 63.
95. *Avertissement* in Calonne, *De l'Etat de la France, présent et à venir* (London, 1790), 439.

fiscal equality and given up new exemptions offered them. Remaining opposition surely could not be, as some were saying, malevolently motivated...

It was a deliberate bid to overawe the Notables by stirring up social resentment, a 'dangerous tocsin' as one of them called it.[96] They were outraged. Even in Boston, declared Lafayette, a pamphlet like this would be seen as seditious. There was only one way the king could disavow his involvement in so blatant an attempt to sow discord among his subjects, and that was to dismiss Calonne. Reluctantly, he did so; but over the next twelve months he seems to have felt a growing resentment towards the nobility in general for resisting reforms whose necessity he had come to accept.[97] And yet the 'tocsin' struck no chord at all. The denunciation of the privileged in the *Avertissement* fell flat. Until late in 1788, in fact, the French would look to the nobility to defend them against the ambitions of 'ministerial despotism'. Over that time, they would take up the cry raised in the Notables when they saw that no satisfactory deal could be done on reform with the king and Calonne's ultimate successor, Archbishop Loménie de Brienne. Only the Estates-General, many Notables were declaring by the time the Assembly was dissolved on 25 May, were competent to authorize the taxes and administrative changes which the kingdom needed.

Calonne had briefly considered the Estates-General for endorsing his plans, only to reject it as too dangerously unpredictable. Brienne thought the same. He was now resolved to push a reform programme through using the traditional procedure of registration by the parlements. But no parlement, whatever reservations individual magistrates might have about the Estates-General, could afford to espouse less than the Notables had called for. All their leading officers, after all, had been members of the Assembly, and some had taken the lead in calling for this greater national forum. Accordingly, when edicts introducing a new land tax and a stamped paper duty were laid before the Parlement of Paris, the magistrates refused to register them, echoing the claim of the Notables when confronted with the same proposals: only the Estates-General were competent to approve new perpetual taxes. Brienne's administration offered everything short of that to expedite registration. A full statement of accounts was prepared, the projected yield of the new taxes was explicitly capped, and spectacular economies were announced in expenditure. The king abandoned the

96. Chevallier, *Journal*, 45.   97. John Hardman, *Louis XVI* (London, 1993), 139.

usual annual transfer of the Court to Fontainebleau for autumnal hunting, resolved to demolish or sell several royal residences, and announced the suppression of a large number of Court offices, sinecures, and pensions.[98] Many courtiers were infuriated at the loss of income and patronage: new noble enemies for Brienne's ministry. The next month there was disgust throughout the army when the archbishop refused to intervene in the Dutch Republic to protect the Patriots against a Prussian invasion. But for the military there was worse to come. A new council of war established during the autumn disbanded several of the prestigious parade regiments of the King's Household and planned economies involving the dismissal of over 5,000 officers. Eventually more than 3,500 were cashiered, but only a handful received the full compensation to which they were legally entitled.[99] New regulations on appointment and promotion, it is true, reassured courtiers that they would retain the pick of the upper ranks and reach them by fast-track procedures. But the cost of this was to offend the petty provincial nobility who provided most of the army's working officers. Explicitly described in the new regulations as 'secondary' or 'lower' noblemen, they were now told in effect that all noblemen were not equal and that they could never aspire to the highest ranks. Noblemen of military tradition were not natural allies of the magistracy, but these army reforms gave them every incentive to back the parlements in their resistance to Brienne's government and its plans. The final crisis of absolute monarchy was played out in the months between August 1787 and August 1788, and many, including Louis XVI himself, thought the fatal blow was delivered by a 'Noble Revolt'.

It was led by the parlements, who supported that of Paris in calling for the Estates-General to consent to new taxation. It was true that the Parisian court, where many peers were now exercising their right to sit, was induced by a bout of exile to contemplate an amended version of Brienne's plans, which included a vague promise to convoke the Estates by 1792. But on 19 November a solemn 'Royal Session', convened to confirm the deal, went spectacularly wrong. It ended with the king's first cousin, the Duke d'Orléans, accusing him in public of acting illegally. He was exiled, and two magistrates who had supported his stance were arrested. After that there was no more hope of any sort of agreement, and the parlement fell to denouncing the *lettres de cachet* under which the three recalcitrants were

98. Egret, *Pré-révolution*, 73–80.   99. Blaufarb, *French Army 1750–1820*, 38–9.

detained. By the beginning of 1788 rumours were circulating of further acts of severity to muzzle the parlements once and for all. There was widespread talk of another Maupeou-like coup. It finally materialized in the second week of May, and proved even more radical in ambition than that of the notorious chancellor. Under laws simultaneously promulgated at military sessions in sovereign courts throughout the kingdom, the parlements were to be deprived of the right to register royal fiscal edicts and to remonstrate against them. These prerogatives were to be vested in a single 'plenary court' made up of princes, peers and senior magistrates: a body not unlike the Assembly of Notables. All its members would be nobles; although Brienne had dreams of supplementing it one day with a sort of lower house of elected landed proprietors.[100] The parlements were at once put into vacation pending a remodelling of their membership and redefinition of their powers. But most refused to disperse until they had passed resolutions condemning the new measures as illegal, and in the days that followed there were protests throughout the kingdom at what was seen as a despotic attack on the defenders of the nation's liberties.

Magistrates could do no more, but other noblemen now took over leadership of the resistance. Members of the peerage itself had already helped the Parisian magistrates to obstruct the arrest of two of their most militant colleagues in the days before the coup. In the provinces, several military commanders held their troops back from firing on rioters, even when they were being stoned.[101] Officers resigned rather than arrest protestors. In Brittany, where the nobility was accustomed to meeting regularly in the provincial Estates, hundreds of noblemen held informal assemblies which sent delegates to Paris to petition against the reforms. The delegates were arrested. No such risks were taken by the nobility of other provinces, but plenty of unauthorized assemblies took place to discuss the crisis. Where provincial Estates did not exist or had fallen into abeyance, nobles were often found signing petitions calling for their restoration alongside the Estates-General. In Dauphiné, a number of gentlemen responded to a call from a petty magistrate, Jean-Joseph Mounier, to meet with self-styled representatives from the Third Estate to consider reviving the Estates of the province. The local military commander did not stop them. They even

100. Egret, *Pré-révolution*, 247.
101. Ibid., 263–5; Samuel F. Scott, *The Response of the French Royal Army to the French Revolution: The Role and Development of the Line Army, 1789–1793* (Oxford, 1978), 46–8.

agreed that the Third Estate in the Estates should have as many delegates as the nobility and clergy combined, and that nobles should contribute to any tax replacing the *corvée*. These 165 noblemen, from a relatively remote Alpine province, were the first to commit themselves publicly to the idea of sharing power with men beyond their own ranks.

But most of those who threw themselves into this nobles' revolt were far more sure of what they were against than what they were for. The Estates-General was a mantra repeatedly invoked, but almost nothing was said about what that might involve. As early as January a perceptive ambassador had mused that the convocation of the Estates, 'so far from calming matters, will only, I believe, redouble internal quarrels. Without mentioning the nature of the questions which might then be raised, I foresee a very large quarrel over the composition of this national assembly, and the choice of those who must represent the nation, given that the parlements do not wish this to depend on the king and that the king will maintain that the old ways for convoking the Estates-General are totally impractical.'[102] These issues were first opened by the government. On 5 July, when it seemed that the initial clamour against the reforms imposed in May might be dying down, a public invitation was issued to anyone with information or ideas about the forms and procedures of the Estates-General to submit them to the keeper of the seals by the end of February 1789. The aim seems to have been to split the opposition by forcing them to make choices, while at the same time leaving the king free to model the Estates as he wished. There was also an implicit promise that they would meet much earlier than 1792. A month later (8 August), this promise was made explicit. The meeting was set for May 1789. But by now the motivation had changed. 'It is become very necessary', observed the Duke of Dorset, the British ambassador,[103] 'to name a period for that important Assembly, was it only to raise the public credit which at present is much on the decline.' Fundamentally, everything that ministers had undertaken since the beginning of 1787 had been to sustain and strengthen public credit, both long and short term. Through all the vicissitudes of these months, it had just about held up. But between May and August 1788 it finally shrank

102. Alessandro Fontana, Francesco Furlan, and Georges Saro (eds.), *Venise et la Révolution française: Les 470 dépêches des ambassadeurs de Venise au Doge, 1786–1795* (Paris, 1997), 156, dispatch 107, 14 Jan. 1788.

103. Browning (ed.), *Despatches from Paris, 1784–1790*, ii, 84, Dorset to Carmarthen, 7 Aug. 1788.

away, as even the financiers whose business it was to lend short-term to the crown withheld their funds. On 16 August the government suspended payments, and all stocks plummeted. And the collapse of credit inevitably triggered the collapse of the ministry too. Within nine days Brienne had gone—and with him, the last attempt made by absolute monarchy to save itself.

* * *

Louis XVI and his ministers believed that their plans had been thwarted by a revolt of the nobility. Revolutionaries shared that view, and enjoyed the irony of what resulted. An intoxicated aristocracy, wrote Barnave, had provoked the revolution of which it became the victim.[104] The nobles, thought Necker's daughter, Mme de Staël, 'lit the fire which produced the explosion', and she concluded that 'no revolution, in a large country, can succeed unless it begins with the aristocratic class'.[105] Many of the greatest subsequent historians of the Revolution have taken the same view.

Certainly, the political drama of 1787–88 was played out among an entirely noble cast. The one attempt to provoke the intervention of the Third Estate and turn the conflict into a class war, Calonne's *Avertissement* of March 1787, met with no response. But the nobility was not united in its attitudes to the problems faced by the state. Many of its members believed that Louis XVI must be supported in his efforts to solve the state's problems, whether because they thought the ministerial solutions were right, or simply because they thought it their duty to accept whatever the king had decided. Not all magistrates in the parlements felt happy about the lengths of resistance to which their companies had gone, or about their public commitment to an Estates-General that could not fail to outshine them in powers and prestige. Nor were the political pretensions of the 'robinocracy' always willingly accepted by nobles who felt their status older and superior. 'The true cause of the difficulties encountered by ... the most necessary of edicts, is that which in all times directs opposition from the parlements' confided the courtier Marquis de Bombelles to his journal

104. Fernand Rude (ed.), *Barnave: Introduction à la Révolution française* (Paris, 1960), 53.
105. Jacques Godechot (ed.), *Madame de Staël: Considérations sur la Révolution française* (Paris, 1983), 114.

in January 1788.[106] 'These sovereign companies have always used pretexts taken from zeal for the public good in order to forward, under cover of this fine motive, their individual interests.' Many observers noticed that, with the exception of Brittany and Dauphiné, resistance to the measures of May 1788 was largely confined to the seats of parlements, urban centres dominated by the interests of courts and lawyers. Paris, they also noted, remained remarkably calm.

There is no doubt that the political stand-off between crown and parlements affected financial confidence. Taxes not registered by the sovereign courts, or registered only under notorious duress, offered questionable security for lenders to government. Public loans which the Parlement of Paris had resisted were also less attractive. But tax revenues for 1789 looked particularly uncertain as well after a huge storm on 13 July devastated the ripening harvest in the vast grain-growing plains around Paris. All these circumstances made short-term loans (*anticipations*) look particularly hazardous. And the financiers who normally advanced these sums knew that this time was intended by Brienne to be the last. His publicly-announced plans were to abolish the financial offices through which regular lenders to government conducted their business. They therefore had no interest in propping him up by making the usual advances. And so it was they who brought Brienne's ministry down by precipitating the suspension of payments;[107] and the 'noble revolt' was only a contributory factor in their fateful decision.

Resistance from noblemen, however, had undoubtedly forced successive ministries to offer repeated modifications to their plans of reform as the crisis developed. They had felt obliged to publish their accounts, to amend their tax-proposals, to modify the structure of provincial assemblies, and at last even to concede the central demand first voiced in the Assembly of Notables and taken up by all opponents since: the convocation of the Estates-General. The fact that resistance went on after the concession was made shows that Brienne's sincerity was still doubted, perhaps justifiably.[108] But nobody who succeeded him could afford to go back on this crucial

---

106. Bombelles, *Journal,* ii 193, 15 Jan. 1788.
107. See J. F. Bosher, *French Finances, 1770–1795: From Business to Bureaucracy* (Cambridge, 1970), 198–9; Egret, *Pré-révolution,* 312–4; Hardman, *French Politics,* 95–6; Doyle, *Venality,* 149–50.
108. See Egret, *Pré-révolution,* 309–11; Kenneth Margerison, *Pamphlets and Public Opinion: The Campaign for a Union of Orders in the Early French Revolution* (West Lafayette, IN, 1998), 23.

concession. The main task facing his successor, in fact, would be to bring the Estates into being. And that could not be done without confronting questions virtually unasked until this moment. Agitation led and sustained by nobles had brought matters to this point. It had also involved more of them directly in public affairs than ever before. Clearly they expected that this enhanced role would become permanent with the Estates-General. Decisions about the Estates would, however, call in question not only the nobility's political role, but also its entire standing in society.

6

Aristocracy Attacked

The Rise and Fall of the Noble Order

The Estates-General represented the three estates or orders of the realm. But when the estates were not in being, only the first order, the clergy, enjoyed any regular institutional existence, in the form of quinquennial assemblies. It was true that in provinces where local estates survived there were usually separate houses for the clergy and the nobility. This created a presumption that the provincial assemblies with which successive ministries experimented between 1778 and 1788 would include similar separate representation.[1] Alarmed, however, when it was proposed to make ownership of property the sole criterion for membership, or to double the numbers of Third Estate members to reflect their numerical weight in society, many nobles threw themselves behind the campaigns of certain parlements in favour of restoring traditional-style estates where noble dominance would be assured. At stake was something which the nobility had never enjoyed before: a permanent and guaranteed role for their order in the government of the kingdom.

In practice, of course, noblemen had always monopolized every position of importance in church and state. But in neither branch had they seen themselves primarily as agents of their own order. Senior clergymen served the church; military officers and magistrates served the king. Nor would most nobles have been content to see great officers of the crown as their representatives, since the latter came overwhelmingly from areas of the order despised, envied, or mistrusted by the rest: courtiers and venal office-holders. And representation, whether in factitious new assemblies or traditional estates, offered no clear models of easy escape from such

---

1. See P. M. Jones, *Reform and Revolution in France: The Politics of Transition, 1774–1791* (Cambridge, 1995), ch. 5.

deep-rooted rivalries. There was no uniformity in how noble representatives in surviving estates were elected. In some provinces a handful of the same families sat by right, in others only holders of fiefs. In Brittany, all noblemen had the right to sit in person, and sometimes hundreds turned up. On the other hand, only those with five degrees of nobility were eligible, and no holder of a judicial office. Everywhere, indeed, the recently ennobled found themselves excluded from representing other nobles in any capacity. Restoring or recreating estates of any sort, therefore, presupposed potentially contentious decisions at every stage; and the Estates-General, not convened since the very different circumstances of 1614, would prove no exception. The widespread fear was that, as implicitly threatened in the declaration of 5 July 1788, the government would use historical ambiguities and uncertainties to invent forms and procedures designed to maintain rather than to limit its own power. There is, in fact, very little evidence that Necker, when he returned to power and made the populist gesture of bringing the Estates forward to January 1789, had given any thought to such questions.[2] But the restored Parlement of Paris, before which the edict of convocation was formally laid for registration on 25 September, took the view that only precedent was proof against ministerial manipulation. In registering the edict, it declared that the Estates should be 'regularly convoked and composed and this following the form observed in one thousand six hundred and fourteen'.

There is equally little evidence that the magistrates had given sustained thought to all that this implied.[3] Their aim was to use legal precedent to tie the hands of an authority that had proved itself by turns slippery and despotic. But the resort to blind precedent took no account of a preceding decade of intensifying debate about every aspect of representation. It ignored the fact that the revival of the estates of Dauphiné, recently sanctioned by the crown in the dying days of Brienne's ministry, was to have a doubled Third Estate and vote by head; whereas the Estates-General of 1614 had three equal orders voting by order. In these circumstances, invoking precedent looked like a bid to establish the permanent hegemony of the clergy and nobility in national affairs. It was no such thing. The

2. The main evidence for his views then comes from works he wrote years afterwards: see Egret, *Pré-révolution*, 338–9; Robert D. Harris, *Necker and the Revolution of 1789* (Lanham, MD, 1986), 311–13.

3. Egret, *Pré-révolution*, 338–9; Bailey Stone, *The Parlement of Paris, 1774–1789* (Chapel Hill, NC, 1981), 166–7.

parlements had a long history of opposing any attempt by the clergy to wield secular power. The magistrates must also have known that in 1614 people like themselves had sat with the Third Estate and vainly resisted the pretensions of the nobility.[4] The dismal and meagre achievements of the 1614 assembly were scarcely encouraging, either. But all these considerations were swamped by the public reaction to the parlement's stance. There were a couple of days of pregnant silence during which history was ransacked to find out what the forms of 1614 had been. But when it emerged that they were a formula which would hand perpetual power to the nobility (given their domination of the clergy), the whole political atmosphere was transformed. The pre-revolutionary struggle against despotism, which had united the educated nation, was over. The task of creating a new political order now began, and its first phase would prove an onslaught against nobility and all its claims.

* * *

A few pamphlets on the composition of the Estates had appeared over the summer, warning that history and precedent were no reliable guide to how the Estates should be constituted.[5] A government still hoping to shape the assembly to its own convenience did nothing to silence this argument; but meanwhile ministers had clamped down on other journalism, arresting many pamphleteers and closing political clubs and discussion groups. Necker abandoned this policy early in September, and the composition of the Estates was the first issue to be discussed by a totally free press.[6]

Two themes predominated in the initial outburst of pamphleteering which followed the parlement's pronouncement of 25 September. One was the ambition and hypocrisy of the magistrates. They wished, it was alleged, to limit the power of the Estates as they had that of the king: and not just by laying down the ground rules. They could also use the precedent of 1614 to infiltrate the Third Estate and so dictate the course of business there.[7] A more important concern took up the pro-ministerial

4. See Hayden, *France and the Estates-General of 1614.*
5. Margerison, *Pamphlets and Public Opinion*, 23–4.
6. Vivian R. Gruder, *The Notables and the Nation: The Political Schooling of the French, 1787–88* (Cambridge, MA, 2007), 106–11,188–9.
7. A theme reported by the Venetian ambassador on 6 October. Fontana et al., *Venise et la Révolution,* 236.

arguments of the previous summer, that the forms of 1614 were not the only precedent.[8] In previous late medieval Estates-General there had been instances both of double representation for the Third Estate, and of vote by head. Responses that even earlier meetings had been more like that of 1614 were beside the point. In the eyes of Mirabeau, the entire historical discussion was beside the point. Even before the parlement had intervened, he had perceived that the organization of the forthcoming Estates would be a social as much as a constitutional question. 'Let us avoid erudition, steer clear of what has been done', he wrote to a friend on the day the government suspended payments.[9] 'War on the privileged and on privileges, that's my watchword. Privileges are useful against Kings, but they are detestable against Nations and ours will never have any public spirit until it is delivered from them.'

This was the sentiment which Calonne had tried so fruitlessly to ignite in March 1787 with the *Avertissement*. Now it was more combustible. And, even more than from the stance of the parlement, the spark came from Necker's next act of policy. Seemingly surprised by the strength of feeling against the parlement, but delighted to see how rapidly the magistrates had squandered their popularity, he decided to seek more impressive advice on the forms and procedures of the Estates. On 5 October a second Assembly of Notables was convoked to provide it. The forms of 1614, he declared in the preamble to the summons, were no longer adequate or appropriate to a kingdom much enlarged since then. Nor was the parlement able to respond to this implicit rejection of its position, since it was now in vacation until November. The summons was, however, a new stimulus to pamphleteers. None failed to notice that the Notables were an exclusively noble body. There were forty new members, mostly replacing those who had died or become incligible since 1787, but the general character of the Assembly was the same, and there was still nobody of unambiguous *roturier* status. Even before the Assembly convened on 6 November, there was little expectation that its members would vote to give up the obvious political advantages which the forms of 1614 gave to what were now beginning to be called the 'privileged orders'.

8. A. F. Delandine, *Des Etats-Généraux ou histoire des assemblées nationales en France, des personnes qui les ont composées, de leur forme, de leur influence, et des objets qui y ont été particulièrement traités* (Paris, 1788); [Guy Jean-Baptiste Target], *Les Etats-Généraux convoqués par Louis XVI* (Oct. 1788). See too Margerison, *Pamphlets*, 25, 27–8.
9. Quoted in Egret, *Pré-révolution*, 332 and 334, letter of 16 Aug. 1788.

And so it proved.[10] Yet there were many nobles outside the Assembly, especially in the sophisticated world of the capital, who accepted that following precedent could only lead to paralysis. Some of them set out to mobilize public opinion, before it was too late, in favour of doubling the numbers of the Third Estate and voting by head. By the time the Notables met, clubs were springing up to debate and promote various political objectives. The most influential was a small circle which began to meet at the house of Adrien Duport, counsellor at the parlement. Later it would be called the Society of Thirty, although for much of its existence it was either smaller or larger.[11] Nine-tenths of its members were noblemen, a blend of great courtiers and magistrates, leavened by experienced publicists like Mirabeau and Condorcet. Three, including Lafayette, sat in the Notables. There were also a few members of the Third Estate, such as the leading advocate Target; clerics like Talleyrand, newly appointed Bishop of Autun; and a secular-minded canon of Chartres, Emmanuel-Joseph Sieyès, who had abandoned his stall to write political tracts in the capital. Their motivations were diverse and often contradictory, but they shared a commitment to seeking a representative government for France, made durable by a written constitution setting clear limits to executive power. It must include proper representation for the Third Estate. And to promote these ends, the Society did not confine itself to lobbying. It employed the considerable wealth of most of its members to subsidize and sponsor pamphlets and model petitions calling for the Third Estate to be given its proper weight.

Some of these, such as Target's *Les Etats-généraux convoqués par Louis XVI* (*The Estates General convoked by Louis XVI*), concentrated still on the ambiguities of the historical record, and pointed to the harmonious example of the orders spontaneously uniting in Dauphiné. Others felt appeals to harmony were not enough. The rights of the nation, argued the Languedoc Count d'Antraigues in his *Mémoire sur les Etats-généraux* (*Memoir on the Estates General*), must be recognized, and the nation was the Third Estate.[12] He did not go on to consider where that left his own order, but in passing

10. Gruder, *Notables and the Nation*, 73–86.
11. The fullest recent survey is Daniel Wick, *A Conspiracy of Well-Intentioned Men: The Society of Thirty and the French Revolution* (New York, 1987). Its conclusions have failed to convince Margerison, *Pamphlets*, 55–9.
12. See Chaussinand-Nogaret, 'Un aspect de la pensée nobiliaire', 449–52.

he declared that hereditary nobility was (in a phrase that would become famous given its author's later counter-revolutionary career) 'the most appalling scourge that heaven, in its wrath, can afflict a free nation with'. It was a nation within a nation, its interests distinct from those of the people. This call for 'doubling the Third' proved one of the most inflammatory and best-selling pamphlets of the autumn. Scarcely less popular was *La Sentinelle du peuple* (*The People's Sentinel*), a pamphlet series by the well-known travel writer Constantin François Chasseboeuf, who adopted the pseudonym Volney. Disgusted by the resistance of the Breton nobility to any change that might loosen their grip on the estates of their province, Volney, like d'Antraigues, declared that the Third Estate was the nation, and that it embodied the public interest. Neither of them dwelt on the contrast between the case they were making for the Third Estate and its political nullity up to their own times. But this was the direction pointed in by the publication in November 1788 (in what can scarcely have been a coincidence) of the posthumous third volume of Mably's *Observations sur l'histoire de France* (*Observations on the History of France*). The second had appeared as long before as 1765[13] and concluded in the sixteenth century. The third, constantly polished by the author until his death in 1785, brought the story to events within living memory, and roundly castigated the parlements, the nobility, and the clergy for colluding in the rise of absolute monarchy. The price had been paid by the Third Estate, which 'is nothing in France, because no man wishes to belong to it. Every middling sort, among us, thinks of nothing but quitting his station to buy offices which give Nobility; and when he has it, he no longer sees himself as part of the community. The people is nothing, in effect, but that populace with no credit, no consideration, no fortune, and incapable of anything by itself.'[14] These were old thoughts; but their relevance to the new situation was made starkly clear by a fresh and more trenchant voice sponsored by the Society of Thirty: Sieyès.

Essai sur les Privilèges was a frontal attack not only on the political claims of the nobility, but on their entire distinct status. 'All privileges', it declared, '... from the very nature of things, are unjust, odious, and

---

13. See above, pp. 78–9, and also Wright, *A Classical Republican*, 154–8. This third volume appeared as part of a new edition of Mably's complete works.
14. Quoted in Egret, *Pré-révolution*, 352.

contrary to the supreme end of every political society.'[15] 'Where … any class of citizens enjoys an exemption from any particular law, it is directly saying to those citizens "You are permitted to do wrong". There is no power on earth which should be authorized to make such a concession. If a law is good, it ought to bind every individual; if bad it ought to be abolished. It is an assault upon liberty.'[16] Sieyès was not interested in an accurate portrayal of the nobility. His essay simultaneously described it as a caste, yet also as an open body which continuously absorbed the wealth of the Third Estate through venal offices and marriages to rich commoners. The privileged class as he described it (implying that only the nobility enjoyed privileges) was vain, greedy, hypocritical, prejudiced, and incapable of exercising the high public functions which it nevertheless monopolized. Scorn was poured on nobles' reverence for ancestors—as if nobody else had them!—their glorification of idleness, their groundless pretensions to superiority, and their sense of entitlement to live at the expense of the public purse. The selfish noble sense of honour was contrasted with a truer sort, which came from the merited esteem of one's fellow citizens:

> There is but one species of real esteem, and yet its language, its character, its appearance are still employed in society for the purpose of prostituting false honours to court sycophants, to favourites, and but too often to the most flagitious of mankind.
>
> In this disorder of manners, genius is persecuted and virtue is turned into ridicule; and, on the other hand, a heap of insignia, ribbands, decorations, strangely figured, imperiously command respect and homage to be paid to mediocrity, to meanness, and even to crimes. How is it possible that dignities conferred in this manner should not extinguish the sparks of real honour, corrupt public opinion, and disgrace the mind?[17]

'It is but too plain', Sieyès apostrophized the nobility, 'that you wish rather to be distinguished *from* your fellow citizens, than *by* your fellow citizens.' And 'it is an absolute fact that the privileged class look upon themselves as another species of beings': an assertion which he substantiated by appending an extract from the deliberations of the Nobility at the Estates-General of 1614.

15. *An Essay on Privileges* in Michael Sonenscher (ed.), *Emmanuel Joseph Sieyès: Political Writings* (Indianapolis, IN, 2003), 71. See also discussion of this pamphlet by Shovlin, 'Political Economy of Honor', 59–60.
16. Sonenscher (ed.), *Essay on Privileges*, 70.   17. Ibid., 73–4.

This was Sieyès' only reference in his polemic to the great issue of the moment; because his purpose was to avoid the procedural and historical technicalities which obsessed so many other pamphleteers in November 1788. He fully shared their desire to escape from the forms of 1614, but his clear strategy for defeating the political pretensions of the nobility was to demolish the social pretensions which underpinned them. The way to awaken the Third Estate was to arouse its social resentment with an inflammatory catalogue of the unjustifiable subordination to the 'detestable Aristocratism'[18] under which it lived. And this strategy did not go unnoticed among the Notables. On 28 November the Prince de Conti denounced the 'scandalous writings which are spreading trouble and division throughout the kingdom',[19] and it seems certain that the Assembly felt intimidated by this rising storm of publicity.[20] Its response was not, however, to bend, but to dig in. In all, it considered fifty-four questions about the organization of the Estates, and any proposal that was seen to further the claims of the Third Estate was rejected. Since, as in 1787, the Assembly never deliberated or voted in plenary sessions, but in six separate *bureaux*, each chaired by a Prince of the Blood, dissident voices were more easily isolated. On what everybody recognized as the key issue of doubling the Third, only the *bureau* chaired by Monsieur voted in favour, and that by the prince's casting vote. Altogether, only thirty-three Notables accepted the principle. It would inevitably open the way, some warned, to vote by head. Perceiving that this would destroy the political power which a traditionally organized Estates promised to the nobility, not a single member supported vote by head in an unequivocal way. All made great show of conceding fiscal equality, but the first Assembly of Notables had accepted this principle long before, so the concession was empty.

The ferment outside the Assembly was certainly making an impact. The parlement, on returning from its vacation shortly after the Notables met, was persuaded by Duport and his magistrate friends from the Society of Thirty to gloss its disastrous demand of 25 September. After considerable discussion and a close vote, the magistrates declared on 5 December that all they had meant by the forms of 1614 was that the deputies should represent bailliages and seneschalcies rather than provinces. The number of deputies for each order was for the king to decide. Certain noble

18. Ibid., 79.   19. Egret, *Pré-révolution*, 354.
20. Gruder, *Notables and the Nation*, 80, 82.

pamphleteers also urged their fellows to give up their various privileges and join with the Third Estate in an equal and patriotic commitment to national regeneration.[21] Yet they were offset by others insisting on the maintenance of noble prerogatives; and in the provinces the example of Dauphiné proved unpersuasive to many nobles excited by the prospect of local power in revived or reformed estates. They seemed more interested in defining who was genealogically qualified to sit as noble than in seeking ways of cooperating with the Third Estate. And the Princes of the Blood claimed to be speaking for the entire nobility when, at the conclusion of the Assembly of Notables on 12 December, five of them addressed an open letter to the monarch on the state of the kingdom.[22] Denouncing the writings that had appeared during the Assembly as 'a reasoned system of insubordination' whose dangerous consequences were unforeseeable, they rejected demands for the number of Third Estate deputies to be doubled. They came close to saying that commoners would be too pusillanimous to use such enhanced power responsibly, but their main argument was that 'the distinction of orders, the right to deliberate separately, and equality of votes' were 'unalterable bases' of the monarchy. By predicting that if the Third's representation was increased the other orders might boycott the Estates they were clearly inciting their fellow nobles to do so. But the king would surely not 'sacrifice, humiliate, that brave, ancient and respectable nobility which has shed so much blood for the country and for kings'. So 'let the Third Estate cease from attacking the rights of the first two orders; rights which, no less old than the monarchy, should be as unalterable as its constitution; let it confine itself to seeking the diminution of taxes with which it might be overloaded'. Then, the nobility might generously give up some of its fiscal prerogatives.

Addressed in the first instance to the king, but clearly directed by the princes mainly to their fellow 'gentlemen', whom they invoked as juridical equals, the tone of this letter was gratuitously offensive towards the Third Estate. Its condescending and disdainful treatment of their claims could only stoke the resentment that was now gathering alarming force throughout the kingdom. Petitions were pouring in by the hundred calling both for doubling the Third and vote by head, and denouncing the attitudes of the

21. Ralph W. Greenlaw, 'The French Nobility on the Eve of the Revolution: A Study of its Aims and Attitudes, 1787–9', (Ph.D. dissertation, Princeton University, 1952), 201–5.
22. Monsieur did not sign. Text in J. M. Roberts (ed.), *French Revolution Documents* (Oxford, 1966), 45–9.

Notables as typical of the whole nobility. By December 1788 a rapid social polarization was under way, and all the arguments advanced theoretically over the preceding century and beyond against the pretensions and powers of nobles were being revived and refined. Now, for the first time, there was isolated talk of destroying hereditary nobility altogether.[23] Moreover the king and his ministers appeared sympathetic to the clamour. He brushed aside the parlement's conciliatory pronouncement of 5 December by declaring that only the Estates-General was capable of offering him worthwhile advice. And he moved with Necker to override the Notables' stance by doubling the Third. Consulting the Notables at such length had already made it impossible to convene the Estates on 1 January as originally intended, and some compensation for this postponement had to be offered to contain the growing uproar. There was resistance from other ministers to setting aside the Notables' solemnly requested opinion, but the king (and queen) were determined to follow Necker's instincts.[24] By the *Result of the Council* of 27 December the great concession was finally made; but there was no vote by head to give practical meaning to the equal numbers now achieved by the Third Estate. In his report to the Council, printed and distributed with the *Result*, Necker invoked the numerical, economic, and cultural weight of the Third Estate—by now a commonplace with anti-noble pamphleteers—to justify doubling. Vote by head, however, must be a matter for mutual agreement between the orders once the Estates met. The minister could foresee occasions when the orders might agree to deliberate in common, but he did not say what these might be. The effect was to satisfy nobody.

* * *

Many nobles were disgusted. 'This new production of M Necker', fumed the Marquis de Bombelles in his diary, 'is a malign or stupid audacity, whose results might tear from the hand of Louis XVI a sceptre which, for so many centuries, was carried with so many advantages for the first

23. *Lettre d'un citoyen dauphinois à Monsieur M.S.D.E.D.D.* declared that 'Les uns veulent détruire la noblesse héréditaire'. Cited in Norman Hampson, 'The "Recueil des pièces intéressantes pour servir à l'histoire de la Révolution en France" and the Origins of the French Revolution', *Bulletin of the John Rylands Library*, 46 (1964), 393.
24. Hardman, *French Politics*, 162–4.

nation in the world. The most seditious writings had fewer drawbacks than this monstrous production.'[25] Scared by the scale and vehemence of Third Estate demands, more timid members of the Society of Thirty withdrew, some to join rival groups with more conservative agendas.[26] Provincial campaigners for revived or reformed estates were also dismayed, especially since the *Result* had made clear that in general local estates would not be the bodies to elect deputies to the greater national assembly. The nobles of Brittany had attempted to buttress the stance of the Notables by organizing a petition in favour of the forms of 1614. It amassed almost 900 signatures. But by the time the Breton estates convened for regular business on 29 December, the town representatives who made up the Third Estate had been galvanized by the autumn's controversies into demanding limits to noble prerogatives and tax privileges. Within days meetings had become so turbulent and recriminatory that the estates had to be suspended.

Doubling the number of their deputies was undoubtedly popular throughout the kingdom among the awakening Third Estate. They sensed that the king and his leading minister were on their side. Necker in his report had even used the term 'privileged orders', whether deliberately or as a result of polemical osmosis, flattering the Third's growing conviction that they themselves had no part in privileges enjoyed by the clergy and nobility alone. Sieyès had done much to propagate this distortion in his *Essay on Privileges*, but he was far from satisfied by a mere increase in the number of Third Estate deputies. In December he left the Society of Thirty, disgusted by the political moderation of most of its noble members.[27] Nor did he think that vote by head would be enough to secure permanent power for the Third Estate. In *Qu'est-ce que le Tiers Etat?* (*What is the Third Estate?*) published on his own initiative in January 1789, he argued that there was no need for the Third to have any dealings with the other two, since it was a complete nation in itself.

Much of the impact of this most celebrated tract of the French Revolution came from its ringing opening sentences:

> What is the Third Estate? *Everything.*
> What, until now, has it been in the existing
> political order? *Nothing.*
> What does it want to be? *Something.*

25. *Journal*, ii, 269, 26 Dec. 1788.   26. Tackett, *Becoming a Revolutionary*, 93–4.
27. Wick, *A Conspiracy*, 298.

Whether the formula was Sieyès's own, whether he got it from Rousseau,[28] or whether it was suggested to him by that ubiquitous ghost writer, Chamfort,[29] who was now openly telling his noble patrons of his total contempt for their order and its pretensions,[30] its impact was volcanic. It told the Third Estate what it now wanted to hear. The Third, Sieyès argued, was a complete nation unto itself, since a nation was a body of people living under laws common to all. Any one claiming exemption from common laws could not be part of the nation, and therefore privileged orders could have no political rights. This was a logical development of arguments and definitions elaborated in the *Essay on Privileges*, and there were echoes of this earlier work throughout, with denunciations of the nobility as a greedy monopolistic caste, and of the 'aristocratism' that pervaded French institutions: 'The noble *order* simply has no place at all in the organization of society—it may be a *burden* upon the Nation, but it cannot be part of it.' Sieyès went on to turn nobles' now-conventional appeal to the authority of Boulainvilliers[31] on its head. 'Why not... send back to the Franconian forests all those families still affecting the mad claim to have been born of a race of conquerors and to be heirs to *rights of conquest?*'[32] And history showed that France had never been a true monarchy at all. Kingly rule at its fullest had been 'undiluted despotism', but for most of the time it had been a '*palace* aristocracy', and it still was. 'What can we see? The aristocracy on its own, simultaneously fighting against reason, justice, the people, the minister, and the King. The outcome of this terrible struggle is still uncertain.' And it could only be resolved to the benefit of the Third Estate if that order woke up and pressed its claims beyond vote by head. So long as nobility existed to dazzle and seduce the ambitions and values of commoners, they would never acquire a clear view of their rights and interests. In the forthcoming elections, nobles should not be allowed to represent the Third Estate, nor should their employees and dependants, all 'agents of feudalism'.[33] Nobles should not, either, be allowed to perpetrate the illusion that by choosing to give up (as if it were not their moral obligation)

---

28. In his posthumously published *Considérations sur le gouvernement de la Pologne* (1782), Rousseau speaks of 'three orders: the nobles, who are everything; the burghers, who are nothing; and the peasants, who are less than nothing'. On Sieyès and Rousseau, see Forsyth, *Reason and Revolution*, 59–64.
29. Dousset, *Chamfort et son temps*, 121. But Paul Bastid, *Sieyès et sa pensée*, 56, 349–50 is sceptical.
30. Auguis, *Oeuvres complètes de Chamfort*, v, 294–9. Chamfort to Vaudreuil, 13 Dec. 1788.
31. See above, pp. 44–6.   32. *What is the Third Estate?* In Sonenscher, *Sieyès*, 99.
33. Ibid., 145.

their tax exemptions they would usher in a time of more general equality. Brushing aside the idea that the French should imitate England and set up a bicameral legislature, Sieyès declared that 'The time for working for conciliation between the parties is over. What hope of agreement can there be between the energy of the oppressed and the fury of the oppressor? ... NO ARISTOCRACY ought to be the rallying cry of all the Friends of the Nation and of good order.'[34] The Third Estate should meet as an entity of its own, a National Assembly, deliberating 'on behalf of the whole Nation, minus two hundred thousand heads'.[35] The latter were 'the privileged class', which, like 'a frightful disease devouring the living flesh of the body of its unhappy victim', is 'harmful ... simply because it exists'.[36]

This was not a call to destroy the nobility. It was an incitement to ignore it, so long as its members claimed any other status than that of citizen. And there is no doubt that Sieyès, in unusually trenchant language, put into words the instinctive feelings of a bourgeoisie whose political and social self-awareness had been aroused by the public debates raging since the early autumn.[37] These feelings would crystallize over the spring, inform what happened when the Estates-General finally met, and help to win Sieyès's (when the identity of the initially anonymous pamphleteer became known) election as a deputy of the Third Estate.[38] The pamphlet sold over 30,000 copies in a few months and went into four editions. Yet its central argument, that the Third Estate should unilaterally constitute itself into the Nation, had a curiously limited impact, attracting little in the way either of support or refutation in subsequent pamphlets.[39] Nor did the ultimate triumph of the Third Estate in June 1789, in which Sieyès himself was closely involved, result in the exclusion of nobles from the National Assembly. But to accept his argument when it appeared at the beginning of the year would have entailed rejecting the whole idea of the Estates-General at the very moment when, and however imperfectly, it was about to become a reality. Writs for election were issued in the last week of January, and even before that men of ambition were beginning to think of

---

34. *What is the Third Estate?* In Sonenscher, *Sieyès*, 147, fn.   35. Ibid., 149.
36. Ibid., 157.
37. See William H. Sewell, Jr, *A Rhetoric of Bourgeois Revolution: The Abbé Sieyès and* What is the Third Estate? (Durham, NC, 1994), 54–6, 60–2.
38. i.e., not the clergy to which he belonged, despite the argument in *What is the Third Estate?* that the Third should not be represented by members of the privileged orders. He sat, elected 20th out of 20 deputies, for the city of Paris.
39. See Margerison, *Pamphlets and Public Opinion*, 97–102.

how to get themselves elected. Few doubted that the proceedings of the Estates would be turbulent and confrontational, but that was all the more reason to try to be part of them, and not to boycott the electoral process. Sieyès himself joined in, first as a drafter of model demands to guide electoral assemblies,[40] then as a candidate for election. The importance of *What is the Third Estate?*, therefore, was to stoke up social resentment in advance of the elections by reiterating all the unmerited advantages enjoyed by the noble order at the expense of commoners, to envenom the atmosphere rather than to establish an influential plan of action.

But, after the intransigence of the Notables, the princes, and the 'iron swords' of Brittany, Sieyès was far from alone in fanning hostility to aristocracy. In fact the lead was often taken by nobles. D'Antraigues, it is true, was already repenting of his earlier radicalism, but other southern nobles carried it further. Mirabeau, desperate to be elected to the Estates, returned to his ancestral Provence hoping, incredibly enough, to be elected for the nobility. But Provençal gentlemen not repelled by his previous unsavoury reputation were outraged by the campaign he immediately waged to break the stranglehold which fief-holders exercised in the newly restored estates of the province.[41] Although nobles without fiefs would have been the main beneficiaries had he succeeded, his egalitarian rhetoric, printed and widely distributed throughout the province, appealed mostly to the Third Estate with its outright denunciation of privileges of all sorts. After a tumultuous spring, he did secure election, but for the Third Estate. Less celebrated nationally, but equally notorious in Provence, was the Marquis and disillusioned former army officer Pierre Antoine d'Antonelle, who as early as October 1788 had produced a *Catéchisme du Tiers Etat* (*Catechism of the Third Estate*) which was republished the following January. Here the Third was described (before Sieyès) as everything, the nation, the breadwinner (*père nourricier*) of the state; whereas the greedy superiority of the other two orders was simply revolting.[42] Meanwhile in Paris, the always impulsive Condorcet was depicting the privileges of hereditary nobility as a species of despotism. The only inequalities should be the unavoidable ones of opinion or of fortune, and 'any nation where there exists a legally

40. *Délibérations à prendre dans les assemblées*, an appendix to electoral instructions issued by the Duke d'Orléans. See Wick, *Conspiracy*, 193–4, and Margerison, *Pamphlets*, 113–7.
41. Monique Cubells, *Les Horizons de la liberté: Naissance de la Révolution en Provence, 1787–1789* (Aix-en-Provence, 1987), 55–6, 64–5.
42. Pierre Serna, *Antonelle, aristocrate et révolutionnaire, 1747–1817* (Paris, 1997), 86–8, 105–7.

established genealogist, cannot be a free nation'.[43] The Viscount d'Aubusson addressed no less than four pamphlets to his fellow noblemen, urging them to reject their 'gothic' prejudices and see their privileges as golden chains forged by despotism to prevent the emergence of a nation of free and equal citizens.[44] Bernardin de Saint-Pierre, still posing as a nobleman, but also as a reclusive sage, reiterated his earlier denunciations of heredity but now ruminated, with characteristic lack of consistency, on how nobles might be saved from poverty and misalliances.[45] He suggested a new order of chivalry, open to all and not transmissible—an idea with a future, but utopian in 1789.[46] *Les grands*, suggested the liberal Grenoble magistrate Michel-Joseph-Antoine Servan, along with the clergy, had been responsible for all the depredations of despotism, public corruption, incompetent government, over-taxation, and generally everything that was wrong with France. '*Les Grands* of feudal times at least had some imposing qualities; most of *les Grands* in this foul age are a disgrace to humanity.'[47]

Pamphleteers from the Third Estate could only agree.[48] A 'Catechism for the use of the Third Estate' detailing a similar general responsibility for all the kingdom's woes concluded an anonymous tract which denounced all noble power as deriving from usurpation by feudal brigands, 'those eternal enemies of Kings and peoples' who were 'nothing but useless and harmful to the state'.[49] Feudal usurpation was the theme of another polemic which argued that nobles holding offices or emoluments should now consider themselves employees of the Nation, lower in status than the free citizens who paid. It called for buying out the whole apparatus of feudalism, and abolition of primogeniture, 'a barbarous law which strips children of the goods of their fathers'.[50] The Nation could 'never be considered free so long as there remain in the laws for any of the Orders in the State marks of servitude and distinctive privileges'. The troubles in Brittany provoked a heavily ironic exchange between a supposed noblemen and a bishop in which they lamented the insubordination of the 'helots' over whom they

43. *Idées sur le despotisme, à l'usage de ceux qui prononcent ce mot sans l'entendre*, in A. Condorcet O'Connor and M. F. Arago (eds.), *Oeuvres de Condorcet*, 12 vols. (Paris, 1847), ix, 153–4.
44. Greenlaw, 'French Nobility on the Eve', 238–9.   45. See above, p. 156.
46. *Voeux d'un solitaire* in *Oeuvres*, 682–6. See also Maury, *Bernardin*, 160–1. Napoleon would see its potentialities with the Legion of Honour. See below, pp. 314–6.
47. *Troisième aux Grands*, quoted in Carré, *Noblesse de France*, 342.
48. See Tackett, *Becoming a Revolutionary*, 107–8.
49. *Pièces du Procès de la Noblesse et du Clergé contre le Tiers Etat* (1789) (BL R46 (14)), 2, 160.
50. *Injustice des Prétentions du Clergé et de la Noblesse* (1789) (BL F13 (2)), 19–20.

had previously ruled unchallenged.[51] 'What will become of us', laments the Marquis, 'if we are deprived of our titles, of all our honours, of all our distinctions: what henceforth will be the line of separation between us and the Third, if all ranks are done away with? What use will our titles of nobility be to us? What will be their advantages? Is nobility nothing more than a brilliant illusion (*chimère*) when all the privileges which are its only merit are taken away?' Few nobles, he says, have the merit to achieve important posts by their own efforts.

Alarmed by the vehemence of pamphlets attacking them and their pretensions, many nobles took refuge in invoking the wisdom of Montesquieu that nobility was essential to the functioning of the monarchy. Third Estate pamphleteers responded by reminding their readers of Montesquieu's preference for his own class, and attempting to demonstrate the flaws in his thinking.[52] One pamphlet devoted entirely to this theme marked the emergence of Philippe-Antoine Grouvelle, who was to become one of the most determined and persistent public enemies of nobility and its claims.[53] A minor playwright and poetaster, Grouvelle had been secretary to Chamfort, and succeeded him in the household of the Prince de Condé. He had thus been able to observe at first hand the ways of one of the grandest of *les grands*, and he followed Chamfort in turning against his former patrons. In the anonymously published *De l'autorité de Montesquieu dans la révolution présente* (*Of the Authority of Montesquieu in the present Revolution*)[54] he sought to discredit their favourite authority, a 'guilty genius' who had enlightened other nations, but was blinding the French. His distinction between monarchy and despotism was specious, and a regenerated nation would have no need of intermediary powers when it gave itself a proper constitution. Meanwhile Grouvelle poured scorn on the intermediaries vaunted in the *l'Esprit des Lois*. The parlements had been craven and selfish; the nobility enjoyed no powers or corporate existence except when the Estates-General met, and then it was positively dangerous. Its historical record was one of disobedience and usurpation, even if a few distinguished

51. *Lettre de M. le Marquis de M****, *Gentilhomme Breton, à Monseigneur l'Evêque de *** ; sur les Débats entre le Tiers et la Noblesse* (BL R46 (13)). This tract also cites Bernardin de Saint-Pierre's *Etudes de la Nature* with approval: 'Remarquez que c'est un noble qui parle ainsi', 26, n.

52. Caracassonne, *Montesquieu et le problème*, 593–635.

53. See below, pp. 231, 245–6, 261–2.

54. BL R Tracts 198 (10). The bitterness of the Condé circle towards Grouvelle is vividly conveyed by the Count d'Espinchal on the eve of the Condés' emigration in July 1789: Ernest d'Hauterive (ed.), *Journal d'Emigration du comte d'Espinchal* (Paris, 1912), 21.

members were now generously promoting 'the people's cause and general liberty'. But the true intermediary powers in public life were good habits (*les moeurs*) and education, whose driving force in modern times was the middle class (*classe mitoyenne*). Montesquieu had totally underestimated it; but then he had been 'a Magistrate, a Nobleman (*gentilhomme*), and Rich, three things which in France guarantee arbitrary power, three things which protect you against a few superiors and subjugate a multitude of inferiors'. The famous maxim linking monarchy and nobility should be reformulated as 'no privilege, no monarch'. Rousseau, Mably, and Sieyès were better guides in framing a constitution enshrining liberty and equality. Grouvelle does not appear at this stage to have thought that nobility could or should be entirely eliminated. He spoke of encouraging nobles to trade (another disagreement with Montesquieu) and pointed to England to show that this posed no danger to their identity. But in the process of giving the nation a constitution, 'what should be ceaselessly kept in view as the only way to political perfectibility is the general and progressive extirpation of Aristocracy in all its forms … That is the hydra which is devastating France.'

The most comprehensive denunciation of nobility in the spring of 1789 was also initially anonymous. It came from the rich Lyonnais lawyer Nicolas Bergasse. Since coming to Paris at the age of 25 in 1775, Bergasse had practised at the metropolitan bar, frequented smart *salons*, and joined or helped to found several fashionable societies, such as the Gallo-American Society, the Friends of the Blacks, and most notably the Mesmerist Society of Harmony, whose bizarre and plausible doctrines he defended in a series of pamphlets.[55] Outraged at the scorn poured by the self-recruiting Academy of Sciences on Mesmerism, already in 1784 Bergasse was calling for the influence of 'ancient aristocracy' to be curbed, and urging crown and people to unite 'to make all citizens noble and all nobles citizens'.[56] The seasoned pamphleteer found the issues of the old order's terminal crisis irresistible. He wrote against the attempted royal reforms of 1788, and warned in February the next year that division within the Estates-General could still permit the triumph of despotism.[57] Seemingly despairing, however, of willingness to compromise among most nobles, he turned in his *Observations sur le préjugé de la noblesse héréditaire* (*Observations on*

---

55. See Darnton, *Mesmerism*, 101–5.
56. *Autres rêveries sur le magnétisme animal, à un academicien de province* (Brussels, 1784), quoted in Darnton, *Mesmerism* 104.
57. *Lettre sur les Etats-Généraux* (Paris, 1789).

the prejudice of Hereditary Nobility) to 'claiming the rights of the greatest part of the Nation, rights common to all men'.[58] The tone was less bitter than that of Sieyès's *Essay on Privileges*, but the indictment just as comprehensive. The historical claims of the nobility were based on usurpation: and the work of Boulainvilliers, on the lips still of countless nobles, should be 'branded with eternal opprobrium'.[59] Montesquieu, too, was implicitly rejected with the assertion that 'any Order of the privileged, whatever it be, between the Prince and the People, is equally harmful to both'.[60] 'Make no mistake: the most redoubtable of despotisms would be that of Aristocracy.'[61] Noble claims to enjoy privileges in return for shedding their blood for the country were dispatched with the observation that commoners did the same without the same reward. All rights deemed innate within any order were unjust usurpations. Reason demonstrated that the only entitlements to public employment were merit and capacity, and these qualifications were not hereditary. And venality made it worse, swelling the numbers of a parasitic class at the expense of productive ones: 'Why buy rights harmful to others, that no man was entitled to sell?'[62] Nor did the education received by nobles, as some claimed, mark them out. Riotous officers regularly disturbed the peace of garrison towns, while in Paris they failed to pay their debts and made the streets unsafe by reckless carriage driving. 'Pride ... that is all they receive from their birth and their education. Is that any ground on which there can ever be hope of founding true virtue?'[63] Bergasse noted that there were some nobles of individual virtue. He named Lafayette, La Rochefoucauld, and his fellow pamphleteer Aubusson. Nevertheless this diatribe brought together every classic argument both from history and from principle against the power and privileges of the noble order; and every recent instance of resulting abuse too, from the Ségur law of 1781 to the way nobles had taken control of the academies when 'their literary titles for the most part, would have had difficulty in withstanding the slightest examination'.[64] Finally, Bergasse reflected, not only France 'groaned under the shackles, more or less weighty, of an imperious aristocracy'. All the nations of Europe suffered in the same way. After such a denunciation, his concluding appeal to the nobility to sacrifice its advantages was scarcely calculated to win an enthusiastic response.

---

58. *Observations*, 1. See also Shovlin, 'Political Economy of Honor', 60, n. 80.
59. *Observations*, 11, fn. 1.   60. Ibid., 18.   61. Ibid., fn. 1.   62. Ibid., 43, fn. 1.
63. Ibid., 31–3, fn. 1.   64. Ibid.,48.

By the spring of 1789, it is true, much of this was the familiar coin of anti-noble rhetoric. But Bergasse also wielded a less-worn stick to beat his prey with. He spent several pages denouncing the absurdities of feudal rights, including the notorious *droit de seigneur* (though admitting it was now defunct), and the supposed obligation of certain Breton peasants to spend nights beating the waters around their lord's moated castle to stop the frogs from croaking.[65] Most attacks on 'feudalism' over the preceding generation, and most notoriously Boncerf's condemned pamphlet of 1776,[66] had focused on its economic drawbacks. And although the character of feudal times had been a central issue in all controversies about the origins of the nobility, the iniquities of feudal rights had not been an important theme in attacks on the principle of nobility. The first signs that embattled noblemen saw these rights as integral to their position came during the second Assembly of Notables. 'Already,' complained the princes in their notorious open letter to the king of 12 December 1788, 'suppression of feudal rights has been proposed, as the abolition of a system of oppression and remnant of barbarism.' To them it seemed to presage an attack on property itself. Sieyès had little to say about feudal rights, perhaps because he too had no desire to see property attacked. But over the spring the link between noble pretensions and feudal lordship attracted increasing attention. Even those whose criticisms of feudalism remained economic were coming to see that its mainsprings were more complex. 'We must look', argued one anonymous pamphlet,[67] 'at what is honorific in feudalism, for pride and vanity Count for much in the maintenance of these rights.' This author drew on the authority of Boncerf, d'Argenson, Mirabeau, Adam Smith, and Filangieri[68] to reject all the claims of nobility before denouncing the more intrinsic evils of fiefs and their 'odious origin'. Awareness of the importance of this issue was no doubt raised by the controversies over the make-up of revived provincial estates, in several of which (Provence, Franche-Comté, Artois) membership of

---

65. *Observations*, 7, fn. 1. This improbable story resurfaced in the debates on the abolition of feudalism on 4 August. See below, p. 211.
66. See above, pp. 142–3.
67. *De la Féodalité et de l'Aristocratie française, ou tableau des effets désastreux des Droits féodaux: & Réfutation des erreurs sur lesquelles la Noblesse fonde ses prétentions* (1789), 18. This author may have had links with Bergasse, whose mysterious collaborator the *Abbé* Pétiot was a long-standing critic of nobility. See Darnton, *Mesmerism*, 103–4.
68. On Filangieri's hostility to nobles, their pretensions, and their defence by Montesquieu, see Vincenzo Ferrone, *La Società giusta ed equa: Repubblicanesimo e diritti dell'uomo in Gaetano Filangieri* (Roma e Bari, 2003), ch. 3.

noble chambers was historically confined to holders of fiefs. Yet the main victims of feudal prerogatives and exactions had so far had little say in the ferment of political discussion. The peasantry had remained silent observers, if increasingly restive ones, during the rigours of the coldest winter within living memory. When the electoral process began in March, however, they had their chance to speak out through the medium of the *cahiers*.

* * *

Although Necker had broken with tradition in authorizing the doubling of the Third, tradition governed almost every other aspect of the process of electing the Estates-General.[69] Only in places not represented in 1614, and in Dauphiné (where the newly-revived estates had seized the initiative in ways it would have been imprudent to quash) were new procedures countenanced. And even here one principle hallowed by precedent was imposed. The election of deputies was accompanied everywhere by the drawing-up of *cahiers de doléances*, grievance lists to concentrate the attention of the assembled Estates of the Realm. Election to the Estates was by order, and in every type of constituency each order produced its own *cahier*.[70] Third Estate *cahiers* were distillations of innumerable parish *cahiers* produced at the first stage of an indirect electoral process, but those of the other orders had the direct participation of all the electors present.

It is clear both from their *cahiers* and accounts of the assemblies in which they were drawn up, that many nobles had been seriously alarmed by the hostility to them and their order which had exploded over the winter.[71] 'M Necker', mused Bombelles as he prepared to set out from Paris for his own assembly,[72] 'has given a disdainful kick to a rock to crush the nobility by its fall. But this rock, as it rolls, has gained a strength whose effects nothing will soon be able to stop.' Bombelles was entrusted with drafting the *cahier*, which endorsed equality of taxation, but 'without abandoning

69. Peter Jones even calls it 'the revenge of the past on a decade of spasmodic attempts to promote ... reform from above'. *Reform and Revolution*, 175.
70. The authoritative works are Beatrice F. Hyslop, *A Guide to the General Cahiers of 1789* (New York, 1936), and Gilbert Shapiro and John Markoff, *Revolutionary Demands: A Content Analysis of the cahiers de doléances of 1789* (Stanford, CA, 1998).
71. A key conclusion of Tackett, *Becoming a Revolutionary*, 115–6.
72. *Journal*, ii, 287, 1er Mar. 1789.

honorific privileges enjoyed since time immemorial'.[73] There was to be 'No sacrifice of any property whatsoever'—including, again, honorific privileges. Presumably this must have meant feudal rights.[74] And to safeguard all this, the Estates-General were to vote by order—an unequivocal stance on the greatest issue of the election. These concerns were widely reflected in noble *cahiers* throughout the kingdom. Over 88 per cent of the 134 extant *cahiers* recognized the justice of equal taxation[75]: only three *cahiers* stood out against it. At the same time fifty-three *cahiers* called for maintenance of honorific rights, with twenty-six demanding enforcement of the noble monopoly on sword-carrying, and smaller numbers seeking confirmation of a wide variety of more specific privileges. Twenty-four *cahiers* calling for the conservation of seigneurial rights and twenty-three specifically supporting lordly jurisdiction suggest a clear awareness that these things were under threat. With eleven noble *cahiers* actually asking for their abolition or redemption, the threat came from inside the order as well as beyond. Finally, Bombelles's *cahier* was in the van of noble opinion on the question of voting in the Estates. The biggest single group, fifty-five strong, gave unambiguous support to vote by order. A further twenty-seven wished for partial retention. But a substantial minority comprising fifty-two *cahiers* either called for, or professed willingness to accept, vote by head.

As always, and now even when presented with the opportunity to stand up and be counted, the nobility lacked solidarity. Like the clergy and the educated elite who produced the final versions of the Third Estate's demands, nobles devoted most of their *cahiers* to the organization of the state, its finances, and its administration. On these matters there was widespread consensus both within and between the orders about the creation of a constitutional monarchy. But the nobility showed no consensus about how best to defend its own interests under a new regime. In the face of the Third Estate's challenge, nobles were torn between concession and intransigence. Even concessions were often insultingly made, as when a Languedoc nobleman urged commoners to 'strive to

73. *Journal*, 290–1.

74. On property rights as noble code for seigneurial rights, see John Markoff, *The Abolition of Feudalism: Peasants, Lords, and Legislators in the French Revolution* (University Park, PA, 1996), 34, 81–5.

75. For a full analysis of noble *cahiers*, see Chaussinand-Nogaret, *La noblesse au xviiiᵉ siècle*, 204–26. This figure comes from p. 212.

make yourselves worthy of one day being raised to [our] level'.[76] However alarmed they were, no nobleman seems to have believed that nobility itself might be under threat, despite the extremist rhetoric of writers like Sieyès. But what constituted noble identity was clearly problematic. The *cahiers* agonized about where its limits lay, and who had the right to define them. None sought to make the order a closed caste, and thirty-two of them thought that nobility should be the reward for virtue, courage, or merit. A clear contrast was drawn with ennoblement by purchase, through the system of venal offices. Over half of noble *cahiers* rejected it,[77] the most important way in which outsiders, and perhaps most of their own ancestors, had entered the order for over two centuries. A variety of more detailed concerns also indicated widespread dissatisfaction with the everyday realities of noble life. There were complaints about inadequate access to regiments, to benefices, to the judiciary, and, more surprisingly, trade.[78] There were calls for greater equality between nobles, and for ways of helping the poor nobility. Provincials resented the way ambitious courtiers came down from Versailles to districts where their long-unvisited fiefs lay, expecting automatic election. Country squires vented their spleen against the magistrates of the parlements, *parvenus* in their eyes, who had too long usurped the right to speak for them. Very few *robins* secured election. There were close votes, both for *cahiers* and for candidates, in many assemblies, and in several, sword-bearing extremists almost came to blows.[79] What seems clear is that very few nobles were content with the order as it was. In fact the most conservative in political terms were frequently the most radical socially. They saw vote by order, now threatened as soon as it had materialized, as opening the way to their own transformation. Guaranteed thus as the leaders of a parliamentary nation, they could fulfil that role as a purified elite, more exclusive but by no means closed, more professional by very virtue of assured distinctions and monopolies.

Needless to say, this was not the vision of the noblemen who had formed and animated the Society of Thirty, and of that minority in most of the noble electoral assemblies who sympathized with them. Their aim was to secure a union of the orders by complementing the doubling of the

76. Jospeh-Gabriel Gleises de Lablanque, quoted in Tackett, *Becoming a Revolutionary*, 116.
77. Doyle, *Venality*, 269.
78. Chaussinand-Nogaret, *La Noblesse au XVIIIe siècle*, 210. Almost a quarter of noble *cahiers* called for the prohibition on trading to be dropped.
79. Tackett, *Becoming a Revolutionary*, 97–8.

Third with vote by head. No more than their conservative opponents did they expect that nobility would disappear, and they often pointed across the Channel to show how a landed elite without guaranteed privileges could still dominate public and parliamentary life. Intended to reassure fellow nobles, this demonstration sent a more ambiguous message to a Third Estate increasingly aroused against the nobility in general. Might not even the removal of every noble privilege be enough to give the Third Estate the power and the opportunities to which it felt entitled by its sheer numerical weight in the nation? But these worries could be confronted once vote by head had been secured. In the general *cahiers* of the Third Estate, vote by head came only behind taxation and guarantees for the Estates themselves as a topic of concern.[80] Discussion of taxation invariably included the demand that all orders should be taxed equally, and that tax privileges of all sorts should disappear. By the spring of 1789 few nobles were prepared to resist this, whether on grounds of natural justice or political prudence.[81] Giving up privileged access to public positions was another matter, but Third Estate opinion was loud in demanding it. Well over half their general *cahiers* called for equal access to positions in administration, the church, the judiciary, and the army—an impressive 72 per cent in the last case for a breach in the most cherished of all noble monopolies.[82] Some noble *cahiers* were prepared to recognize the justice of such claims, but few in comparison. Where the orders came closest was in rejecting venality as a criterion for anything, whether public positions or access to the social elite. As the *cahier* of Châtillon-sur-Seine put it, 'nobility should be the reward of virtue and service'.[83] Granted changes to facilitate this, most of the Third Estate seem to have expected, not to say positively desired, the continuance of nobility as the embodiment of the nation's elite.[84] The idea of abolishing the nobility entirely, only fifteen

---

80. Markoff, *Abolition*, 30. Provincial estates came higher, but it can be presumed that vote by head was a primary concern in all discussions of this topic.

81. Although there were exceptions: three noble *cahiers* rejected fiscal equality: Chaussinand-Nogaret, *La Noblesse au XVIIIᵉ siècle*, 209. The electoral assembly of Rouen voted that there was 'no need' to surrender fiscal privileges: Tackett, 98.

82. Shapiro and Markoff, *Revolutionary Demands*, 312. See also the complementary figures, indicating massive Third Estate support for careers open to talent, in George V. Taylor, 'Revolutionary and Non-Revolutionary Content in the Cahiers of 1789: An Interim Report', *French Historical Studies*, viii (1972), 498.

83. Quoted in Doyle, *Venality*, 272.

84. For Third Estate acceptance of a reformed nobility among writers later elected to the Estates, see Tackett, *Becoming a Revolutionary*, 106–7.

months before it happened, only occurred in a handful of the general *cahiers*.[85]

But perhaps it was a significant handful, since they were all *cahiers* of rural provenance. Even in the countryside, the drafters of parish *cahiers* were more concerned about taxation and other burdens imposed by the state than about the exactions of lords.[86] But a consistent current runs through them of complaint about both direct lordly demands in cash or kind, as well as harmful seigneurial monopolies such as hunting rights and the keeping of prestigious vermin like pigeons and rabbits.[87] Nor did most of these complaints envisage reform or moderation of such practices. They asked for their abolition without compensation—precisely the sort of attack on property rights feared by noble *cahier* drafters. Few peasant *cahiers* called for the abolition of the entire apparatus of feudal exactions, although such a generalized demand was sometimes distilled at Third Estate level from a multiplicity of parish attacks on specific rights. 'We are truly serfs,' complained the Third Estate of Vannes, exaggerating for dramatic effect, in strife-torn Brittany, 'slaves of our lords through the dues we have to pay; feudalism is our greatest scourge, the need to abolish it is urgent: it is the universal cry of all the parishes.'[88] Nobles were scarcely in a position, even if so inclined, to check whether such claims were true. What they could not fail to notice was the rising disorder in the countryside in the course of the electoral campaign, as a long, cold winter was succeeded by a spring of increasing bread prices and unemployment, the delayed but inexorable consequences of a catastrophic harvest in 1788.[89] Amid the market riots and attacks on grain convoys that were normal in times of scarcity, reports began to trickle in of peasants repossessing feudal payments in kind, attacking castles, invading parks to hunt, attacking gamekeepers and assembling to demand limitations on the rights of lords.[90] There were also isolated incidents of noblemen being physically assaulted.[91] Not all lords were nobles, but most nobles were, or aspired to be, lords; and

85. Taylor, 'Revolutionary and Non-revolutionary Content', 498 (Table 4).
86. Markoff, *Abolition*, 30–2, 36–8.   87. Ibid., 42–7.
88. Quoted in Edmé Champion, *La France d'après les cahiers de 1789* (Paris, 1897), 138–9. Serfdom of any sort only survived in Franche Comté and parts of Burgundy. Even here it was not serfdom in the East European sense, but mainly a lord's ability to prevent a vassal from alienating feudally-held property.
89. Nicolas, *Rébellion française*, 260–5.
90. Jacques Godechot, *The Taking of the Bastille, July 14th 1789* (London, 1970), 129–31; Markoff, *Abolition*, 220–9.
91. Carré, *Noblesse de France et l'opinion*, 343–4.

popular hostility to the manifold facets of feudalism was readily seen by many noblemen as threatening to the essence of their status in society.[92] On top of all this came the results of the elections, steadily declared throughout the month of April. Bombelles was appalled, grimly congratulating himself on having refused to be a candidate.[93]

> To wish to sit alongside Monsieur de Mirabeau and a crowd of coxcombs would be to wish either to join in their folly or to open oneself fruitlessly to be swept aside by enthusiasts for a new form of government. There is no sign of a sheet-anchor in the entire nobility of the kingdom. One will appear, let us hope, in the Estates-General; but so far who is in? Decent people blush at the colleagues they will have. Young lords who, without this circumstance, would never have been anything much ... The worst characters in the Third Estate of France are the ones who have got themselves elected ...

* * *

A subsidiary issue in the debates about the forms and procedures of the Estates-General since the second Assembly of Notables had been whether a member of one estate could be elected for another. Partisans of the Third Estate feared that, as in 1614, nobles would usurp the representation by prevailing on the instinctive deference of non-noble electors. They need not have worried. No less than fifty-eight holders of nobility were indeed elected to the doubled Third Estate,[94] but none of these were from the metropolitan elite. The only one of any previous national notoriety was the renegade Mirabeau. Most of the rest were recently ennobled or holders of incomplete nobility, prominent in their localities but with no acquired commitment to their incipient status. There was also one well-known cleric: Sieyès. He and Mirabeau would certainly provide leadership to the Third Estate at vital moments, but not to bring it under the sway of the 'privileged orders' from which they came. The elections to the First Estate, meanwhile, brought the first important defeat for nobles in the French Revolution. So far from dominating their order as they had in 1614, bishops found themselves reduced to a mere 14 per cent of clerical deputies;[95] and only about a third of the entire contingent

92. Markoff, *Abolition*, makes this point repeatedly in his exhaustive reading of the treatment of feudalism in the *cahiers* of the nobility.
93. *Journal*, ii, 296, 17 Apr. 1789.   94. Tackett, *Becoming a Revolutionary*, 44.
95. Ibid., 24.

was of noble extraction. Exercising a free vote, the diocesan clergy of the kingdom, overwhelmingly commoners, had massively rejected the aristocratic superiors who had hitherto controlled the church and milked its most lucrative benefices. In the tightly integrated professional world of the clergy, motives for voting against the hierarchy were complex, and the social antagonisms that had begun to suffuse the laity over the winter were no doubt only one factor. But the social extraction of the clerical majority would make it instinctively susceptible to appeals from the Third for solidarity against aristocracy during the contentious first six weeks of the Estates-General.

In contrast, the elections to the Second Estate were a triumph for hierarchy. Nobles in general voted for their betters and rejected their inferiors.[96] No commoners were elected, and only a small percentage from families ennobled within living memory. Seventy-three per cent came from that small minority of the order who enjoyed titles and, for all their grumbling, provincial electors still returned metropolitan carpet-baggers like Lafayette, who suddenly appeared among them soliciting votes. Many opulent courtiers, with fiefs in several provinces, had little trouble in securing election in at least one constituency; and princes, peers, and other *grands* were well represented. The great losers were the robe nobility, who for most of the preceding century had been the order's only spokesmen, and kept the wheels of government turning too. Sword nobles had always looked down on them, even as they envied them their power. Now they had their revenge. The biggest single group elected by an order which still liked to justify itself by its military vocation were serving or former officers in the army or navy. It was true that the most conservative of all nobles were not represented: the Breton nobility, on the rejection of its demand that its deputies should be chosen by the province's estates, refused to send any at all. This could only give greater weight to those favouring accommodation with the Third, led by the eighteen members of the Society of Thirty who sat as noble deputies.[97] Perhaps three times as many more were prepared to follow their lead in the great confrontations of the first six weeks of the Estates.[98] But they remained a small minority among noble deputies, many of whom

96. Ibid., 28–31.   97. Wick, *A Conspiracy*, 304–5.
98. See James Murphy and Patrice Higonnet, 'Les députés de la noblesse aux états-généraux de 1789', *Revue d'Histoire moderne et contemporaine*, xx (1973), 236.

were explicitly mandated by their *cahiers* to resist the claims of the Third Estate.

Those claims, articulated in hundreds of pamphlets and sanctified by the *cahiers*, were overwhelmingly for a union of the orders. But, from the start, everything emphasized their continued separation. In the opening ceremonies, the orders processed separately and were commanded to dress differently, with the nobility wearing swords, plumed hats, lace, and cloth of gold, and the Third in sober black. In church, the Third was hustled to the back, because (they were told) this was where they had sat in 1614. After all the controversies of the winter about the forms of that last meeting, the rationale could scarcely have been less diplomatic. And when the first working sessions began, the Third found themselves alone in the hall. The two other orders had been assigned separate meeting places. Each order, it appeared, was expected to verify the credentials or 'powers' of its own members.

The problem had been foreseen, at least by those active in the struggles of the preceding months. Most of the new deputies knew few others, but those from provinces like Dauphiné and Brittany were already used to working together against the instinctive separatism of the privileged orders. Along with members of the Society of Thirty, they recognized that nothing must be done to confer any sort of legitimacy on separate action. They persuaded their as-yet unfocused colleagues that they should refuse to organize themselves. Instead, an invitation was sent to the other two orders to begin verification of powers in a common assembly.[99] But there was no consensus about what to do in the event of a refusal. The Bretons, soured by the experience of noble intransigence at home, favoured a Sieyèsian course: for the Third or 'Commons' (as they immediately began to call themselves) to declare themselves unilaterally a national assembly. The Dauphinois, whose own experience was that nobles could be made amenable, pressed for conciliation and informal contact with the other two orders. They were vigorously supported in this by most affiliates of the Society of Thirty sitting in all three orders. On 7 May a huge majority of the Third Estate authorized the Dauphinois leader, Jean-Joseph Mounier, to seek avenues of cooperation with the nobility and clergy.

But there, too, the issue had been anticipated. Among the clergy, a cluster of prelates with wide experience of managing clerical assemblies evoked the

99. Tackett, *Becoming a Revolutionary*, 127.

widespread anti-clericalism, voiced over the spring, in order to deter parish priests from responding too impulsively to calls for Third Estate solidarity.[100] The cry of the church in Danger, however cynically raised, proved far more persuasive. Nevertheless when the Third's plenipotentiaries asked them to appoint commissioners to explore ways of working together, the clergy agreed. Among the nobility, however, there were immediate moves for the order to verify its own members' powers and constitute itself quickly for business. A vocal minority, mostly former members of the Thirty now operating as the 'Viroflay Club', urged delaying prematurely irrevocable decisions, and insisted that common verification did not entail vote by head; but few were convinced. Obviously well-prepared speakers from the other side vehemently denounced any sort of compromise. 'They are trying', warned the Count de La Gallissonnière, 'to plunge you into a fatal security over the intentions of the Third Estate, when everything speaks to you of a deeply laid project to equalize and *level* all conditions, and to destroy the ancient constitution of the realm to put in its place a new order of things, whose forms you can neither foresee nor measure.'[101] Others echoed these fears, and a motion was carried by 188 votes to 46 for the nobility to verify its own powers. Commissioners to do it were immediately appointed, and by the end of the next day their task was completed. Representatives of the Third Estate bringing Mounier's message were kept waiting until they had reported, and were only received after the order had voted itself constituted. By now the voting disparity had widened to 195 against 29. It was then agreed to open talks with the Third; but with dinner time approaching there was no discussion about what they should cover.

The disdain was obvious, and it suffused the language of many of the speakers. Nor did it diminish with the passage of time. Yet many of the most eloquent had credentials sneered at by their colleagues. Duval d'Eprémesnil, the hero of the parlement during the constitutional confrontations of 1788, had barely completed his family's passage to nobility, but his lawyer's eloquence expressed what those unused to public speaking inarticulately felt. Scarcely less of a *parvenu* was Jacques Antoine Marie de Cazalès, son of an ennobled Toulouse *capitoul*, but now an outspoken defender of the 'rights' of the noble order. The lineage of his fellow southerner d'Antraigues

---

100. Ibid., 129–32.
101. Olga Ilovaïsky (ed.), *Recueil de documents relatifs aux séances des Etats-Généraux*, ii (I) (Paris, 1974), 219.

was older, but he had been refused the Honours of the Court, a snub which might have helped inspire his famous denunciation of hereditary nobility the year before.[102] To the dismay of the Third Estate, he now grandiloquently foreswore his radical past and denounced vote by head. He did persuade his fellow nobles to declare a commitment to fiscal equality, but by now there was nothing new in this. 'It will not do', reflected one deputy calling himself a member of the 'Commons', 'for the nobles to make us the real or apparent sacrifice of their pecuniary privileges, it is also of the greatest importance that they should not have an unreasonable influence in the formation of the Constitution … to leave them as an order apart which could oppose decisions taken by the Commons would be to grant them a right of prevention or "veto".'[103] Torn between assuring himself that there was no desire to destroy the noble order 'quite absurd though it is', and exasperation at its obduracy, he ended these reflections by speculating what the nation would be like without a nobility—with virtue, merit, and talent recognized, the king universally popular, and his kingdom flourishing.

All the 'conciliatory' talks between the orders achieved, in fact, over the fortnight in which they took place, was to polarize positions on all sides. The Estates remained deadlocked. An attempt by ministers to broker compromise between 28 May and 4 June also failed. And while the talks went on, nothing else happened. An expectant public witnessed only political paralysis, and the deputies of the 'Commons', reporting home to their constituents, left them in no doubt about who was to blame. Mirabeau advised his Provençal constituents to think about following American models: 'Begin by annihilating in France the nobility and the government; then set up a single assembly of the nation's representatives and a senate to take the place of the monarch and his council.'[104] Sensing their increasing isolation, the nobility drew back even from the semblance of negotiation. Even before agreeing to accept ministerial conciliation, they voted that nothing implying vote by head was constitutionally acceptable, and the victorious margin (207:38) was wider than ever.[105] Honour prevented them,

102. See above, pp. 172–3.
103. Jean Marchand (ed.), *Jacques-Antoine Creuzé-Latouche: Journal des Etats-Généraux et du début de l'Assemblée nationale, 18 mai–29 juillet 1789* (Paris, 1946), 14.
104. *Courrier de Provence*, Lettres à ses commettans, i, 12 May 1789. Quoted in Lewis Rosenthal, *America and France: The Influence of the United States on France in the xviiith Century* (New York, 1882), 168.
105. See Tackett's masterly summary of the noble mood in *Becoming a Revolutionary*, 132–8.

one noble participant declared, from reconsidering any decision. Honour was repeatedly invoked, in fact, to justify any stance, and outsiders could see that reason and argument were fruitless against it.[106]

It was at this point that Sieyès intervened. Determined attempts had been made to keep him out of the assembly, and he was the last member of the Parisian Third Estate delegation to be chosen. The elections in the capital took place after the Estates convened, and the delegation only took its seat on 27 May. Like everybody else, Sieyès had to wait until the failure of conciliation was formally announced on 9 June, but by then he had already discussed a plan of action with radical deputies now known as the 'Breton Club'. On 10th, introduced by Mirabeau, he moved that the Commons should invite the other two orders to join them at once in common verification of powers as 'representatives of the Nation'. If they refused, verification should proceed without them. After some modification of harsh words, the motion was adopted by 247 votes to 41. The invitation went to the other orders the next day; and on 12th, without waiting for their response, a roll-call of the deputies returned for each electoral district began.

Nobody expected any nobleman to break ranks, even though everybody knew there was a sympathetic minority among them. Sieyès's motion was aimed primarily at the much more evenly divided clergy, to whom repeated appeals for union had been sent over the previous weeks. It was clear that the procrastination of the bishops was decreasingly effective. On 13 June it finally gave out. Amid rapturous scenes, three parish priests appeared when their delegation's name was called. By the time the roll-call was complete, eight more had joined them, and others followed over the next few days. The separation of the orders had been breached. The nobility affected indifference, spending leisurely days debating the Third's invitation and attempting to advertise a greater concern for the public welfare than the other two orders by discussing the rising price of bread. But few were now interested in anything they did. The gesture of a handful of frustrated parish priests had completely undermined the principle of separate orders, and the assembly they had joined seized the moment to proclaim itself no longer either Third Estate or Commons, but something much more comprehensive. The obvious name had been bandied about for weeks, and even the king had used it in one of his messages to the three

106. Creuzé-Latouche, *Journal*, 77, 9 June 1789.

orders: National Assembly.[107] Sieyès had advocated it in *What is the Third Estate?,* although not including the other orders.[108] He now proposed a tortuous formula which he perhaps hoped would not be adopted. Other even more fanciful proposals went the same way before it came down once more to National Assembly. A deputation from the nobility was pointedly kept waiting until the matter was settled, but on 17 June it finally was. The envoys found themselves addressing a self-proclaimed National Assembly, whose president told them that the only message it was interested in hearing was that the nobility would accept the invitation to join it.

An audience of thousands had watched this discussion from the galleries, and wildly cheered the result. When, immediately afterwards, the Assembly cancelled and at once re-authorized all taxes, it made the full implication clear. This was a seizure of sovereignty on behalf of the French Nation. And it would be a nation without privileges. 'Through this ...', wrote one deputy, 'we have obliterated all distinctions of privilege by order.'[109] Most clergy, whose solidarity had already begun to crumble, accepted the new situation almost immediately. On 19 June the clerical order voted by 148 to 135 to join the National Assembly, several bishops voting with the majority. But on 20th, arriving to make their triumphant entry, they found the hall closed and guarded by soldiers. It was being re-arranged, they and all other arriving deputies were told, to accommodate a special Royal Session. Fearing that this meant an imminent dissolution, the Assembly convened in a nearby indoor tennis court and took their famous oath not to disperse until they had given France a constitution.

The king, whose customary indecision had been compounded by grief at the death of his elder son and heir a few days earlier, was convinced by Necker that he must now act or lose his authority entirely. Highly placed conservative deputies from both the nobility and clergy were also sending desperate messages through their friends at Court urging firm action to preserve the separate orders. But once a Royal Session was decided upon, there was bitter conflict among royal advisors about what the king should announce. The queen and the king's brothers insisted on a more uncompromising declaration than Necker thought prudent, and in

---

107. Robert H. Blackman, 'What's in a Name? Possible Names for a Legislative Body and the Birth of National Sovereignty during the French Revolution, 15–16 June 1789', *French History*, 21 (2007), 22–43.
108. See above, p. 180.   109. Quoted in Tackett, *Becoming a Revolutionary*, 148.

protest Necker stayed away from a ceremony which had originally been his idea.[110] Whether it would have succeeded even as he had conceived it seems doubtful. It was too late now to offer a lead that should have come six weeks earlier. But Necker had thought that by ignoring rather than confronting the declaration of a National Assembly, while at the same time commanding the orders to deliberate together on general matters and reiterating the need for fiscal equality, the king might manage to regain some sort of initiative. As it was, the Third Estate were admitted last, and seated separately at a ceremony reminiscent of the beds of justice in which absolute monarchs had dictated their will to parlements. The king began by declaring that the proclamation of a National Assembly had been illegal and unconstitutional. It was pronounced null and void. The 'old distinction of the three orders of the State' was to be 'kept in its entirety'; as was voting by order. The estates were indeed 'exhorted' to deliberate in common on matters of general importance. Two of them had already flouted such exhortation for two months, but their usual grounds for resistance were removed by cancelling all binding mandates. Yet the king was explicit that 'the ancient and constitutional rights of the three orders' and 'feudal and seigneurial properties [and] the useful rights and honorific privileges of the first two orders' were matters for those orders alone. Fiscal equality was commended, but left dependent on formal renunciation by the first two orders of their pecuniary privileges. There was a wide range of other constitutional concessions culled from the *cahiers,* and the king hinted that he would proceed to implement this programme even without the Estates if they failed to agree on it. The session concluded, after barely half an hour, with the monarch ordering the deputies to return to their respective chambers.

Shouts of acclaim and applause greeted these announcements from the noble benches. The Third heard them in dismal silence. Several noticed the satisfied smirks of noble deputies as they filed out. The Third's response was to refuse to move from what was already being called the National Hall. Summoned to do so by a master of ceremonies notorious for citing the forms of 1614 in all his pronouncements, the deputies cheered Mirabeau when he declared that only bayonets would force them out. The king, confronted on emerging with a letter of resignation from Necker, was too confused to order them to be forced out. He spent the rest of the day

110. Egret, *Necker,* 288–96.

in frantic efforts to persuade Necker to stay. The Assembly, including the clerical majority who had voted to join it a few days earlier, proceeded with business, pretending nervously that nothing had happened.

By the end of the day Necker had agreed to stay, implored by the queen and princes who had earlier sabotaged his strategy. But that strategy could not now be resurrected. It was as dead as theirs, and before anything new could be formulated, the National Assembly had consolidated its position. The next day, troops were posted to exclude spectators and prevent deputies of one order from joining another, but, with ominous indiscipline, they allowed outsiders in and showed the clerical majority how to avoid locked doors and join the Assembly. On 25th, all except a handful of the remaining clergy followed them. And so, at last, did a minority of noblemen. Ever since the failure of ministerial mediation, there had been rumours that the senior noble deputy, the Duke d'Orléans, was preparing to lead a secession. After the proclamation of the National Assembly, he formally moved that the nobility join it, but was only able to muster eighty-nine votes. On 22 June three noblemen from Dauphiné appeared in the Assembly, but their delegation had not yet formally been recognized by the noble Estate, so they could not be said strictly to have broken ranks. The failure of the Royal Session, however, brought home the crisis, and those who had always voted for cooperation with the other orders spent the night of 24/25 considering their position. A number of them, like Lafayette, still felt agonizingly bound by mandates to maintain the separation of orders.[111] But on the morning of 25th, forty-seven who were not so bound agreed that the moment to abandon their 'brothers' had come. Orléans was among them, although not their leader. There were also several Dukes and courtiers who had funded the campaigns of the Society of Thirty, magistrates like Duport, and American veterans like the Lameth brothers. Their appearance in the Assembly that morning caused a sensation, and was greeted by fifteen minutes of ecstatic applause. They had come, they said, (with studied circumspection) only to verify their powers in common as members of the Estates-General. They spoke of their pain and regret at breaking with their order. But by the end of the day their verification was complete, and the newcomers had accepted membership of various committees which the Assembly was establishing.

111. Louis Gottschalk and Margaret Maddox, *Lafayette in the French Revolution: Through the October Days* (Chicago, IL, 1969), 66–9.

Vainly the separated majority of the nobility tried to carry on. They voted to accept the royal declarations of 23 June, including the abrogation of binding mandates—implying that this gave room for flexibility. But a deputation sent to announce this decision to what they still called the Third Estate was denied recognition except as a group of individual deputies. And from the other side, the king was preparing to deal them a final blow. Alarmed by popular disorder in Versailles, and reports of worse from Paris, and increasingly unsure whether troops could be relied upon to control it, the demoralized monarch was now desperate for calm. He responded to the nobility's vote to accept his programme by asking 'my faithful nobility' to join themselves at once with the other two orders 'to hasten the accomplishment of my paternal intentions'. The message threw them into complete confusion. Many were reluctant to comply, and it took further intervention from the hero of the intransigents, the Count d'Artois, before the royal request was accepted. But late on 27 June, when most of the National Assembly had dispersed for dinner, the rest of the nobility finally stole into the National Hall. They were angry and deeply ashamed. 'This joining,' reported the moderate conservative Marquis de Ferrières, 'which ought to have been marked by love of concord and peace, was appalling, from the grim silence in which it came about.'[112]

* * *

'Nothing,' reported the Duke of Dorset in his ambassadorial despatch, 'can equal the despondency of the Nobility upon this occasion, forced as they have been by an extraordinary and unexpected impulse to sacrifice in one moment every hope they had formed and the very principles from which they had resolved and flattered themselves that no consideration whatever should oblige them to depart.'[113]

The hope they sacrificed as they yielded to royal entreaties, having spurned those of the rest of their compatriots, was that of a guaranteed role in the life of a parliamentary nation. On 27 June 1789 the nobility gave up nothing that they had previously enjoyed. They had already resigned themselves to the loss of fiscal exemptions, but they had thought the

112. Henri Carré (ed.), *Marquis de Ferrières. Correspondance inédite, 1789, 1790, 1791* (Paris, 1932), 77. Ferrières to Mme. De Medel, 28 June 1789.
113. Browning, *Despatches*, ii, 227, Dorset to Duke of Leeds, 28 June 1789.

compensation of political power, such as they had never before enjoyed, more than adequate. A union of orders, with a doubled Third and voting by head, destroyed these hopes for ever.

Whether it would ever have worked out as well as they hoped seems improbable. That would have demanded a consistent solidarity seldom achievable in any political assembly, and one which in any case they had shown themselves unable to reach even when playing for the highest stakes. The months since September 1788 had laid bare all the deep-rooted divisions and antagonisms within the nobility, and the elections had produced a slate of noble deputies unable to achieve unanimity on anything. Noblemen had also lost control of the clergy, so there was no chance that the so-called 'privileged orders' could ever forge a permanent working alliance even voting still by order. As things stood in 1789, the forms of 1614 could only have produced chaos.

But in pursuing their utopian dreams, the nobles of France said and did things which at once embittered their opponents and made them all the more determined to thwart noble ambitions. Nobles entered the process of building a post-absolutist France as heroes and leaders of the Nation. In the course of the struggle to set up representative institutions, they squandered this goodwill, most of them preferring to seek power for their own order rather than for the wider educated, propertied elite of which they formed only a part. Too many of them dreamed of restoring a past, a nobility even, which had never existed, rather than helping to build a more rational future. The language in which they expressed their aspirations was suffused with superiority and condescension. It provoked commoners to respond in kind, pouring critical scorn not only on nobles' political pretensions but also their long-standing social claims. And these criticisms, at a moment when government had abandoned attempts to control printing and journalism, were far more widely diffused than ever before. In the spring of 1787, Calonne had failed spectacularly to raise the anger of the Third Estate against the 'privileged orders'.[114] Two years later, resentment against those orders suffused all public discussion about the political future of the kingdom, and there was, in the oft-quoted[115] phrase of the Swiss observer and journalist Mallet du Pan, 'war between the Third Estate and the other two orders'.

114. See above, pp. 160–1.
115. Most famously by Georges Lefebvre, *Quatre-Vingt Neuf* (Paris, 1939), 58.

And by then, nobles were not just proud and ambitious. They were afraid. Voting by head opened the prospect not only of political disappointment, but of empowering a resentful Third Estate. And all sorts of privileges, not just political ones, were now under attack. Feudal rights, deemed since time immemorial an essential ornament of noble identity, were being denounced. The drawing up of *cahiers* of grievance (*doléance*), as they were officially called, encouraged such denunciations and lent them legitimacy. For nobles, separation became more urgent than the promise of political power. It now appeared as essential protection against the social revenge of exasperated commoners. A minority saw that digging in could only now seem like futile provocation; but most, whether in electoral assemblies, or as deputies chosen and mandated by them, thought anything else too risky. The two-month struggle to merge the orders compounded the bitterness on all sides. The outcome was a humiliation for an order which claimed to hold honour dearer than life. And, as they had feared, it opened the way to far worse.

7

Aristocracy Abolished
The Destruction of Noble Power

'The whole business now seems over, and the revolution complete.' So wrote the English traveller Arthur Young, who was in Versailles to witness the end of separate orders on 27 June.[1] 'The King has been frightened by the mobs into overturning his own act of the *séance royale*, by writing to the presidents of the orders of the nobility and clergy, requiring them to join the Commons, full in the teeth of what he had ordained before.' Young believed that Louis XVI had surrendered royal power for ever, and that the traditional institutions of the kingdom, including the nobility, would soon 'find themselves all in danger of annihilation'. To his amazement, nobody he spoke to accepted his lurid expectations. Some noble deputies told him that the orders would unite only for the verification of powers, and for constitutional business. And indeed a majority of the nobles continued to congregate separately in advance of the plenary sittings which began on 30 June. They still claimed to be bound by their mandates not to deliberate in common. Even those who did not feel so bound persisted in sitting together when common deliberations began, as did the clergy. Others, meanwhile, left Versailles to seek new instructions from their electors. They included some of the more vociferous intransigents, many of whom did not return for several weeks. Yet nobles who showed themselves willing to cooperate with 'Commons' deputies[2] found themselves welcomed with warmth, and even deference. Immediate efforts were made to draft members of the former privileged orders on to committees, and to elect them to positions of responsibility.

---

1. Constantia Maxwell (ed.), *Arthur Young: Travels in France during the Years 1787, 1788, and 1789* (Cambridge, 1929), 159.
2. 'Third Estate' was a term now carefully avoided, except among diehard separatists from the other two orders.

And on 7 July a final salve to tender consciences was offered when Talleyrand, the extremely aristocratic young Bishop of Autun, moved that all binding mandates should be abrogated. The only mandate of elected deputies, he argued, should be to judge according to their conscience what was in the best interests of the Nation as a whole. This way, all three orders renounced their mandates together, and nobles whose scruples were sincere could point to the example of the other two orders. The motion did not pass uncontested, notably among Talleyrand's fellow clerics. A solitary noble protested, presciently enough, that if it passed, all distinctions between orders would disappear for ever. His fears were widely shared, but after the Assembly gave its overwhelming approval to Talleyrand's proposal, separate meetings of noble intransigents withered rapidly away.[3]

The abrogation of mandates was an essential precondition for all the later reforms undertaken by the National Assembly—a breakthrough in its way just as significant as the assumption of sovereignty on 17 June. But, if it eased the dilemma of *cahier*-bound noble deputies in the short run, in the longer term it opened the way to action far beyond anything imagined by the electors of any Estate in 1789, including all the losses which the nobility would suffer over the next twelve months. Nor was the warm relief directed at cooperative noble deputies universal. Months of defiant and condescending noble rhetoric and weeks of resistance to common action in the Estates had left many Third Estate deputies suspicious and resentful, as well as apprehensive of the impact of hundreds of former diehards now voting on all issues before the Assembly. Nor could anti-noble sentiment in the nation at large, steadily fostered and built up over nine months of electoral activity, simply be dispelled. An American visitor who had watched it grow since his arrival in February, noted on 4 July that 'The Current is setting so strong against the Noblesse that I apprehend their Destruction, in which will I fear be invoked consequences most pernicious, tho little attended to in the present Moment.'[4]

Nor, he explained to a correspondent the same day,[5] had the nobility behaved wisely in confronting such opinion. They 'have rather opposed Pride than Arguments to their Assailants. Hugging the dear Privileges of Centuries long elapsed ...'. He said it with evident regret, for the instincts

3. Tackett, *Becoming a Revolutionary*, 160, 163. By mid-July they had completely disappeared.
4. Beatrice Cary Davenport (ed.), *A Diary of the French Revolution by Gouverneur Morris 1752–1816, Minister to France during the Terror*, 2 vols. (London, 1939), i, 134.
5. Ibid., Morris to Carmichael, 4 July 1789.

of Gouverneur Morris were conservative; but radical precedents from his native America were clearly fuelling the anti-noble drift. On 11 July Lafayette, unchained by the abrogation of mandates, moved the proclamation of a declaration of rights. The idea, inspired by the example of American state constitutions, had been in Lafayette's mind since the beginning of the year, and he had discussed it several times with Jefferson.[6] His proposal declared that 'Nature has made men free and equal; distinctions necessary to social order are founded only on general utility.'[7] Laws were to be the same for all citizens. A first draft in January, sent by Jefferson to Madison,[8] had explicitly condemned nobility, 'arbitrary distinctions between citizens', hereditary power and offices, primogeniture and entails. In an atmosphere of bruised noble feelings, such unequivocal provisions would clearly have been inflammatory, and they were now dropped. Instead (despite Jefferson's disapproval) honour was set out as one of man's inalienable and imprescriptible rights. The egalitarian implications of Lafayette's proposal were nevertheless quite clear, and aroused some alarm even in sympathetic fellow deputies. But greater alarms cut short any debate on this initiative, with the news the next day that the king had dismissed Necker.

It seemed the prelude to an attempt to reverse the Revolution with the aid of thousands of troops who had been converging on the capital over the preceding fortnight. Louis XVI had steadfastly refused to withdraw them, despite frantic pleadings from the Assembly. Whatever the precise plan behind these manoeuvres,[9] they were clearly conceived by courtiers, and even at their most benign would have been unlikely to leave in place anything that had happened since 23 June. The nobility would certainly have recovered some of what it had lost since then, and national sovereignty and other gains of the Third Estate would have been repudiated. The uprising of Paris, which culminated in the taking of the Bastille on 14 July, prevented all this. It saved the Revolution. But the plotters who had hoped to arrest its course identified themselves by their reaction to their failure. On the night of 16 July the Count d'Artois and the Prince de Condé left Versailles in secret, heading for the frontier. Watching Condé

---

6. Gottschalk and Maddox, *Lafayette in the French Revolution*, 13–16, 81–90.
7. In Stéphane Rials, *La Déclaration des Droits de l'Homme et du Citoyen* (Paris, 1989), 590–1.
8. *Jefferson Papers*, xiv, 438–9; Rials, *La Déclaration des Droits*, 528–9.
9. For a full discussion, see Munro Price, *The Fall of the French Monarchy: Louis XVI, Marie-Antoinette and the Baron de Breteuil* (London, 2002), 75–94.

leave his ancestral palace at Chantilly was Grouvelle, still his secretary, and professing surprise at his departure. But the prince's entourage knew his true sentiments, and left cursing him as a rascal, a hypocrite, and a monster.[10] Other ministers and royal advisers also left over the next few days, setting a new example to anyone who found the direction of the Revolution unacceptable: emigration. 'We were very relieved', recalled one of the first émigrés, 'to find ourselves out of France, and to hear no longer the jeers against the nobility and the cries of "Long live the Third" that even children were screaming out.'[11]

More than jeers against the nobility continued to be published. In the first week of July an embittered cleric, inspired by Sieyès, denounced noble claims to hereditary superiority as based on illegitimate conquest, usurpation, and prejudice. 'The yoke of aristocrats, however wise, however moderate they appear to be, will always appear insupportable to a courageous people ... Apart from the crown, there are no functions that are not better performed through election than through entail.'[12] Some weeks later, a self-styled 'Philanthropic Frenchman'[13] poured scorn on the way 'a self-important tone, a few parchments and the word *honour* are a substitute for many people for any morality'. Nobility was part of 'the rust of feudal barbarism', although most nobles now derived their status from usurpation or venality. None of it provided any basis for excluding non-nobles from positions of power and authority, yet recently 'all avenues open to unsupported talents have been closed'.[14] This had not prevented the nobility in their *cahiers* from claiming yet more exclusive access to the best employments in the army, the magistracy and the church, not to mention a collective role as intermediaries between the throne and the Nation. The effect would be 'to raise up from the dust the appalling colossus of feudalism.'[15]

But the danger of that would soon be past. In the aftermath of the fall of the Bastille, feudalism came under more than intellectual attack. While in Paris, as the British ambassador noted, 'the execration of the Nobility is universal amongst the lower order of people',[16] in the countryside news

---

10. Hauterive, *Journal d'Emigration du comte d'Espinchal*, 21.   11. Ibid., 24.
12. Abbé de Bignon, *Que'est-ce que la Noblesse?* (Paris, 1789), signed 1 July 43, 54 (BL F tracts 90 (6)).
13. *Le Français philanthrope ou considérations patriotiques relatives à une ancienne & une nouvelle aristocratie* (s.l, 1789) (BL R tracts 46 (12)). Mention of a sitting of the Assembly on 17 July suggests a publication date late in that month.
14. Ibid., 104–5.   15. Ibid., 108.
16. Browning, *Despatches*, ii, 241, Dorset to Leeds, 16 July 1789.

of metropolitan upheavals brought to a climax a tide of attacks on the institutions and symbols of lordships which had been gathering momentum throughout the social and political confrontations of the spring. It took days, sometimes weeks, for news of the capital's defiance and the beginning of noble emigration to reach the provinces. But in many parts, as the annual season for collecting dues approached, peasant communities had been repudiating the authority of their lords for weeks or even months. Dues were being refused or repossessed, monopolies flouted, game reserves violated, and those who attempted to enforce feudal claims threatened. Alarm at all this prompted the king's promise on 23 June that feudal and seigniorial rights would be 'constantly respected'.[17] But nothing came of that, and by early July there were reports of castles and country houses being attacked, muniment rooms ransacked, terriers and rent rolls found there burnt, and symbols of authority like weather vanes and coats of arms vandalized.

In the later weeks of July the incidents merged into a series of generalized rural panics about invaders, brigands, marauders and plotting aristocrats which became known as the Great Fear.[18] From the perspective of Paris, and the National Assembly sitting in Versailles bombarded with daily reports of violence and outrages against property and (occasionally) persons, it looked as if social order was entirely breaking down. From 20 July the deputies were discussing how to appeal for calm, but the very next day there were renewed and bloody disturbances in Paris, with high noble officials lynched and their heads paraded on pikes. On 25th, news arrived of a castle blown up in Franche Comté, allegedly by its own lord, who was subsequently murdered. It triggered a wave of attacks on other seats of lords and aristocratic monasteries. A crescendo of alarm peaked around 28th.[19] During all this time the National Assembly tried to address what it now proclaimed to be its primary task, the drafting of a constitution. Relief at the relatively peaceful outcome of the crisis of 12–17 July in the capital had produced unprecedented harmony among the deputies.[20] The diehard president of the former noble order, the Duke de Luxembourg, had emigrated, and in his absence separate meetings of nobles were abandoned.

---

17. 'Déclaration des intentions du roi', no. xii, in Roberts, *French Revolution Documents*, 119. See also above, p. 199.
18. The classic survey is Georges Lefebvre, *The Great Fear of 1789* (London, 1973, trans. of the Paris edition of 1932). See also P. M. Jones, *The Peasantry in the French Revolution* (Cambridge, 1989), 67–81; and Markoff, *Abolition of Feudalism*, 218–29; 427–48, and *passim*.
19. Markoff, *Abolition*, 437–9.   20. Tackett, *Becoming a Revolutionary*, 164–5.

The Duke de Liancourt was elected president of the Assembly, and if Lafayette was distracted from legislative business by the need to organize the new National Guard of which he had been made commander, other former members of the society of Thirty now took the lead in sketching out the elements of the new constitution. By the last week in the month a Declaration of Rights was once more under discussion, with much raking over of competing phraseology, philosophic differences, or 'syllables', as Mirabeau contemptuously called them.[21]

Many deputies shared his view. These discussions seemed to them a pointless distraction when much of the kingdom was in anarchy and there were no reliable forces to restore order. Some became convinced that only a dramatic gesture by the Assembly could bring back calm. In the first days of August a group of deputies known as the 'Breton Club' began to discuss a plan for bouncing the Assembly into this. The club had begun as an informal gathering of Third Estate deputies radicalized by the intransigence of nobles during the pre-revolutionary clashes in Brittany. They had done much to sustain resistance to noble and clerical separatism before the union of the orders, and by July they had been joined by representatives of other provinces and by sympathetic liberal nobles, too. On 3 August one of their founder members, the half-ennobled Rennes lawyer Isaac René Guy Le Chapelier, was elected president of the Assembly, and he was in the chair when the club's plan went into operation.[22] The business of the day on 4 August concerned a proclamation appealing for order. The Breton idea was to propose an amendment to include the abolition of certain feudal rights and dues. To make the maximum impact, the amendment was to be moved by a great nobleman with extensive feudal rights of his own. The Duke d'Aiguillon, son of a former foreign minister and a member of the Richelieu family, had been a founder member of the Society of Thirty and a leading activist in the liberal minority of noble deputies. He had inherited his dukedom only the year before, along with one of the largest landed fortunes in the kingdom.[23] He was primed to intervene on one of the first evening sittings of the Assembly, perhaps because it was thought the house

21. J. Bénétruy (ed.), *Etienne Dumont: Souvenirs sur Mirabeau et les deux premières assemblées législatives* (Paris, 1951), 100.
22. The fullest account in Patrick Kessel, *La nuit du 4 août 1789* (Paris, 1969). See also Tackett, *Becoming a Revolutionary*, 171–5; Fitzsimmons, *The Night the Old Regime Ended*, 12–17; Jean-Pierre Hirsch, *La nuit du 4 août* (Paris, 1978).
23. On the d'Aiguillon fortune, see Lucien Laugier, *Duc d'Aiguillon, Commandant en Bretagne, Ministre d'Etat* (Paris, 1984), 259–265.

would be thin. But when the moment came, the hall was unusually full, and he was pre-empted at the tribune by another young liberal, American veteran[24] and fellow member of the Thirty, the Viscount de Noailles. Noailles was not rich, but the ducal family to which he belonged was. Impulsive and opinionated, he shared the taste for self-publicity of his brother-in-law Lafayette. The people would only be calmed, he declared, by giving them what they wanted, which was reform of the taxes and an easing of seigneurial rights. To this end he proposed:

$1°$ ... that taxation will be paid by all individuals in the kingdom, in proportion to their income.

$2°$ That all public burdens shall in future be borne equally by all.

$3°$ That all feudal rights shall be redeemable by communities, in money, or compounded at a fair price, namely at the yield of one ordinary year in ten.

$4°$ That seigneurial labour services (*corvées*), serfdom (*mainmortes*) and other personal servitudes shall be abolished without compensation.[25]

As long beforehand as the Assemblies of Notables, spokesmen for the nobility had conceded proportional fiscal equality.[26] All that was new in Noailles's proposals on this was that the National Assembly should endorse it. The proposals to redeem some feudal rights and abolish others outright, however, were sweepingly radical. This was everything that conservative nobles had dreaded since the autumn of 1788. Noailles certainly went further than d'Aiguillon had intended, as the latter made clear when he lamely followed him to the tribune.[27] While claiming that the Viscount had taken the words out of his mouth, the Duke was in fact much more careful in what he proposed. Feudal rights were property, he declared, and could not simply be abolished outright. If they were to be ended, there must be a 'just indemnity'. Those subject to them should be free to pay them off at 3.3 per cent,[28] or whatever rate the Assembly chose to set. D'Aiguillon endorsed the principle of equal and proportional taxation, but extended it beyond individuals to corporations (*corps*), towns or communities enjoying 'particular privileges or personal exemptions'. Feudal dues, meanwhile,

---

24. And Cincinnatus.   25. Quoted in Kessel, *La nuit*, 138.
26. See above, p. 159.   27. Kessel, *La nuit*, 138–41.
28. *Denier 30* in contemporary usage.

should be levied as normal until fully paid off. And d'Aiguillon made no mention of abolishing any without compensation.

D'Aiguillon's proposals were therefore both more radical and more conservative than those of Noailles. To attack corporate privileges and exemptions went far beyond the advantages enjoyed by nobles alone. But to make all feudal rights subject to redemption recognized that they were all equally legitimate forms of property. No concessions were made to the unqualified renunciations and suppressions of rights which were being forced out of lords up and down the country even as d'Aiguillon was speaking. Yet the differences between the speeches of the two courtier deputies appear to have passed almost unnoticed in the heat of the moment. The planners of the attack on feudal dues had calculated that the sight of great noblemen acknowledging fiscal equality and renouncing their most distinctive privileges would work 'a sort of magic'[29] in the Assembly. They were right. Wild applause greeted both speeches, and there began a rush of excited speakers to the tribune which went on for six hours. Feudalism was repeatedly denounced in lurid terms. The Breton wine and cloth merchant, Le Guen de Kérengal, dressed as he had been since May to look like a peasant, said that the abolition of seigneurial rights was long overdue. The Assembly should learn from the example of America, where none existed. He evoked absurdities, like the duty to silence frogs: clearly this self-styled peasant had read Bergasse in the spring.[30] To repeated ovations, other non-noble speakers reeled off lists of grotesque and burdensome feudal exactions in their own provinces. Then, to general surprise, the Duke du Châtelet rose to denounce 'all rights linked to former feudal servitude'.[31] The Duke was widely hated as the martinet commander who had provoked his regiment of French Guards into mutiny during the July crisis. Crowds had threatened his life on several occasions in the lawless days that followed. The experience had terrified him into a populist, some thought. Now, at any rate, he concluded an impassioned speech by renouncing any personal servitudes owed him by his vassals. His example set off a chain reaction of personal renunciations by noblemen overcome by what the Marquis de Ferrières called 'patriotic intoxication'.[32] 'There

29. The words of Jean-Nicolas-Jacques Parisot, Third Estate Deputy for Bar-sur-Seine, in reporting this session to his constituents on 5 August: Lemay, *Dictionnaire des Constituants*, ii, 732.
30. See above, p. 186.   31. Kessel, *La nuit*, 147.
32. 'Ivresse patriotique': *Correspondance*, 144, Ferrières to Rabreuil, 7 Aug. 1789.

was no chance', recalled an observer from the galleries, 'to reflect, to object, to ask for time; a sentimental contagion carried hearts away.'[33] There is no evidence that most speakers were party to the original plan. The enthusiasm was spontaneous. 'I groaned inwardly,' confessed one of the session's noble secretaries, 'not to have any personal sacrifice to offer' while recognizing at the same time that people were no longer in control of themselves.[34] Soon, indeed, the original plan was completely swamped by denunciations of all manner of practices, from burdensome taxation to laws against Protestants, from unearned pensions to judicial fees, from colonial slavery to the ecclesiastical tithe, from provincial and municipal privileges to heredity of offices, from trade guilds to the sale of offices. The offers and proposals came so thick and fast that the Assembly's secretaries were overwhelmed and many points did not find their way into the hurried summary read out before the session closed at past two the next morning. The last decisions were to proclaim Louis XVI 'Restorer of French Liberties', to order a celebratory *Te Deum*, and to decree the striking of a commemorative medal. It was clear that everyone present thought that they had achieved something quite momentous. But, until the drawing up of formal decrees over the next few days, few of them seemed at all sure what.

* * *

They had, in fact, ordered the destruction of the institutional, and much of the social, structure of pre-revolutionary France—what people were already beginning to call the *ancien régime*. The Night of 4 August was the most radical single episode of the entire French Revolution. No province, no town, no taxpayer, no litigant, no priest, no peasant, would be unaffected by the decisions taken then: and certainly no noble. The initial plan, indeed, had been to restore order to the countryside largely at the expense of the nobility by the removal of feudal rights. And the ploy of letting noble deputies start the process succeeded beyond all expectations: perhaps three quarters of the proposals and renunciations of that night came from noblemen or prelates.[35] Within days, too, they

---

33. Dumont, *Souvenirs sur Mirabeau*, 99.
34. The Count de Lally-Tollendal, quoted in Kessel, *La nuit*, 158.
35. Tackett, *Becoming a Revolutionary*, 173, counts 60 per cent nobles and 25 per cent clergy; but most of the clerical speakers were noble-born bishops.

felt able to congratulate themselves that their sacrifices had been effective and immediately worthwhile. Although the effervescence in the country at large had passed its peak as an abundant harvest absorbed the bulk of peasant energies, news of returning calm in the days after 4 August seemed like the consequence of that night's concessions.[36] Perhaps it emboldened those who sought, in prolonged debates between 6 and 11 August, to limit the practical impact of the grand gestures of principle made the week before.

The decrees of 11 August 1789 certainly began with a grand gesture. The National Assembly proclaimed Article 1 'entirely destroys the feudal regime'. Serfdom (*mainmorte*[37]) and personal servitude were suppressed without any compensation to the lords who benefited. This was much what Noailles had proposed when opening the 'never to be forgotten session' and what du Châtelet and others had offered in a personal capacity in the course of it. A handful of noble voices raised against uncompensated abolition were brushed aside. But then few lords were affected. The king himself had emancipated the last serfs on the royal domains in 1779, piously expressing the hope that private landlords would follow his example. Few did, and the Parlement of Besançon, in whose jurisdiction most French serfs were to be found, resisted registration of the edict for nine years. Nevertheless, in 1789 there were only about 140,000 left in the kingdom, largely in Franche Comté and Burgundy, and most were vassals of monasteries rather than individual noblemen.[38]

Other rights difficult to quantify but of undoubted prestige were also abolished without compensation. They included monopolies of keeping pigeons and rabbits, and exclusive entitlements to kill them: a constant irritant to peasant cultivators who saw these lordly luxuries as destructive vermin. Exclusive hunting rights and reserves likewise disappeared uncompensated. So did seigniorial courts and jurisdiction, useful perhaps in enforcing lords' rights while feudalism existed, but pointless if it was now abolished. In recent years, in any case, many lords had been finding the costs of maintaining such courts and their apparatus of officers and buildings

36. Markoff, *Abolition*, 443.
37. Reflecting the primary fact that land held on these terms could not be sold outside the fief, and hereditary vassals remained bound to it and the dues and services owed in return for tenure.
38. Marcel Marion, *Dictionnaire des institutions de la France aux xviiᵉ et xviiiᵉ siècles* (Paris, 1923), 508–9. Revenues of such monasteries, of course, often ended up in noble pockets, such as those of their commendatory abbots.

far more burdensome than their advantages seemed to justify.[39] Even so, they were not to disappear at once. They were to continue to function until an entire new judicial order was put in place. There would be work for them to do as well, for the Assembly's clear intention was that all other feudal burdens should be redeemable, and continue to be levied until they were fully bought out. This had been the original objective of those who had planned and launched the onslaught of 4 August, and it was spelled out no less than twice in the decree of 11th.[40] The details were left for later elaboration. It took seven months of patient committee work to produce them.[41] But there was no support for abolishing quantifiable rights without compensation. One clause in the decree (vi) even allowed the possibility of creating new ones, provided they were redeemable. Feudal rights were property; they had a tangible market value. Only their less material gothic trappings were to be suppressed outright.

In the long run, and in fact quite soon, these attempts to safeguard the material value of feudal rights would prove unenforceable. Most former vassals simply ceased paying or performing their obligations to lords, and attempts by the latter to enforce the letter of the law were often met with violence.[42] It would, however, be some years before former lords could compute their losses from the way feudalism had been abolished. Looking back on 4 August ten months later, the Marquis de Ferrières did not mention the loss of feudal dues as fatal to the nobility.[43] He thought the loss of seigneurial courts and symbols important, and the abolition of primogeniture,[44] but what he emphasized most was the loss of pecuniary privileges, and the proclamation of equal admission to civil and military appointments. Both had an explicit clause to themselves in the decree of 11 August, and both took effect immediately. Most nobles had been resigned for many months to the eventual loss of fiscal and professional privileges, but the advent of civil equality marked a fundamental transformation of their status in society. The law would no longer recognize their claims to innate superiority by rewarding them with unearned advantages. Richer nobles might continue to enjoy all that wealth and property made available,

39. See Anthony Crubaugh, *Balancing the Scales of Justice: Local Courts and Rural Society in France, 1750–1800* (University Park, PA, 2001), 1–130.
40. Articles i and vi.   41. See below, pp. 227–8.
42. See Jones, *Peasantry*, 83–5, 90–4, 103–23; Markoff, *Abolition*, 450–5, 462–9.
43. Correspondance, 207. Ferrières to de Chacé, 20 June 1790.
44. See below, pp. 227–8.

but henceforth their birth would confer no automatic entitlements. Poorer ones had no such safeguards: their loss of privilege was absolute. All they had left to console them was the distinction of their ancestry.

Yet paradoxically that quality was now set to be enhanced. In the small hours of 5 August, just when the momentum of abolitions and renunciations seemed to be flagging, one obscure deputy from Lorraine moved the suppression of the sale of offices.[45] The Assembly greeted his proposal 'with transports'. It was clear from the summary drafted at the end of the session, from later discussion on 11 August, and from the definitive decree promulgated later that day, that this was seen largely as a judicial matter. Free justice was invariably associated with it. No thought seems to have been given to any social implications. But for the best part of three centuries venality had been the main vehicle of French social mobility; and at the summit of the system the 4,224 ennobling offices were the portal through which ambitious men of wealth could make their families noble.[46] Each year between 500 and 700 individuals passed through it.[47] The abolition of venality slammed it shut. Nobody challenged the rights of the king as the sole source of legitimate ennoblement; but venality had been the normal, largely impersonal way through which he had exercised them. The effect, therefore, was to transform the French nobility at a stroke from the most open elite in Europe into a virtually closed caste.

Pre-revolutionary opinion had overwhelmingly considered venality to be indefensible.[48] Half the *cahiers* of the nobility in the spring of 1789 had condemned venal ennoblement,[49] and one of the main fault lines within the nobility was between those who flaunted a lineage untainted by purchase and those unable to conceal such origins. These distinctions would continue to preoccupy nobles and their nineteenth- and twentieth-century descendants and to perpetuate the pre-revolutionary 'cascade of disdain' among them. But the outer limits of nobility were now definitively drawn. Nobody who was not fully and demonstrably noble in August 1789 could legitimately claim, for themselves or their descendants, to enjoy the status. And a revolution which sought to dispel the infectious mystique of nobility

---

45. Doyle, *Venality*, 1–2, 279–81. The future terrorist Bertrand Barère recalled in his memoirs that this abolition was planned in advance along with that of feudal dues. A magistrate from a parlement was to move it. (Leo Gershoy, *Bertrand Barère: A Reluctant Terrorist* (Princeton, NJ, 1962), 76). But this motion came late, and its mover was a magistrate in a petty jurisdiction. It seems more likely that, like so much on the Night of 4 August, it was unpremeditated.
46. Ibid., 78–81.   47. Ibid., 165.
48. Ibid., ch. 8, *passim*.   49. See above, p. 190.

would have the effect of deepening it by making it henceforth both clear and unattainable. Even when, under subsequent regimes, ennoblements resumed,[50] their beneficiaries would never enjoy the prestige, or the unalloyed legitimacy, of families set apart for ever by the closure effected under the decree of 11 August, which declared venality of judicial office 'suppressed from this moment'. In June of the next year, the National Assembly would decree the entire abolition of nobility itself; but nobility as it had functioned under the absolute monarchy had already come to an end, frozen in time, with the disappearance of venal ennoblement.

✳ ✳ ✳

At the time, these implications seem to have passed unnoticed. The most virulent second thoughts about the proceedings of 4 August came from the clergy, who lost their tithes and vestry fees with no compensation other than the promise of future salaries, and heard ominous threats of the entire confiscation of church lands.[51] Few nobles spoke up for them, despite the huge losses to be expected by younger brothers who were bishops, abbots, and canons. Most nobles in the Assembly seemed resigned, for better or worse, to changes in their status which had been threatening for months. 'The Nobility can do nothing better', wrote Ferrières to his sister, 'than to join in good faith with the Third, and to raise up to itself the honest and solid citizen of the middle class. It is the wisest course, and, at the same time, the soundest way to recover, through personal consideration, the authority it has lost by giving up its feudal dues and its privileges; the Upper Third will be flattered by the regard shown by the Nobility.'[52] As was his principle, he said nothing in open session. Other nobles now took the lead, however, in returning to the proposed Declaration of Rights.

On 12 August three key committees were established to give detailed substance to the general decree of the previous day. One was for the liquidation of feudal rights, one for judicial reorganization, and one for finalizing the Declaration of Rights. Nobles were well represented on all three, and on 17th Le Chapelier ceded the presidency of the Assembly to one of the most vocal former members of the Society of Thirty,

---

50. See below, pp. 326–30.   51. Tackett, *Becoming a Revolutionary*, 180–1.
52. *Correspondance*, 120. Ferrières to Mme. De Medel, 10 Aug. 1789.

the Count de Clermont-Tonnerre. He would be in the chair when a final series of projects and proposals for the Declaration of the Rights of Man and the Citizen were discussed.[53] The longest discussions, as in the debates before 11 August, were over the clergy's resistance, this time to religious toleration. By contrast, the principle of civil equality was endorsed unanimously.

'Men are born and remain free and equal in rights:' declared the very first article, 'social distinctions can only be founded on common utility.' Equal and proportional liability to taxation (Art. 13) also passed with little debate. Equal access to 'public dignities, offices and employments according to ability, and with no other distinction than that of virtues and talents' (Art. 6) provoked more debate, but only about whether 'capacities' was a better word than 'ability'. Some worried that capacity implied wealth, and so a new form of aristocracy.[54] As finally agreed, these clauses confirmed the civil and fiscal equality proclaimed on 4 and 11 August; but nothing remained of the explicitly anti-noble drafts of the spring, or of honour as a fundamental human right.[55] A proposal to state in Article 6 that birth was no qualification for public office was struck out at the suggestion of the president himself.[56] The Declaration therefore avoided explicit humiliation of nobles. And for those, overwhelmingly noble, destined to suffer loss of property as a result of 4 August, there was reassurance in the seventeenth and final clause of the Declaration, voted at the last minute at the proposal of Adrien Duport, magistrate and original animator of the Society of Thirty. It declared property an inviolable and sacred right. Nobody might be deprived of it except by legally certified public necessity, and then only on condition of just and prior compensation. One Duke expressed worries that, given the sheer scale of the suppressions to be compensated, prior indemnity might be completely impractical.[57] He would be proved right, but now his concerns were swept aside. Deputies on all sides were tired of debating first principles, and were anxious to begin practical constitution-building.

Yet the principle of aristocracy was raised by the very first questions they addressed. No country, the Declaration of the Rights of Man had stated,[58] in which the separation of powers was not provided for, could be said to

---

53. Rials, *La Déclaration*, 199–266; Tackett, *Becoming a Revolutionary*, 182–4.
54. Rials, *La Déclaration*, 227–33.   55. See above, p. 206.
56. Rials, *La Déclaration*, 232–3.
57. The Duke de Mortemart, a member of the judiciary committee: Doyle, *Venality*, 281–2.
58. Article 16.

have a constitution. But separation of what powers? To the constitutional committee, sitting since 6 July and dominated by the eloquence of Mounier, the leader of the previous year's revolution in Dauphiné,[59] separation of powers of the sort found in Great Britain was the only one suitable for a monarchical state. That meant a king and a legislature of two chambers, each with a veto. Mounier set these ideas out in detail in August in a pamphlet sanctioned by the committee.[60] It was clearly meant to prepare public opinion for the official recommendations of the committee, which he read to the Assembly on 31 August and 4 September. The effect, however, was not as Mounier had hoped. A royal veto, said many Parisian journalists and more radical deputies, was the high road back to despotism; while a second chamber would re-institutionalize the reign of aristocracy. In vain did Mounier argue the virtues of checks and balances, evoke the manifest success of such a constitution in Great Britain, and point to the way that the Americans, at state and more recently at federal level, had adopted these principles. His second chamber, he emphasized, would not be a hereditary House of Lords, but an elective Senate or 'Chamber of Conservators' of older, richer men sitting for twice as long as the lower house.[61] Mounier was supported by an eloquent group of deputies who were coming to be known as the *monarchiens* from their outspoken commitment to an absolute royal veto. But it was known that the constitutional committee was not united either on the veto or on the second chamber. Even the advocates of the latter disagreed on its precise composition: Mounier was for electing senators, but Lally-Tollendal, another member of the committee, favoured lifetime senators nominated by the king.[62] When Sieyès joined the debate on 7 September it was to denounce the proposal of his own committee. The king should have no veto of any sort, he insisted, and as for a second chamber, 'it would reawaken the destructive germ of aristocracy which ought to be wiped out forever'.[63]

59. See above, pp. 163–4. Mounier's dominance was not uncontested, but dissidents like Sieyès, Le Chapelier, and Talleyrand were in an impotent minority. They chose to let him be defeated on the Assembly floor before succeeding to a dominance of their own in the new committee elected on 12 September.
60. *Considérations sur les gouvernements et principalement sur celui qui convient à la France* (Paris, 1789).
61. Ibid., 39–41. Compare the Napoleonic Senate, below, pp. 316–7, sometimes called the 'conserving senate'.
62. His eloquent speech of 31 August, not printed in the *Moniteur*, is in François Furet and Ran Halévi, *La Monarchie républicaine: La constitution de 1791* (Paris, 1991), 345–64.
63. Quoted in Jean-Denis Bredin, *Sieyès, la clé de la Révolution française* (Paris, 1988), 149.

Opinion in the Assembly was deeply and genuinely divided over the royal veto, but a clear majority favoured some sort, and in the final vote on 11 September the majority for a suspensive or delaying veto was over two to one.[64] The vote on a second chamber the day before was much more conclusive. The proposal only mustered 89 votes, with 122 abstentions, and no fewer than 849 against.[65] It was easy to see why Third Estate deputies wanted no truck with a senate. They had spent the spring resisting the idea of separate, veto-wielding houses in the National Assembly. They did not wish to create something similar for the future. And although *monarchien* speakers in these impassioned debates denied any intention of creating a new noble order or chamber of peers, and insisted that an upper house would be open to all men of ability, this only fanned a widespread suspicion that its eloquent advocates saw themselves as destined to sit there first. Nor were deputies impressed by their endless invocations of British and American precedents. Sieyès long before, not to mention Rousseau,[66] had scornfully pointed out the flaws in the vaunted British constitution, and in any case the men of 1789 already felt that their revolution was an opportunity to go beyond the imperfect products of different foreign histories. But the majority rejecting an upper house could not have been so large if great numbers of the former privileged orders had not also voted against it. Many members of the lesser nobility saw an upper chamber as consolidating hated hierarchies with entry dependent on Court or ministerial favour. 'The Senate of Mounier and Their Lordships' noted Ferrières with grim satisfaction, 'will not pass ... they will not obtain it, and justly so.'[67] And a British observer reported that 'The greater part of the Noblesse could not bear the idea, that persons of no rank or consideration in the Country should be raised to a dignity so important as this, and should be put upon a level with themselves. They therefore unite in opposing an Upper House. You may depend upon this fact, I have heard many of them say it myself, and glory in their victory.'[68]

The rejection of a second chamber destroyed the last chance that some principle of aristocracy might be built into the new constitution.

64. Tackett, *Becoming a Revolutionary*, 193.
65. Ibid., 192; Jean Egret, *La Révolution des Notables. Mounier et les Monarchiens, 1789* (Paris, 1950), 152.
66. *What is the Third Estate?*, ch. 4, sections 6 and 7; *Social Contract*, Bk.III, ch.xv.
67. *Correspondance*, 145–50. Ferrières to Mme. de Medel, 18 Sep. 1789.
68. Browning, *Despatches*, ii, 261. Jenkinson letter, 17 Sept. 1789. The author, son of a Baron, would later become prime minister as Earl of Liverpool.

With both that and the absolute royal veto defeated, the constitutional committee that had proposed them resigned. Only known dissidents like Sieyès, Le Chapelier, and Talleyrand were re-elected to its successor. Their task now was to elaborate constitutional proposals which ignored the concept of nobility entirely, and make any sort of aristocracy impossible in the regenerated Nation. 'The term Aristocrat is used here', reported Thomas Paine a few months later from Paris to Edmund Burke, whom he still unwittingly thought naturally sympathetic to the French cause,[69] 'similar to the word Tory in America;—it in general means an enemy of the Revolution, and is used without that peculiar meaning formerly fixed to Aristocracy'.

* * *

Great principles were decided in the debates of August and September, but they were not decided in calm isolation. Many of the votes were taken in an atmosphere of passion and violent emotion, sometimes altruistic, sometimes vengeful, and always in fearful awareness that the kingdom was on the verge of anarchy. Many deputies were clearly afraid that popular resentments might at any moment be turned against them. The Assembly's deliberations were watched from crowded public galleries where popular speakers were applauded and unpopular ones loudly jeered. Many of the spectators came from Paris, and they brought constant rumours about popular opinion in the capital. The centre of political agitation there was the Palais Royal, the pleasure garden opened to the public by the Duke d'Orléans in the previous decade. From there on 30 August a march set out to force the Assembly at Versailles to reject any idea of a royal veto. It was led by an eccentric nobleman, the Marquis de Saint-Huruge, and although it was turned back by Lafayette and a detachment of National Guardsmen, the idea of a march on Versailles kept surfacing throughout the debates of September. Threatening letters were received by *monarchien* spokesmen. And even after their defeat, the manifest reluctance of the king to give explicit sanction to the decrees of August kept the Palais Royal in ferment. In a context of rising unemployment in the Parisian luxury

---

69. Alfred Cobban and Robert A. Smith (eds.), *The Correspondance of Edmund Burke*, vi, *July 1789n December 1791* (Cambridge, 1967), 68, Paine to Burke, 17 Jan. 1790.

trades and among servants, as alarmed noblemen reined in their ostentatious expenditures, and renewed rumours of bread shortages, a march eventually materialized on 5 October. This time Lafayette and his National Guards were unable to stop the thousands of women who converged on Versailles, invaded the Assembly and the royal palace, massacred guardsmen, and threatened the life of the queen herself. Nor was anybody able to resist the demands of the insurgents the next day that the royal family and the National Assembly should accompany them back to Paris. From now on, both would be prisoners of the capital and its volatile people, and a sense of intimidation would be a permanent element in revolutionary politics.

Mounier was in despair. He was president of the National Assembly during the 'October Days'. His election ought to have reassured him that, despite the earlier defeat of his constitutional proposals, his influence and his following were far from extinct.[70] The popular violence would in fact produce an authoritarian backlash over the autumn from which he might have profited.[71] But instead he fled to his native Dauphiné in the vain hope of rousing the provincial Estates to reject the authority of Paris. There was talk of a mass-resignation of over 300 deputies,[72] although in the end only forty-eight, evenly divided between the three orders, left the Assembly before the end of the year.[73] Other former *monarchiens* simply fell silent.

There was much exultation in the popular press that the people had once more thwarted the machinations of aristocracy: but also a clear awareness that it had taken direct revolutionary action to do it. The Assembly was still full of the Nation's enemies, the incendiary journalist Marat warned the readers of his *Ami du Peuple* at the end of the year, so 'if some unforeseen event brings a new general insurrection, take advantage of the occasion to expel the nobles and the prelates from the National Assembly. As representatives of orders which no longer exist, they have no right to sit there.'[74] The orders had indeed melted away. Until 4 August clerical and noble deputies had still tended to sit in distinct areas of the Assembly. Afterwards, more and more they congregated with those, regardless of

70. Tackett, *Becoming a Revolutionary*, 193–6.
71. Barry M. Shapiro, *Revolutionary Justice in Paris, 1789–90* (Cambridge, 1993), 99–123.
72. Egret, *Révolution des Notables*, 192–3.
73. Tackett, *Becoming a Revolutionary*, 199–200. But they included Lally-Tollendal.
74. 29 Dec. 1789, quoted in Gérard Walter (ed.), *La Révolution française vue par ses journaux* (Paris, 1948), 88.

orders, who shared their political sympathies. At the *Te Deum* to celebrate 4 August, most non-clerical deputies abandoned the formal costumes worn at the inaugural service in May, and on 15 October, on the motion of several noble deputies, they were abolished. On the same day it was decreed, again on the motion of a nobleman, that substitute deputies for vacant seats should be elected without distinction of orders.[75] Rumours now began to circulate that the entire suppression of nobility itself was being planned. 'What enormous changes all at once!' wrote a worried nobleman from Paris to a correspondent in Belgium, 'It is like dreaming while wide awake ... it is claimed that ... nobility, distinctions, etc. will be dealt with, and that all titles of Duke, Count, Marquis and even all distinguishing signs: the king's Orders, saint-Louis, etc., will be abolished.'[76]

Such questions were certainly being discussed outside the Assembly. An anonymous pamphlet of the late summer,[77] taking stock of the sacrifices made in August, urged a general review of ennoblement. Neither money nor favour, it asserted, offered a legitimate entitlement, and nor of itself did birth. All those claiming nobility should be reviewed by a national commission every twenty years to see if they remained worthy of the status in terms of public services rendered. But for one Lambert, writing under a pseudonym later in the autumn, it was too late for any sort of nobility.[78] He called for its outright abolition, beginning with the words of d'Antraigues a year earlier[79] that hereditary nobility was the greatest scourge with which Heaven in its anger could afflict a nation. All the gains of the summer, 'won, so to speak, by assault', would remain insecure 'if we allowed to subsist among us a distinguished caste of individuals still looking to take advantage of circumstances which offer to recover the ground they have lost and to resurrect gothic pretensions which, for eight or nine centuries, have made the nation groan in most shameful servitude. The more spectacular their downfall, the less should we be tranquil over

75. Fitzsimmons, *Night the Old Regime Ended*, 118. The proposer was the Viscount de Beauharnais, husband of the future Empress Josephine.

76. Comte de Seneffe to J. B. Cogels, 6 Nov. 1789, in Pierre de Vaissière (ed.), *Lettres d''Aristocrates': La Révolution racontée par des correspondances privées 1789–1794* (Paris, 1907), 159.

77. *Essais politiques et philosophiques sur ce qu'on appelle les Trois Ordres de France* (Paris, 1789) datable from internal evidence to late August or September. (BL F tracts 14 (1)).

78. *Abolition de la noblesse héréditaire en France, proposée à l'Assemblée nationale; par un philanthrope, citoyen de Belan* (BL F tracts 92 (9)) Undated, but clearly from internal evidence after September 1789. Authorship is attributed by Carré, *Noblesse de France et l'opinion publique*, 453, n.1.

79. See above, p. 173.

the stability of the revolution, so long as titles and hereditary distinctions pass on to them the memory of their political influence and the desire to recover it.'[80] This author praised the Americans for outlawing nobility in their constitutions: he had read and approved the attack of the 'New Jersey Farmer' on John Adams.[81] He denounced Montesquieu's defence of nobility as not relevant now that absolute monarchy had gone, and reminded his readers that Rousseau and d'Argenson had been against it.[82] He offered the draft of a decree to outlaw hereditary nobility and titles, except for members of the royal family. But members of the nobility, he concluded, were unlikely to accept it without repugnance: 'the chance of birth is such a great merit for those without any other!'

It was true that some of the more obstinate standard-bearers of noble separatism had belatedly given in to the inevitable. Late in August, the nobility of two Breton bailliages (Nantes, Quimper) broke ranks with their provincial fellows who had refused even to send a delegation to the Estates-General. They told the Assembly that they now accepted everything that had been done.[83] But another former bastion of noble power was more equivocal. As decrees began to pour from the Assembly as it resumed its task of constitution-making, the question arose of whether, like former royal legislation, the new laws needed to be registered by the parlements. Ever since the ill-judged intervention by the Parlement of Paris in September 1788 in favour of the 'forms of 1614',[84] the sovereign courts who had done so much to precipitate the Revolution had enjoyed no public support. As the results of the elections showed,[85] even their fellow noblemen took pleasure in humiliating the proud self-styled 'senators'. On the Night of 4 August, a motion to abolish the parlements was only deflected by the intervention of the liberal Parisian magistrate Fréteau de Saint-Just, currently serving as one of the Assembly's secretaries, who offered the Assembly the respect of all the sovereign courts and moved the sacrifice of their special privileges, including heredity of offices and nobility. But the idea kept resurfacing in subsequent debates. And on 17 August Bergasse delivered a report from the Constitutional Committee on the future organization of the judiciary, which made clear that there

80. Marhoff, *Abolition*, 5.
81. Ibid., 23–4. See also above, pp. 135. He shared the erroneous conviction that the author was Governor William Livingston.
82. Marhoff, *Abolition*, 25, n.1.   83. Fitzsimmons, *The Night*, 116.
84. See above, p. 169.   85. See above, p. 193.

would be no place for anything like the parlements or their powers under the new order.[86] A number of provincial courts did not hesitate to express their dismay, if not outrage, and in response on 3 November Alexandre de Lameth moved that, since the parlements were now in their annual vacation, they should not be allowed to reconvene. The vacation chambers which normally handled judicial business during these times should continue to sit until provision had been made for the total replacement of the parlements.[87] These courts, he declared, had once set limits to the depredations of despotism, but now there was no doubt that 'so long as the parlements retain their old existence, the friends of liberty will not be without fear, or its enemies without hope'. His motion was passed 'almost unanimously'. Two days later the vacation chambers were ordered to register decrees of the Assembly at once, with the unspoken implication that the days of remonstrances and delayed registration were over. Most of the vacation chambers obeyed, but with an ill grace, blaming the Assembly for the disorders now afflicting their districts and the kingdom at large. Some went so far as to call the powers claimed by the Assembly illegal. The magistrates at Rouen, Dijon, and Rennes were replaced for their defiance, those of Metz largely escaped, while the entire Bordeaux chamber was summoned to Paris to be publicly reprimanded. These incidents punctuated the winter months, provoking violent exchanges in the Assembly between left and right wherever they were reported or discussed.[88] They only served to stoke anti-noble opinion and emphasize how once-powerful noblemen remained unreconciled to their losses. When, in January 1790, the Viscount de Mirabeau lamely tried to defend the defiance of the magistrates of Rennes, his elder brother, the notorious Count, unleashed a torrent of vituperation which amazed the British observer Arthur Young:

> These are men whose pretensions have long insulted any idea of social order; ... who ... after placing themselves between monarch and subjects so as to enslave the people by dominating the prince, have deceived, threatened, and betrayed by turns the one and the other at the whim of their ambitions, and set back by several centuries the day of reason and liberty ... [they] ... are nothing but the champions ... of a system which brought France two hundred years of public, individual, political, fiscal, feudal and judicial oppression.[89]

86. *Moniteur*, i, 340–7.
87. Ibid., ii, 131. See also Henri Carré, *La fin des parlements, 1788–90* (Paris, 1912), 125–138.
88. Carré, *La fin*, 139–97.   89. *Moniteur*, iii, 99–105, 9 Jan. 1790; Young, *Travels*, 250.

Young, back in Paris after six months, also noted a pervasive fear of plots to spirit the king out of Paris.[90] The corollary was sustained suspicion towards any sort of nobleman. The Paris National Guard decided to disarm and expel all former nobles in its ranks, on the grounds that weapons in such hands were too dangerous.[91] 'The abolition of noble Titles,' reported a British diplomat, 'and the extinction of orders from the St. Esprit down to the Croix de St. Louis, it is said, are to come on next.'[92] This rumour was premature, but the febrile atmosphere came to a climax in December with the revelation of a real plot. On Christmas Eve agents of the Paris commune arrested Thomas de Mathy, Marquis de Favras.[93] A familiar of Monsieur, the king's brother, Favras had been dabbling, with the discreet connivance of his patron, in schemes to restore royal independence ever since 14 July. In the course of his machinations he had made potentially incriminating contact with many influential figures and he now proved a scapegoat for all of them. Within five days of his arrest he was put on trial, accused of fomenting a conspiracy to remove the royal family from Paris, dissolve the National Assembly and murder several leading public figures. After a show trial lasting almost two months, in which the accused resolutely incriminated nobody by name, Favras was condemned to death on 18 February 1790. He was executed the next day. The trial had been extensively reported throughout by the popular press as a record of the iniquity of noble counter-revolutionaries. The verdict and sentence were greeted with jubilation throughout the capital. There was particular satisfaction that Favras was condemned to hang, rather than suffer execution by the former noble privilege of decapitation.[94] Up to 50,000 spectators watched him die, and when it was over, they called out for more. Everyone was sure that many other conspirators just as guilty had been saved by Favras's cover-up trial.

They were certainly right. From the start the Favras trial had been orchestrated by Lafayette, who felt as commander of the National Guard

90. Ibid., 251, 10 Jan. 1790. On plot mania, see Tackett, Becoming a Revolutionary, 245–7.
91. M. de Lescure, Correspondance secrète inédite sur Louis XVI, Marie-Antoinette la cour et la ville, 2 vols. (Paris, 1866), ii, 402, 20 Nov. 1789.
92. Browning, Despatches, ii, 277, Fitz-Gerald to Duke of Leeds, 6 Nov. 1789.
93. See Shapiro, Revolutionary Justice, 124–74, for a definitve discussion of the Favras affair and its significance. For the position of Lafayette, Louis Gottschalk, and Margaret Maddox, Lafayette in the French Revolution: From the October Days through the Federation (Chicago, IL, 1973), ch. 6.
94. Equality of capital punishment had been explicitly decreed by the National Assembly only as recently as December 1789: Shapiro, Revolutionary Justice, 169.

that he held the Nation's destiny in his hands. By heaping all the blame for counter-revolutionary plotting on to the hapless Marquis, Lafayette hoped to efface rather than exacerbate political divisions.[95] At the same time he was urging the king to discountenance further conspiracies by declaring unequivocal support for the work of the Revolution and putting himself at the head of it. Rumours that such a gesture was imminent circulated throughout January, and it finally materialized on 4 February, before the Favras trial was over.[96] With studied lack of ceremonial, the king walked from the Tuileries to the Assembly and there declared, in a speech largely written by Necker, his personal commitment to constitutional monarchy and the achievements of the Revolution. He exhorted his fellow citizens to harmony and reconciliation but warned against extremism. He appealed for particular restraint in legislating for religion, and pleaded for the deputies to respect the 'transmission of titles' of an 'honoured race' whose 'continuity of services' was 'a distinction that nothing can destroy'.[97] Frenzied applause, and a patriotic euphoria similar to that of 4 August, swept the chamber, as the deputies responded to the royal gesture with a new oath of allegiance to the Nation, the law, the king, and the constitution. Over subsequent weeks the oath was widely subscribed up and down the country. But the euphoria did not last. Many nobles remembered how the monarch had consistently failed to protect them ever since the doubling of the Third, and the royal pledge of commitment to the Revolution reassured none of those who saw it as an accelerating disaster. Alone in the hall, a group of noble deputies refused to join the applause; and on leaving, the younger Mirabeau ostentatiously broke his sword, observing that the king had just broken his sceptre.[98] Reflective patriots, meanwhile, might have noted the implicit challenge in the king's assertion that nobility could never be destroyed. Were there really limits to the power of a National Assembly which was already rapidly demolishing so many other aspects of the old regime?

Practical limits to the Assembly's power were in fact already visible to anyone willing to recognize them. With the executive paralysed, the army demoralized and afraid to act, and the old local and judicial institutions about to be dissolved and replaced, authority and order was widely perceived to have broken down. 'From the Provinces', reported

95. Gottschalk and Maddox, *Lafayette ... from the October Days*, 114–7, 203–9.
96. See Tackett, *Becoming a Revolutionary*, 275–7.   97. *AP*, xii, 430, 4 Feb. 1790.
98. M. F. Barrière (ed.), *Mémoires de Weber, frère de lait de Marie-Antoinette, reine de France* (Paris, 1885), 2912.

the British *chargé d'affaires* on 5 February, 'we have repeated accounts of violences committed on the part of the Peasantry against the Gentry, and of endless contestations'.[99] Rural disturbances were in fact rising to a new peak, with clear echoes of the atmosphere before 4 August 1789.[100] Ever since that month, the Feudal Committee of the National Assembly had been methodically working to codify the general legislation agreed then. It scarcely seems a coincidence that the Committee's preliminary report was presented to the Assembly on 8 February. The next day the Viscount de Noailles, who had launched the great wave of abolitions and renunciations on 4 August, called for the report to be discussed and implemented at once, but it was not until more influential figures like Lafayette took up the call two weeks later (22 February) that the committee's recommendations began to be discussed on the floor of the chamber.[101] The effect was nothing like as emollient as the grandiloquent renunciations of 4 August, for these recommendations spelled out in unprecedented detail which feudal rights were to be compensated before disappearing, and which were to be abolished outright. In some respects the committee's recommendations marked a retreat from the grand gestures of the previous summer,[102] slimming the list of uncompensated abolitions, even qualifying the abolition of serfdom, and stipulating reimbursement wherever a feudal right could be categorized as a contractual obligation on property. Accordingly the losses to former lords promised to be less drastic than many had feared in the confusion of the previous August. This did not prevent a number of noble deputies from denouncing the whole operation in the bitterest terms as an act of unjustified spoliation.[103] Their posturings were a reminder of the resentment harboured by many noblemen towards the Revolution's work, and the whole debate on the Feudal Committee's proposals, stretching intermittently over three weeks, was a reminder of the full panoply of former feudal dominion. Nor, for nobles, was there any avoiding of the full consequences of a proposal that had passed almost unnoticed on 4 August: the end of primogeniture. Feudal law had invariably conferred extra property and other advantages on

---

99. Browning, *Despatches*, ii, 291, Fitz-Gerald to the Duke of Leeds, 5 Feb. 1790.
100. Markoff, *Abolition*, 276, 283.
101. Gottschalk and Maddox, *Lafayette...from the October Days*, 242–3.
102. See Mackrell, *Attack on 'Feudalism'*, 174–6; Jones, *Peasantry*, 87–91; Markoff, *Abolition*, 460–2, 533–42; Fitzsimmons, *The Night*, 149–162.
103. *AP* xi, 687, 25 Feb. 1790. The Marquis de Foucault denounced the 'violence and atrocity' of certain abolitions.

eldest sons as the bearers of a family's title and principal fiefs. The precise range and proportion of privileges under the *droit d'aînesse* varied from province to province according to custom, but noble successions were invariably unequal because of it.[104] With the disappearance of fiefs and all other types of property deemed noble, distinctive forms of succession also lapsed, and children of intestate fathers acquired equal claims on all their property. Henceforth noble patrimony would be inherited on the same terms as that of commoners. It followed (though not spelt out in the debate)[105] that titles were now divorced from property, with no public law to determine their transfer. And whereas distinctions now without a rationale might seem harmless enough, this made them stand out all the more clearly as anomalous relics and reminders of a vanished and discredited order.

The effect was seen repeatedly throughout April, when further decrees clearing up residual feudal rights were discussed and passed. When one participant in the debates was described in the official record as a 'Breton gentleman' (*gentilhomme breton*), there was general applause for the objection raised by the Breton deputy Lanjuinais that such a description was inappropriate. It was an 'old and absurd usage' when only the quality of citizen was entitled to recognition.[106] A letter sent to the *Moniteur* the same day warned that the Revolution was not yet accomplished in French minds, that 'aristocracy, dethroned by the constitution, reigns on in habits', and that deference to nobles and respect for titles and ribands was still instinctive.[107]

Another reminder of old iniquities came early in April, with the publication of the so-called *Livre Rouge* (*Red Book*), a list of secret 'gratifications' distributed by the crown since 1774. Pensions and other handouts had been assumed from the start of the Revolution to be one of despotism's more insidious instruments, and on 22 September 1789 the National Assembly had authorized the publication of a list of names subsidized by the king. When the first instalment, comprising annual payments of over 30,000*l*. appeared in November, the popular press exploded with

---

104. See above, p. 15.

105. The full debate on this clause, 25 Feb. 1790, in *AP* xi, 599–601. On how the implications were ignored, see Garaud, *Histoire générale du droit privé français*, 97.

106. *Moniteur*, iv, 205, 26 Apr. 1790.

107. Ibid., 196–7, 25 Apr. 1790. The letter was anonymous, but some of the phraseology is reminiscent of Grouvelle's attack on duelling: see below, p. 231.

righteous outrage at the opulent 'beggars' and 'vampires' of the Court who monopolized these large sums.[108] But nobles outside Court circles shared the disgust, and took the lead in Assembly debates on the pensions question in denouncing these privileged 'spoilt children'.[109] It was decreed in January that no pensions over 3,000*l.* would continue to be paid, and the Assembly ordered its pensions committee to demand the release of a more secret list of payments for nominally diplomatic purposes. This was the *Red Book*, and initial resistance by Necker to its publication whetted the public appetite for its revelations. They did not disappoint. A good quarter of 228 millions distributed since the beginning of the reign had gone to princes, ministers, and favourites, many already substantial beneficiaries of other pensions and sinecures. Thousands queued to buy the first printed instalments,[110] and the details they contained dominated the popular press for much of April. But this time it was not just the parasites of the Court who were denounced. Camille Desmoulins, who had criticized the pensions list with heavy irony in the very first issue of his notorious *Révolutions de France et de Brabant* in November 1789, now asked how anyone could regret the old order after reading the *Red Book*.[111] Men of title, he observed:

> cannot bear the thought of being equal in rights to so many citizens, with whom they could in no way bear to compete in virtues, talents, services. Ah! If Mirabeau himself, dear Mirabeau, who has deserved so well of the nation, and for whom it would seem the name of Demosthenes should suffice, if he still signs himself *Count de Mirabeau*, if I read underneath M. de Lafayette's portrait, *M. le Marquis*, can I believe that this multitude of former princes and dukes, such nullities, so contemptible, so imperceptible in themselves... could bring themselves to return to the class of insects and the smallest of the small?[112]

No journalist failed to notice, either, that two of the Lameth brothers, leading radical orators in the Assembly and moving spirits in the rapidly expanding Jacobin Club, had had their education paid for by a secret grant from the king, secured by the intercession of the queen. Right-wing commentators gloated at their embarrassment, patriots huffed and puffed to

108. Carré, *Noblesse de France et l'opinion*, 438–41. For the main debates, *AP* xi, 51–4.
109. Baron Félix de Wimpffen: ibid., 54.
110. Ruault, *Gazette d'un Parisien*, 188–9, 193, 195–6, 198–9.
111. *Révolutions de France et de Brabant*, no. 23, 340.
112. Ibid., 456: 'la classe... des infiniment petits'.

defend their youthful innocence, while the brothers themselves borrowed money to pay their grants back into the treasury.[113]

Everything now happening seemed to reflect badly on the nobility. Throughout the autumn, American speculators had been advertising the delights of settlements along the river Scioto, in the still-virgin territory of Ohio.[114] In February 1790 Duval d'Eprémesnil and his wife bought 11,000 acres, urging their noble friends to join them in financing a colony there. But their plans were closely followed by the popular press, which accused them of robbing the kingdom of coinage and able-bodied inhabitants in the search for a noble paradise far from French turmoil, where they could 'rebuild their castles with their towers and the right of cuissage and dovecotes'.[115] The controversy ran on throughout the spring. Then late in March, the press began to report a new conspiracy, in which an experienced soldier, the Count de Maillebois, was alleged to be plotting an armed return of the Count d'Artois from his current base in Turin with the aid of an uprising in the south.[116] Maillebois had fled to the Dutch Republic by the time the news broke, but the story underlined how counter-revolutionary many nobles still were. Other issues also rumbled on throughout the spring. As the old structure of the church was dismantled, and a new Civil Constitution of the Clergy was elaborated, attention was repeatedly drawn to the way noblemen had monopolized ecclesiastical power before 1789. The closure of monasteries and convents, and the prohibition of binding vows, brought a spectacular end to age-old noble appropriation of the revenues and facilities of the cloistered life. A particularly complex issue was that of the Order of Malta, based in a sovereign territory outside France but enjoying extensive ecclesiastical privileges and properties within. It was chiefly notorious, however, for the stringency of the proofs of nobility required of entrants with no other commitment to the order's purposes than to advertise their families' pedigrees.[117] The suppression of the order was discussed in the Assembly several times between November 1789 and April 1790. In March the official genealogist of the order sought to defend

113. *Révolutions de Paris*, 39, 6–12 Apr. 1790; *Mémoires de Weber*, 293.
114. Jean Bouchary, *Les compagnies financières à Paris à la fin du xviiie siècle*, 3 vols. (Paris, 1943), iii, 127–151.
115. *Révolutions de France et de Brabant*, 8 Mar. 1790, quoted by Bouchary, Les compagnies, 135.
116. Shapiro, *Revolutionary Justice*, 175–87.
117. For example, the admission of Chateaubriand in 1788: *Mémoires d'outre-tombe*, liv. 5, ch. 5. For the Order of Malta, see Alain Blondy, *L'Ordre de Malte au xviiie siècle: Des dernières splendeurs à la ruine* (Paris, 2002), esp. pp. 282–97.

it by a general reminder of the value of nobility.[118] He clearly feared that the quality itself was under threat, despite the services which noblemen had always rendered and could still, with certain minimal reforms encouraging a return to their traditional military vocation. And he warned, echoing the king on 4 February, that 'the glory of our forefathers is a benefit that we cannot lose and that cannot be wrested from us'.[119]

Such repeated attempts to defend the indefensible must have alarmed all those who hoped that nobility might wither away under the impact of the countless losses it had sustained since the National Assembly had come into being. To radicals, no aspect of noble behaviour was now beyond suspicion. There was disquiet, for example, at the persistence of duelling as a way of settling political disagreements. Noble deputies had made duels a regular feature of life among members of the National Assembly. Such behaviour disgusted Grouvelle, already one of the most persistent public enemies of the nobility and its values.[120] He was one of the first non-deputies to join the Jacobin Club, and early in the year he persuaded it to print and distribute to its affiliates a *Projet d'Adresse à l'Assemblée Nationale sur le duel* (*Proposed Address to the National Assembly on Duelling*)[121] in which he complained that 'Aristocracy, dethroned by the constitution, still reigns in habits' such as duelling. But this was a 'monument of degenerate feudalism, the abuse of abuses', based on 'false honour', 'shameful illusions', and 'the prejudices of a few families'. The club had a number of noble members, including Cloots and the Count de Moreton-Chabrillan, who had so outraged commoner sensitivities at the theatre in 1782.[122] Perhaps they supported Grouvelle to emphasize renunciation of their former privileged position. It was certainly alleged later that the anti-noble stance of Alexandre de Lameth, the leading orator in these early months of the club, was assumed in order to further his political ambitions.[123] Perhaps, too, the Lameth brothers were hoping to expunge the memory of their inclusion in the *Red Book*. What is certain is that by April their activities had begun to alarm other men of ambition. Despairing of countering Lameth's grip on the Jacobins, they supported

---

118. *Hommage à ma patrie: Considérations sur la Noblesse de France. Par M. De la Croix, généalogiste de l'Ordre de Malte* (Paris, 1790), dated 18 Mar. 1790.
119. Ibid., 22. See above p. 226.
120. For his earlier interventions in public debates, see above, p. 183–4.
121. See F. A. Aulard (ed.), *La Société des Jacobins: Recueil de documents*, 6 vols. (Paris, 1889–1897), i, 225–39.
122. See above, pp. 146–7.
123. Berville and Barrière (eds.), *Mémoires du Marquis de Ferrières*, 3 vols. (Paris, 1822), ii, 62–3.

moves to set up a rival club by a group of like-minded moderates who had already been congregating informally since late the previous year: the Society of 1789.[124]

Conceived by Sieyès and Condorcet, the new society aimed to combine the qualities of a political club, an intellectual circle, and a vehicle of public instruction. Juggling these diverse roles proved impossible, and the society scarcely survived a year. But during the first four months following its official launch on 12 April, it was taken up by Lafayette and his allies as a counterweight to the Lameth-dominated Jacobins.[125] At the same time they tried to steer public business in the Assembly in moderate directions by concerting action in an informal committee. It met at the house of the Duke de la Rochefoucauld-Enville, whose liberal credentials went back to the translation he had made in 1783 of the constitutions of the new American states.[126] And it was there, on 4 June, that the practicality of abolishing hereditary nobility and its outward signs appears to have been seriously discussed for the first time among men with the power to bring it about. The evidence comes from Mirabeau, who was present in the hope of concerting a plan to bolster the monarchy with Lafayette.[127] The Count was clearly frustrated by the time devoted by the committee to an idea that he had himself been the first to advocate openly back in 1784. Now he laughed at such plans, seeing the plight of the king as altogether more urgent. But they seem to have gone ahead, and it seems possible that the king himself had some forewarning. Early in June he ordered the secretary of state Saint-Priest to write to Chérin, the Court genealogist, with instructions to discontinue scrutiny of proofs of ancestry as a qualification for any office under the crown.[128] The letter was published, prompting speculation that the king wished to pre-empt the abolition of noble credentials themselves by making them useless.[129] On 17 June, meanwhile, the Society of 1789

124. See K. M. Baker, 'Politics and Social Science in Eighteenth Century France: The Société de 1789', in J. F. Bosher (ed.), *French Government and Society, 1500–1850: Essays in Memory of Alfred Cobban* (London, 1973), 208–230; Mark Olsen, 'A Failure of Enlightened Politics in the French Revolution: The Société de 1789', *French History*, 6 (1992), 303–34.

125. Gottschalk and Maddox, *Lafayette . . . from the October Days*, 316–20.

126. See above, p. 125.

127. A. de Bacourt (ed.), *Correspondance entre le Comte de Mirabeau et le Comte de La Marck pendant les années 1789, 1790 et 1791*, 3 vols. (Paris, 1851), ii, 34, Mirabeau to La Marck, 4 June 1790.

128. *Gazette de Paris*, 16 June 1790.

129. See Jean Chalon (ed.), *Mémoires de Madame la Duchesse de Tourzel* (Paris, 1969), 81.

held a glittering banquet to celebrate the first anniversary of the formation of the National Assembly, that moment when the Third Estate turned its back on a separatist nobility. What more appropriate occasion to complete the work?

* * *

The proposal, when it came, looked unplanned. In the chair on 19 June was Jacques-François de Menou, a Baron of old stock who had voted consistently against noble separatism and was a long-standing member of the Jacobin Club. He had been president of the Assembly during the first fortnight of April, and was now deputizing for the absent Sieyès. Some thought, in retrospect, that Sieyès's absence was deliberate, and perhaps concerted.[130] Camille Desmoulins claimed that the whole session was the product of a 'momentary union of the two clubs',[131] but Alexandre de Lameth, in his memoirs, insisted that it was 'the result of a spontaneous movement and not of a plan settled in advance'.[132] It was certainly not part of the official order of the day. That was about arrangements to celebrate the first anniversary of the fall of the Bastille.[133] The Assembly even began by setting up a new exclusive body: an armed and uniformed company of accredited 'Conquerors of the Bastille'. It then admitted the 'Deputation of Foreigners' led by Cloots,[134] and when it had left Alexandre de Lameth proposed that by 14 July the enslaved figures at the foot of Louis XIV's statue in the Place des Victoires should be removed as 'monuments of pride which should not survive under the reign of equality'. These were the words which, by accident or design, prompted Lambel to propose that the

130. Ferrières, who witnessed the scene, claimed in his memoirs that the Lameths had fixed on Menou to preside: *Mémoires*, ii, 64.
131. *Révolutions de France et de Brabant*, xxxi, 346.
132. Alexandre de Lameth, *Histoire de l'Assemblée constituante*, 2 vols. (Paris, 1828), i, 446. See also Doina Pasca Harsanyi, 'The Memoirs of Lameth and the Reconciliation of Nobility and Revolution', in Jay M. Smith (ed.), *The French Nobility in the Eighteenth Century: Reassessments and New Approaches* (University Park, PA, 2006), 279–302.
133. *Moniteur*, iv, 675, 19 June 1790. In some ways, this body was curiously reminiscent of the American Society of the Cincinnati—a veterans' organization, though not hereditary. When on 25 June the 'Conquerors of the Bastille' petitioned the Assembly not to grant them any privileged place in the 14 July ceremonies, Roederer observed that they were following the example of the Cincinnati when they renounced heredity: *AP*, xxvi, 464.
134. See above, p. 3.

use of titles be forbidden. He also appears to have proposed the proscription of hereditary nobility itself.[135] Lambel was unknown, seemingly even to the Lameths,[136] but when loud applause from the left greeted his intervention, they clearly sensed a moment to seize. The elder brother Charles supported the proposal to prohibit titles as remnants of abolished feudalism, and denounced hereditary nobility as inimical to political equality and the encouragement of civic virtue. The title of noble, he said, was a 'puerile distinction'. Lafayette, who had long claimed (in private) to share these views, now rushed to add his own support. Outshone in radicalism by a political rival, he rather sourly observed that such a necessary motion scarcely needed support, but that it had his if it did. He took care, however, to intervene several times subsequently to declare various other speakers too timid. The first opponent to speak, the Marquis de Foucault, recalled that abolishing nobility had been moved on 4 August but rejected. He may not have been correct,[137] but his intervention certainly placed abolition in the logic of the Assembly's previous achievements. The discussion was then given focus by Goupil de Préfelne, a leading Jacobin, who declared that he had long before prepared a draft decree for abolishing titles, which he now read out. Clearly here was somebody who had come prepared, if not for this moment, then one quite soon.[138] Quick-witted conservatives now claimed that this was a constitutional issue, and that the Assembly had recently voted to discuss such fundamental matters only in the morning, much less the Saturday evening that this was. Postponement would, of course, give opponents time to rally their forces; but the left, now in full cry, insisted that the debate go on. Lafayette himself joined them, arguing that abolition of nobility would not be part of the constitution, but merely its 'necessary consequence'.[139]

An atmosphere which many compared to that of 4 August was now developing, with noblemen joining an orgy of renunciations. The Viscount

---

135. Only the proposal on titles is recorded in the *Moniteur* and *AP*. But Charles de Lameth's speech immediately afterwards mentions a 'second proposition' in connection with hereditary nobility.

136. Lameth, *Histoire de l'Assemblée constituante*, i, 435.

137. There is nothing in the scanty and ambiguous records of the Night of 4 August about the outright abolition of nobility.

138. Fitzsimmons, *The Night*, 125, reports, without citing a source, that Goupil's proposal was two months old; Tackett, *Becoming a Revolutionary*, 292, speculates that he might have hoped to introduce it on 20 June, the anniversary of the Tennis Court Oath.

139. *Moniteur*, iv, 678; *AP* xvi, 376. See also Gottschalk and Maddox, *Lafayette ... from the October Days*, 421–3.

de Noailles, anxious to repeat his spectacular intervention then, called for liveries to be forbidden as humiliating to citizens. Virtues alone should confer distinctions, as in America; and he invoked among others the example of Franklin, whose recent death had been solemnly acknowledged by the Assembly only a week before with three days of mourning.[140] President de Saint-Fargeau of the Parlement of Paris, a Marquis and a Count several times over, proposed that only family names should henceforth be authorized, and asked that he should be allowed to sign his motion with his own, Le Peletier. The Count de Montmorency, from one of the oldest noble families whose head called himself the premier Baron of Christendom, made up for arriving late[141] by advocating the abolition of 'marks which most recall the feudal system and the chivalric spirit': coats of arms. For a time the tide was stemmed by the most eloquent of conservative deputies, the *abbé* Jean-Siffrein Maury, who was already in a mood of continuous outrage at reforms concurrently being debated for the Church. He tried to swing the discussion back to the statues in the Place des Victoires, but with characteristic verbosity could not resist the bigger issue. 'In France', he declared, 'the nobility is constitutional; if there is no longer a nobility, there is no longer a monarchy.' Nobody took issue with this stark (if impeccably Montesquieuan) analysis; but when Maury in a second long intervention claimed that the nobility was not feudal in origin but went back to the Gauls, he was interrupted with cries of 'Read Mably!'[142] The left was now clamouring for a vote on a new composite draft decree from Le Chapelier, incorporating the various proposals made since Lambel's first intervention. They were urged on by cheering from the public galleries. Stunned noble deputies on the right frothed inarticulately as Menou gave priority to speakers who sought to refine rather than reject Le Chapelier's draft. Taken by surprise, they lacked the numbers and the collective discipline to block the drift of an increasingly emotional evening. Those who managed to speak tended to invoke an authority long superseded: the *cahiers* of their constituents instructing them to vote for nothing to the detriment of their fellow nobles. Several declared that if

---

140. *Moniteur*, iv, 600–601, 10 June 1790.
141. This he admitted in his speech, perhaps inadvertently revealing evidence of preconcerted plans.
142. This clearly refers to Bk. I, ch. 5 of Mably's *Observations sur l'histoire de France* (1765, reprinted in *Oeuvres completes*, 1785): 'De l'origine de la noblesse parmi les Français'. See also above, pp. 78–9.

the decree passed, they would feel obliged to secede from the Assembly forthwith. But, ignoring the warning of Count Landenberg-Wagenbourg that nobility was a quality of the blood that nothing could remove,[143] the Assembly passed the decree 'amidst applause and shouts of joy':

> Hereditary nobility [it declared] is abolished forever; ... in consequence, the titles of prince, of Duke, of Count, of Marquis, Viscount, vidame, Baron, knight, milord, esquire, noble, and all other similar titles, shall neither be taken by nor given to anybody;
>
> ... No French citizen shall assume other than the true name of his family;
>
> ... nor shall he either wear or have worn livery, or have a coat of arms;
>
> ... titles of my lord or lords shall not be given to any body, or any individual, nor the titles of excellency, highness, eminence or greatness.[144]

Echoing conciliatory fears expressed by some deputies that its provisions might encourage gratuitous destruction of the symbols of nobility, the decree forbade any interference with monuments in churches or other public places, charters, or private muniments. Nor was the decree to take effect until after 14 July in Paris, and three months later outside. But those who hoped in this way to soften the consequences of the decree were only deluding themselves.

* * *

Concerted or not, the decree to abolish hereditary nobility and the display of its attributes was not a bolt from the blue. Alexandre de Lameth was right to recall that 'Already, for some time, the idea of suppressing nobility was brewing in the minds, not of the people, but of the elite of the Third Estate.'[145] He went on: 'when one lives in comfort, having received a good education and become knowledgeable, one ... is reluctant to bear superiorities whose justification one finds insufficient. This natural sentiment was given new force by events and the principles of equality that, every day were professed from the platform. Orders having been destroyed, distinctions which recalled them, wounding to the deputies of the third, appeared to them in contradiction with the new system, and it cannot be doubted that they were ready to demand, sooner or later, their abolition.'

---

143. See above, p. 5.   144. *Moniteur*, vi, 679; *AP*, 379.
145. *Histoire de l'Assemblée constituante*, i, 445–6.

In that sense Jefferson's former secretary was right when he wrote to him from Paris that 'Saturday evening last may be considered the complement of the 4th August.'[146]

Yet, with the exception of Lambel, it was not aggrieved members of the former Third Estate who took the lead on either occasion. The running was made by noblemen, mostly of distinguished lineage. Several—Lafayette, Noailles, the Lameths—had served in America, and there imbibed a republican indifference (at the very least) to European social distinctions. Perhaps this made them all the more ready to sacrifice nobility in a political auction to advertise their rival revolutionary credentials. Others, such as Fréteau (vocal in both sessions) and Saint-Fargeau appear to have been genuinely convinced that nobility and its prerogatives, however residual, were an impediment to the regeneration of the Nation as an egalitarian and meritocratic community. Outside the Assembly, and in the radical press of Paris especially, hostility to the very principle of nobility and, increasingly, the persons of nobles, had been widespread and perhaps growing over the winter of 1789–90. But it took the collusive populism of deputies seeking easy ways to demonstrate their patriotism and lack of regret for the *ancien régime*, to give the overthrow of nobility the force of law.

The Marquis de Ferrières was appalled by the decree, and even more by the circumstances in which it was passed. But even if more deputies on the right had been present, he thought, it would still have passed.[147] Suppression of the nobility had for too long been 'the object of public wishes in the great part of the Nation'.[148] On reflection, he even saw a bright side. The decree 'only attacks opinion, and law never did destroy opinion. Nobility had gone in fact...what was left for nobles? Opinion, an old habit of respect. But would the decree prevent any man from being his father's son, and Nobility from being passed on, as it once was, by tradition?'[149] The important point was for nobles 'not to expose themselves by useless resistance to the drunken rage of a deluded people'; for sooner or later nobility would re-emerge. Ferrières carefully followed this line of conduct, returning after the end of the Assembly to his estates in Poitou, and there cooperating with every succeeding regime. But when, after nine more years, he came to write his memoirs, the perspective lent by intervening

146. *Jefferson Papers*, 16, 571, William Short to Jefferson, 25 June 1790.
147. *Correspondance*, 214–5, Ferrières to Mme. de Medel, 22 June 1790.
148. Ibid., 207, Ferrières to Monsieur de Chacé.   149. Loc. cit., n. 147.

events had darkened his analysis. Public opinion, he was sure, 'would have achieved without effort, within a few years, what this decree risked never bringing about.'[150] But the attempt to abolish nobility at the same moment as other long-hallowed bodies came under attack had proved disastrous. 'Until then', the Marquis reflected, 'nobles had borne, with a good deal of patience, everything that the National Assembly had done against them. Most, indeed, of the provincial gentry, had watched the new constitution establish itself without regret. From this moment, a proud illusion made them its irreconcilable enemies. A league was formed between the nobility, the clergy, the parlements; these three bodies, which detested each other before the Revolution, came together in common cause, and worked with equal activity to overthrow an order of things in which no place was left for them.' The abolition certainly gave them a common cause, and no doubt the activity of the various elements who worked to reverse it was equal. But they proved no more capable of working in unison than they ever had. The revolutionary struggle would, in fact, provide nobles with new reasons to despise one another.

150. *Mémoires*, ii, 74.

8

Ci-devants, 1790–1792

A s on 5 August 1789, members of the National Assembly awoke on 20 June 1790 wondering quite what they had done, and what it would mean. Although the Assembly went on later in the day to embody the decisions of the previous evening into a formal decree, and refused to accept any protests against it, it showed no appetite to take matters further. When on 25 June Menou called for the suppression of orders of chivalry, and their replacement by a single 'national order', he was shouted down.[1] For the deputies were already aware that popular reaction to the decree in Paris had been practically instantaneous. Liveried servants were attacked, and coaches displaying coats of arms pursued with hostile shouts. Foreign diplomats, specifically exempted from the decree, were thrown into alarm, and petitioned in vain for government protection.[2]

Mirabeau, in the second of the secret notes of advice which he was now sending to the king,[3] denounced the abolition decree as a 'madness… in which Lafayette was, either stupidly or perfidiously, entirely complicit; a madness that I regard as the spark for civil war through the excesses and violence of all sorts of which a decree, even more senseless by the way it was passed than by its provisions, will inevitably become the cause.' But Lafayette was worried too. However much he opposed nobility in principle, he had been bounced into taking a public stance at a moment not of his own choosing, and he appears to have hoped that the decree could be modified.[4] The way to achieve this was to persuade the king to veto it. The king had yet to make use of the suspensive veto accorded him under

1. *AP* xvi, 464, 25 June 1790; Ferrières, *Correspondance*, 220. Ferrières to Mme. de Ferrières, 26 June 1790.
2. Fontana et al., *Venise et la Révolution*, 430, 29 June 1790; Oscar Browning (ed.) *The Despatches of Earl Gower* (Cambridge, 1885),7, 25 June 1790.
3. Bacourt, *Correspondance*, ii, 38–9, 20 June 1790.
4. Gottschalk and Maddox, *Lafayette…from the October Days*, 426, 429–31.

the constitution the previous September, and this seemed an ideal occasion to demonstrate the legislative independence of a constitutional monarch. On 25 June Lafayette took this proposal to a meeting with ministers, and here he learnt that others had had the same idea. In council, Necker and other ministers had urged Louis XVI to refuse his sanction. But the king ignored them. 'He had persuaded himself,' one minister recalled,[5] 'that by its mistakes and bad measures the Assembly would fall into disrepute' and that 'the kingdom would be revolted by its excesses.' Lafayette now appealed to him at least to defer announcing his sanction, but he was ignored, too. Necker, increasingly frustrated by royal inertia or *politique du pire*, decided, as he so often had before, to appeal to the public. On 29 June he published the letter which he had drafted for the king to send to the Assembly setting out the grounds for his veto.[6]

The idea was not to reject the law out of hand, but to ask the Assembly to reconsider it in the light of certain 'observations'. After all the advantages of which the nobility had been justly deprived by the Revolution, Necker asked, what extra purpose was served by additionally proscribing nobles' 'honorific distinctions which form part of their heritage, and whose loss must be more painful to them than that of the pecuniary advantages which they had possessed?' These new penalties were useless to the Nation, and might even impel 'a numerous class of citizens' to 'seek to enjoy in other countries the advantages which they hold from their birth.' They were economically damaging too, in throwing out of work the makers of braids and ribbons adorning liveries. Neither liveries nor coats of arms, in any case, were any longer a noble monopoly. There was a serious risk in the decree of 'misleading the people on the true meaning of that word *equality,* which can never signify, in a civilised nation and in an already established society, equality of rank and property.' And all these consequences would follow from a decree that in many respects was fundamentally unenforceable. Repeating the claim that he had put into the king's mouth on 4th February,[7] Necker asserted that 'no decree, no law … no authority' could destroy heredity. If its outward show could be prohibited in France, French laws could not bind other nations to deny

---

5. Baron de Barante (ed.), *Comte de Saint-Priest. Mémoires,* 2 vols. (Paris, 1929), 24–5. See also Egret, *Necker,* 420–3.

6. *Observations de M. Necker, relativement au décret de l'Assemblée nationale concernant les titres, les noms et les armoiries.* Reprinted in *AP* xvi, 387–9.

7. See above.

nobles recognition, and in the final analysis, 'decrees cannot wipe out the value of opinions'. 'It is never by law that ancient opinions are destroyed in a kingdom as vast as France; these opinions are the work of time, and time alone can destroy them; all great changes need to be prepared.'

Many of these sentiments had already been expressed in protests sent by noble deputies to the president of the Assembly. But the new president, elected on 21 June, was Le Peletier, who had moved the clause in the decree prohibiting the use of other than family names. He refused to accept the protests, and they were not published in the official record, the *Moniteur*.[8] Deputies who had been absent on 19 June denounced the way the decree had been passed, in an evening session with no advance notice on the order paper. Others who had been there complained that their attempts to intervene had been ignored. Several observed that the throne itself was hereditary and that to abolish nobility was to impugn the monarchy from which it was inseparable. Some declared that noble status was a form of property, and as such was constitutionally guaranteed under Article 17 of the Declaration of the Rights of Man and the Citizen. And most made the point that legislation could not deprive them of a quality inherited in the blood of their ancestors. The constituents who had elected him, declared Count François d'Escars[9] (whose proven nobility went back to 1281) 'would not believe that any human power could prevent them from passing on to their descendants the quality of *gentleman*, which they had received *only from God*'. Eventually 138 noble deputies, over half those remaining in the Assembly by this time, signed and published a formal protest against the decree.[10] It was the signal for a new wave of protests from beyond the Assembly. They invoked the age-old glorious service to king and nation of a brave and honour-bound order. They invoked the historical endorsement of Montesquieu. They noted the absence of any demand in the *cahiers* of 1789 for nobility to be terminated. They claimed it as a property guaranteed by the Declaration of Rights. They warned with Necker of damaging economic repercussions. Above all, they seized on the claim that no power on earth could deprive nobles of their illustrious ancestors and the bloodline derived from them. Some of the protests came from individuals prepared to pay to print their

---

8. They are to be found in *AP* xvi, 379–386. Several were also printed and published separately.
9. Ibid., protest of 21 June 1790. It was subsequently published in the *Gazette de Paris*, 25 June 1790.
10. *Protestation de cent trente-huit gentilshommes ... contre le décret du 19 juin 1790* (Paris, 1790).

opinions. Others came from informal local assemblies of outraged squires and men of title.[11] None appear to have come from non-nobles, with the solitary exception of Mounier, who had already turned his back on the Assembly and all its works.[12] Many consigned their indignation to the conservative press, which now seemed to unite for the first time around a single issue.[13] Nothing, declared the *Gazette de Paris* on 23 June, was now unthinkable if this could happen, and the king might as well say, *No more monarchy*. Would people, asked the satirical *Actes des Apôtres*, whose surnames happened to be Earl, Knight and Noble be able to use them in future?[14]

The prohibition of proper titles took effect immediately. The most title-holders felt able to do was to qualify their family name with 'formerly' or *ci-devant*. This changed the meaning of *ci-devant* for ever. Ever since, it has only been used to describe those who were noble before the Revolution. Le Peletier gave the lead, and most duly followed, although few could be persuaded to start calling Mirabeau Riqueti or Lafayette, Motier. Among the Assembly's secretaries signing the official decree was Maximilien *de* Robespierre, but this was the last occasion on which he used his usurped particle. Camille Desmoulins even suggested that the new law required Louis XVI to be known as Capet,[15] and the king's opportunistic cousin Orléans cheerfully adopted this family name at once. Enforcing this part of the decree became a sort of crusade for the jobbing journalist Jacques-Antoine Dulaure. Long a foe of the curious and irrational distinctions of pre-revolutionary society, Dulaure now started to compile a concordance of the titles and family names of prominent figures, embellished with scurrilous anecdotes about them.[16] Most of you, he told *ci-devants* in a

---

11. Fitzsimmons, *The Night*, 129–131; Patrice Higonnet, *Class, Ideology and the Rights of Nobles during the French Revolution* (Oxford, 1981), 61–2.

12. J. J.Mounier, *Réflexions politiques sur les circonstances présentes* (Geneva, undated), 5–51.

13. Murray, *The Right Wing Press*, 105–6.

14. *Actes des Apôtres*, cxxix, 154–61. The French names are Lecomte, Chevalier, Lenoble.

15. *Révolutions de France et de Brabant*, no. 620, 7.

16. *Liste des noms des ci-devant nobles, nobles de race, robins, financiers, intrigans, et de tous les aspirans à la noblesse, ou escrocs d'icelle; avec des notes sur leurs familles* (Paris, l'An second de la liberté) (BL FR tracts 127 (16)). It was reissued in revised form in 1791 as *Etrennes à la Noblesse, ou précis historique et critique, sur l'origine des ci-devant ducs, comtes, barons, etc., excellences, monseigneurs, grandeurs, demi-seigneurs et anoblis* (BL FR tracts 128 (23)). Another example of the genre is Louis Brossard, *Les Métamorphoses, ou liste des noms de famille et patronimiques des ci-devant ducs, Marquis, comtes, barons etc., excellences monseigneurs, grandeurs, demi-seigneurs et anoblis* (1790).

preface,[17] owe your nobility to money, often made in far from noble ways. And how many in their genealogies did not have 'high and mighty lords who deserved to be hanged... if you do not wish to inherit their dishonour, you must necessarily renounce inheriting their glory'. He also wished to 'bring down the insolent pride of some nobles of recent date, who have even more arrogance than former nobles of race... by exposing the story of their ennoblement to the eyes of the public.' At the same time Dulaure was writing a 325-page 'critical history of the nobility where are exposed its prejudices, its brigandage, its crimes, and where it is proved that it has been the scourge of liberty, of reason, of human knowledge and constantly the enemy of peoples and of kings.'[18] 'Everything' he concluded,[19] 'which contributes to the happiness of people, to the prosperity of empires, and to the glory of the human spirit, has been the work of non-nobles. Everything which has contributed to chaining up reason, brutalising the mind, degrading government and mankind, has been the work of the nobility.' But why did all this need to be said now that it had been abolished? Here Dulaure was closer to Necker than he might have cared to admit.[20] 'I reply that, if the body of the nobility is destroyed, pretended nobles are not, that the prejudice of their elevation above other men, still exists in its entirety. All the laws of an empire can be renewed in an instant; but it takes centuries to change opinions, it is not in a day that prejudices established among almost all peoples, strengthened and consecrated by more than twelve centuries, are wiped out.' How many people read Dulaure's anti-noble polemics is unknown, but one who did was a young Corsican officer, of petty noble extraction himself.[21] From Dulaure Napoleon Bonaparte learnt how worthless the rule of a hereditary nobility could be; but perhaps also that there were deep-rooted prejudices in favour of nobility that it was more advantageous to harness than to flout.

But this was not the mood of the radical press and pamphleteers in the weeks after the abolition decree.[22] They exulted in the final downfall of the once mighty. 'The gothic monuments of domination and pride

---

17. *Liste des noms*, 4–5.
18. *Histoire critique de la noblesse, depuis le commencement de la monarchie, jusqu'à nos jours* (Paris, 1790).
19. Ibid., 316.   20. Ibid., vii.
21. Jean Tulard, *Napoléon et la noblesse d'Empire* (3rd edn., Paris, 2001), 18.
22. Jack Richard Censer, *Prelude to Power: The Parisian Radical Press, 1789–1791* (Baltimore: MD, 1976), 42–3, 48–9.

have just been overturned,' crowed Marat on 23 June.[23] 'They have gone forever from the face of the kingdom, and the French, freed from the hands of illusion, have at last remembered their common origin.' But he was suspicious of the participation of nobles in their own downfall, and warned his readers to be on the lookout for plots. And by the end of the month he was echoing one of the noble participants in the debate of 19th. In a desperate call to have the issue discussed in a morning session, Count de Faucigny had responded to heckling from the left by asking why the Assembly was overlooking 'bankers and usurers'.[24] Marat agreed. 'What will we have gained' he asked in one of the Revolution's most celebrated rhetorical questions,[25] 'in destroying the aristocracy of nobles, if it is replaced by the aristocracy of wealth? And if we must groan under the yoke of these jumped-up newcomers, it would have been better to keep the privileged orders.' For Camille Desmoulins, however, there was no equivocation.[26] 'The decree of 19 June, the most decisive for democrats, the most mortal for aristocrats, that has ever been passed... deserves to be written in letters of gold on the triumphal arch in the Champ de Mars.'[27]

Desmoulins and a number of other pamphleteers devoted considerable space to attacking Necker's *Observations*. Ferrières believed that if Necker had not intervened the decree would have been rapidly forgotten, since all other protest had come from predictable quarters.[28] But the popular press now hated the once-idolized minister. All he had ever cared about was money, sneered one pamphleteer.[29] As for the economic damage to luxury industries, said another,[30] 'How can he not blush to suggest that, to make a constitution, we should consult the interest of braid mer-chants?' Nothing else could be expected, opined Desmoulins,[31] from the Baron de Coppet—a reference to Necker's estate in Switzerland. Both sides of mid-century arguments about the historical origins of the nobility were invoked, but neither Frankish conquest nor feudal usurpation were

23. *L'Ami du Peuple*, no. 142.   24. *AP* xvi, 374. See also Tourzel, *Mémoires*, 110–11.
25. *L'Ami du Peuple*, no.149.   26. *Révolutions de France et de Brabant*, no. 33, 405.
27. Meaning the special arch built for the Festival of the Federation on 14 July 1790.
28. *Correspondance*, 251. Ferrières to Mme. de Medel, 25 July 1790.
29. François Paul Nicolas Anthoine, *Lettre à M. Necker, sur son opinion relativement au décret concernant les titres, les noms et les armoiries* (Paris, 5 July 1790), 5. (BL FR tracts 128 (8)).
30. Aubin Louis Millin, *Réfutation du pamphlet de M. Necker, contre le décret de l'Assemblée nationale qui supprime les titres, les armoiries & les livrées* (Paris, undated), 12. (BL FR tracts 128 (11)).
31. *Révolutions de France et de Brabant*, no. 33, 421, 425.

deemed legitimate bases for subsequent noble power. Blending the two, one Loyseau, publishing from the presses of Jacques-Pierre Brissot's *Patriote français*, declared that titles perpetuated the memory of illegitimate pretensions. 'It is certain that this *gentrified* nobility (*noblesse gentillâtre*), which flooded Europe so suddenly, comes from the establishment of fiefs by a few titled brigands.' And the author ominously attacked Necker with a claim also advanced by Desmoulins: nobody had the right to criticise a law once it was passed.[32] To say that no authority could destroy heredity, Desmoulins raged, was 'a blasphemy against the nation's omnipotence'. Legislation, on this analysis, articulated a Rousseauistic general will which was never wrong, and so not subject to challenge. It was an attitude that was to underpin much revolutionary violence after the fragile consensus of 1789 crumbled.

'So everything,' concluded another of Necker's anonymous critics, 'with respect to birth, is nothing but chimera, folly, illusion and lies.' And what, he asked Necker, 'would Washingtons and Franklins, and all free men who have known the rights of the human race debased, think of your outrageous opinions?'[33] The Society of 1789 knew the answer to this one. Most of its founders, who had first mooted the idea that abolishing nobility was a practical possibility,[34] were passionate admirers of America and its noble-free society. In the sixth issue of its newly-launched *Journal* (10 July) was a long article by the indefatigable Grouvelle[35] denouncing Necker's intervention: 'If there are titles, there is still a nobility; if there is a nobility, the constitution has only strengthened this privilege, and rooted error in ... to suppress ennoblements without suppressing nobility and titles would be singularly to push up the value of these supposed advantages.' Grouvelle followed up this polemic a week later by publishing for the first time the letter which Franklin had given to Mirabeau in 1784 to incorporate in his pamphlet denouncing the Cincinnati—a key document in focusing the century's arguments against nobility.[36] A translation and adaptation by Morellet of Franklin's scornful letter to his daughter about the

---

32. Loyseau, *Réponse aux observations de M.Necker, sur le décret qui supprime la noblesse, qui défend de porter des titres, les noms de fiefs et les armoiries* (Paris, 5 July 1790), 3, 9. (BL Fr tacts 128 (10)); *Révolutions de France et de Brabant*, no.33, 423.

33. *Réponse à M. Neker [sic] sur ses opinions relativement aux livrées, armoiries & noblesse héréditaire* (undated), 7–8. (BL FR tracts 128 (13)).

34. Se above, p. 232.

35. 'Considérations sur le décret du 18 juin [sic] et sur l'opinion de M. Necker à ce sujet', *Journal de la Société de 1789*, vi, 10 July 1790, 19–42. The first issue had only appeared on 6 June.

36. See above, p. 122. See also Durand Echeverria, 'Franklin's Lost Letter on the Cincinnati', *Bulletin de l'Institut français de Washington*, iii (1953), 119–126.

Cincinnati, it contained the essence of the doctor's anti-noble arguments, including his notorious calculation of thinning blood down the generations. Grouvelle reminded his readers of Franklin's recent death, and the public mourning decreed by the Assembly. Was it likely, he asked, that in America, the descendants of such a great man would receive any credit for his achievements if they had none of their own?

In denouncing Necker, Grouvelle had confidently predicted that nobles would soon lose track of the documents which attested to their former status. In a few more years, Chérin himself would no longer be in a position to distinguish between Parisians and Philadelphians.[37] But Chérin's genealogical labours had already been made redundant by the king's decision no longer to seek proofs for any appointment.[38] And, most sensationally of all, the hereditary genealogist himself welcomed the Assembly's decree. In a pamphlet of transparent anonymity,[39] the former arbiter of noble pretensions renounced the *ancien régime* (using that newly fashionable term twice) where he had occupied an honoured place. The 'new order of things has cost me my fortune; I have perhaps acquired through that the right to show myself its partisan, & to say *& I too am a citizen*.' Speaking with all the authority of his former profession, Chérin rejected the claims of Boulainvilliers (and Maury on 19 June) that nobility existed before feudalism. He was with Dubos and Mably in seeing titled nobility as inseparable from fiefs. That being so, the abolition of feudalism made the end of titles, arms and liveries—'that gothic debris'—a logical consequence. 'It is quite extraordinary that nobles, who had embraced the part of the commons in good faith, should not have foreseen that it was necessary to come to it sooner or later, & should not have made merit of voluntarily abdicating titles that it was impossible for them to retain any longer, without contradicting themselves, without wounding the principles of equality which they claimed to profess.' But nobility and titles were not the same thing. True nobility, derived from ancestral distinction, was a matter of memories that could not be extinguished. It was never harmful to nations, because great actions were always within the reach of anyone, and some nobles (among others he mentioned Montmorency, Lafayette, Clermont-Tonnerre) were living up to their ancestors through

---

37. *Journal de la Société de 1789*, vi, 33.   38. See above, p. 232.
39. *Considérations sur le décret de l'Assemblée nationale, relatif à la noblesse héréditaire, aux noms, aux titres & aux armoiries* (undated), signed L.N.H.C. (BL FR 128 (16)).

new opportunities to distinguish themselves provided by the Revolution. Could genuinely old and famous families regret the end of a nobility they had shared with *parvenus* whose only qualification was money? Their distinction would survive current upheavals. Meanwhile, however, Chérin invoked the authority of Mably and Rousseau to urge his compatriots to let time do its work. And he ended by commending Necker, not for his objections to the Assembly's decree, but for his long record of service to the Nation, and for the conciliatory intentions of his intervention.

* * *

But it was too late for conciliation. Most nobles now blamed the foreign, Protestant banker for their predicament. His financial mismanagement had precipitated the Revolution, he had betrayed them by doubling the Third Estate and refusing to support the king's rearguard action at the royal session of 23 June 1789. Now they revelled in his vilification by the demagogues he had unleashed. Yet the consolation was slight. The king himself had betrayed his truest supporters by sanctioning the decree, and now even Chérin, the gatekeeper of the higher nobility, had turned against them. So, it appeared, had most of their compatriots. While Third Estate deputies exulted privately in the humiliation of those who had humiliated them for so long,[40] outsiders took more direct and open action. They did not wait for the deadline of 14 July to demand that coats of arms be erased from buildings and coaches, and many chose to turn the Festival of the Federation into a celebration of aristocratic downfall.[41] When it rained, as it did for most of the day, it was called the tears of the aristocracy.[42] Reluctantly, nobles began to paint out or cover over armorial bearings, although this scarcely reduced the mansions and vehicles displaying them to anonymity.[43] By the autumn, officers of the Paris commune were sending inspectors around the streets to check whether the job had been done thoroughly and safely, in a way not easy to undo if times changed.[44] 'The *Aristocrats*' reported an Irish peer on 27 September,[45] 'are melancholy and

40. Tackett, *Becoming a Revolutionary*, 293–4.
41. Carré, *La Noblesse de France et l'opinion*, 473.
42. Lescure, *Correspondance secrète*, ii, 458. 16 July 1790.
43. Mercier, *Le nouveau Paris*, 520, ch. cxxxiv, 'Armoiries'.
44. Fitzsimmons, *The Night*, 131–2.
45. Lord Mornington, quoted in J. M. Thompson (ed.), *English Witnesses of the French Revolution* (Oxford, 1938), 94.

miserable to the last degree; this makes the society at Paris very gloomy; the number of deserted houses is immense, and if it were not for the Deputies, the Ambassadors, and some refugees from Brussels,[46] there would scarcely be a gentleman's coach to be seen in the streets.'

It seems improbable that the ultimate attack on nobility did not play some part in the military mutinies of the next month.[47] Nowhere was the social gulf between noble and commoner more stark than in the army, and nowhere else did commoners daily experience the arrogant indifference of superiors who were frequently absent from their posts, and often blissfully unprofessional when they were not. Military discipline had begun to crumble in the spring of 1789, and mutinous French Guards played a crucial role in the taking of the Bastille. By the following spring insubordination was rife in a number of regiments, and it was encouraged by the National Assembly's reluctance to authorize vigorous repressive action. Throughout late June public attention was attracted by a clash between the younger Mirabeau, a leading 'aristocrat' in the Assembly, and the regiment of which he was colonel, based in Perpignan. It culminated in the bad-tempered Viscount confiscating the regimental colours, being arrested in possession of them, but claiming a deputy's immunity. Both sides appealed to the Assembly, but even as he did so, Mirabeau was denouncing the decree abolishing nobility.[48] No doubt this stance influenced the Assembly's decision to uphold the protests of his regiment. Mirabeau's reaction was to leave the Assembly, and the country, in mid-August, condemning the entire work of the Revolution as soon as he reached foreign territory. By then, however, news had arrived in Paris of a full-scale mutiny by three regiments stationed in Nancy. The trigger was attempts by noble officers to strengthen discipline and prevent men in the ranks from fraternizing with local Jacobins. But military men in the Assembly, including Lafayette, saw this as an opportunity to restore order in the army more generally by making an example of the mutineers. General Bouillé, an American War veteran, was sent with a small army to storm Nancy, rescue officer hostages and arrest ringleaders. The siege was swift and bloody, and in the aftermath 23 Swiss soldiers of the Châteauvieux regiment were executed and 41 more condemned to penal servitude in the galleys. The incident appalled 'patriots', and perhaps somewhat reassured demoralized noble

46. Noblemen fleeing the anti-Austrian uprising in the southern Netherlands.
47. Scott, *Response of the French Royal Army to the French Revolution,* 80–97.
48. *AP* xvi, 386.

army officers, but it only added to the sense of embattlement felt by many noblemen in the face of popular hostility. An increasingly hysterical mood seemed to grip even those who remained active in the Assembly. Deputies on the left were scoundrels (*scélérats*) yelled the vocal conservative orator Cazalès, a Languedocian hothead of very recent noble extraction, and he forced Barnave, whom he called the most rascally of all, into a duel. It was Cazalès who was nearly killed; but if he had shot Barnave, reflected the appalled Ferrières, there would have been popular mayhem.[49] Two weeks later Faucigny, still incandescent at the abolition of titles, declared that a state of war existed within the Assembly, which could only be resolved by attacking 'those clowns there' on the left 'sabre in hand'.[50] He was saved from the penalties of contempt by the pleading of friends, and a prompt apology, but weapons came out again early in November. This time the conservative Duke de Castries wounded Charles de Lameth, a popular hero. When the story became public, a large mob sacked Castries's house in the heart of the fashionable faubourg Saint-Germain, causing 300,000*l*. worth of damage. 'Let us admit,' sighed Ferrières,[51] 'that the Aristocrats have no common sense, and that they act with an unwisdom, a carelessness which bring down on them the misfortunes that they incur.' Their 'insolence and thirst for vengeance' only increased hatred against them.

And these were men who had chosen—so far—to continue living with the new regime. Increasing numbers felt they could not. None of those who left the kingdom during the summer of 1789 expected to be away long. Sooner or later, they thought, order and calm would return, and so would they. Country gentlemen of the eastern and south eastern provinces whose castles had been sacked and burned during the disturbances of July and August might have been seeking safety across the Rhine or the Alpine passes, but most of the first émigrés were rich and metropolitan, scarcely distinguishable from summer tourists or at worst escaped debtors. Only those who gravitated to the circle of Artois now established in Turin were unequivocally advertising their political hostility to the new order. But

---

49. *Correspondance*, 263–4. Ferrières to Mme. de Ferrières, *c*.12 Aug. 1790.
50. Ibid., 271–2, to Mme. de Ferrières, 24 Aug. 1790: 'ces gaillards-là'. See also Tourzel, *Mémoires*, 110–111.
51. Ibid., 320. Same to same, 14 Nov. 1790. See also Duc de Castries, *Maréchal de Castries, serviteur de trois rois* (Paris, 1979), 150–4. On duels, and particularly the significance of this one, Pierre Serna, 'Le duel durant la Révolution. De la joute archaïque au combat politique', in D. M. G. Sutherland (ed.), *Violence and the French Revolution* (Historical Reflections/Réflexions historiques, 29, no.3, 2003), 409–431.

their numbers began to grow after the violence of the October days closed down the Court of Versailles and made the royal family the prisoners of Paris. Hundreds of deputies even applied for passports, although only a handful made immediate use of them.[52] Over the winter a steady trickle of carriages was observed crossing into Switzerland, and growing colonies of aristocratic expatriates established themselves in the Netherlands and the residential cities of the Rhineland. Few admitted to leaving out of fear. Count d'Espinchal, who left with the Prince de Condé in the aftermath of the fall of the Bastille, appears to have been motivated at first by simple loyalty to the prince, who had long been his patron at Versailles. Later, in the very full journal he kept of his wanderings, he justified his absence by invoking the recklessness of the Assembly and the spinelessness of the king. He persisted in believing that the French people had been misled into 'persecuting those who, in unhappy times, were always your true protectors against the cruel and continued tyranny of... bourgeois, that infernal race of pen-pushers [*gens d'écritoire*] of whom you are today the blind instruments.'[53] Yet most nobles were still reluctant to take the fateful step, realizing that it could only inflame their enemies. Some worried that 'a few hotheads, a few intriguers, a few fools, were exploiting the honour, the devotion, the bravery of the Nobility' to destroy it far more effectively than any decrees.[54]

The Assembly as yet appeared unconcerned: citizens of a free country must be allowed freedom to travel abroad. But the growing number of famous names in ostentatious exile escaped nobody's attention, nor the surge in departures produced by each major reform. The decree abolishing nobility produced the biggest exodus since October, and it was denounced by nobles abroad as well as those now considering departure.[55] Nor was the younger Mirabeau the only army officer feeling driven into exile by the endemic insubordination of the ranks. If Bouillé's firm action against the Nancy mutineers steadied wavering nerves, the attack on Castries produced a minor panic. 'Two hundred families' reported the

52. Over the whole course of the Constituent Assembly only 20 noble deputies (or 6 per cent of the order) left their seats in order to emigrate: Edna Hindie Lemay, *La vie quotidienne des députés aux Etats-Généraux de 1789* (Paris, 1987), 171.
53. *Journal d'émigration*, 421, 17 Sept. 1792.
54. Baron de Frénilly, cited in Carré, *Noblesse de France et l'opinion publique*, 479.
55. *Sentiments généreux et patriotiques concernant l'opinion libre d'un noble françois réfugié à Madrid sur le décret du 19 Juin 1790 HEUREUSEMENT sanctionné par le ROI, contre la noblesse héréditaire* (Madrid, Aug. 1790) (BL FR tracts 128 (5)). See also Espinchal, *Journal d'émigration*, 139.

British ambassador,[56] 'have applied for passports to the Mayor since the pillage of Mr de Castries's house; he obtained one under a feigned name and is now out of the French dominions.' A few weeks earlier the final closure of the parlements, prefigured since the spring, allowed a whole fresh category of *ci-devants* to contemplate emigration. Reduced to minimal vacation chambers since the autumn of 1789, most parlements disappeared quietly, although some passed secret protests.[57] Only that of Toulouse issued a public condemnation of the whole course of the Revolution, whereupon all its signatories fled to Spain. By this time too, bishops unable to accept the new Civil Constitution of the Clergy had begun to abandon their sees, confident that the still-silent Pope would not condemn them. They knew, in any case, that they would soon be confronted with an oath (decreed on 27 November), refusal of which would entail loss of their benefices. By the end of 1790, in fact, the volume of noble emigration was so great that calls were being heard for a co-ordinated resistance to the Revolution under the leadership of Artois and Condé.[58] Leading these calls, from the safety of England, was the disgraced former minister Calonne, whose *The State of France, present and future*, appeared in Paris in a print-run of thousands, in early November.[59] A comprehensive denunciation of the Revolution's fruits, it devoted a withering series of pages[60] to the 'incredible decree of 19 June' in terms now familiar from innumerable noble protests. It had, Calonne claimed, 'reduced three hundred thousand noblemen to the desperate option of leaving France, or defending their rights there with arms in their hands.' The only solution to the kingdom's self-induced problems, he concluded, was a counter-revolution, a 'league of Duty', led by Artois, 'that worthy scion of the great Henry, whom persecution itself seems to have reserved for the salvation of France, by forcing him to leave.'

Still the Assembly affected indifference, or perhaps good riddance, to those who rejected its work by leaving. On 22, December it is true, it passed its first legislation against émigrés: pensioners and office holders in public pay were summoned to return on pain of loss of their

56. Browning, *Despatches of Earl Gower*, 43, 19 Nov. 1790.
57. Carré, *Fin des parlements*, 229–31, 273–4.
58. *Appel au devoir de la noblesse française, par M. le Marquis de L.P.C.B.D.G.S.D.P.D.M.A.O.D.C.* (Paris, 1790), 16–19. (BL FR tracts 127 (11)).
59. *De l'Etat de la France, présent & à venir. Par M. de Calonne, ministre d'Etat* (London, Oct. 1790).
60. pp.232–250.

emoluments. Nothing else was done, however, even when news arrived in the spring that the Prince de Condé was organizing an émigré army in Germany. Vengeance was left to a mob which invaded and ravaged his park at Chantilly.[61] The great political preoccupation of the first months of 1791 was the growing religious schism brought into relief by the clerical oath. In the end, only seven of the all-noble bench of bishops took it, confirming, in patriotic eyes, the anti-revolutionary instincts of the higher nobility from which most prelates were recruited. But popular attention was momentarily concentrated on the choices made by ordinary parish priests, and some people thought that hostility to nobles was dying down. A new monarchical club was founded to combat the influence of the Jacobins; and a provincial nobleman in the capital on business reported to his wife[62] that 'Paris is more reasonable than the provinces. The nobility retains all its consideration here, and merchants and workers are strongly regretting the spending and the decorations that made them a living.'

Increasingly, the touchstone of political speculation was the king. Although he had given his sanction to the Civil Constitution of the Clergy and to the clerical oath, he was suspected of waiting only for the Pope to break his silence in order to repudiate both. He was resourceful in avoiding the sacraments administered by priests who had taken the oath, and when in February he authorized his two pious aunts to make a pilgrimage to Rome, he appeared simultaneously to be endorsing emigration and resistance to the Civil Constitution. For much of the month there was agitation in Paris, and intermittent debate in the Assembly, about the issue. A crowd of market women arrived only just too late to prevent the ladies' eventual departure on 19th, and they were repeatedly stopped on their way south. After tumultuous debates, the Assembly insisted that they were free to proceed, but day after day huge and suspicious crowds surged around the chamber and the Tuileries palace, apparently expecting further royal departures and determined to prevent them. By the end of the month the safety of the royal family seemed in danger, and when on 28th an armed stranger was discovered in the queen's apartments, hundreds

61. Browning, *Despatches of Earl Gower*, 59, 11 Feb. 1790. On Condé, see Frédéric d'Agay, 'A European Destiny: The Armée de Condé, 1792–1801', in Kirsty Carpenter and Philip Mansel (eds.), *The French Émigrés in Europe and the Struggle against the Revolution, 1789–1814* (London, 1999), 28–42.
62. Marquis de Mesmon to his wife, 17 Mar. 1791, in Vaissière, *Lettres d' 'Aristocrates'*, 278.

of young noblemen converged on the palace with hunting knives and an assortment of other weapons, proclaiming their determination to die if necessary defending the throne. 'Had any one pistol gone off by accident,' shuddered the British ambassador,[63] 'a massacre must have ensued'. But the intruders were disarmed by National Guardsmen, and this 'day of daggers' came to nothing. It was a reminder, nevertheless, that Paris was full of young *ci-devant* hotheads, seemingly organized in some way, prepared to flout the law (which forbade arms within the royal palace), and perhaps intending to abduct the king rather than defend him.

The king for his part repudiated their support. The only protection he needed, he disingenuously proclaimed, was that of the National Guard. He was, in fact, already laying plans for the very escape that the Parisian crowds professed to fear.[64] The departure of his aunts brought new proposals from the left in the Assembly to curb emigration, but they were heavily voted down, again on grounds that it was invidious to restrict the movement of free citizens. A new surge in spectacular departures resulted: at Rouen, ten magistrates of the former parlement chose the Easter weekend to leave the city together in ostentatious disdain, spurning by the same gesture the sacraments offered by 'constitutional' priests.[65] The king hoped to avoid this by more discreetly performing his Easter duties at Saint-Cloud, where he had often gone during 1790. But the royal coach was turned back by suspicious crowds at the gates of the Tuileries, the National Guard refusing to obey Lafayette's orders to force a passage. After this ignominy, several courtiers of the Royal Household resigned and headed for the frontier. The idea was now floated that nobles might be subjected to a civic oath similar to that imposed on the clergy,[66] but quite apart from the ambiguous and divisive results of the latter, becoming clearer by the day, under the law of June 1790 nobles enjoyed no civic existence, so could not be legally identified.

Nobody could mistake that the volume of emigration was increasing, and the émigré princes gaining in confidence and optimism. The reconquest of the insurgent southern Netherlands by the Emperor Leopold I opened a whole new and inviting frontier, nearer and easier to cross than the Rhine or the Alps. The Prince de Condé, established since March at Worms on the

63. Browning, *Despatches of Earl Gower*, 67, 4 March 1791.
64. Price, *Fall of the French Monarchy*, 113, 119–35.
65. Jean Vidalenc, *Les Émigrés français, 1789–1825* (Caen, 1963), 67.
66. Lescure, *Correspondance secrète*, ii, 518, 9 Apr. 1791.

territory of the Archbishop-Elector of Mainz, was now actively assembling officer deserters into regiments. So was the younger Mirabeau, recruiting a black-uniformed 'legion' under the ominous banner of a death's head. Émigrés were now regularly urging their relatives still in France to join them in taking the 'road of honour'. Others simply emphasized, striking a chord that few metropolitan nobles could resist, that emigration was the fashionable thing to do.[67] That was certainly what it became on and after 21 June. On that day the royal family itself finally made its long-rumoured bid to escape the captivity of Paris. Almost a year to the day after he had refused to block the abolition of nobility, the First Gentleman of France acknowledged that those who had been leaving the kingdom in his brother's wake since July 1789 had been right. There seemed no place in the new Nation for any sort of hereditary authority or distinction; and the king was joining the émigrés.

✳ ✳ ✳

Or so it appeared. He was certainly heading towards a frontier beyond which his brother-in-law's troops were massing, and where his fellow embattled monarch Gustav III of Sweden was eagerly waiting. His brother Monsieur, who left at the same time by a different route, crossed safely into Austrian territory. The king left behind him a manifesto which he had composed himself, denouncing his captivity in Paris, disavowing the sanction he had given to revolutionary legislation as accorded under duress, and saying he could not blame those 'forced to expatriate themselves' out of fear for their lives or properties. Most modern scholars believe that he did not intend to leave the country, but rather to dictate terms to the National Assembly from the frontier fortress of Montmédy.[68] Since the royal flight was stopped at Varennes, we can never know for certain. Much clearer is that most of the king's former subjects believed he was trying to emigrate.[69] In their eyes, for good or ill, Louis XVI had finally aligned himself unequivocally with the most intransigent opponents of

67. Vidalenc, Émigrés français, 65–70.
68. See Hardman, Louis XVI, 185; Price, Fall of the French Monarchy, 169–70, 186–7, and ch. 9, passim; Timothy Tackett, When the King took Flight (Cambridge, MA, 2003), 50; Joël Félix, Louis XVI et Marie-Antoinette. Un couple en politique (Paris, 2006), 542.
69. Tackett, Becoming a Revolutionary, 188–193.

the Revolution, with nobles who had found continued life in France intolerable.

The émigrés had been commanding more and more attention in the days preceding the flight to Varennes. On 17 June the Assembly formally summoned Condé to return to France within a fortnight, or publicly disavow hostile intentions, on pain of confiscation of all his properties.[70] And at this very moment the temptations for noblemen to join the increasingly militarized émigrés were growing. There was renewed unrest and insubordination in the ranks of the army,[71] and on 11 June all officers were subjected to a new oath to the nation, the law and the king (in that order) which seemed designed to weed out those whose commitment to the new regime was dubious. Its likely effect was still untested when the news of the flight to Varennes broke, but when in the aftermath of the flight the oath was amended to exclude the king altogether there was no refuge in ambiguity. Within six weeks 1500 officers had refused it.[72] Others simply deserted, feeling absolved from their previous oath to the king alone by the patent fact that he was no longer a free agent, not to mention his own claim that he had not been one since October 1789. The flight also served to legitimize emigration, and the lead was given by Bouillé, who had been complicit in the escape plans. He tried to take public blame for the king's 'abduction' but he did it from beyond the frontier. By the end of the year no less than 6,000 army officers, between half and three quarters of the army's entire complement, had left the country.[73]

The flight to Varennes, in fact, consolidated the alienation of a great part of the nobility which had set in in June 1790. So long as the king had appeared prepared to accept whatever the National Assembly enacted, including if need be the attempt to abolish their own identity, they could convince themselves that they owed him their support, despite everything. So long as there was a monarchy, hopes of a noble revival were perhaps not entirely vain. These delusions now vanished. Noblemen who had refused to despair of the king found that he had abandoned them. Brought back from Varennes in shame, he was now a discredited captive. 'The whole enterprise,' lamented Ferrières,[74] who had hitherto always hoped

70. Browning, *Despatches of Earl Gower*, 95, 17 June 1791.
71. Scott, *Response of the Royal Army*, 98–103.   72. Ibid., 106.
73. Ibid. Also Donald Greer, *The Incidence of the Emigration in the French Revolution* (Cambridge, MA, 1951), 26.
74. *Correspondance*, 368. Ferrières to Mme. de Ferrières, 24 June 1791.

for the best, 'is the height of folly, and unfortunately indicates, in the king, the guilty project of carrying civil war, with foreign troops, into the bosom of the country. He has abandoned to the fury of the people, the Nobility, the Clergy, the right wing in the Assembly, his friends, his servants, his ministers, laying France open to the incalculable evils of civil and foreign war. This conduct is atrocious, and all to satisfy the arrogance, the vengeance, the greed of the Queen, of a few bishops, of contemptible courtiers.' But this disillusionment did not tempt Ferrières to join the 'Aristocrats' in the Assembly, much less to contemplate emigration. 'One of the great faults of the counter-revolutionary party,' he reflected,[75] 'is not to have known public opinion, and how should they know it? These people live only among themselves, only listen to each other, only read papers which speak as they do.' But the Marquis, though a deputy, was more typical than perhaps he realized. He saw that whatever happened was to be endured with patience rather than denounced in helpless and provocative fury. When the Assembly ended, he returned to his native Poitou and kept his head down until the most skilful *ci-devant* to have played the revolutionary game restored order with the new century. The old monarchy had gone, but prudent conduct might yet ensure that noblemen would survive to perpetuate their bloodline.

This must have been the attitude of the great majority of noblemen who did not leave the articulate record of Ferrières. If the eye was caught at the time, and all too often since, by the posturings of the émigrés and the great names who embellished their ranks, it is easy to overlook the fact that they never numbered much more than around twelve per cent of the entire nobility.[76] The historical problem is that they claimed to speak for them all. Condé simply called his army 'The Nobility', and in their letters home urging their friends and relatives to join them, émigrés sought to portray theirs as the only possible or honourable response to what had happened in France. Their attitude was entirely understandable, and doubtless they were able to shame many a waverer into serving the captive king from beyond the frontier against their better judgement.[77] One result was to intensify general suspicion of all nobles, and in such an endogamous group every

---

75. *Correspondance*, 371, same date.
76. See Greer, *Incidence*, 132, where a figure of 16,431 noble émigrés is given. Higonnet, *Class, Ideology and the Rights of Nobles*, 284, suggests 25,000, though the basis for this is unclear. The total size of the nobility is taken as 140,000: see above, p. 16.
77. Vidalenc, Émigrés *français*, 66–70, 74–5.

émigré must have left far more relatives behind. And the bitterness between those who went, to a future almost invariably frustrating and disappointing, and those who stubbornly refused all their urgings, preferring to remain in a land incomprehensibly changed, only added a further set of divisions and antagonisms to those which had already riven the nobility in and before 1789.

The king's attempted emigration certainly made it more difficult for others to succeed where he had seemingly failed. For several weeks after his return, the frontiers were closed. And if the National Assembly spent a frightened summer filling the Constitution with last minute amendments designed to promote conciliation and a harmonious launch of post-revolutionary political life, little was done to reconcile *ci-devants*. Unfinished business, rejected when Menou proposed it in late June 1790,[78] was revisited on 30 July when Camus presented a report on behalf of several committees, about orders of chivalry.[79] They were, he said, contrary to the spirit of equality and unity that the Constitution should enshrine. They were private corporations, often with conditions of entry incompatible with other laws, particularly in terms of proofs of nobility; and 'When nobility no longer exists, it is impossible to conceive of any corporation recognised by the law of the State, into which one could only enter by proving what no longer exists.' All the French were now noble, he declared (to derisive laughter from the right) in the sense that they stood for liberty, equality and the virtues, whereas 'nobility as it was formerly understood, was merely the right to become a court valet'. Camus was an old adversary of the Order of Malta,[80] and he clearly had it in mind when he went on to recommend that no French citizen should be eligible even for foreign orders where proofs of nobility were required. He thought the personal distinction denoted by the Order of Saint-Louis could be retained, but others disputed even this. Could there be knights of Saint-Louis when the title of knight had been abolished, asked one. And Anthoine, who had written against noble pretensions the year before,[81] noted (erroneously) that in America even the order of Cincinnatus had been abolished. He proposed, like Menou in June 1790, a single nationally-awarded medal for public service which would replace the cross of Saint-Louis. Others took the opportunity to complain that parties to legal documents were still describing

78. See above, p. 239.   79. *AP* xxix, 35–43.
80. See above, pp. 230–1. Also Blondy, *Ordre de Malte*, 298–9.   81. See above, p. 244.

themselves as noble, or using their old titles preceded by *ci-devant*. This complaint may have been an opportunistic move to pre-empt the idea of restoring nobility as part of the drive for reconciliation.[82] If so, it certainly worked. The longest clause in a decree passed at the end of this session prohibited the use of such descriptions. It somewhat overshadowed the main clause of the decree, which abolished 'any order, any corporation, any decoration, any external sign which presupposes distinctions of birth'. It also promised to consider a new national decoration to replace existing military insignia, and removed citizenship from any Frenchman entering a foreign order requiring proofs of birth. Camus exulted in what he clearly saw as a final triumph over the Order of Malta. Members of the Order, however, considered that he had been duped, and were soon applying for passports to leave the country as foreigners.[83]

Most went, of course, to Germany, not Malta. And now they could claim exemption from the first general legislation passed against émigrés. On 1 August, French citizens were forbidden to leave the country, and those who had left since 1 July were ordered to return on pain of tripling their tax obligations. It was a recognition that the attractions of emigration had increased enormously after Varennes. Hitherto, the support of the great powers in which they placed so much hope had never been forthcoming, but when news of his brother-in-law's flight reached Leopold I, he issued the Padua Circular (6 July) urging all his fellow monarchs to recognise the dangers which the plight of the king of France presented to all rulers. The émigré princes were ecstatic, and even more so when weeks later the Emperor and the King of Prussia resolved long-standing differences. When the two monarchs agreed to meet at Pillnitz on 27 August they were pursued there by Artois and his current leading advisor, Calonne. They carried away with them the text of a joint declaration in which the rulers promised to 'act promptly, with mutual agreement, with the necessary forces' to 'put the King of France in a state to establish, in the most perfect liberty, the bases of a monarchical government conformable equally to the rights of Sovereigns and to the wellbeing of the French Nation.' The commitment was far from open-ended. In fact it was so conditional that the Emperor regarded it as practically meaningless.[84] But

---

82. 'The session of 30 has reassured the public on the project of re-establishing nobility' noted one observer: Lescure, *Correspondance secrète*, ii, 540, 6 Aug. 1791.
83. Blondy, *Ordre de Malte*, 299.
84. See T.C.W. Blanning, *The Origins of the French Revolutionary Wars* (London, 1986), 86–89.

Artois was allowed to publish the Declaration of Pillnitz as he saw fit, and he did so under an open letter, written by Calonne, signed by himself and Provence,[85] and supported by a declaration of the Condé princes, which called upon Louis XVI to reject the amended Constitution now being hurriedly finalised. The princes vowed not to recognize any acceptance he might give, and denounced the entire work of the National Assembly, including its violation of 'the rights of the Nobility which, more sensitive to the outrages done to the Throne of which it is the support than to the persecution it is undergoing, is giving up all to demonstrate by outstanding zeal, that no obstacle can prevent a French knight from remaining faithful to his king, his country, his honour.' The Courts of all Europe, the princes claimed, were ready to intervene to help him.

Nothing could have been further from the truth, and the reception of the declaration in France suggests that most people realized this. When news of it arrived on 19 September the press across the political spectrum dismissed the threats as empty.[86] In any case, the king had already declared his official acceptance of the Constitution the week before (13 September). Few could believe that this acceptance was sincere, but the Emperor, who knew that for certain, saw it as a pretext for carrying his threats no further.[87] Émigrés who felt betrayed by Louis XVI yet again now faced a bitter choice. The promulgation of the Constitution was accompanied by a general amnesty, which implicitly repealed the law of 1 August, and so allowed them to return without penalties. On the other hand the final version of the Constitution accepted by the king contained a preamble additional to the Declaration of the Rights of Man and the Citizen which made clear that nobility and its appurtenances were gone for ever. 'There is no longer,' it declared, 'either a nobility, or a peerage, or hereditary distinctions, or distinctions of orders, or feudal regime, nor patrimonial justice, nor any of the titles, denominations or prerogatives derived from them, nor any order of chivalry, nor any of the corporations or decorations, for which proofs of nobility were required, or which presupposed distinctions of birth, nor any other superiority but that of public functionaries in the exercise of their functions. There is no longer either venality or heredity of public office. There is no longer, for any part of the nation, or for

85. Text in L. G. Wickham Legg, *Select Documents Illustrative of the History of the French Revolution. The Constitutent Assembly*, 2 vols. (Oxford, 1905), ii, 128—136.
86. Murray, *Right Wing Press*, 143.   87. Blanning, *The Origins*, loc. cit., n. 81.

any individual, any privilege, or exception to the common law of all the French.'

* * *

Thus ended the Constituent Assembly. Elected as the Estates-General, with a quarter of its seats reserved for an order of nobility, and a somewhat higher proportion of sitting deputies born noblemen,[88] it rapidly transformed itself into an assembly without orders which stripped nobles of most of their material advantages before attempting to proscribe the very quality of nobility itself. And in the orchestration of these measures individual noblemen played a disproportionately prominent role. Most nobles inside the Assembly, and in the kingdom at large, were appalled at the turn of events, but few thought they could be reversed, and even fewer committed themselves to the attempt. Most of those who did, emigrated; and were conspicuous by their rank, the ostentation of their departure, the void left by their absence, and now too their refusal to return. Calling themselves the representatives of the vast majority of the French nobility, on 2 October 536 émigrés residing in Coblentz issued a *First Sommation of the French Nobility to the French People.*[89] They called upon them to elect a new Constituent Assembly which would revise the constitution and revoke the decree which had abolished nobility. They admitted that the old order had seen abuses, and even that some nobles had behaved badly, 'but because a fruit is diseased, stony or rotten, do you cut down a tree which carries two thousand full of flavour?' They dwelt much on the code of chivalry, which made nobles courageous, generous, and committed to defending widows, orphans, and oppressed victims of injustice. They warned that, 'in destroying what you call an ARISTOCRACY, you break the counterweight of a more odious aristocracy, in that it is viler, more insolent and more humiliating; the ARISTOCRACY OF WEALTH, born in the den of greed, vexation, oppression, which breeds all the vices and with them every ill.' The old nobility 'provided a living (through vanity if you will, by ostentation, but so what? It was a living)' to 'the excellent French people' who did not

88. Almost a third of the clerical deputies and a handful of Third Estate ones were noble; but some noble seats, notably those from Brittany, were never occupied.
89. *Première sommation de la noblesse française au peuple de France* (Coblentz, 2 Oct. 1791) (BL FR tracts 129 (1); and R tracts 45 (7)).

hate the nobility, had not sought its abolition, and was now adjured to abandon an 'absurd law' which 'prevented nobles from indicating what our forefathers were.'

There were curious echoes in this of arguments put forward only a week earlier by Marat.[90] Always ambivalent about the unintended consequences of attempting to abolish nobility,[91] the People's Friend had denounced the ineptitude, perfidy even, of those who had first proposed the idea and then made it into a fundamental law of the state. They had created unnecessary enemies for the Revolution, and it would be wiser to give the *ci-devants* back their 'titles and toys'. But, as so often, Marat's was an isolated voice among Patriots.[92] More typical was the impassioned response of an anonymous pamphleteer to 'that feudal horde which wearies Europe with its absurd claims; which wishes to involve all the powers of heaven and earth in upholding the pretensions of pride against the eternal principles of justice, and the sacred rights of humanity; which believes that too much human blood cannot be shed to keep its vain titles, puerile honours, and above all odious and tyrannical privileges.'[93] The French should forget that nobility had ever existed in their land, and expunge titles from their vocabulary. That also remained the view of nobility's most persistent nemesis, Grouvelle, who was now the co-editor of a journal of civic education, the *Feuille Villageoise*, which he had helped to launch in September 1790.[94] Early in 1792 he printed a letter[95] purporting to come from villagers worried that their former lord, though a paragon of patriotic virtue, obedient to the law, and popular among his former vassals, refused to acknowledge the point of abolishing titles and arms, arguing that they were now 'distinctions without consequence, imaginary signs, which might have consoled us for so many more real losses.' All prohibition had done, in this former nobleman's view, was to 'humiliate thousands of families into despair; even irritate all foreign nobles, that is, all governments; arming

---

90. *Ami du Peuple,* 29 Sept. 1791. See also Louis Gottschalk, *Jean-Paul Marat: A Study in Radicalism* (New York, 1927), 98.

91. See above, p. 244.

92. And his scorn was perhaps directed less at the principle than at the hated figures who had carried it: Lafayette and the Lameths.

93. *Réflexions sur la ci-devant soi-disant noblesse* (undated) which claimed to have been printed on 20 October 1791; 10 (BL R tracts 47 (3)).

94. See Melvin Edelstein, '*La Feuille Villageoise,* the Revolutionary Press, and the Question of Rural Political Participation', *French Historical Studies,* 7 (1971), 175–203. Also, on this particular issue, Shovlin, *Political Economy of Virtue,* 180.

95. *Feuille villageoise,* no.18, 26 Jan. 1792.

the whole of Europe against France; at the risk of ten years of external and internal war.' But Grouvelle brushed these arguments aside. As in July 1790,[96] he asked 'if titles and other signs of nobility mean something, can they be allowed to go on? If they are nothing, why regret them? Why are men like you prepared to have two hundred thousand throats cut to recover this *nothing*? ... signs, however chimerical, recall and represent a superiority, prerogatives, power that were only too real. Not to destroy them would be to sanctify, to authorize them. They announce to all eyes, they proclaim to all ears, that formerly you had the honour of being born to tyrannise over your fellows ... For your mania is still to form a nation separate from the French nation.' The Americans had seen these dangers. So had Mirabeau, in denouncing the Cincinnati, whose insignia, banned across the Atlantic, only now 'served to feed the foolish vanity of a few Frenchmen.'[97] Grouvelle concluded his article by once more reprinting Franklin's letter of 1784 against the Society.

✳ ✳ ✳

Such polemics did little to reassure nobles about their security. Very few émigrés took advantage of the Constituent Assembly's final amnesty, and they were far outnumbered by a further exodus of *ci-devants* unprepared to continue living under an explicitly anti-noble constitution and the rule of a newly-elected Legislative Assembly where only a handful of their fellows now sat. 'What confirms our worst expectations,' wrote an observant Parisian on 20 October,[98] 'is the emigration of what are left of the great lords of Paris since the acceptance. Around thirty of them who had not set foot outside France since 1789 left last week bound for Coblentz which is the general meeting place of these gentlemen. They are taking advantage of the *unlimited freedom* to travel granted at the same time as the general amnesty to swell the malcontent party in Germany. Those I speak of came to make public farewells to the king, to the queen ... and take leave of their Majesties at the Tuileries; they left loudly for Coblentz, as if on an embassy or open mission.'

96. See above, pp. 245–6.
97. Newcomers continued to be admitted to the French Cincinnati until February 1792. See above, p. 131.
98. Ruault, *Gazette d'un Parisien*, 262.

The king for his part professed to deplore emigration. On 14 October he issued a proclamation condemning it, and urging those who had left to return. His only true friends, he declared, were those who did so, and who would work for the consolidation of the new order.[99] There was no reason to doubt his sincerity, as his brothers in Coblentz organized a Court in exile deliberately more lavish than his own, and disavowed everything he did on the grounds that he was not a free agent.[100] But many in the new Assembly, elected in the febrile atmosphere after Varennes and deeply suspicious of anything the royal couple said or did, believed that pious words from a discredited monarch would never dispel the standing threat to the new order that emigration represented. The Assembly spent much of its first fortnight organizing itself for business, but took note throughout that time of repeated reports of officer desertions[101] and stories of exiles drilling beyond the frontiers. On 20 October it began a debate on emigration which lasted several days. It marked the parliamentary debut of Jacques-Pierre Brissot (no longer calling himself de Warville), whose newspaper *Le Patriote français (The French Patriot)* had become one of the leading radical organs during the Constituent Assembly. His speech[102] electrified his audience, and was cheered from the galleries. Previous measures taken against émigrés, he argued, had failed because they had targeted the branches of the tree rather than its trunk. Instead of taking sanctions against a 'crowd of enthusiasts for their old parchments, who, misled by perfidious advice, were abandoning hearth and home' the Assembly should strike at the leaders of emigration, the king's two faithless brothers, and the foreign princes who protected and sheltered them. 'It is beyond the Rhine that we should strike, and not in France.' This meant summoning the princes to return, on pain of loss of their rights of succession to the throne, and property in France. But it should also mean, Brissot argued, 'forcing foreign princes to forsake the rebels.' If France 'spoke the language of free men' to foreign powers, not only would emigration cease, but those who had gone would come flooding back, 'for the unfortunates taken thus from their country are deserting in the firm persuasion that numberless armies will fall upon France, and re-establish nobility there. It is at last time to end these chimerical hopes.' In a word, France should threaten the émigrés's protectors with war. The

99. Vidalenc, Émigrés français, 27–8. See also Higonnet, *Class, Ideology and the Rights of Nobles,* 296–7.
100. Ibid.   101. On the scale of this problem, Scott, *Response of the Royal Army,* 109–111.
102. *AP* xxxiv, 309–317.

so-called great powers were all distracted, weaker and less resolute than they appeared. The lesser princes, including those offering hospitality to the émigrés, were puny. None could resist the forces of a France regenerated by liberty. Insofar, then, as Brissot saw the cause of the émigrés as that of nobility, as this language repeatedly implied, the way to ensure that France remained free of nobility was to threaten war against the rest of an aristocratically-ruled continent.

Although Brissot had argued that effective action against the émigré leaders, hosts, and protectors would make measures to restrict or punish emigration unnecessary, speakers who followed him clamoured for the reactivation of the law of 1 August at the very least. And those who left the country were freely described as counter-revolutionaries, conspirators, and even traitors. Few deputies sought to stand against the emotional torrent that engulfed the Assembly during these debates. Condorcet, one of the few nobles among the newly-elected deputies, was certainly converted by it.[103] The result was two decrees. On 31 October, Monsieur, designated under the Constitution to become regent if the king should die, was reminded that this provision required him to reside within the kingdom. He was instructed to return within two months or lose his right to the regency. At the same time a committee was appointed to draft a more general law on emigration. It produced a decree, eventually passed on 9 November,[104] which declared all French people 'assembled beyond the frontiers of the kingdom' to be 'suspected of conspiring against the country.' They were required to return by 1st January or be declared guilty, and subject to the death penalty. Princes were explicitly included, and their revenues confiscated in the interim. Civil and military officers were forbidden to leave the kingdom, and attempts to induce anyone to join the emigration were made punishable by death. A final clause instructed the Assembly's diplomatic committee to formulate measures to deal with 'adjoining foreign powers who allow assemblies of French fugitives on their territories'.

Although nobles as such were not mentioned in the decree, and although it was beginning to be noticed that not everybody now arriving in the centres of emigration was noble,[105] nobles were inevitably the main targets of this decree. Obsessed at the same moment by the machinations of the nonjuring clergy, the deputies saw the new regime that they were

---

103. Vidalenc, Émigrés français, 28.   104. AP xxxiv, 724–5.
105. Fontana, et al., Venise et la Révolution, 630, despatch of 23 Oct. 1791.

attempting to make work as mortally threatened still by the unregenerate remnants of the two former privileged orders. The introduction of the death penalty into their sanctions showed the unprecedented extent of their fears and suspicions, as did the idea that it might take a war to dispel the threat once and for all. These fears could only be intensified by the king's response to their decree, three days later. For the first time since becoming a constitutional monarch, Louis XVI deployed his veto.

A proclamation of 12 November explained why.[106] The king thought the volume of emigrations was decreasing, and might even soon be reversed. Such a severe decree might stop these trends. The use of the veto should also convince the émigrés that he was a free agent. And so he ordered them once more to return to the kingdom, bringing back with them their wealth and the energies to which the abolition of 'distinctions and titles' offered enhanced opportunities. Privately he let it be known that he could never sanction a decree which held the death penalty over his own brothers,[107] but his public stance was to reject anything which polarized his compatriots. In the same spirit, two weeks later, he vetoed a decree imposing harsher penalties on nonjuring priests. In Patriot eyes these vetoes made explicit the king's support for the forces of counter-revolution. They were not surprised: one purpose of framing the decrees in such extreme terms was precisely to force the king into this corner. But they were surprised by his next move. On 29 November the Assembly wrote formally to him requesting that he take 'energetic' steps to require the Electors of Trier and Mainz and other princes of Germany to expel the émigrés from their territories.[108] 'Tell them... that if the princes of Germany continue to favour preparations directed against the French, the French will visit on them, not fire and flame, but liberty... let the nation know who are its friends and its enemies.' Two weeks later the monarch came in person to the Assembly to announce that he would do it.[109] He had told the elector of Trier (whose capital was Coblentz) that he must remove from his territories, by 15 January, 'all gatherings and all hostile dispositions on the part of the French who have fled there'. Otherwise the king would regard him as an enemy of France, and declare war. It proved the high point of Louis XVI's relations with the Legislative Assembly. Increasingly excited by talk of war since Brissot's speech of 20 October, the deputies

---

106. *AP* xxxv, 103–4.   107. Lescure, *Correspondance secrète*, ii, 559. 12 Nov. 1791.
108. *AP* xxxv, 443.   109. Ibid., xxxvi, 110–11. 14 Dec. 1791.

were ecstatic to find the king in agreement, and those who had hoped to compromise him further were disconcerted. What disconcerted them even more was that the Archbishop-Elector hastened to comply, ordering the émigrés on his territory to cease their military preparations and to disperse.

* * *

The Elector was happy to be given the excuse to act against his troublesome guests. Nor was he the first to declare their presence unwelcome. On 22 October the Emperor Leopold himself had ordered French émigrés out of the Austrian Netherlands, a precedent noted with gratitude by Louis XVI in his speech to the Assembly on 14 December. The Emperor's main motivation had been to help his brother-in-law's efforts at conciliation by removing a standing provocation to French sensitivities just across a common frontier. But the émigrés were also undeniably disruptive in a territory that had been in turmoil even longer than France. If they brought in money which they spent freely, this imported inflation into the local economy. They were also as careless of running up debts as nobles had notoriously been in France before 1789. 'The French are abundant here' wrote one newly-arrived émigré from Brussels in October 1791,[110] 'but are little liked.' They took no trouble to hide their disdain for the Belgians and their ways, and were indifferent to the alarms caused by their constant drilling and armed manoeuvres. They brought similar problems to the Rhineland electorates further south, and in Coblentz at least they were compounded by the presence of Louis XVI's brothers. A prince of the Saxon royal house, the Archbishop-Elector was their uncle, as well as a priest horrified by the growing religious schism in France. But in offering them asylum and lending them palatial quarters he found himself host to a Court in exile which Artois modelled as closely as he could on Versailles. It soon outshone the Elector's own, and brought thousands of French nobles flocking into his territory in search of princely favour or simply a fashionable refuge. It was initially sustained by modest subsidies from the King of Prussia and the Russian Empress, which many grumbled would

---

110. Guillemeau de Saint-Soupplets to his brother: Vaissière, *Lettres d' 'Aristocrates'*, 336. See also Vidalenc, *Émigrés français*, 80–2.

have been more fruitfully spent on military preparations like those of the more serious army of Condé further up river at Worms.

But nobody was satisfied at Coblentz. 'I had imagined finding here,' wrote a new arrival on 23 November 1791,[111] 'a court with a bearing appropriate to people marked by two years of ill-fortune, that is to say a tone of dignity which misfortune cannot cast down, an outward gravity, thoughtful conduct, maturity of plans. I thought that, with great political combinations absorbing everything, intrigues, secret plottings and above all the fatal influence of women would have been banished forever.' But what he found was 'lightness and triviality, boundless pretensions, frivolous ways, every man looking to himself, none to public matters, ambition beyond measure, disputes over rank, authority divided and in several hands, tossed by favour and intrigue ... despotism in political opinions, reason thrust out among a few wise people who dare not speak out, who are neither listened to, nor consulted, nor employed ... scandalous luxury, mad expense ... while in the camps there are gentlemen bearing every privation and the full rigour of the weather.' Even those who knew the ways of courts were disgusted. 'My stay in Coblentz,' wrote the former farmer-general and intimate of Monsieur, J. M. Augeard,[112] 'seemed to me like Versailles in an even more hideous way: it was a sewer of intrigues, cabals, stupidities, depredations and apings of the old court ... I left Coblentz ... shaking the dust from my feet, firmly promising myself never to step back into such a nasty place.'

To ape Versailles was to recreate its hierarchies, and even to prolong quarrels abruptly foreclosed in 1789. The pre-revolutionary reign of Louis XVI had seen the steady shrinkage of the king's military household in the teeth of protests from courtiers who regarded service in parade regiments as their birthright. One of the exiled princes's first acts on establishing their court was to re-establish several of these regiments, one defunct as long before as 1775.[113] Their genealogical conditions of admission were just as stringent, although the circumstances of the emigration also made indispensable, as one entrant put it,[114] 'a fine and good horse between your legs, [and] money in your pocket to feed, equip and maintain yourself.' Fierce competition for the princes's limited patronage only reinforced the

111. Bengy de Puyvallée to d'Abzac in Vaissière, *Lettres d' 'Aristocrates'*, 366.
112. Evariste Bavoux (ed.), *Mémoires secrets de J.M.Augeard* (Paris, 1866), 281.
113. Philip Mansel, *Louis XVIII* (London, 1981), 67.
114. Clermont-Gallerande to Sarcé, 24 Oct. 1791: Vaissière, *Lettres d' 'Aristocrates'*, 365.

prejudices of those who thought they had prior claims on it;[115] and lineage counted for more among the émigrés than ever it had before, now that the king was no longer in a position to short-circuit precedence with promotions, sales, or new creations. There was no abatement, either, of what d'Espinchal called[116] 'that old and unalterable jealousy of provincial gentlemen towards the inhabitants of Paris and Versailles'; whilst traditional sword contempt for the robe fell with full force on magistrates, blamed for fatally weakening the monarchy with their judicial obstructionism, as well as for their always inadmissible social pretensions. They were still seen as having their uses: there was talk of putting together a plenary court of émigré parlementaires to condemn the whole Revolution as illegal once the king was set free.[117] But the restored regime of which the princes dreamed would have no place for institutional opposition from what they found comforting to regard as moneyed upstarts.

And to traditional snobberies and antagonisms fossilized by the revolutionary earthquake, the experience of emigration added a new criterion for social appraisal. New arrivals in émigré society were closely scrutinized on their reasons for coming, on why they had chosen this moment for departure, and on what this said about their political views. Émigrés of the longest standing, who saw themselves as thereby entitled to the most consideration, called themselves 'Pures'. Along with their natural leader Artois, they abominated everything that had happened in France since July 1789 at the latest. Monsieur, on his own admission, was not as Pure as his younger brother. After all, he waited almost two years before taking the road of honour. But as the senior (if less active) prince he avoided the censure reserved for others who had waited just as long. These were known witheringly as *Monarchiens*, after the ill-fated constitutionalists of September 1789 who had attempted to produce a workable constitution on British lines, with two chambers.[118] They were scarcely forgiven for once thinking that the Revolution might have been made to work. Noble deputies who had delayed in abandoning their seats were not forgiven at all. When in July 1791 Cazalès, one of the most eloquent and determined defenders of conservative causes, including the rights of the nobility, in the Constituent Assembly, resigned his seat and appeared in Coblentz, he found himself

---

115. Gérard Walter (ed.), *Le Comte de Las Cases: Le Mémorial de Sainte-Hélène*, 2 vols. (Paris, 1956), i, 942.

116. *Journal d'Emigration*, 246, 27–30 July 1791.   117. Carré, *La fin des parlements*, 265–9.

118. See above, pp. 217–9.

shunned, and returned to France. Would he have been better received if his own nobility had gone back further than 1737? Certainly Maury, an equally fierce and eloquent conservative spokesman, but a priest with no pretensions to nobility, was made far more welcome when he crossed the Rhine after the Constituent came to an end. There was a welcome, too, for the handful of non-nobles who joined the princes's colours. Their presence was a token that support for the cause transcended the old noble order. These were the real heroes, noted Chateaubriand, 'because no personal interest was mingled with their sacrifice'.[119] But they wore a distinctive drab uniform, while the former officers who filled the ranks of most of the émigré armies peacocked in their old regimentals or broke themselves to buy specially designed new ones in spectacular colours. If and when war broke out, most of them believed, it would be a military promenade, and they would be welcomed back by most of the disenchanted French population with open arms. And should that moment come, their contempt for the Jacobins and democrats who had ruined the country would scarcely be greater than that for fellow-nobles who had remained at home and let it happen.

✱ ✱ ✱

Yet, as 1792 dawned, the longed-for moment seemed to be receding. Their subsidies from sympathetic monarchs were running out, and not being renewed. The Archbishop-Elector of Mainz followed his neighbour's example and ordered émigrés on his territory to disperse. The king of Prussia denied them passage through his own territories, except as unarmed refugees, and in groups of no more than ten.[120] Only the Archbishop of Strasbourg, that same Cardinal de Rohan whose folly had done so much to embarrass Louis XVI and Marie Antoinette in the diamond necklace affair of 1785, offered them some asylum. He was now an émigré himself, but retained control of his see's territories east of the Rhine. Some dreamed of converging from there on the city itself, and making it a fortified centre of resistance on French territory. But few émigrés, and certainly not their princely leaders, thought that they could act without the support of greater powers.

---

119. *Mémoires d'outre-tombe*, bk.ix, ch.9.   120. Vidalenc, *Émigrés français*, 87.

The Emperor was as reluctant to intervene as ever. But, even as they hastened to comply with French threats, the archbishop-electors appealed to him as their suzerain to protect them if the armies which France was now mobilizing along its eastern frontier should violate the boundaries of the Empire. France had, in fact, already debauched the Empire's integrity. As early as 4 August 1789, in its attacks on feudalism, the Constituent Assembly had unilaterally abrogated the rights of a number of German princes and prelates in Alsace. In its various later reforms it continued to do so. Though French since the days of Louis XIV, Alsace remained part of the Holy Roman Empire, and the princes appealed for redress to the Imperial diet. Though powerless without the collusion of the Emperor and other German princes, on 6 August 1791 the diet formally annulled French actions. On 3 December Leopold II endorsed the decision, and three weeks later ordered his troops to protect the Rhenish electorates if the French should attack them. With the émigrés under notice of expulsion, there was now no reason for that, and in retrospect these gestures seem like a clumsy attempt to intimidate blustering French demagogues for whom the Austrians had little more respect or understanding than the émigrés.[121] But the effect was to provoke them, and throughout December and January Brissot used the Jacobin Club as a platform to proclaim the case for war, not so much now because of the émigrés, but as a tonic to the Nation, and a way of sorting out once and for all who were true patriots and who aristocrats. Only Robespierre stood out against this, pointing out the risks of both defeat and victory. But he was not a member of the Assembly, and when the Austrian threats were reported to it, Brissot and his allies were able to work the deputies into a state of frenzied patriotic indignation. They laid down an ultimatum to the Emperor requiring him explicitly to renounce designs against French sovereignty by 1 March.

On that very day Leopold II suddenly died. In his last days he had probably accepted that war was all but inevitable. In any case his son and successor Francis II shared none of his reluctance to cross swords with the French. His Prussian allies were now positively eager for that. And in Paris, by the time news of the Emperor's death arrived on 15 March, a new, more bellicose set of ministers were about to bring the executive fully into line with the legislature. They received no more diplomatic satisfaction

121. See J. H. Clapham, *The Causes of the War of 1792* (Cambridge, 1899), 130–33; Blanning, *Origins of the French Revolutionary Wars*, 102–4.

from the new King of Hungary[122] than their predecessors had from his father. With the wholehearted support of Louis XVI, who far preferred to be rescued by the armies of sympathetic kings than a fractious horde of disobedient émigrés, it was decided on 16 April to declare war. Four days later the king came in person to recommend this course to the Assembly. Only seven deputies voted against a declaration that would determine the entire subsequent course of the French Revolution, and its impact on the rest of Europe.

* * *

Wishful thinking underlay the attitudes of almost all parties in the outbreak of war in 1792. The émigrés were no exception. Although their activities were the occasion for the rising international tension over the preceding winter, by the time hostilities were declared their importance had shrunk. If the declaration of war began by castigating Austria's 'overt protection for French rebels' and its attempts to 'divide French citizens, and to arm them against each other', the issues of Alsace, hostile alliances, diplomatic bad faith and a military buildup threatening the 'independence and security of the French nation' took up much more space. And it was underpinned by long-standing disgust and frustration with an Austrian alliance which since 1756 had brought little but humiliation and given France an Austrian queen hated throughout the nation.

The declared war aims of France were entirely defensive. But the declaration invited émigrés from Austrian rule to come and fight under French colours—which suggested support for regime change in the enemy's Belgian provinces at least. And throughout the buildup to war there had been much talk of exporting liberty to the groaning subjects of despots. Nor was this simply a warning to kings. A war waged by a French nation which had abolished nobility would not spare foreign aristocrats who fought against it. That was certainly the expectation of the *ci-devant* imperial Baron who claimed credit for the achievements of 19 June 1790. By now calling himself Anacharsis,[123] and nothing less than the 'Orator of the Human Race', Cloots was allowed to address the Legislative Assembly on 13 December

122. He had not yet been formally elected Holy Roman Emperor.
123. He first adopted the name on 3 June 1791: Mortier, *Anacharsis Cloots*, 169.

as a well-known foreign convert to French revolutionary values. He urged them to strike at the émigrés and push France's frontiers to the Rhine. At this prospect, he predicted that the oppressed peoples of twenty countries would rise up to break their chains. On 1 December he repeated these predictions at the Jacobin Club, to the scorn of Robespierre but of few others in his euphoric audience. The French Revolution, he proclaimed over the spring, was the beginning of a world revolution.[124] Among other things, it would destroy everywhere the principle of nobility, which could only have been born in times of ignorance and mindlessness when degraded mankind consented to be seen as vile and boorish. Posturing windbag though he was, Cloots often made prophecies which turned out not far wide of the mark; and in innumerable ways the war launched in April 1792 would indeed throw down a mortal challenge to nobles throughout Europe.

And it would turn the French émigrés, and later anyone who could be linked with them, into traitors. The first attempt to do this had been contained in the decree of 9 November 1791 vetoed by Louis XVI.[125] But in the fevered atmosphere of the new year he did not dare withhold his sanction again from a new decree which specifically indicted his two brothers with high treason, as well as Condé, Calonne, the younger Mirabeau and other known émigré leaders. It was a gesture which the Assembly had no power to implement, but it marked a further advance in the perception of émigrés as guilty of treason and, by implication, deserving of its penalties. What the Assembly could do was punish the émigrés by the seizure of the assets and properties they had left behind in France. The idea had been periodically mooted for some time, but difficulties of identification and categorization had always made legislation appear impossibly difficult. Sanctions had been confined to stopping the emoluments of those in public pay. But during the campaign against emigration over the winter much emphasis had been laid on the economic damage, whether in terms of wealth taken abroad, unemployed dependants left behind, or the cost of defensive preparations. The idea arose of seeking compensation at the expense of émigré properties, and on 9 February, after an acrimonious debate, it was decreed that the possessions of émigrés

---

124. Anonymous 'Arrêté du Tiers Etat de l'Univers' published in *Chronique de Paris*, 13 Feb. 1792. Quoted in Mortier, *Anacharsis Cloots*, 272.
125. See above, pp. 264–5.

should be 'placed under the hand of the nation, and under the oversight of the administrative bodies'. No details were specified, no clear definitions stated. Only seven weeks later, during the final countdown to war, was a first attempt made to clarify what an émigré was, and what sort of properties they were liable to lose (law of 30 March 1792).[126]

They were defined as citizens absent abroad since 1 July 1789 without legitimate reasons.[127] They were not defined as nobles, and indeed under a constitution which no longer recognized nobility they could not have been. Yet at the moment when war broke out those who had left the country in rejection of the Revolution were overwhelmingly noble. To confiscate émigré property was, therefore, largely to dispossess nobles, to prolong a process of loss that the decree of 19 June 1790 ought notionally to have completed. But in attempting to extinguish their very identity, the revolutionaries had driven a significant number of *ci-devants* to abandon their country and to embrace armed resistance to the new regime. It was a step most nobles declined to take, but those who took it, amid extravagant claims to be speaking and acting for the nobility as a whole, inevitably cast doubt and suspicion on others left behind. The émigrés wanted war. Their activities played a major part in bringing it about. But so far from restoring a vanished world, and the authority they had enjoyed there, the war would defeat and scatter them. And nobles who chose to remain in the land of their birth, fatally compromised by those who had gone, would now feel the full punitive force of a defiant Nation which no longer trusted any of them.

126. Vidalenc, Émigrés français, 32–3.　　127. A wide range of such reasons was specified.

9

Persecution, 1792–1799

Although noble emigration had severely depleted the officer corps in the months leading up to war, command of the French armies was still entrusted to noble generals. The heroes of France's last successful war, Lafayette and Rochambeau, along with Luckner, a German Baron long in French service, were given armies confronting the Austrians and (soon enough) the Prussians. Troops safeguarding the Alpine frontier were commanded by the former constituent and Marquis, Montesquiou-Fezensac. When commands were later switched, the army of the Rhine fell to Biron, who as Duke de Lauzun had taken a personal expedition to America in 1780, but had made most of his pre-revolutionary conquests in the boudoirs of Versailles and fashionable Paris.[1] The record of most of these *ci-devants* proved lamentable. Ordered to advance with troops he considered inadequately trained, Rochambeau resigned within weeks. Aware no doubt of the same problems, Luckner lumbered timidly in and out of enemy territory. Lafayette, meanwhile, was more concerned with events in his rear. Thwarted in an attempt to be elected mayor of Paris, no longer confident of the unanimous support of the National Guard, he hoped that command of regular troops would make him once more the arbiter of the political scene. It was just as Robespierre had feared and predicted in the Jacobin Club. On 16 June Lafayette denounced Jacobin activities in a public letter to the Legislative Assembly, posing as the spokesman of brave soldiers let down by spineless politicians. After a menacing mob invaded the Tuileries and threatened the king on 20 June, the Hero of Two Worlds left his post, returning to Paris to repeat his strictures on the Jacobins in a speech at the bar of the Assembly. The reception was tepid and suspicious, and was followed by a motion to impeach him for dereliction of duty.

1. His notorious memoirs are largely a catalogue of amorous adventures and Court frivolity.

By then he had returned to the front, to find his own men disgusted by his behaviour. When, after the fall of the monarchy on 10 August, he appealed to them to follow him in a march on Paris, they spurned him. Accompanied by a small party of officers including his old rival, Alexandre de Lameth, on 19th he gave himself up to the advancing Prussians, no longer able to control or even influence a revolution that he had helped to launch. The romantic republicanism of a lifetime had been shattered by the prospect of what destroying a monarchy meant.

It was war which brought down the monarchy. This had been precisely the intention of many of its promoters. But noblemen played an important part in precipitating the moment, and not simply through their inadequacy as generals. The émigrés, who had occasioned the war in the first place, were galvanized by the prospect of returning at last in triumph, and spent the first few months of hostilities frenziedly organizing themselves for action. They assumed that they would be in the van of invading forces, and would be welcomed back by the revolution-weary inhabitants of the provinces through which they passed. But they despaired, in advance, of Paris. That centre of republican anarchy could only be overawed by massive intimidation, and as war approached in March the princes had urged the new ruler in Vienna to publish a manifesto of war aims, including threats against any who might harm the royal family. Louis XVI and his queen lent secret support to the idea once hostilities began, and, with the encouragement of the trusty Fersen, a draft document was produced by the émigré Marquis de Limon.[2] It was approved by the princes, endorsed by the Prussians, and accepted by the Austrians. Signed by the allied commander, the Duke of Brunswick, it was published from Coblentz on 25 July as his forces prepared to cross into France. The Brunswick Declaration[3] proclaimed that the main war aim of the invaders was to restore the king and royal family to liberty, and not to make conquests or interfere in French internal affairs. But the inhabitants of Paris were explicitly warned that if any violence or 'outrage' was offered to the king or his family, the city would be subjected to 'exemplary and unforgettable vengeance, in delivering up the town of Paris to military execution and total subversion'. The queen was predictably delighted by these ferocious

2. Barton, *Count Hans Axel von Fersen*, 160–5, contains the fullest and most accessible account of the origins of the Brunswick Manifesto.
3. Text in Thompson, *French Revolution Documents*, 186–92.

threats, but when Brunswick's declaration reached Paris on 3 August the effect was to accelerate the long-mooted attack on her husband's throne. It was taken as clear evidence that the royal family were in league with the Nation's enemies. A week after it appeared, the Tuileries Palace was stormed and the monarchy overthrown.

The king was now a prisoner, his authority suspended, and the formal proclamation of a republic only a matter of time. Émigrés might still hope for his rescue if Brunswick moved quickly, yet the French frontier was only crossed on 17 August, and days were spent besieging fortresses. And the allied commanders took good care to keep their émigré auxiliaries well behind the front line and short of supplies, regarding them as little more than an undisciplined embarrassment.[4] Hardly any of them got to fire a shot in anger, and when they came into contact with their invaded compatriots they were shocked to receive no welcome and no defections. 'We believed above all,' Las Cases told Napoleon in 1815,[5] 'repeating it endlessly to ourselves, and I believed firmly that the immense majority of the French nation was for us; however I was disabused when our companies reached Verdun and beyond; for not one came to join us, everybody on the contrary fled as we drew near.' Attempts to synchronize the invasion with internal insurrection had long since fallen apart. The Marquis La Rouërie, an American veteran and Cincinnatus, had been encouraged by the princes over the spring to organize nobles in his native Brittany into a conspiracy to subvert local garrisons. The plot was betrayed and its organization pulverized by arrests even before the monarchy fell, and La Rouërie died in despair only a few days after the king's execution. The ultimate shock for émigré hopes came on 20 September when the Prussian army, the terror of Europe since mid-century, was stopped in its tracks by accurate and disciplined French artillery fire at Valmy. The army had evidently not collapsed in the absence of so many of its old officers—although its commanders on that day were still former noblemen. It was not in a position to harry the subsequent retreat of the invaders, but atrocious weather and epidemic disease soon ensured that their defeat was total. As the demoralized Prussians marauded and pillaged their way back to Germany, the émigrés struggled after them through sodden and stripped country littered with decaying corpses.

---

4. See Vidalenc, *Emigrés français*, 154–7.   5. *Mémorial de Sainte-Hélène,* i, 448.

The French forces now turned their full strength against the Austrian Netherlands. The only use the Austrians made of the émigré auxiliaries assembled there by the Duke de Bourbon was to escort the baggage train of the fleeing governor after their own troops had been defeated at Jemappes on 6 November.[6] Émigrés who had chosen Belgium as a refuge now decamped in panic towards the Dutch Republic and the Rhineland, but the German princes and prelates who had welcomed them a year earlier were under threat themselves from French invasion. Much of the Rhineland was overrun by French troops by the beginning of November, and rulers still free of them were anxious not to hand them a pretext for invasion. By the end of the year there was no safe haven left west of the Rhine and, with the exception of Condé's army, which never reached the front and saved itself only by a total submission to the Austrian high command, émigré military organization fell apart. On 23 November, as a condition of the King of Prussia offering them asylum on his territory, the princes formally dissolved their forces.

✷ ✷ ✷

The threat from noble émigrés, insofar as it had ever seriously existed, was now at an end. But the damage it had done to the fortunes of the French nobility certainly was not. Even before war broke out, the Legislative Assembly had defined persistent emigration as an offence punishable by death, but this was the decree which Louis XVI had notoriously vetoed.[7] In the declaration of war émigrés were described as rebels, but no further sanctions were taken against them until late in July. On 29th a blanket prohibition on leaving the country and a revocation of previously issued passports were aimed at preventing the further swelling of their ranks. Two days earlier, however, a crucial new principle was established. The goods and revenues of proven émigrés were declared confiscated for national use.[8] It would be many months before effective force could be given to this decree,[9] but eventually these 'National goods of second origin' would add substantially to those of the church (first origin) already marketed. They would underpin huge new issues of *assignats*, and deal the wealth of the

6. Vidalenc, *Emigrés français,* 158.   7. See above, p. 264–5.

8. Vidalenc, *Emigrés français*, 36–7.

9. See Bodinier and Teyssier, *L'Evénement le plus important de la Révolution*, 125–6.

nobility a blow from which it would never fully recover.[10] Having lost their feudal revenues and distinct status, nobles who actively resisted the course of the Revolution now found themselves dispossessed of their property too.

Meanwhile the overthrow of the monarchy unleashed a spate of new legislation. 'The evils which afflict France', declared a law of 15 August, ' ... are caused by the treasons and plots of citizens who have emigrated'.[11] No fewer than eighteen new measures were directed against them between 10 August and the meeting of the Convention elected to frame a republican constitution on 20 September. The most important presumed the complicity of relatives left behind, and placed them under special surveillance as public hostages. A law of 9 September penalized them further by requiring them to provide equipment and pay for two soldiers for every one of their children who had emigrated. These were laws which presumed guilt by association and kinship. Embodying no procedures for verification or proof, they were perhaps more populist than punitive in intent,[12] but they were evidence of the boundless suspicion towards nobles created by the emigration, and they set a sinister precedent for later legislation.[13]

After Valmy, a new and more urgent issue arose with the capture of the first émigrés bearing arms. Their captors were not sure what to do with them, but the Convention now ruling France had no doubts. The royal veto on the law of 9 November 1791 had lapsed with the fall of the monarchy: the law therefore dictated that they must die. Accordingly, a first group of nine went to the guillotine (the new instrument of execution in use since April) in Paris on 23 October. Four non-noble servants had been taken with them, but they were reprieved. That same day, émigrés were forbidden to return to the country on pain of death. Three weeks later (15 November) any who had already returned were subjected to the same penalty unless they left again within a fortnight.

The legal flaw in these comprehensive condemnations was that nothing still defined unambiguously what an émigré was. It was all too easy to presume that anybody, and especially any nobleman who had disappeared since 1789, had joined the princes, but the possibilities for abusive and

10. See below, p. 294−5.
11. Quoted in Higonnet, *Class, Ideology and the Rights of Nobles*, 99; Vidalenc, *Emigrés français*, 37−8.
12. The argument of Higonnet, *Class, Ideology and the Rights of Nobles*, 99−102.
13. See below, p. 293.

malicious invocation of increasingly draconian laws were obvious. Nobody wished to penalize citizens away, for however long, on legitimate business. Only in March 1793 were these matters codified, and even then not without ambiguities.[14] Émigrés were now more closely defined as French citizens absent without legitimate cause between 1 July 1789 and 9 May 1792, or who had left since without authorization. There was a wide range of carefully framed exceptions, but local authorities were ordered to keep open lists of these public enemies, who were to be banished in perpetuity, and their goods forfeit to the Nation. And whereas public notoriety was enough to result in a listing, removal from the lists was a cumbersome process requiring written certification from eight competent witnesses. Contested, erroneous, and multiple entries were to dog the whole history of émigré lists, not to mention the efforts of historians to reach accurate conclusions about them.[15]

✳ ✳ ✳

The onset of war could not fail to intensify suspicion of all nobles, even those with no demonstrable link to, or sympathy with, the émigrés. 'Nobility!' exclaimed Vergniaud, who before the Revolution had been secretary to a magistrate persecuted by his colleagues on account of his undistinguished birth,[16] 'Ah, that word alone is an insult for the human race!'[17] The most vocal proponents since the previous autumn of a war launched without clear aims beyond clarifying domestic allegiances, he and his political friends and allies found it increasingly attractive, as suddenly victorious French armies poured eastwards, to portray the struggle as essentially anti-noble. It was they who carried, on 19 November 1792, a decree promising French 'fraternity and assistance' to all peoples seeking to 'recover' their liberty. More ominously, just less than a month later, the Convention ordered its generals to enforce the social policy of the Revolution wherever they took control.[18] They were to proclaim 'the

14. Vidalenc, *Emigrés français*, 39–42; Jacques Godechot, *Les Institutions de la France sous la Révolution et l'Empire* (2nd edn, Paris, 1968), 376–7. An English translation in John Hall Stewart, *A Documentary Survey of the French Revolution* (New York, 1951), 414–23.
15. On these problems, see Greer, *Incidence of the Emigration*, 5–17.
16. See Doyle, 'Dupaty', 49–50.
17. Quoted in Higonnet, *Class, Ideology*, 97.
18. Decree of 5 December 1792. English text in Stewart, *Documentary Survey*, 381–4.

suppression of all established authorities and of existing imposts or taxes, the abolition of the tithe, of feudalism, of seigniorial rights … of real and personal servitude, of hunting and generally of all privileges'. The policy was summed up in the famous slogan, reputedly coined by Chamfort, *War on the Castles, peace to the Cottages!*

These principles were never to be consistently pursued. The triumphant circumstances in which they were proclaimed vanished within a few months as the French invaders were driven back onto their own territory. When the French returned, in and after 1794, their policy towards local elites would prove unexpectedly pragmatic. Meanwhile, however, the first sudden explosion of French republican power threw the other nobilities of Europe into a panic. Until now they had contemplated the fate of their French counterparts with indifference or at best pitying detachment, an attitude exemplified by Edward Gibbon's Olympian observation on the émigrés two years before he fled Switzerland for cross-Channel security: 'These noble fugitives are entitled to our pity; they may claim our esteem; but they cannot, in the present state of their mind and fortune, much contribute to our amusement.'[19] Before 1792 the entrenched aristocracies of Europe beyond the Rhine continued to see the main threat to their hegemony coming from domestic despots rather than French democrats. By the end of 1789, for example, the Emperor Joseph II's attempts to restructure the servile economy of the Habsburg hereditary lands had brought many noble landlords to the brink of open revolt. In the weeks before his death in February 1790 the Emperor had begun to back down, revoking his most radical measures. His brother and successor Leopold II confirmed the revocations, and by promising conciliation delivered to his own conservative son and successor the noble support he needed to confront the French declaration of war. Yet even before Francis II was crowned, another monarch was assassinated by discontented nobles. Dazzled by, and keen to imitate, the Court of Versailles, Gustav III of Sweden had surrounded himself with well-born sycophants, and sought to revive the martial glories of the previous century by provoking war with the Russians.[20] But the noble house of the Swedish diet persistently obstructed his plans, while mutinous army officers undermined his strategy.

19. Georges A. Bonnard (ed.), *Edward Gibbon: Memoirs of my Life* (London, 1966), 185.
20. See H. Arnold Barton, *Scandinavia in the Revolutionary Era, 1760–1815* (Minneapolis, MN, 1986), chs. 7 and 8.

The king felt betrayed by those he thought should have been his natural supporters. So did many of the Swedish population when the war against Russia went disastrously wrong. The king used this patriotic revulsion to browbeat the diet into handing him almost unlimited power in February 1789. The Act of Union and Security, which embodied this royal *coup d'état*, appeared to achieve what Louis XVI had seemed to be moving towards some weeks earlier in doubling Third Estate representation in the Estates-General: an alliance of crown and commoners against aristocracy.[21] And although Gustav III declared that he had simply saved the nobility from itself, most nobles saw him as bent on the destruction of traditional Swedish liberties in reckless alliance with fickle and unpredictable popular forces. There was a widespread noble boycott of royal service which, combined with fears that the king would drag the country into a pointless war to save Louis XVI, culminated in the fatal shot at a masked ball on 16 March 1792. But by the time the king died of his wounds two weeks later all but a handful of the Swedish nobility had come to realize that in Jacobinical times they had worse enemies than a headstrong monarch. 'This unfortunate event', wrote the elder Fersen, a long-time opponent, 'has put an end to all resentments ... The consternation is general and our future appears sinister and foreboding.'[22]

It had taken nothing so sudden to convince the most eloquent voice raised outside France in defence of nobility, fully two years before this. The French abolition occurred while Edmund Burke was still writing his *Reflections on the Revolution in France*. Burke had spent much of his public career as the pensioner or placeman of wealthy English peers. No wonder he believed that 'Nobility is a graceful ornament to the civil order. It is the Corinthian capital of polished society ... It is indeed one sign of a liberal and benevolent mind to incline to it with some sort of partial propensity.'[23] He had publicly proclaimed his hostility to the Revolution as a whole ten months before his great tract appeared in November 1790, and no doubt much of it had been written by the time the Constituent Assembly abolished nobility. Certainly discussion of this came relatively late in the text. Burke could not believe that the French nobility had done anything to deserve what had befallen them. 'What have they ... done that they

21. See above, p. 177.   22. Quoted in Baron, *Fersen*, 155.
23. First edition (1790), 205. See also Amanda Goodrich, *Debating England's Aristocracy in the 1790s: Pamphlets, Polemics and Political Ideas* (Woodbridge, VA, 2005), 34–41.

were to be driven into exile, that their persons should be hunted about, mangled, and tortured, their families dispersed, their houses laid in ashes, that their order should be abolished, and the memory of it, if possible, extinguished, by ordaining them to change the very names by which they were usually known? Read their instructions to their representatives. They breathe the spirit of liberty as warmly, and they recommend reformation as strongly, as any other order. Their privileges relative to contribution were voluntarily surrendered.'[24] And before 1789 they had been 'for the greater part composed of men of an high spirit, and of a delicate sense of honour ... They were tolerably well-bred; very officious, humane, and hospitable; in their conversation frank and open; with a good military tone; and reasonably tinctured with literature.'[25] They had been more easy with their inferiors than British noblemen, fair if conservative landlords, and not oppressive. They had their faults: they were too ready to ape the worst habits of their British neighbours, often dissolute, too open to 'that licentious philosophy which has helped to bring on their ruin',[26] and not open enough to outsiders. But none of this was beyond hope of reform. In short:

> All this violent cry against the nobility I take to be a mere work of art. To be honoured and even privileged by the laws, opinions, and inveterate usages of our country, growing out of the prejudice of ages, has nothing to provoke horror and indignation in any man ... He feels no ennobling principle in his own heart who wishes to level the artificial institutions which have been adopted to give a body to opinion, and permanence to fugitive esteem. It is a sour, malignant, envious disposition, without taste for the reality or for any image or representation of virtue, that sees with joy the unmerited fall of what had long flourished in splendour and honour.[27]

Burke's *Reflections* were destined to become the most celebrated and influential denunciation of the French Revolution in any language. Sooner or later they were translated into most of the other major ones. But his defence of the stricken French nobility formed only a part of a grander design to point up the contrasts between British wisdom and French folly. Notoriously it was provoked by the assertions of Richard Price[28] that the American and French Revolutions embodied the same principles as that of 1688 in Great Britain. And Price, though a long-standing opponent of

---

24. *Reflections*, 200.   25. Ibid., 202.   26. Ibid., 204.   27. Ibid., 205.
28. In his sermon on *The Love of Country* at the Revolution Society on 4 November 1789.

nobility,[29] made no specific reference to nobles in the famous sermon which so infuriated Burke. But the Irishman's impassioned defence of the French nobility drew the particular fire of most of those attempting to refute him. They descanted on the haughtiness, pomp, pride, ambition, gothic prejudices, and general 'feudal barbarism'[30] of 'an immense insulated *cast, separated from society by every barrier that prejudice or policy could raise*'.[31]

None went so far in this as Tom Paine, who had spent the winter months of 1789 in Paris as the anti-noble impetus was gathering momentum. Having made his name in America as an opponent of hereditary power,[32] he saw the revolution in France as a continuation of the same struggle. He could see no fundamental difference between the British social elite and the French nobility. England, like pre-revolutionary France, was in thrall to the descendants of barbaric conquerors—in this case the Norman followers of William the Bastard. The idea of the Norman Yoke was far from original,[33] but Paine found it irresistible, as had Sieyès with the myth of Frankish conquest of the Gauls,[34] in challenging the legitimacy of aristocratic rule. 'What is called Aristocracy in some countries and Nobility in others', Paine declared in *Rights of Man* (the first part published in March 1791) 'arose out of the Governments founded upon conquest.'[35] Titles, meanwhile, were 'but nicknames, and every nickname is a title. The thing is perfectly harmless in itself, but it makes a sort of foppery in the human character, which degrades it ... It is, properly, from the elevated mind of France that the folly of titles has fallen. It has outgrown the baby cloaths of *Count* and *Duke*, and breeched itself in manhood ... the punyism of a senseless word like *Duke* or *Count* or *Earl* has ceased to please. Even those who possessed them have disowned the gibberish[36] ... Is it, then, any wonder that titles should fall in France? Is it not a greater wonder that they should be kept up anywhere?'[37] Titles were a farce, a folly, whose value would disappear 'when society concurs to ridicule them',[38] but, in addition, 'to exterminate the monster Aristocracy, root and branch—the

29. See above, p. 127.   30. Goodrich, *Debating England's Aristocracy*, 51-3.

31. James Mackintosh, *Vindiciae Gallicae: Defence of the French Revolution and its English Admirers against the Accusations of the Rt. Hon. Edmund Burke* (3rd edn, London, 1791), 255.

32. See above, p. 91.

33. Christopher Hill, 'The Norman Yoke', in *Puritanism and Revolution: Studies in Interpretation of the English Revolution of the Seventeenth Century* (London, 1958), 50-122.

34. See above, p. 179.   35. Everyman edition (London, 1915), 61.

36. This optimistic assessment perhaps came from Lafayette, who was Paine's main French contact during his months in France over the winter of 1789-90.

37. *Rights of Man*, 59.   38. Ibid., 60.

French Constitution has destroyed the law of PRIMOGENITURESHIP. Here then lies the monster; and Mr. Burke, if he pleases, may write its epitaph.'[39]

Paine preferred to avoid the term 'nobility' in his attacks, except to pun on it as 'no-ability'.[40] He preferred 'aristocracy' as its meaning had developed in French political usage since 1788,[41] and which in the British context made clear that he was not just referring to members of the House of Lords, but to everybody involved in the exercise of hereditary authority. This was a new meaning in English,[42] but it instantly became a commonplace among radical pamphleteers. There would thus be little in their view to distinguish the traditional British ruling orders from the old French nobility or indeed any other in Europe. This was certainly the position adopted by Paine's American friend Joel Barlow. A writer of bad and interminable patriotic verse, Barlow had come to Europe to help promote the Scioto company.[43] His largely unsuccessful dealings with would-be émigrés seemed to have turned him against all *ci-devants*, and in 1792 he produced *Advice to the Privileged Orders in the Several States of Europe resulting from the necessity and propriety of a general revolution in the principles of government*. His advice was actually less to the privileged orders than to their opponents. He called for the abolition everywhere of primogeniture and entail, as pernicious products of the feudal system. He denounced the idleness which feudal values made a criterion of nobility, and which produced a swarming horde of parasites on the body politic.[44] He scorned the idea of honour as an imposture to vindicate the killing of men in battle,[45] 'for it is no great figure of speech, to say that the nobility of Europe are always fed upon human gore. They originated in war, they live by war, and without war it would be impossible to keep them from starving. Or, to drop the figure entirely, if mankind were left to the peaceable pursuit of industry, the titled orders would lose their destinations, mingle with society, and become reasonable creatures.'[46] Nowhere, Barlow observed, had rank and hereditary titles commanded as much respect as in France before the Revolution; yet 'the national character of that people within four years has

---

39. *Rights of Man*, 62. The dangers of primogeniture were a favourite theme of Jefferson, another of Paine's informants about the early French Revolution. See above, pp. 94–5.
40. *Rights of Man*, 90.   41. See above, p. 220.
42. Goodrich, *Debating England's Aristocracy*, 57–60.   43. See above, p. 230.
44. David Brion Davis, (ed.) *Advice* (Ithaca, NY, 1958), 22–3.
45. Ibid., 36–7.   46. Ibid., 40

undergone almost a total change with regard to the estimation of exterior marks of distinction of every kind.'[47]

Barlow's tract was one of many triggered by Paine's rejoinder to Burke. Among the flood of reformist pamphlets appearing in Great Britain during the year after the first publication of *Rights of Man* in March 1791, few failed to repeat Paine's comprehensive denunciation of aristocracy.[48] Buoyed by this groundswell of support, in February 1792 Paine produced a second part containing detailed reform proposals. Here the author of *Common Sense* again denounced monarchy as 'the master-fraud, which shelters all others'.[49] And among those it sheltered were the aristocracy, who 'are not the farmers who work the land and raise the produce, but are the mere consumers of the rent; and when compared with the active world, are the drones, a seraglio of males, who neither collect the honey nor form the hive, but exist only for lazy employment'.[50] Moreover, 'the Aristocracy have quartered their younger children and connections upon the public, in useless posts, places and offices, which when abolished will leave them destitute, unless the law of primogeniture be also abolished or superseded'.[51] On the morning of publication, the author met Gouverneur Morris, recently arrived in London from Paris. 'He seems Cock Sure of bringing about a Revolution in Great Britain', confided Morris to his diary; but, having already read Part II, 'I tell Payne that I am really afraid he will be punished.'[52] His warning was not groundless. Within three months Paine found himself arraigned for seditious libel as the government issued a royal proclamation against subversive pamphleteering. It was the opening of a campaign against one who, as Pitt the prime minister put it, had 'struck at hereditary nobility, monarchy, religion and the established form of government'.[53] The aim was to drive him out of the country rather than bring him to a dangerous show trial deliberately set for months ahead. Accompanied by a campaign of informal harassment, the strategy worked, and in September Paine left for France. He was accorded honorary French citizenship and elected to the Convention. Joel Barlow followed him across the Channel, and had his *Advice* commended to the Convention by the new deputy. The exiles met regularly at White's Hotel with other expatriate sympathizers. There on 18 November they welcomed Lord Edward Fitzgerald, fifth son of the

---

47. Ibid., 103–4.   48. See Goodrich, *Debating England's Aristocracy*, 60–84.
49. *Rights of Man*, 205. See also above, p. 91.   50. Ibid., 231–2.   51. Ibid., 263.
52. *Diary of the French Revolution*, ii, 368, 16 Feb. 1792.
53. Quoted in John Keane, *Tom Paine: A Political Life* (London, 1995), 335.

Duke of Leinster, the premier peer of Ireland. Long an open sympathizer with French principles, Lord Edward toasted French victories and 'the speedy abolition of all hereditary and feudal distinctions', grandiloquently renouncing his own on the spot.[54]

By now such gestures were viewed from Great Britain as little short of treasonable. The victories in Belgium, toasted by Lord Edward, had convinced Pitt, as even Burke had not been able to do, that republican France now posed a mortal threat to British security. And the onset of war against a traditional enemy now also godless and soon to be regicide, shrivelled the anti-aristocratic groundswell that had seemed to be building in Great Britain throughout 1791 and 1792. Defenders of established British elites now began to argue that they had little in common with the old French nobility in any case. Far from a caste of greedy parasites (or indeed Burke's polished Corinthian capital), the British ruling orders were depicted as open to all, and their summit in the House of Lords as integral to the kingdom's free and commercial constitution.[55] In any case, aristocracy of any sort became progressively easier to defend in the light of the bloody and vindictive persecution visited on surviving nobles in France over the next two years.

✳ ✳ ✳

Organized noble attempts to reverse the Revolution came to an end with the collapse of the émigrés' military structure. Even the execution of Louis XVI in January 1793 only provoked a solitary protest—although that was spectacular enough. The day before the execution, the deputy Le Peletier, who had moved the prohibition of titles on 19 June 1790,[56] was assassinated in the Palais Royal. His killer was Michel Antonin de Paris, a former royal bodyguard outraged that a nobleman by birth should have voted for the death of the king. Thus the first republican martyr was a *ci-devant*, murdered by a brother noble. His body was interred in the Pantheon and a commemorative portrait of the martyred corpse commissioned from David. But Le Peletier was not the only nobleman to sit in the Convention, or to vote for the king's death. Forty of the 749 deputies had enjoyed

54. Stella Tillyard, *Citizen Lord: Edward Fitzgerald, 1763–1798* (London, 1997), 139.
55. Goodrich, *Debating England's Aristocracy*, ch. 5.   56. See above, p. 235.

noble status in 1790,[57] the most notorious being the king's own cousin, the former Duke d'Orléans, now styling himself Philippe-Egalité. Hundreds (like young Captain Bonaparte) remained as republican army officers. But as soon as the seemingly effortless victories of the autumn of 1792 turned to renewed defeat the next spring, it was all too tempting to attribute reverses to the treason of aristocratic generals. When Dumouriez met unexpected defeat at the hands of the resurgent Austrians in Belgium, he followed the example of Lafayette and defected. The patriotic credibility of Custine, the conqueror of the Rhineland, never recovered from the loss of Mainz in July 1793, and within six weeks the Revolutionary Tribunal had sent him to the guillotine. When internal rebellion broke out in the Vendée and Brittany in March, the peasant rebels instinctively sought out noblemen of military experience, returned émigrés like Charette and d'Elbée, to lead the Catholic and royal army. Biron, the former Duke, was seconded from the eastern front to put the rebellion down, but his uncharacteristic lack of vigour was interpreted as sympathy for the rebels, and he followed Custine to the scaffold.

Could any former nobles be trusted? The *sansculottes* of Paris certainly thought not. Their sectional assemblies made repeated calls for nobles and their servants to be disarmed; for them all to be arrested; for them to be expelled from the army, if not indeed all public employment. Some even thought that all these 'irreconcilable enemies of equality and the whole of humanity' should be deported.[58] The authorities did nothing to discourage these effusions. They ordered the public burning of all patents and proofs of nobility, and the ransacking of public libraries to weed out all 'nobiliaries and similar works' to add to the bonfires.[59] 'The most absurd of all distinctions', intoned Roland, minister of the interior, 'that according to which some men were born above other men, no longer exists; but its ridiculous vestiges still remain in various places.'[60] In July 1793 the same fate was decreed for all documents establishing feudal

---

57. Higonnet, *Class, Ideology and the Rights of Nobles*, 139.   58. Ibid., 122–4.

59. The impact of this among the émigrés was inordinate. The son of the Marquis de Bombelles, now in self-imposed exile in Switzerland, was 'afflicted ... so much as to make him cry [by] the decree to burn all the archives of nobility' noted a young English acquaintance. But she saw in him 'not the noble pride which pleases but the cursed French vanity, false politeness and misplaced gentility. In short he is a silly boy who thinks more of a long genealogical tree than of a poor but noble and virtuous heart.' Anne Fremantle (ed.), *The Wynne Diaries*, 3 vols. (Oxford, 1935–40), i, 154–5.

60. Adolphe Schmidt (ed.), *Tableaux de la Révolution française*, 3 vols. (Leizig, 1867), i, 102, Lettre circulaire, 20 Nov. 1792.

entitlements. By this time the Republic's sense of embattled emergency induced by military reverses and the Vendée peasant insurrection had been compounded by the so-called 'Federalist' revolt of the great cities of the south against a Convention supposedly in thrall to the bloodthirsty populace of Paris. Few former nobles were involved in fomenting or leading this defiance. If the mayor of Federalist Bordeaux, François Armand Saige, was a second-generation nobleman, most of his collaborators were commoners, and the Jacobin perception was that Bordeaux's true crime was 'tradeism' (*négociantisme*).[61] At least fifty-nine nobles were active in the revolt of Lyon, but their fellow 'Federalists' numbered several thousands.[62] In Marseille, a mere thirty-one of almost a thousand defendants before the Revolutionary Tribunal were *ci-devants*;[63] while in Toulon only the surrender of the naval port to the British brought the appearance of nobles expecting a return to pre-revolutionary deference.[64]

Yet the loss of Toulon spelt more tribulations for former nobles, in that news of it triggered the acceptance by the Convention of a policy of government by Terror. The machinery that would enforce Terror had been in existence since the first emergencies of the spring: a committee of public safety with executive powers, a Revolutionary Tribunal, local watch committees, and deputies on mission outside Paris invested with the full authority of the republic. But only after the *sansculottes,* electrified by the fall of Toulon, mobbed the Convention during the first days of September was Terror proclaimed the order of the day. From the start it was clear that nobles were to be a special target. Once again spokesmen for the Parisian populace demanded a purge of all former nobles from public employment, and the Convention agreed to draw up lists. These would certainly facilitate their identification under the Law of Suspects passed on 17 September. Under this law, watch committees (from which nobles had been excluded at the outset) were empowered to imprison all suspect persons at their own expense until the end of the war. Among the categories defined as suspects were 'former nobles, husbands, wives, fathers, mothers, sons or daughters, brothers or sisters, and agents of the émigrés,

61. Michel Figeac, *Destins de la noblesse bordelaise (1770–1830)*, 2 vols. (Bordeaux 1996), i, 395–411.
62. Bill Edmonds, *Jacobinism and the Revolt of Lyon, 1789–1793* (Oxford, 1990), 258.
63. William Scott, *Terror and Repression in Revolutionary Marseilles* (London, 1973), 207–8, 350.
64. Malcolm Crook, *Toulon in War and Revolution: From the* ancien régime *to the Restoration, 1750–1820* (Manchester, 1991), 133, 142.

who have not steadily manifested their devotion to the Revolution'.[65] Under so wide a definition of suspicious behaviour, almost anybody could incur denunciation and arrest at the hands of personal as much as political enemies. And once in custody, suspects were more readily open to further investigation which could lead to indictment before the Revolutionary Tribunal or other courts set up to deal with political crimes. The stage was set for government as social revenge.

Nobody knows how many French citizens were imprisoned as suspects; much less how many nobles. Estimates have varied between half a million and a mere 70,000. But in Paris it is known that 9,249 suspect persons were arrested between August 1792 and July 1794,[66] of whom 546 were noble men and 220 noble women. The average length of imprisonments was around eight months. And whereas in many cases suspicion was undoubtedly well deserved, in others frivolous or malicious denunciation by former servants, tenants, vassals, or disappointed litigants brought the same result. Among 102 detained nobles listed in Bordeaux in April 1794, in conditions which even the representative on mission described as 'a true tomb, not fit for the living', were people who had merely 'never shown themselves favourable to the Revolution', held 'moderate opinions', been 'besotted with their nobility', or in one instance been 'unpopular because she only mixed with people of her caste'.[67] The memoirs of those who survived this ordeal, or who escaped it thanks to risks taken by friends or more faithful retainers to hide them or spirit them away, breathe with the horror of the experience—compounded as it was with the constant fear that formal charges would be brought that might lead them to the guillotine. And even if it never came to that, imprisonment in generally insanitary conditions substantially increased the chances of early death.[68]

The number of nobles executed under the Terror is much more certainly known. Out of 16,594 persons officially condemned to death by extraordinary courts, 1,158 were nobles of one sort or another.[69] This is less than 1 per cent of the entire order,[70] and only 8.25 per cent of the total

65. Stewart, *Documentary Survey*, 478.
66. J.-L. Matharan, author of an unpublished thesis on this subject, contributing to Albert Soboul (ed.), *Dictionnaire historique de la Révolution française* (Paris, 1989), 1000–8.
67. Figeac, *Destins*, i, 371–3.
68. Donald Greer, *The Incidence of the Terror during the French Revolution* (Cambridge, MA., 1935), 31–4.
69. Ibid., 163. This total conflates separate figures for 'nobles' and 'noblesse de robe'.
70. If we accept Michel Nassiet's estimate of 140,000 nobles in 1789. See above, p. 16.

number of the Terror's victims. Over half (666, ominous number!) perished in Paris, although this preponderance perhaps reflected the centralization of revolutionary justice in the capital from the spring of 1794: 501 died there in June and July of that year alone. Despite all the anti-noble rhetoric, relatively few were arraigned before the end of 1793. The most famous was perhaps Egalité, always widely suspected of monarchical ambitions despite his democratic posturing. He went to the guillotine on 6 November, condemned for his links to the fallen Girondins and the traitor Dumouriez. But the bloodiest Terror of the autumn and winter months took place in the reconquered centres of 'Federalism', and in Nantes, where captured Vendéans and Breton *chouans* were concentrated; and, as noted earlier, noble involvement in these outbreaks had not been prominent. From March 1794, however, the number of noble victims began to mount.

Among them was Cloots.[71] Although he had been its president as recently as November, he was expelled from the Jacobin Club on 12 December after a blistering speech by his old enemy Robespierre. The Incorruptible denounced Cloots's wealth, his internationalism, his atheism, and above all the fact that he was a German Baron. The Club voted to expel all former nobles along with him, however impeccable their patriotic credentials. Two weeks later, along with Tom Paine, he was deprived of his seat in the Convention. In a republic at war with the rest of Europe, foreigners, however ostensibly Francophile, were no longer to be trusted.[72] But the former Prussian Baron was, if anything, more suspect than the Anglo-American publicist. 'Democratic barons', observed Robespierre, who orchestrated this expulsion too, 'are the brothers of Coblentz marquises and sometimes red caps are nearer to red heels than one might think.' Two days later the Orator of the Human Race was arrested. But it was only three months later that he came to trial, included almost as an afterthought in a motley batch of incautious populists (the so-called Hébertists), speculators, and other foreigners. They all went to the guillotine on 24 March 1794. Since his appearance in the Constituent Assembly on the day nobility was abolished, Cloots had become a French citizen, a deputy in the Convention, and an unrepentant advocate of diffusing the benefits of the French Revolution beyond the territory of the republic. He had voted for

---

71. See Mortier, *Cloots*, 434–83.
72. Sophie Wahnich, *L'impossible Citoyen : L'étranger dans le discours de la Révolution française* (Paris, 1997), 185–200.

the death of the king. But none of this outstanding revolutionary record could save a man who had never learnt when to keep his mouth shut. And although he gloried in the renunciation of his own nobility, this accident of birth was one of the principal accusations levelled against him. On that distant day in 1790, and frequently since, noblemen had protested that nobility was indestructible. Even their enemies now seemed to accept that it was at least unforgettable; and that spring and summer hundreds more nobles had reason to rue the fact.

Nobody went to the guillotine merely for being noble; but after years of anti-aristocratic propaganda and scapegoating, having been noble was becoming prima facie grounds in itself for presuming further guilt. Under the law of 27 Germinal (17 April) which centralized political justice in Paris,[73] all citizens were enjoined to report to the authorities any 'uncivic speech and acts of oppression of which they have been victims or witnesses'. Introducing the proposal with a speech which surveyed the whole course of the Revolution, Saint-Just inferred that all nobles were, and always had been, its declared enemies.[74] It was an open invitation to denounce any action since 1789 which in retrospect appeared counter-revolutionary. The new law declared that 'anyone convicted henceforth of having complained of the Revolution, and living by doing nothing' should be deported to Guiana. Who this meant seemed clear enough; but if it was not, the law further provided that all ex-nobles should be expelled from Paris, from fortified towns and from seaports. They were also to be excluded from public office, and local authorities were ordered to send lists of resident ex-nobles to the governing committees. The only exceptions to these measures were persons deemed useful to the republic by the committee of public safety—and in discussion it was made clear that this protected deputies who had once enjoyed nobility. But even they were scarcely reassured by the law of 22 Prairial (10 June) two months later. This notorious measure gave the Revolutionary Tribunal the sweeping remit of punishing enemies of the people, who were defined in terms even wider than those of the Law of Suspects. Now 'moral' evidence against them was accorded equal weight with material, and hearing witnesses was dispensed with—as were defence counsel. For nobles, the defencelessness was complete.

---

73. *Moniteur*, no. 207, 27 germinal An II.
74. Charles Vellay (ed.), *Oeuvres complètes de Saint-Just*, 2 vols. (Paris, 1908), ii, 378.

Accordingly, although the Revolutionary Tribunal still did deliver occasional acquittals, cases of *ci-devants* were not among them. During the
period of the so-called 'great' Terror in Paris from the Prairial law until
the fall of Robespierre on 9 Thermidor (27 July) the great majority of
the condemned were still ordinary people; but the proportion of nobles
rose from 6 per cent over the preceding eight months to 20 per cent.[75]
During this period the guillotine did not operate in the centre of Paris.
The governing committees feared that the sight of daily carnage as they
attempted to keep the prisons from overflowing would sicken even the
most bloodthirsty *sansculotte* spectators. So executions took place outside
the city's eastern gate, the *barrière du trône* (or, as it was now known,
trône renversé: throne overthrown).[76] Nor was there time to dispose of so
many bodies in an orderly way. They were simply piled into two huge
and stinking common pits not far from the execution site, in a former
monastic garden. Just over 1,300 headless corpses were buried there in six
weeks, at least 473 of them noble, including 51 women.[77] They represented
the whole range of the old nobility: princes and princesses, dukes and
duchesses (three of the latter from the Noailles family alone), generals
(including Alexandre de Beauharnais, first husband of the future empress
Josephine), magistrates (half of the entire parlement of Toulouse), a former
minister, high officials and tax farmers, a bishop and several canons and
canonesses, and scores of army officers. A striking number of commoner
victims had also been in the service of noble families—as much grounds
for suspicion in these times as actually being noble. In the next century the
Garden of Picpus became a place of pilgrimage not only for the relatives of
those interred there, but for all nobles who felt touched by the Terror. An
expiatory memorial chapel was built, and adjoining land became a favoured
burial ground even for noble families who escaped its ravages—a curious
gesture of solidarity with martyrs to shared blue blood. Among them lies
Lafayette, who through his flight survived the Picpus victims by forty
years—although in 1794 several years in German prisons still lay ahead of
him. It seems inconceivable that many of the others buried there would
have been happy to be alongside one who had done so much to precipitate
their tribulations.

---

75. Greer, *Incidence of the Terror*, 166.
76. Daniel Arasse, *The Guillotine and the Terror* (London, 1989), 107–9.
77. At least, because some of the 131 ecclesiastics of both sexes were certainly noble by birth.
    G. Lenôtre, *Le Jardin de Picpus* (Paris, reprinted 1989), 185.

The preponderance of non-noble victims in those ghastly pits shows that even the last, Parisian phase of the Terror, the 'Great Terror' of Dickensian memory, was not primarily a policy for eliminating nobles. Its weight simply fell on them disproportionately since it was almost impossible for them, as the law stood in a time of national emergency, to avoid compromising themselves. Inevitably most of their friends and acquaintances had been other nobles. They were intricately intermarried. With 16,431 members of the nobility having emigrated[78]—perhaps more[79]—very few could have been without some potentially incriminating associations. In such circumstances, once a *ci-devant* had fallen under suspicion, innocence was very hard to establish. As one judge told a former magistrate of the Bordeaux parlement, to escape condemnation he would need to prove that he would have been torn to pieces in the event of a counter-revolution.[80] And such an easy target was almost irresistible in providing justification for a Terror that seemed to be accelerating even as the national emergency which had given rise to it was easing.[81] Most victims of the Terror, in its most destructive phase over the winter of 1793–4, died for what they had done in the provincial revolts. But it seems clear that many nobles condemned later, in Paris, whatever the technical charges, perished largely for what they were.

* * *

Nor was it only lives that were lost. Under a law of 10 March 1793, condemned traitors had their property confiscated by the Nation, disinheriting their heirs. This property was added to the 'National goods of second origin' forfeited by émigrés since February 1792. On 17 December 1793 forfeiture was extended to the parents of émigrés, and on 26 February 1794 even the property of suspects was subject to sequestration.[82] Some of these measures were soon revoked. Detained suspects recovered most of their property when they were released *en masse* in the weeks following the downfall of Robespierre in July 1794. In April 1795 the relatives of

---

78. Greer, *Incidence of the Emigration*, 131.
79. Higonnet, *Class, Ideology and the Rights of Nobles*, 284, suggests approximately 25,000, but no ostensible calculations underpin this estimate.
80. Doyle, *Parlement of Bordeaux*, 312.   81. Higonnet, *Class, Ideology*, 145–52.
82. Legislation on national goods is conveniently summarized in Bodinier and Teyssier, *L'Evénement le plus important*, 25–32.

émigrés recovered theirs, and two months later even the unsold goods of the Terror's victims were restored to their heirs.[83] But by then some at least of these later confiscations had been sold off alongside earlier ones. Altogether emigration and Terror brought a massive loss of property for the nobility.

Ironically, when lands of first origin, confiscated from the church, were originally marketed in 1791, there were many noble buyers.[84] They largely disappeared from the market between 1792 and 1794, but by 1795 they were reappearing, and now buying goods of second origin, too. Mostly, however, this was a matter of seeking to reconstitute family patrimonies devastated by confiscation—in effect buying back rights of succession in the property of dead or absent relatives, either directly from the state or from previous buyers. In this way whole estates, or at least their choicer parts, were often recovered over time, and in many a department the greatest landowners under Napoleon were the same families as before 1789, despite intervening confiscations.[85] Such recoveries must be set against more ostensible losses. Nevertheless only between a fifth and a quarter of lost lands were repurchased by the families of former owners,[86] and in the end there was no district in which the overall holdings of the nobility were entirely reconstituted. The best estimates suggest that thanks to the Revolution around a tenth of noble landed wealth had disappeared from their hands for ever.[87] The loss of other assets is almost impossible to estimate. Many nobles were substantial creditors, and this form of property also accrued to the state in the event of confiscation. There were also vast amounts of movable goods taken from a group for whom ostentation was second nature: furniture, works of art, books. When sequestered dwellings were closed up by the authorities, they were often pillaged by thieves and vandals before their contents could be sold, and the market places of revolutionary France were a treasure-trove for bargain-hunters.[88] Merely identifying the assets and possessions of nobles condemned to lose them could be complex and haphazard. The landed wealth of many of the great families was often widely scattered across the country. It was

83. See below, p. 299.   84. Bodinier and Teyssier, *L'Evénement le plus important*, 262–4.

85. Robert Forster, 'The French Revolution and the "New" Elite, 1800–50', in Jaroslaw Pelenski (ed.), *The American and European Revolutions, 1776–1848* (Iowa City, IA, 1980), 186–8.

86. Bodinier and Teyssier, *L'Evénement le plus important*, 268.   87. Ibid., 271.

88. Constantia Maxwell, *The English Traveller in France, 1698–1815* (London, 1932), 206. Also Bodinier and Teyssier, *L'Evénement le plus important*, 419.

very easy for absent proprietors to be listed as émigrés, and complex to get erroneous listings cancelled. The daughter of an old friend, noted an English visitor to Paris in 1797, 'is ... endeavouring to procure the definite expunction of her father and husband's names from the list of émigrés, for, in fact, they never quitted France. But during the Reign of Terror, wherever you had an estate and happened not to reside upon it, the kind vassals or peasants set you down as emigrated.'[89] Whether products of ignorance or malice, such errors could only compound the traumatic impact of confiscation on the nobility as a whole. Overall, at least 17,589 nobles either emigrated or were condemned in the Terror. These numbers could surely be doubled if parents of émigrés and interned suspects are added. The property of anything up to half the nobility therefore stood notionally liable to confiscation or temporary sequestration.[90] And when, under the Restoration, a huge indemnity was granted to 25,000 families claiming to have suffered losses through emigration, the majority of those indemnified, and certainly all those receiving the largest grants, were nobles.[91]

These blows fell upon a nobility already weakened by material losses incurred in the earlier stages of the Revolution. Most of them followed from decisions taken on the Night of 4 August 1789. It had already been clear for months before that memorable session, and most nobles appear to have been resigned to it, that fiscal equality was inevitable.[92] That meant two things. First, it meant the end of exemption from the *taille*, although its material value had been steadily diminishing as the crown had sought to shift taxation to more flexible levies.[93] But the true advantage of *taille* exemption was more social and cultural. It was the ultimate badge of superior status,[94] and its disappearance robbed nobles of official recognition

---

89. Henry Swinburne, *The Courts of Europe at the Close of the Last Century*, 2 vols. (London, 1895), ii, 250–1.
90. Again assuming a total of 140,000 (see above p. 16.) a third of whom are likely to have been children.
91. André Gain, *La Restauration et les biens des* émigrés, 2 vols. (Nancy, 1929). See also Robert Forster, 'The Survival of the Nobility during the French Revolution', *Past and Present*, 37 (1967), reprinted in Douglas Johnson (ed.), *French Society and the Revolution* (London, 1976), 136; although the estimates made are based on a higher, and now discredited, estimate of the total number of nobles in 1789.
92. See above, p. 190.
93. See Harris, *Necker*, 190–1; Mireille Touzery, *L'Invention de l'impôt sur le revenu: La Taille tarifée, 1715–1789* (Paris, 1994), 189–90.
94. Michael Kwass, *Privilege and the Politics of Taxation in Eighteenth Century France* (Cambridge, 2000), 31–2.

for their separateness. Second there was the subsequent introduction of a new range of direct taxes from which nobody enjoyed exemption, and whose uniform weight absorbed more income than most nobles had ever contributed before.[95]

Then there was the loss of feudal revenues: marginal for some, massive for others. 'We never recovered from the blow to our fortune delivered in that nocturnal session', reminisced the Marquise de La Tour du Pin thirty years later, '…since then we have only lived by expedients, from the product of selling what was left, or from employments whose burden have almost always been heavier than the income they produced. And it was thus that we went down over many years, step by step into the depth of the abyss where we shall remain until our lives' end.'[96] The greater part of the revenues itemized by the Marquise was in the form of tolls, and these were abolished without compensation.[97] Most other feudal dues were indeed initially classified as redeemable, and this principle was underlined by the definitive decrees on feudal property promulgated in March 1790.[98] But they proved impossible to enforce. Most vassals stopped paying soon after August 1789, and there was no power capable of making them comply with the final decrees. With the advent of a populist republic, prudent former landlords stopped trying to secure compensation; and on 17 July 1793 a totally unsympathetic Convention decreed the immediate and uncompensated suppression of all feudal or related payments. Public bonfires of title deeds were authorized, and former lords who failed to hand them over were to be imprisoned. The regime of bonfires only lasted until the following October, and (happily for historians) vast numbers of title deeds survived.[99] Scarcely veiled forms of feudal rent and tenure sometimes continued to operate, too, far into the nineteenth century.[100] Nevertheless most feudal revenues simply dried up. In a region like that around Toulouse, that meant an average loss to lords of almost 19 per cent

---

95. Forster, 'Survival of the Nobility', 135.
96. Christian de Liedekerke Beaufort (ed.), *Mémoires de la Marquise de La Tour du Pin: Journal d'une femme de cinquante ans (1778–1815)* (Paris, 1979), 107–8.
97. See Anne Conchon, *Le Péage en France au xviiie siècle: Les privilèges à l'épreuve de la réforme* (Paris, 2002), ch. xii.
98. See above, pp. 227–8.
99. See Albert Soboul, 'Le brûlement des titres féodaux', in *Problèmes paysans de la Révolution* (Paris, 1976), 136–46.
100. Ibid., 147–66, 'Survivances féodales dans la structure rurale du xixe siècle'.

of landed revenues.[101] In a province like Brittany, the proportion was often much higher.[102]

Substantial noble capital was tied up in venal offices—also formally abolished on 4 August 1789. Although noblemen held only between 4 and 5,000 of the kingdom's 70,000 offices, they comprised all the most prestigious ones and accounted for perhaps three-quarters of the capital invested in the venal system.[103] Despite occasional threats, the revolutionaries never reneged on their initial commitment to compensate office holders for the abolition of their property. But the terms of the compensation did not reflect the current market value of offices, and the sums paid out were in revolutionary paper money, the rapidly depreciating *assignats*. Many offices were encumbered with mortgages, and lenders had first claim on any reimbursement. Add to this the loss of guaranteed employment, emoluments, and access to the former privileges of nobility for those buying office for social advancement, and the loss to the rich segment of the nobility investing in venality becomes serious. Permanent too, since although lost landed fortunes could be reconstituted in calmer times, venality at this level was never restored.

Individual histories varied enormously, and it often took years for the full scale of losses to become clear. One who tried to sum up the experience as early as 1796 was Count Dufort de Cheverny, by no means a magnate, but a courtier who before 1789 had been the presenter of ambassadors at Versailles. As a revolution which appalled him progressed, he spent more and more time on his estates near Blois, seeking, as he put it, 'to be forgotten'.[104] He did not emigrate, and remained at liberty until May 1794, when he was arrested as a suspect, ostensibly on account of 'feudal signs' still on display at his chateau. He remained in prison for four months, devastated by regular news from Paris of the execution of less fortunate friends. Returning at last to his vandalized seat, he tried to compute his losses. 'I had lost', he calculated:

---

101. Jean Bastier, *La Féodalité au siècle des lumières dans la région de Toulouse (1730−1790)* (Paris, 1975), 260. Bastier believes the 8% suggested by Forster, 'Survival of the Nobility', 133, to be too low.

102. Jean Meyer, *La Noblesse bretonne au xviiie siècle* (Paris, 1972), 220−1.

103. Doyle, *Venality*, 77−9.

104. Robert de Crèvecoeur (ed.), *Mémoires du comte Dufort de Cheverny*, 2 vols. (Paris, 1909), ii, 164.

in the first three years of the Revolution, twenty-three thousand livres of income in seigneurial dues...my pension from the royal treasury granted by Louis XV, and several other items...I had had to suffer incursions by national guards, enormous taxes imposed by the Jacobins, all sorts of requisitions, seizure, under the name of patriotic donation, of what was left of my silverware...My four months imprisonment had involved excessive expenditure...I had planted a four-deep avenue of poplars, in a straight line of three and a half leagues: it was proposed to fell them all to remove the air of feudalism, at one point I thought it might be done. My best trees were taken for the navy, and not a week went by when I did not have to take my requisitioned grain to military stores in Blois...I make no mention of trees of liberty taken from my park, of the burning of all feudal title-deeds, of the decree, later rescinded, under which they confiscated all books and prints bearing coats of arms,...of firearms impounded and only partially returned...[105]

✱ ✱ ✱

'Since the 9 Thermidor', Cheverny continued, 'everything became easier, but our ills were at their height. And only little by little were we able to get back to a better situation.' Within days of Robespierre's fall, however, executions fell away and prisons began to empty. The Law of Suspects remained in force, but soon the Convention was deluged with petitions alleging groundless imprisonment, and it wished to distance itself as soon as possible from the reign of Terror and arbitrariness.[106] Suspicion of nobles would remain endemic: the language of politics, after all, had been saturated with it since the earliest stages of the Revolution. But, as Jacobins and sansculottes who had led the persecution of ci-devants increasingly found themselves the target of reprisals, a sense that conditions were easing for their former victims steadily spread. Former nobles in the Convention now took increasingly prominent roles in formulating policy. Barras, a Viscount of old Provençal stock and a seasoned army officer, had commanded the troops who arrested Robespierre. Merlin de Douai, ennobled by office in 1782 and the architect in 1790 of the doomed redemption of feudal dues,[107] led a drive to renounce all extraordinary and emergency laws. Cambacerès, a former sovereign court magistrate, even proposed a general amnesty for

105. de Crèvecoeur, *Mémoires du comte Dufort de Cheverny*, 184–5.
106. Bronslaw Baczko, *Comment sortir de la terreur? Thermidor et la Révolution* (Paris, 1989), 99–106.
107. See above.

those convicted of counter-revolutionary acts. It was too soon for that when he brought it forward on 7 December 1794, but the next day the law of 27 Germinal excluding nobles from public functions[108] was abrogated. Some weeks before (25 October) had come the first concession to émigrés: those who could prove that they had not left the country were to have lands confiscated since their presumed emigration restored. Emigration had slowed to a trickle, in some districts drying up almost entirely, since the start of the year.[109] Now émigrés began cautiously to slip back into the republic. Their presence became so noticeable that on 15 November a new law reiterated the death penalty for any attested émigrés found on French soil, and similar draconian punishment for those proved to have assisted them. But local authorities no longer had much interest in enforcing such rigour. By the spring of 1795, the Republic's armies had defeated the Dutch and brought the Prussians to negotiate peace. 'I have been officially informed', wrote the commander of the Alpine front,[110] 'that since the announcement of the signature of peace preliminaries on the two banks of the Rhine, Condé's army is disbanding and émigrés are seen arriving from all sides having thrown away their uniforms and now seeking, under different disguises, to re-enter France. They have false passports from different departments and internal municipalities with signatures traced from true ones.' The city of Lyon was said to be a 'factory of false residence certificates'.[111] Meanwhile, as the policies and the personnel of the Year II (September 1793–September 1794) were inexorably dismantled and disavowed, the more extreme land confiscations began to be reversed. A determined publicity campaign was mounted by Morellet, who had once advised Franklin in his attacks on heredity,[112] to rectify the injustices borne by relatives of émigrés and the victims of Terror. A pamphlet series which he began in December 1794 with *Le cri des familles* (*The Cry of Families*) eventually ran to seven titles comprising some 500 pages.[113] It had its effect. In March 1795 the sale of condemned persons' property was suspended. In April, the property rights of parents of émigrés were restored; on 6 June, the unsold goods of the Terror's victims were given back to their families.

That month, however, brought a new crisis. On 8th, Louis XVI's son and heir died in his republican prison. When the news reached the

108. See above, p. 291.   109. Greer, *Incidence of the Emigration*, 35–7.
110. Quoted in Renée Fuoc, *La Réaction thermidorienne à Lyon (1795)* (Lyon, 1957), 48.
111. Ibid., 49.   112. See above, p. 122.
113. Jean-Pierre Gucciardini (ed.), *Mémoires de l'Abbé Morellet* (Paris, 1988), 389, 409.

Count de Provence at the émigré Court in exile in Verona, he proclaimed himself Louis XVIII and issued an uncompromising declaration.[114] In it he promised, when restored, to bring back the entire old regime, including the three orders and 'that scale of subordination without which society cannot exist'. In this he consciously aligned himself with the most intransigent elements among the émigrés. Vague hints at reform scattered throughout the declaration deceived nobody. By the time of Louis XVII's death, many in France had been beginning to wonder whether a restored but constitutional monarchy offered the best hopes of re-establishing stability. The declaration of Verona blighted those prospects. And even before news of it reached France, how a restoration of social subordination might come about was demonstrated by the arrival on the coast of Brittany of an émigré army. Ever since the outbreak of the Vendée rebellion and the more diffuse *chouan* insurgency in Brittany, the British had been fascinated by the idea of helping to spread this rural opposition to the Revolution. The rebels in turn constantly appealed for British help from the sea. As the reaction against Terror gathered force, they welcomed proposals from a seasoned counter-revolutionary plotter, the Count de Puisaye, for an armed descent on the Breton coast to link up with the *chouans* for a march on Paris.[115] The van of the expedition was to be made up of émigrés recruited largely in England, the largest and safest refuge since the republican victories on the continent. Eventually five regiments, comprising 3,300 men, were landed in the last week of June on the Quiberon peninsula. But half the ranks were made up of pressed French prisoners of war, the *chouans* who welcomed them were chaotically organized, the chain of command was unclear, and the émigré core of the invaders proved as factious and undisciplined as their predecessors during the invasion of 1792. It only took General Hoche, the republican commander, three weeks to defeat the invasion and take over 6,000 prisoners. Of these, over 500 died of disease and 748 were shot. Six hundred émigrés, taken with arms in their hands, perished according to the law of 1792:[116] 278 were noble officers. Others were killed in the fighting; some of the *chouan* leaders who died were also nobles. It would be remembered in émigré circles for years as 'that cursed expedition to the shores of France, in which so many of our exiles perished

---

114. Text in Paul H. Beik (ed.), *The French Revolution: Select Documents* (New York, 1970), 325–9.
115. See Maurice Hutt, *Chouannerie and Counter-Revolution: Puisaye, the Princes and the British Government in the 1790s*, 2 vols. (Cambridge, 1983).
116. See above, pp. 264, 277–8; Hutt, *Chouannerie*, ii, 322; Vidalenc, *Emigrés français*, 119.

uselessly'. These were the words of the Chevalier de Latocnaye, who spent his own emigration tramping around the British Isles and recording his impressions.[117] 'There was hardly a French family in London', he noted in July 1795, 'that had not to deplore the loss of a father, a husband, or a brother: people shunned each other—all the bonds of society seemed to be broken; a blind and sullen grief seemed to alienate the few friends who remained.'

Across the Channel, meanwhile, all this seemed evidence that nothing could reconcile émigrés to the achievements of the Revolution. The trend towards indulgence stalled. It is true that over that summer royalists were lured back into public life in reaction to the last attempts by the *sansculottes* to coerce the Convention in the spring. But when, in the first week of October (13 Vendémiaire) they tried coercion of their own to prevent two-thirds of the deputies from retaining their seats under a new constitution, the insurgents were shot down by troops under the command of Barras and his military *protégé*, Bonaparte. Barras's reward was to be chosen one of the five Directors under the new constitution. Bonaparte's was to be given command of the army sent to invade Italy in the spring of 1796. By then this republican *ci-devant* had married another, the widow of the guillotined General de Beauharnais, introduced to him by Barras. Rose (now better known as Josephine) Tascher de la Pagerie was herself noble, from a family which had sought to restore its fortunes in the slave-worked plantations of Martinique. She was now one of the leaders of a revived social life more extravagant than any seen since the glittering times of the late 1780s, in which the greatest cachet was to be related to a victim of the Terror. At so-called 'victims' balls' released suspects flaunted their own survival and applauded reports from the provinces about the 'White Terror' of murder and mayhem against the 'blood drinkers' of 1793–4. With so many of the levers of power controlled or manipulated by other near-victims, they felt confident that their grisly revels would bring no renewed danger.

As long as they eschewed open royalism, they were right. Men kept in power by the two-thirds law were more afraid of a revived popular movement than of *ci-devants* more intent on fashion and pleasure than on restoring a monarchy at incalculable political cost. Only two days after

117. John A. Gamble (ed.), *De Latocnaye: A Frenchman's Walk through Ireland, 1796–7* (Belfast, 1984), 2, 3–4.

the Vendémiaire rising, the Law of Suspects was finally repealed. It was true that two weeks later (3 Brumaire Year IV) public office was denied to émigrés and their relatives, but the unspoken implication was that some émigrés had now safely returned. The Irish revolutionary Theobald Wolfe Tone travelled from America with two of them. Committed to the overthrow of the aristocratic ascendancy ruling his native island, Tone reflected that 'It is a pity they should be aristocrats, yet I can hardly be angry with them. Aristocracy has been most terribly humbled in France and the reverse of fortune is too much for them. It is not only their own downfall but the exaltation of others whom they were accustomed to despise, which mortifies them; ... it is not fair however to judge too hardly of them, now they are down, but I confess I should be most sincerely sorry to be a witness of their resurrection; there is however no great danger of that event taking place, and they seem to be sufficiently sensible of that.'[118]

Yet the ostentatious contempt of the resurgent rich for the misery of the defeated populace over two successive winters of frozen hardship played its part in keeping Jacobinism alive and plotting. Former nobles who had embraced revolutionary radicalism were among the leaders of the 'conspiracy for equality' thwarted by the Directory shortly after Tone and his émigré friends arrived. Babeuf himself, the plot's nominal leader, had learnt his egalitarianism as a *feudiste*, advising landlords about how to maximize their feudal dues at peasant expense before the Revolution. His co-conspirators of old stock included Buonarroti, the Italian descendant of Michelangelo who would do most to preserve the memory of the conspiracy for posterity;[119] Félix Le Peletier, half brother of the first Jacobin martyr;[120] and Antonelle, whose commitment to the Jacobin cause, like Le Peletier's, had survived expulsion from the Club in 1793, and subsequent imprisonment on grounds of noble extraction.[121] In 1795, Antonelle was still declaiming hotly against his former status. Nobles, he wrote in the *Journal des Hommes libres* (*Freemen's Journal*), 'wish to be distinguished as a race ... think not that this mania ... is easy to destroy. I would almost say it

118. Diary entry for 7 March 1796 in T. W. Moody, R. B. McDowell, and C. J. Woods (eds.), *The Writings of Theobald Wolfe Tone*, 3 vols. (Oxford, 1983–2007), ii, 101. One of Tone's companions, Aristide Dupetit-Thouars, was later killed in the Republic's service, commanding a ship of the line at the battle of the Nile in 1798.
119. In his *Conspiration pour l'Egalité, dite de Babeuf* (Brussels, 1828).
120. See above, p. 286.   121. Serna, *Antonelle*, 223–33.

is impossible ... I state as incontestable fact that nobles are and always were foreigners.'[122] As such, except in a few cases of outstanding service to the republic, they should be stripped of citizenship. When the conspiracy was broken up in May 1796, Le Peletier fled, and Buonarroti and Antonelle were among those arrested and tried. But only the commoners Babeuf and Darthé suffered execution. The nobles, it was rumoured, were saved and protected by Barras.

The Directory had begun in October 1795 in a mood of relative indulgence towards Jacobinism, in reaction against the royalist threat of Vendémiaire. One result had been Babeuf's conspiracy. Accordingly, the months between then and the first scheduled elections under the new constitution in the spring of 1797 witnessed a conservative reaction. The objective was less to encourage royalism than support for a conservative republic; but inevitably it led to the election of many royalists amid a generally conservative landslide. The new majority in the legislative councils was deeply fractured, but its first act was to elect Barthélemy, a former noble who had ridden out the Revolution as ambassador to émigré-infested Switzerland, to the first vacancy in the Directory. They were able to agree, too, on indulgence for émigrés: on 27 June the law of 3 Brumaire Year IV, excluding them and their relatives from public office, was repealed. The first spectacular consequence was the appointment, two weeks later, of one of the best-known returned émigrés as foreign minister. The former bishop Talleyrand had left the country in September 1792 with official approval, but was later deemed to have emigrated. Back in September 1796, as soon as he felt it was safe, he found old friends ready to lobby for him to be given office. Barras, perhaps sensing that this was no ordinary émigré, pushed the appointment through. Within weeks, in any case, the directors who had opposed Talleyrand were swept from power. Afraid that the conservative offensive would accelerate into full scale counter-revolution as émigrés poured back into the republic, Barras and two other directors planned a coup. They secured the support of Bonaparte, who feared that the fruits of his brilliant campaigns in Italy would be squandered by a giveaway peace. Soldiers under his ultimate command were therefore on hand on 3 September when the 'triumvirs' deposed two of their fellow directors (including Barthélemy), ejected fifty-three conservative deputies, and annulled elections in forty-nine departments.

122. Quoted ibid., 278.

This 'coup of Fructidor', intended as it was to save the republic from the monarchy of an intransigent émigré prince, was followed by the most extreme anti-noble legislation of the entire Revolution.[123] The law of 3 Brumaire Year IV was at once reactivated to exclude émigrés and their relatives from public office. More important now, all unexpunged émigrés were required to leave the territory of the republic instantly, on pain of death. Émigrés who had re-entered the country more or less openly since the spring elections now left again in panic to escape what became known as the 'Directorial Terror'. It proved nothing like as murderous as its Year II namesake, but returners who chose to stay ran real risks. Between October 1797 and March 1799, 131 were condemned to death by special military courts.[124] In any case, as Mme de la Tour du Pin recalled,[125] 'This put a sudden and irremediable end to all arrangements made with acquirers of national goods, and it may be affirmed, rightly, that the events of 18 Fructidor were as fatal to individual fortunes as the Revolution itself, because they stopped short all the deals which, at this time, holders of properties just sold to the profit of the nation were considering.' She and her husband, back in the country for barely a year, saw the process of reconstituting their devastated properties ended for ever by their hurried flight to England.

These measures were ordered by the new Directory—joined now by Merlin de Douai. But the purged legislative councils were even more zealous. Unprompted by the Directors,[126] the Council of Five Hundred now called for the exclusion of all former nobles from public office. It also established a commission to consider how 'measures of ostracism, exile and expulsion' could be used against '*ci-devant* nobles and ennobled'. The commission's spokesman was Antoine Boulay de la Meurthe, but the language of its report[127] marked it out as largely the work of another member, Sieyès. Although he had, in his own notorious words, survived a Terror which cut down so many of the Revolution's early leaders, Sieyès had carried the hatred of nobility which had made his

---

123. A full discussion of this aspect in Higonnet, *Class, Ideology and the Rights of Nobles*, 234–43.

124. Carré, *Noblesse de France et l'opinion publique*, 544.

125. *Journal d'une femme de cinquante ans*, 255.

126. Laurence Chatel de Brancion (ed.), *Cambacérès, Mémoires inédits*, 2 vols. (Paris, 1999), i, 403.

127. BL F Tracts 89 (12), *Conseil des 500. Rapport fait par BOULAY (de la Meurthe) … Séance du 25 Vendémiaire An 6.*

name in 1788 and 1789[128] unmellowed throughout his years of prudent inactivity. According to Benjamin Constant, who knew him well, it was the dominant passion of his life.[129] Nobles would have been obvious beneficiaries if the new conservative intake into the councils had been given free rein, and with their overthrow Sieyès saw the opportunity to realize what he had fruitlessly proposed in *What is the Third Estate?*: the complete exclusion of nobles from the citizen body.[130] Nobility and the republic, his mouthpiece Boulay argued, were fundamentally incompatible, as the historical record of the Revolution had shown. Descendants of foreign conquerors, nobles should be expelled from the territory where their ancestors had usurped power and authority. In any case, nobles had never accepted the abolition of 1790, and the Revolution had never been able to perform the 'miracle' of purging their hearts of a sense of innate superiority and separateness.[131] This was striking admission of what many noble apologists had always claimed—that the attempt to abolish nobility was a failure. But now it was deployed not as an argument to abandon the ambition but rather to extend it. The commission recommended that former nobles should be deprived of their French citizenship unless they could demonstrate an exemplary record of military or civilian service in defence of liberty, or swear an oath of contempt for hereditary power and privilege, and the 'insolent…cowardly and shameful superstition' which supported them. Former courtiers, officers of the crown, holders of orders, and anybody who had protested against the abolition of 1790 were to be expelled from the country, their property confiscated and sold.

The proposal proved very contentious. Many deputies, while not disputing the necessity of the Fructidor action, argued that specific victimization of nobles was unnecessary, if not positively unconstitutional, and that to stigmatize members of a caste which no longer enjoyed legal existence would be tantamount to recreating it, not to mention alienating members who had never opposed the republic.[132] Others countered that French

---

128. See above, pp. 173−5, 178−180.
129. 'L'abbé Sieyès' in Alfred Roulin (ed.), *Benjamin Constant: Oeuvres* (Paris, 1957), 965−6.
130. Bastid, *Sieyès et sa pensée*, 194−8 ; Margerison, *Pamphlets and Public Opinion*, 94−5.
131. *Rapport fait par BOULAY*, 11.
132. BL F tracts 88 (5) *Opinion de P. F. Duchesne, Député de la Drôme, sur le projet d'une commission, relatif à l'exclusion provisoire des ci-devant nobles de toutes fonctions publiques. Séance du 7 vendémiaire an VI*; F tracts 89 (5) *Opinion de BEYTS, député de la Lys, contre le projet de résolution tendant à exclure les ci-devant nobles des fonctions publiques. Séance du 8 vendémiaire an VI.*

nobles were in effect part of an international 'corporation' dedicated to the destruction of liberty and the republic, and that their solidarity with nobles in other countries (who continued to recognize their nobility) would always outweigh their commitment to their fellow citizens. But not even in the Year II had mass deportation of nobles been considered. 'The public', recalled Cambacérès, who felt seriously alarmed for his own safety, 'seemed to rouse itself from the state of stupor which had hung over France since 18 Fructidor',[133] and the volume of protest forced a modification of the proposals. Deportation was now abandoned, but they remained radical enough: nobles were to be deprived of their citizenship and be subject to all the conditions of foreigners living in France. To purge their nobility, they would be required to go through a seven-year process of progressive naturalization. The only exceptions would be directors, ministers, soldiers, and members of revolutionary assemblies. The bill was hotly debated in the Council of Elders for three days late in November.[134] To some elders it seemed unjust, not to say unconstitutional, that all nobles should be punished when many had accepted and even promoted the work of the Revolution. Others said that since legally nobles did not exist, to persecute them was to pursue phantoms. Several pointed out that Bonaparte, the victor of Italy himself, might fall victim to the proposed law. Its supporters responded that 'it is to the nobility that are owed all the evils in the Revolution',[135] and that it was no coincidence that the foes of Gaulish freedom, in Frankish times or now, had come from Germany. That the German powers had now acknowledged defeat was not considered. On 9 Frimaire (29 November 1797) the law was passed. Not only did nobility no longer exist in France, those who had once enjoyed it were no longer recognized as French.

The Directors, who had never intended to go so far, and thought the decree was ridiculously extreme,[136] observed with relief that it was unenforceable. Certainly they made no consistent effort to enforce it. Worried by the new leftward swing they had set in train, their main

---

133. *Mémoires*, ii, 402.

134. BL F tracts 89 (9), also F tracts 91 (3), *Rapport fait par J. A. Creuzé-Latouche, au nom de la commission chargée d'examiner la résolution relative aux ci-devant nobles. Séance du 26 Brumaire, an 6*; F tracts 89(6) *Opinion de P.C. LAUSSAT (des Basses-Pyrénées) sur la résolution du 29 vendémiaire an 6, relative aux ci-devant nobles & anoblis. Séance du 6 Frimaire an 6*; F tracts 89 (8), *Opinion de LARMAGNAC, sur la résolution du 29 vendémiaire an 6, relative aux ci-devant nobles & anoblis. Séance du 9 frimaire an 6.*

135. Charles-François Oudot, quoted in Higonnet, *Class, Ideology*, 243.

136. Bastid, *Sieyès*, 195.

preoccupation was to reinforce the forces of conservatism before the 1798 elections, and persecuting nobles indiscriminately scarcely served those ends. Nevertheless the law was not repealed, and when it was proposed on 17 Germinal (6 April 1798) that nobles or émigrés who had proved their attachment to the republic should once more be eligible for public office, there was such hostile clamour in the Council of Five Hundred that the proposal was not even voted on. The law of 9 Frimaire was a tool which could be used against individuals, and occasionally was,[137] but nobles who remained politically quiescent were undisturbed until the new war emergency of 1799.

As in 1792, the crisis was noble-induced, but this time it was largely the work of a single *ci-devant*: Bonaparte. His expedition to Egypt of 1798, hastily endorsed by the Directory to get an overmighty general out of the country, set off a diplomatic chain reaction which resulted, by the following spring, in a new coalition against the French Republic which threw its armies on to the defensive for the first time since 1793. Emergency legislation reminiscent of the Year II was now passed: universal compulsory conscription, a forced loan levied on the rich, and, on 12 July 1799, a Law of Hostages in which many at once saw a new Law of Suspects.[138] Resistance to conscription had been one of the mainsprings of rural revolt in 1793, and now it flared up again. One of the ploys of republican generals to contain previous insurrections had been to take relatives of rebels, known or suspected, hostage for the good behaviour of their districts. The Law of Hostages generalized this principle. When an area was 'notoriously in a state of civil disturbance', local authorities were to be empowered to take hostage 'the kinsmen of émigrés, their relatives by marriage, and former nobles' as well as those of notoriously rebellious non-nobles, against the future good behaviour of their communities. They would be held at their own expense, and if they absconded, treated as émigrés. Whenever a public official, acquirer of national goods, soldier, or known supporter of the Revolution was attacked, four hostages were to be deported, their property sequestrated, and each to be fined 5,000 *francs*. Passed when neo-Jacobins once more seemed in the political ascendant, the Law of Hostages would be remembered by nobles as the ultimate act of political proscription against them, making them legally liable for all forms of resistance to republican government.

---

137. Higonnet, *Class, Ideology*, 238; Carré, *Noblesse de France*, 545–6.
138. Text in Stewart, *Documentary Survey*, 746–52.

But it is not clear how far it was ever seriously invoked,[139] and by November, as French armies went on the offensive once more and internal disorder appeared less menacing, repeal was being considered. Almost as alarming as this law for nobles, in July 1799, had been the appointment of Joseph Fouché, one of the most notorious terrorists of the Year II, as police minister. But this too proved a false alarm. Fouché had been protected by Barras since his Jacobin days, and one of his first acts was to close down a neo-Jacobin club. He then turned his attention to the list of émigrés, and began to remove high-profile names. He was soon inundated with requests for further removals. And so the number of returning nobles was once more the talk of Paris when, on 16 October 1799, General Bonaparte himself reappeared in the capital after abandoning his army in Egypt. The very next day he called on Cambacerès, now minister of justice. 'The conversation was quite long', recalled the future consul and imperial arch-chancellor.[140] 'It dwelt essentially on legislation concerning the émigrés.'

* * *

It was the first hint that a decade of tribulation for the French nobility would soon be over. The man of the hour saw, even before his seizure of power, that the routine demonization of nobles since 1797 made no sense. A nobleman himself, he knew better than anyone that it 'was wrong to attack entire classes, when a revolution like ours had done its work among them'.[141] Nobles had never been unanimous in opposing the Revolution, at any stage. Only a minority of the order emigrated; an even smaller proportion were condemned in the Terror for their presumed treachery; and nobles could be found in every revolutionary grouping, from the earliest Jacobins of 1789 to the egalitarian conspirators of 1796. Noblemen had taken the lead in abandoning their own privileges, and in abolishing their very status. Whatever Robespierre (minus his particle) might claim in the Year II, or Fructidorian hotheads in 1797, there was no natural and predestined enmity between those born noble and the revolutionary republic. To suggest this was, in a curious way, to accept that these people

---

139. Morellet, who wrote a tract denouncing the law, says that it was applied in certain frontier regions: *Mémoires*, 420.
140. *Mémoires*, i, 431.   141. Las Cases, *Mémorial de Sainte-Hélène*, i, 451.

did possess the sort of innate qualities which the law of 1790 had tried to abrogate as meaningless prejudice.

On the other hand it is scarcely surprising that most nobles were appalled by a revolution which repudiated and then persecuted them with increasing fervour. Not content with removing their privileges, and the income and property bound up in them, the Revolution took away their status and public identity, the focus of their ancestral loyalty in the monarchy, not to mention the church to which they were bound in so many material as well as spiritual ways. Yet these attacks did not reinforce the solidarity of a group already deeply divided before 1789. They simply created new divisions even among those who never tried to embrace the Revolution—between émigrés and remainers; between 'pures' who left early and various degrees of late-comers; between remainers who stayed quiescent and others who joined internal plots and rebellions; and between those who dreamed, in exile or at home, of a total restoration of the old order and those who accepted that compromises with the work of the Revolution would be necessary. The traumas of failure, defeat, imprisonment, and massacre did nothing to soothe these antagonisms. They merely deepened them with recrimination. So fractured already in 1789 that it was incapable of uniting to defend its most vital interests, over the revolutionary decade the nobility of France became even more helpless in the face of its enemies. Nobles who tried to resist met with repeated and complete failure.

It ought, then, to have been increasingly clear from late 1792 onwards that nobles offered no real threat to the revolutionary republic. And yet over the next two years they were treated with ever-increasing suspicion and severity, and later leftward swings in directorial politics produced ever more extreme gestures of hostility. The less threatening nobles became, the more ferociously they were threatened. The first historian to highlight this paradox[142] attempted to explain it in terms of the ideological ambiguities of a bourgeoisie simultaneously committed to political equality and the defence of private property. For bourgeois politicians to attack the former social elite and blame it for whatever went wrong was a cheap and easy way to foster popular support and establish egalitarian credentials. Nobles were an obvious scapegoat in a revolution which repeatedly failed to develop as expected or desired. Yet they would not have been as easy to blame

---

142. Higonnet, *Class, Ideology and the Rights of Nobles.*

if their self-appointed spokesmen had not been so vocal and active from the beginning in denouncing the Revolution; much less if, between the declaration of Pillnitz and the fiasco of Quiberon, a large segment calling itself alone the nobility had not taken up arms against the land of its birth. On his tramp through Ireland in 1796, the émigré Latocnaye came upon a group of French republican prisoners in County Cork. He found them 'polite enough' and 'with pleasure I perceived that the ferocious enthusiasm which distinguished the partisans of the Revolution at its commencement no longer possessed them. But I noticed among them a sort of blind and unreasoning fury against the émigrés; they accused them of many things of which I had never thought, and reproached them with having borne arms against France.'[143]

Cambacérès offered no details of what General Bonaparte said to him about the émigrés on 17 October 1799; but for the general to raise this of all subjects on his first day back in Paris suggests that he thought it highly important. France was at war with a coalition of powers, governed by nobles, and these regimes gave shelter and support to remnants of the old French nobility with no interest, as things stood, in accepting the government of their native land. A general intent on seizing power for himself had every interest in drawing this sting. To win over the émigrés would be to detach them from France's enemies, not to mention the deposed Bourbons. It would signal the end of persecution to other nobles who had resisted the lure of emigration. Besides, General Bonaparte had a sneaking respect for the émigrés' courage, and he thought that they would prove friends in the future to strong government.[144] The most fervent enemies of the old nobility, on the other hand, the triumphalists of Fructidor, the architects of the Law of Hostages, were viewed by the general as 'anarchists' and defenders of Terror and its legacies. When he took power a few weeks later, he would claim to be saving the republic from their clutches. And by the time he lost that power, fifteen years later, nobles would once more be the honoured instruments of monarchical government.

143. *A Frenchman's Walk*, 92–3.
144. Isser Woloch, *Napoleon and his Collaborators: The Making of a Dictatorship* (New York, 2001), 56–7.

10

Ambiguous Aftermaths

When Napoleon Bonaparte seized control of French government on the second week of November 1799, he proclaimed himself saviour of the republic. Despite his earlier Jacobin reputation, only Jacobins feared him from the start. Even monarchists, from the pretender Louis XVIII downwards, thought he might, like General Monck in England 140 years earlier, prove the instrument of a restoration. French nobles certainly greeted the advent of a fellow *ci-devant* with cautious optimism. They were encouraged by the very first gestures of the interim government. Four days after taking power it brusquely abrogated the Law of Hostages. The forced loan on the rich was also rescinded. Bonaparte in person symbolically released several imprisoned hostages from the Temple prison, declaring that an unjust law had robbed them of their liberty. This gesture towards nobles who had never left the country was followed by one to reassure those who had. On 14 November 1795, a matter of weeks into the Directory, a party of émigrés bound for India under the British flag had been shipwrecked off Calais. They included members of some of the most illustrious noble families—a Montmorency, a Choiseul. They were arrested under the fearsome law of 1792 as bearing arms against France. But two successive military commissions refused to try them, and they had languished in prison ever since. On 9 December 1799, a month after taking power, the consuls who had replaced the Directory released them. Yet the signal was mixed. Although the decree condemned their imprisonment as 'contrary to the law of civilized nations'[1] they were still deported; and when a week later the new consular constitution was promulgated, its 93rd article stated that the laws against émigrés remained in full force, and that their property was 'irrevocably vested in the republic'.[2]

1. John Eldred Howard (ed.), *Letters and Documents of Napoleon*, i, *The Rise to Power* (London, 1961), 317, Decree of 18 Frimaire Year VIII.
2. Ibid., 323.

The loss of confiscated lands, whether of the church or the émigrés, was to remain a fundamental principle of Napoleonic rule. A regime determined to build a bedrock of support among all property owners considered this guarantee essential to reassure acquirers of revolutionary confiscations. But loss of lands did not preclude repurchase by former owners with the means, and to allow this was a positive invitation to accept the legitimacy of the new regime. Émigrés who returned in order to foment royalist rebellion were still shown no mercy: the Count de Frotté was shot in February 1800 when caught stirring up *chouannerie* in Normandy. But two weeks after his execution a decree of 2 March stipulated a wide range of exceptions to the laws against émigrés, and they began to flood back. 'It is an epidemic', lamented a royalist countess who watched most of her society melting away in Hamburg. 'Most of them have no idea why they left and know even less why they are going back.'[3] But many were simply homesick. Faucigny, who had decamped to London after three years of fruitless opposition to reform in the Constituent Assembly, now missed his wife and children he had never seen grow up. If he could be with them in his native Burgundy, he confessed to Roederer, once a fellow deputy and now a confidant of the first consul, 'I swear to you that you will hear no more of me…I confess to you that I have had emigration enough to bury me. For pity's sake, get me out.'[4] It was still necessary for returners to have their names struck from the official emigration lists, and that could strictly only be done by proving, by means of certificates signed by ten citizens, that they had never left the country. But false certificates were easy to buy. Espinchal, among the very first to leave the country in 1789, was able in 1801 to establish that he had been resident continuously in obscure locations since 1792.[5] A 'commission on émigrés', established at the ministry of justice to review claims to return, was notoriously venal and subject to influential pressure. It became a fashionable meeting place for all sorts of 'returned nobility' (*noblesse rentrée*). They could only feel reassured on 3 March by the closure of the emigration list. No further public gestures of reconciliation were made, however, until the security of the new regime had been firmly established by the victory of Marengo in the following June.

Then, having informed Louis XVIII that he had no intention of being the instrument of Bourbon restoration (7 September), the first consul turned his

3. Quoted in Vidalenc, *Emigrés français*, 133.
4. Quoted ibid., 134. For Faucigny in the Constituent Assembly, see above, p. 249.
5. *Journal d'émigration*, 530.

full attention to wooing as many as he could of those who had joined the pretender in exile. At the urging of Fouché, who had ridden out the change of regime as minister of the interior, the consuls decreed on 20 October (28 Vendémiaire, Year IX) that several large categories of émigrés would be abrogated.[6] At a stroke, the numbers on the list were almost halved. Like the majority of the émigrés, most of those benefiting were not nobles, but most of those still listed were. They included anyone who had borne arms against the republic, or who had served the Bourbon princes or their allies and protectors. But many émigré nobles had done none of these things, and the effect among them was to accelerate returns. Returners were merely required to take a new oath of loyalty which included a promise to accept the revolutionary land settlement. Fouché's ministry still kept a watch on better-known figures, and not all behaved with discretion. 'You would find it difficult to imagine,' observed a republican general, 'the insolence of these gentlemen'.[7] Nevertheless the relaxation of rules was so successful in 'rallying' émigrés who did not feel irrevocably committed to the Bourbons that on 25 April 1801 (6 Floréal, Year X), a general amnesty was proclaimed. Reception offices were opened in major ports and frontier towns where returners could take the oath of loyalty and swear to have no links with enemies of the state. The ranks of the latter were in any case diminishing fast. By then the Emperor Francis had been defeated, negotiations with Rome were well under way for restoring Catholic worship in France, and even the British were moving towards the negotiations which would culminate, a year later, in the peace of Amiens. Louis XVIII, so long the focus of émigré loyalty, was a penniless dependant on the shifting whims of the King of Prussia and the Russian Czar. Most émigrés now accepted that royalism had no future—whereas monarchy, and the order and stability it embodied, had virtually been restored in France in the person of the first consul. He had proclaimed in December 1799 that the Revolution was over. The response of the émigrés to his conciliatory policy showed that most of them now believed it.

For his part, Napoleon harboured a grudging respect for military men who had sacrificed everything for a monarch. He was sure he could use them. He knew, too, that his amnesty would destroy any residual royalist solidarity they might have. On 26 April 1802, to the echo of celebrations

6. Vidalenc, *Emigrés français*, 52–3.
7. Quoted in Louis Madelin, *Histoire du Consulat et de l'Empire*, iv, *Le Consulat* (Paris, 1939), 25.

marking the promulgation of the peace of Amiens and the concordat with the Catholic Church, the list of émigrés was reduced to a thousand named individuals, known royalist intransigents. The rest, it was implied, the first consul had no quarrel with. And the Napoleonic regime would be served by many returned noblemen. Talleyrand was the most famous, reappointed foreign minister in December 1799. He had abandoned his bishop's mitre long before emigrating, but other bishops now returned to accept sees under the restored Church. One of them, Archbishop Boisgelin de Cucé, formerly of Aix but now of Tours, preached at the service celebrating the concordat. The way to religious reconciliation had been smoothed by the publication of Chateaubriand's *Génie du Christianisme*, which made the name of an author who had slipped back into France in April 1800. He too agreed to serve the new order—although Napoleon's kidnap and execution of the Bourbon Duke d'Enghien in 1804 stung him into resignation. And the posthumous reputation of the emperor would later be comprehensively refurbished by the writings of another *rallié*. The Marquis de Las Cases, a naval officer from ancient Languedoc nobility, had emigrated early, served under Condé, and returned to France only after the amnesty. He entered imperial service as a Court chamberlain as late as 1809, but he sailed with the defeated emperor to St Helena and recorded his every word and movement over thirteen months to produce, after Napoleon's death, a Bible of Bonapartism in the form of the *Mémorial de Sainte Hélène*.

* * *

In the ample time he had in that distant exile for talk and recollection, the fallen emperor touched on every aspect of his career, policies, and motivation. Among them was the Legion of Honour, which was first mooted within days of the final reduction of the list of émigrés.[8] 'The diversity of orders of chivalry' he told Las Cases,[9] 'and their special rewards sanctified castes, whereas the single decoration of the Legion of Honour, open to all,[10] on the contrary typified *equality*. The one maintained distance among classes, whilst the other was bound to bring on cohesion of citizens ... bringing together all that was most *honourable* in the State.'

8. Tulard, *Napoléon et la noblesse d'empire*, 36.   9. *Mémorial*, i, 571–2.
10. 'avec l'universalité de son application'.

Similar arguments had been heard from Menou in the Constituent Assembly in the days after the abolition of nobility,[11] and during later debates on suppressing orders of chivalry.[12] Unlike the republican revolutionaries of America, successive revolutionary regimes in France had never set their faces unequivocally against public rewards for public service. Nevertheless a number of the first consul's nominees to public office, at every stage of the legislative process in May 1802, denounced the project laid before them. With its cross and red riband (reminiscent of the old order of Saint Louis), its life membership and its hierarchical organization, the Legion seemed like the restoration of an exclusive order of chivalry. It was when, during the discussion at the Council of State, one member called it a collection of playthings (*hochets*),[13] that Napoleon intervened with his famous observation that men were governed through playthings. All the French cared about was honour, he said, and to feed this sentiment they had to have distinctions. But the final vote was narrow, and the same objections surfaced in discussions in the Tribunate.[14] The Legion was denounced as a return to the old regime, and the germ of a new nobility. Votes in the Tribunate had no status, although thirty-eight of the ninety-four tribunes present recorded their opposition. In the Legislative Body, whose only function was to vote, 166 were in favour, but 110 voted against. Defeat was never likely, but the first consul later admitted that perhaps the bill had been brought forward too hastily.

The Legion of Honour was not in itself an attempt to create a new nobility, despite its chivalric trappings. In fact the original oath (later modified) required of new members pledged them to 'combat by all means ... any measure tending towards re-establishing the feudal order, or bringing back titles and qualities which were part of it'.[15] The purpose of the Legion was to recognize an elite of proven service to the state, which in 1802 effectively meant the person of the first consul. This reality was only underlined that same month by the proposal to grant him the consulship

11. See above, p. 239. Appropriately, Menou was made Grand Officer of the Legion of Honour in 1804.
12. See above, p. 257.
13. Literally, 'rattles'. See Tulard, *Napoléon et la noblesse d'empire*, 37–9; Claude Ducourtial-Rey in Tulard, *Dictionnaire Napoléon*, 1055.
14. Tulard, *Napoléon et la noblesse*, 39–42; Irene Collins, *Napoleon and his Parliaments* (London, 1979), 73–4.
15. Jacques Godechot, *Les institutions de la France sous la Révolution et l'Empire* (2nd edn, Paris, 1968), 698.

for life. And apart from their distaste for echoes of defunct feudal chivalry, the fear of many opponents was that the Legion would supplant what they saw as the natural elite of wealth and property which the Revolution had sought to empower, and which they had looked to a successful general to guarantee. These fears at least were groundless. The original consular constitution of 1799 set up what Sieyès, its main architect, privately called 'a nobility of well off (*aisés*) notables' in the form of the 'lists of confidence'. They were made up of a hierarchy of lists of adult male citizens, each a tenth in number of the one below it, from which the consular authorities would choose their collaborators or officials. At the top came a national list of around 6,000 men of note. Under the original constitution each list was freely chosen by the level below it; but when the life consulship was established in 1802, the opportunity was taken to stipulate that at every level only those paying the highest taxes might be chosen. The lists were now to be called electoral colleges, and at departmental level their members had to be chosen among the department's 600 most highly taxed. Once chosen, they sat for life. And although their only function was to nominate short lists of candidates for vacant offices, with the government making the final choice, the electoral colleges integrated the national elite of wealth and property—what Napoleon liked to call the 'masses of granite'—firmly into the structures of his regime quite independently of the Legion of Honour. And given how important nobles remained as landowners and therefore taxpayers, in many districts, they qualified for the electoral colleges in large numbers. Though strictly coincidental, this was a step every bit as important as the amnesty to émigrés in reconciling *ci-devants* to the new order.

A much more exclusive approximation to a new nobility was the Senate. Conceived (again by Sieyès) as a 'conserving' body entrusted with maintaining the spirit and purity of the constitution, its more practical function was to reward the leading 'Brumairians', who had helped to overthrow the Directory, with authority, prestige, and a life interest in the new regime. Most of the original sixty-three senators had been members of successive revolutionary assemblies, and nine had been nobles. In addition to life membership, senators enjoyed substantial salaries from assigned national lands and a crucial (if increasingly confirmatory) role in promulgating fundamental legal and constitutional changes through *senatusconsulta* modelled on the pronouncements of their ancient Roman namesakes. Both the so-called constitutions of the Year X (1802) and the Year XII (1804) which respectively instituted the life consulship and then the empire, were instituted by *senatusconsultum*. Until the role they played in 1814 in the overthrow of the emperor,[16] the senators were politically supine. But they constantly sought further rewards for their complaisance. From the start, some senators called for landed endowments, but the first consul was apprehensive of the independence that this might give them. Only with the constitution of the Year X, which replaced the principle of co-optation to the Senate with direct nomination by the life-consul, did he feel confident enough to establish a number of *sénatoreries*, landed estates attached to seats in the Senate.[17] Not all senators were to enjoy them: only thirty-one were established at the start. They were widely scattered, too, and, made up largely of unsold national lands, they seldom came in one block. Accordingly they were difficult and time-consuming to manage and financially disappointing—far from the semi-feudal power-bases which some thought they might become.

In any case most senators were much more attracted by the idea of heredity, which would turn them into something like a peerage. So long as the consulate lasted, such un-republican thoughts could scarcely be articulated. But when in 1804 it was proposed to make the first consul a hereditary emperor, the question arose of whether other leading figures in the state should not also pass on their status to their children. The Senate, argued Roederer, now a councillor of state, senator since 1802 (and an ennobled magistrate in the Parlement of Metz before 1789), was best placed to guarantee the heredity of the imperial dignity if the dignity of its own members was also hereditary: 'Just as the proprietor is the sole faithful guarantor of property, the hereditary magistrate is the sole assured guarantor of the supreme heredity.'[18] Roederer touted this idea widely during the preparations to proclaim the empire, and it is clear that his senatorial colleagues found it attractive. They gingerly proposed it in an addendum to their address asking Napoleon to take the imperial title. The response was swift and unequivocal. The new monarch declared, in full council of state, that he did not intend to be encumbered with 'an English-style constitution' or an oligarchy like the House of Lords.[19]

On the other hand he recognized at once that a monarch needed a Court, a magnificent stage full of dignitaries and a hierarchy of servitors.

---

16. See below, p. 326. 17. Tulard, *Napoléon et la noblesse*, 28–32.
18. Quoted in Woloch, *Napoleon and his Collaborators*, 115.
19. Louis Madelin, *Histoire du Consulat et de l'Empire*, v, *L'avènement de l'Empire* (Paris, 1939), 112.

He had already been surrounded by a considerable Court as first consul, and it had been located in the former royal palace of the Tuileries. It had evolved its own protocols and ceremonies, and many foreign visitors remarked that it was already more lavish than most royal courts elsewhere.[20] But could there be a Court without a nobility? The question was being openly discussed by the end of 1802, much to the delight of conservative observers. The transition to a hereditary empire intensified the speculation. Archives were now ransacked for ancien regime precedents, a budget was established for the imperial household, and hierarchies of salaried dignitaries officially established. Princely titles were conferred on the new emperor's brothers and sisters, and each was given his or her own household. And just as with the disappearance of the republic, *Monsieur* and *Madame* returned to supplant *Citizen* as standard forms of address, at Court there were once more Highnesses (*Altesse*) and My Lords (*Monseigneur*) to defer to. A majority of the great officials of the imperial Court were in fact nobles of old stock, and those who had known Versailles under Louis XVI were constantly consulted on the niceties of etiquette. Among the most difficult was the question of who qualified to be at Court. Bourbon precedent suggested, apart from office-holders, only those who had been presented to the monarch. But before 1789 only nobles of ancient lineage qualified for this honour.[21] Here Napoleon's respect for courtly traditions reached its limit. There would be no return to the Honours of the Court.[22] Army officers and imperial officials down to the middle ranks would be entitled to presentation, but anybody else could also apply. The final decision rested with the emperor himself.

He made his decisions by three criteria: service, wealth, and—previous nobility. In that order, these were also the principles underpinning the imperial titled hierarchy created in 1808. Cambacerès traced its origins to the *senatusconsultum* of 14 August 1806, which authorized the creation of entailed estates in the male line.[23] The revolutionaries had abolished entails and primogeniture,[24] although the Civil Code promulgated in 1804 had allowed heads of families a certain amount of testamentary freedom. Napoleon approved of partible inheritance as a general principle. 'It consolidates your power,' he told his brother Joseph, 'for by its means

---

20. Philip Mansel, *The Court of France, 1789–1830* (Cambridge, 1988), 48–54.
21. See above, pp. 21–2.   22. See above, p. 11.
23. *Mémoires*, ii, 207.   24. See above, pp. 227–8.

all wealth not in the form of entail disappears, and no great families remain ... That is why I recommend a Civil Code and why I established it.'[25] But he was prepared to promote exceptions wherever they enhanced his power. In 1804 France had acquired an emperor, but not yet an empire more extensive than the former republic and its north Italian sub-state. From 1805, however, Napoleon began to make new conquests, and he saw in them a resource for rewarding his leading collaborators. In 1806 he began to establish entailed 'fiefs', in territories ceded the previous year by the defeated monarchs of Germany. They were to be called duchies, and transmitted by primogeniture. When the next year he made his brother Joseph king of Naples, he instructed him to make Talleyrand and Bernadotte hereditary princes of the former papal enclaves of Benevento and Pontecorvo. Their titles, he explained to the new monarch, 'are titles, and no more; the essential thing is the money that goes with them: 200,000 *livres* a year will have to be set aside for this purpose. I have made it a further condition that each holder of a title shall keep up a house in Paris; for that is the centre of the whole system, and I want to have there 100 fortunes, which have all been built up alongside the throne, and which are the only estates of any size remaining in the country, for they are entailed, whereas all others, under the working of the Civil Code, gradually disappear.'[26]

Seeing that the emperor was determined to create a privileged elite, Cambacérès argued that if new titles were to be accorded, those who had held titles before the Revolution should be allowed to resume theirs, on the grounds that this would make the new creations more prestigious and authentic. But Napoleon was emphatic.[27] 'I do not wish to re-establish what has been destroyed, for good or ill. You know that, according to your advice, I have worked steadily to reorganize the social body on new interests. So do not talk to me about older interests. Let people of quality, noblemen, attach themselves to my dynasty; let them serve me in good faith; I shall give them without difficulty a part in the new institution, and I shall give them not the title they bore, but one which corresponds with the new functions they have performed, and the services they have rendered.'

Despite this rebuff Cambacérès, now arch-chancellor of the empire, was entrusted with drafting the laws which would establish the new elite, and presenting them to the Senate for endorsement by *senatusconsultum*. On

25. J. M. Thompson (ed.), *Letters of Napoleon* (Oxford, 1934), 149, 5 June 1806.
26. Ibid.   27. Cambacérès, *Mémoires*, ii, 208–9.

11 March 1808 he tabled two imperial decrees, one authorizing a hierarchy of titles, the other allowing their holders, in appropriate circumstances, to set up hereditary, entailed estates called *majorats*. At no point, either in the statutes or in Cambacérès's speech, was the word *nobility* used. The 'new order of things' was declared entirely compatible with equality before the law. 'Careers still remain open to the virtues and useful talents,' he proclaimed, 'the advantages ... conferred on proven merit will do no harm to merit still unknown; on the contrary, they will be so many grounds for hope towards which just and praiseworthy emulation will turn.'[28] Nevertheless the experience of centuries had shown that hereditary distinctions entered into the essence of monarchy, and were the source of that sense of honour which was its guiding principle. These were the precepts of 'one of our greatest publicists'.[29] It was not necessary to name Montesquieu, although this was the first official praise he had received for almost two decades. At the same time, however, Cambacérès argued that the new system of imperial titles was the best way to rob old ones of their prestige, 'to tear up the last roots of a tree which the hand of time has felled'.[30] This was his master's voice. 'This scheme', Napoleon had written to him the previous summer, 'is the only means by which the old nobility can be completely rooted out. The titles of Duke, Marquis and Baron are reappearing: coats of arms and liveries are coming into use again. It was easy to foresee that, unless one replaced these old customs by new institutions, they would soon begin all over again.'[31]

And so a new, titled hierarchy was established, ranging from prince via Duke, Count, and Baron down to knight.[32] The highest titles decorated the imperial family and the great officers of state—like Cambacérès himself, Duke of Parma. Ministers and other high functionaries became counts; senior judges and provincial notables were now barons; and all members of the Legion of Honour might call themselves knights. Additionally the emperor reserved the right to bestow any level of title in return for outstanding services. But, apart from prince, these were titles for life. They only became hereditary if the holder could demonstrate a certain level of wealth and petitioned to entail it by means of a *majorat*. Establishing a working framework for these was the object of the second decree

28. Cambacérès, *Mémoires*, ii, footnote 1.
29. Quoted in Tulard, *Napoléon et la noblesse*, 73. See also above, p. 47.
30. Quoted ibid., 74.   31. Thompson, *Letters of Napoleon*, 201, 12 August 1807.
32. There were no marquises, too often a title of literary ridicule before 1789, and no viscounts.

presented on 11 March. Thus a hereditary Duke would require an entailed estate producing an income of at least 200,000 *francs*, a Count 30,000, a Baron 15,000 and a knight, 3,000. The emperor might choose to endow a *majorat*, wholly or in part; but anyone with the requisite wealth was encouraged to apply to a specially established Council for the Seal of Titles for authorization to establish one. Nevertheless they were accorded by special favour and were in no sense automatic. All this reflected Napoleon's conviction that authority, whether social or political, must be underpinned by secure wealth. Coming himself from a large family of poor nobles, he knew how precarious unsecured means could be. 'It is very hard', he reflected on St Helena, 'to see a fool, who inherits a fortune built up over five hundred years, lose it by the throw of a dice or squander it on an actress to the ruin of his family.'[33]

This, then, was in no sense a restoration of the old nobility. It was a titled aristocracy of service, not a hereditary elite. Heredity was an incidental reward rather than a defining characteristic. And entry, though in practice only accessible to men of some financial means, could not be bought. Napoleon despised the 'ridiculous nobility' of 'people who had done nothing... who had acquired nobility as mayors or king's secretaries... By what right should the son of a king's secretary go in front of you? Personally, I have never thought anything of that sort of nobility.' What he admired were 'men who had rendered service to the State'.[34] And yet he was anxious from the start to recruit 'families which had a certain lustre. I looked for them everywhere.'[35] Sieyès had told him, early in the consulate, that he could never regard his power as fully established until he saw 'the Faubourg Saint-Germain in his antechamber'. By this Sieyès meant 'former dukes, former marquises'.[36] The name of the fashionable quarter south of the Seine, now recolonized by old families, was shorthand these days for titled remnants of the Bourbon Court. Sooner than Sieyès had ever thought, Napoleon was able to tempt numbers of such *ci-devants* into his service, but the seduction was slow. The proclamation of titles and *majorats* brought an initial surge of applications, old nobles like Las Cases

33. Paul Fleuriot de l'Angle (ed.), *Général Bertrand: Cahiers de Sainte-Hélène, 1816–17* (Paris, 1951), 237, 27 June 1817.
34. Paul Fleuriot de l'Angle (ed.), *Général Bertrand: Cahiers de Sainte-Hélène, 1818–19* (Paris, 1959), 98–9, 29 Mar. 1818.
35. Ibid.
36. Las Cases, *Mémorial*, ii, 192; Bertrand, *Cahiers, 1818–19*, 202, Nov. 1818.

among them. But many, thought Cambacerès,[37] were only interested in entailing their estates to safeguard the future of a family patrimony. Then in December 1809 no fewer than 137 new posts of chamberlain were created at Court, with the barely concealed purpose of attracting old nobles. Many younger sons applied for them, and were eagerly accepted. But so long as the usurper remained childless and repeatedly ready to risk his life on the battlefield (he was struck by spent ordnance in 1809 at the siege of Ratisbon) the preference and hope of much of the Faubourg Saint-Germain was for a Bourbon restoration. 'The whole nobility was attached to the principle of legitimacy' reminisced Count Molé, a future prime minister too young to remember pre-revolutionary times, 'and it would have been to foreswear themselves to recognize a king who did not hold his crown from his ancestors.'[38] Only when Napoleon divorced Josephine, and in 1810 married the Habsburg princess Marie Louise and immediately had a son, having once more defeated all his continental enemies and extended his realms across much of Europe, did the dreams of the Faubourg begin to fade. If only, they despairingly sighed, he were legitimate …[39]

Napoleon, however, thought he was. Was he not now a great nephew by marriage of Louis XVI?[40] Allied to the oldest ruling dynasty in Europe, he became more determined than ever to reinforce his new titled elite with old blood. More people must be induced, he wrote in June 1810,[41] to apply for hereditary titles in this 'national institution'. 'One of the most appropriate ways of strengthening this institution would be to associate former nobles with it.' He particularly wanted 'historic names, which it is useful to preserve' but 'they must above all have retained some wealth'. And to attract them, 'there must be privileges … The system would be incomplete if no thought was given to this important part.'[42] Here Napoleon showed his appreciation of what *ci-devants* missed most. There could be no question of restoring their pre-revolutionary tax-exemptions, but they could be given coats of arms, and the higher echelons allowed to display them over their portals and on their coaches. Shields and crests would be of a new design, their symbolism reflecting the official function of the holder: but a family with a famous name might be allowed to incorporate its old heraldic devices. A hierarchy of honours, commensurate with titles, was also

37. *Mémoires*, ii, 209; see also Tulard, *Napoléon et la noblesse*, 109–10.
38. Marquise de Noailles (ed.), *Souvenirs de jeunesse de Mathieu Molé* (Paris, 1991), 323.
39. Las Cases, *Mémorial*, ii, 289.
40. Marie-Louise was the great-niece of Marie-Antoinette.
41. Quoted in Tulard, *Napoléon et la noblesse*, 149.   42. Quoted ibid., 151.

introduced: dukes swore fealty between the hands of the emperor himself, other ranks had differential access to the Court. Finally the distinction between ranks was stretched by the stipulation that the title of knight borne by all members of the Legion of Honour could only become hereditary if three successive generations were members—a clear echo of the old principle of gradual nobility.[43]

But in case these inducements were not enough, Napoleon took active steps to dragoon as many as he could of the old nobility into the new. When in 1811 the upper judiciary was reorganized, lists were drawn up of surviving members of the former parlements, with notes on their financial circumstances. As a result a number found themselves back on the bench. The Emperor even considered resurrecting the parlements themselves, only to recognize the idea's daunting complexity.[44] Lists were also drawn up of noblemen of military age who might be sent (as Napoleon himself had been) for officer training; and eligible aristocratic heiresses who ideally had to be prevented from marrying within their families' traditional circles. 'Most old families', wrote the interior minister Savary (Duke de Rovigo) in 1811, 'only look to marry among themselves because they are persuaded that they can revivify and burnish titles which the government does not recognize and which today are nothing more than rewards for those who have rendered numerous services in civil careers. These unions also have the aim on the part of these families of perpetuating in their posterity the spirit of opposition which animates them against the present dynasty; they would think themselves demeaned if they joined families whose fathers have so gloriously shed their blood for their country.'[45]

* * *

In the end just over 700 members of the pre-revolutionary nobility were recruited by Napoleon into his new titled elite. This was around 22 per cent of the grand total of 3,263,[46] and represented perhaps a fortieth or less

43. See above, pp. 11–12. See also Tulard, *Napoléon et la noblesse*, 153–7.
44. Paul Fleuriot de l'Angle (ed.), *Général Bertrand: Cahiers de Sainte-Hélène, janvier 1821–mai 1821* (Paris, 1949), 51, 27 Jan. 1821.
45. Quoted in Tulard, *Napoléon*, 158–9.
46. All these figures from Tulard, *Napoléon*, 93–8, but this total includes only knights of the empire, recognized as a separate category in 1810. It does not include the 30–35,000 members of the Legion of Honour also entitled to call themselves knights.

of the adult male complement of *ci-devants*.[47] The tally was unimpressive from both viewpoints. Napoleon was clearly dissatisfied, and the Faubourg could congratulate itself on the extent to which his blandishments had failed. The reintroduction of heredity was somewhat more successful. Just under half of all imperial title-holders (1,531) established *majorats*.[48] But many new holders scarcely had the time, in the six-year lifetime of the new class, to build up the necessary level of solid wealth, for the vast majority of them were honoured for their military prowess rather than other resources, and they were away on active service for much of the time. They constituted a new sword nobility perhaps, but scarcely more wealthy overall than their pre-revolutionary counterpart. All except a handful of the rest of this imperial aristocracy received their titles as servants of the civil state, ministers and senators, bishops, and councillors of state, down to magistrates, presidents of electoral colleges, and mayors of larger communes. This was further removed from the recreation of another branch of the old nobility, that of the robe: magistrates were a small minority within it. It was more a nobility of the pen, an administrative rather than a judicial elite. But, recruited from families which had had the means to buy them a superior education, most non-military imperial nobles were already well placed to entail a comfortable underpinning for a hereditary title. A further difference from the old nobility was that the imperial elite was not just French. It was intended to be the aristocracy of a multinational empire, and in fact many of those admitted to it after the initial creation of 1808, and the near doubling of its complement in 1810, came from Italy, Germany, and the Netherlands.

In exile, Napoleon reproached himself with not having embraced the old nobility soon enough. Aristocracy was 'the true, the only support of a monarchy ... the State without it is a ship without a tiller, a true balloon in the air. Yet the good thing about aristocracy, its magic, is in its age, in time; and these were the only things that I could not create.'[49] But even before his downfall he recognized that his attempt to fuse old and new into a new service elite was not working. Former revolutionaries, he declared during the retreat from Moscow, in 1812, resented any favour shown to nobles, yet it was in France's interest that he should conciliate holders of illustrious names

---

47. Assuming 28,000 heads of family in 1789; but revolutionary depredations must surely have diminished that number to an unmeasurable extent.
48. Félix Ponteil, *Napoléon 1er et l'organisation autoritaire de la France* (Paris, 1956), 126.
49. Las Cases, *Mémorial*, i, 895.

and still-extensive properties. He had shown them that he did not take them for enemies, and in general they had served him well. It would, however, take time, at least another ten years, before 'all these jealousies' disappeared.[50]

* * *

Time was what Napoleon did not have. His imperial aristocracy only lasted six years, and by the end of 1812 his grip on the elite he had tried to create to underpin his throne was visibly weakening. On the pretext that the emperor had died in Russia, Malet, a former noble promoted to general under the Directory, attempted to seize power in October. The coup collapsed within hours, but Napoleon was appalled that none of the conspirators had thought of proclaiming the succession of his son. Intransigent royalists, encouraged by his quarrel with the Pope which resulted in excommunication, were now setting up shadowy networks to plot a restoration of church and king. Napoleon realized that nobles remained his most inveterate enemies. They were prime targets of the establishment in April 1813 of four regiments of 'Guards of Honour' for the sons of rich families who were also required to fund and equip them. It was in effect a new Law of Hostages, holding the heirs of great names under military discipline as a security for their families' good behaviour.[51] It did nothing to stop the waning of the emperor's authority, and one of these regiments triumphantly escorted the restored Louis XVIII into Paris in May 1814. And although it was military defeat which ultimately brought him down, his abdication was precipitated by his own Senate, convoked by Talleyrand. Created by Napoleon in his days of triumph, his new institutions and the nobles and notables who filled them simply abandoned him at his moment of defeat.

Yet he had no alternative, when he returned from Elba in his hundred-day bid for restoration in 1815, to relying on many of them afresh. Eleven months of rule by the returned Bourbons made men raised up by Napoleon more than ready to welcome him back. Restoration of the legitimate dynasty, on the other hand, had brought old nobles out in their true colours. The last of the émigrés now returned, feeling vindicated. The intransigents

---

50. Jean Hanoteau (ed.), *Mémoires du Général de Caulaincourt, duc de Vicence, Grand Ecuyer de l'Empereur*, 3 vols. (Paris, 1933), ii, 330–1, 340.
51. Tulard, *Napoléon et la noblesse*, 159–60.

of the Faubourg Saint-Germain felt the same, while *ci-devants* who had served the usurper now openly squared their consciences and happily reclaimed their old status. Struck on his return by the popular hostility towards nobles shown both by the peasantry and the people of Lyon, Napoleon took his revenge on the group whom he had tried for so long to amalgamate into his new order. On 13 March 1815, even before reaching Paris, he decreed that all émigrés who had returned with Louis XVIII should leave again at once and their goods be confiscated. He further declared, explicitly invoking the legislation of the Constituent Assembly, that feudal rights, and nobility itself, were abolished. The only nobility he would recognize would be the one he had created himself. And so the petty *ci-devant*, who throughout his years of success and glory had extended a welcoming hand to any others prepared to serve him, turned in the end against them—three months before suffering his final defeat at the hands of noble younger sons like himself, one of an Irish earl, the other a Mecklenburg Baron.[52]

* * *

Even if Napoleon had succeeded in re-establishing himself, it is unlikely that he would have had any more success than the Constituent Assembly in attempting to abolish nobility. His real success was the creation of a new one. For all his later lamentations about lack of time, the six-year-old imperial aristocracy did not disappear with the empire. Nor did other institutions, seen when they had been created as suspiciously aristocratic. The Senate which, under Talleyrand's guidance, invited Louis XVIII to take the throne in 1814, received its reward under the Charter which became France's new constitution by transmutation into a Chamber of Peers. In its first draft of what became the Charter, the Senate declared that 'The former nobility resumes its titles; the new keeps its own by heredity. The Legion of Honour is retained with its prerogatives.'[53] These words reappeared almost integrally two months later in the text of the Charter itself,[54] the first time that Napoleon's titled elite had been officially described as a nobility. Yet the question of heredity remained ambiguous. Imperially

52. Wellington, of course, and Blücher.
53. Quoted in Pierre Rosanvallon, *La monarchie impossible: Les Chartes de 1814 et 1830* (Paris, 1994), 193.
54. Ibid., 257, Arts. 71 and 72.

created senators were still dreaming of it in their draft, but the Charter (Art. 27) reserved to the king the right of nominating either hereditary or life peers. Nor did it state that imperial titles could be inherited. The capital point, however, was that the restored king recognized the titles bestowed by the usurper. A brand new nobility had had its credentials and character confirmed overnight by a legitimate monarch—so much for the patina of time which even Napoleon had thought so essential.

Recognizing this upstart elite was one of the many compromises which Louis XVIII knew he had to make in order to reassure his new subjects. Few of them reassured old nobles who had yearned so long for the king to enjoy his own again. There was to be no challenge to the revolutionary land settlement, any more than under Napoleon. Lands lost were lost for ever. So were feudal dues. The king made a special point of emphasizing this at his second restoration,[55] so disturbingly had the returned Napoleon played on fears aroused by the imprudent pretensions of some nobles in 1814. Civil and fiscal equality were also proclaimed: there would be no return to a world of noble privilege. There was little enough solace, either, in renewed recognition of old titles, since only a small minority of nobles before 1790 had been titled,[56] whilst all Napoleonic nobles were. When Louis XVIII attempted to compensate by bestowing hundreds of courtesy titles during the first Restoration, he was accused of debasing them all. But one debasement practised by his ancestors did not reappear. Venal offices, much less ennobling ones, were not reintroduced. Over half of the noble *cahiers* of 1789 had denounced venal ennoblement;[57] and the Revolution, in abolishing all forms of venality, had coincidentally gratified this wish. The nobility was thus virtually closed to further recruitment even before the status was suppressed. In 1814 Louis XVIII reopened the gates, reserving the right to create nobles as he saw fit.[58] Between then and 1830 he and Charles X created or confirmed 2,143 titles, over a thousand fewer than Napoleon in almost three times as many years.[59] The rate of creation, though uneven (Charles X was more sparing than his brother in the first flush of restoration)[60] was much more comparable with that of

55. Ibid., 266–8, Proclamation of Cambrai, 28 June 1815.
56. See above, p. 10. Also Philippe Du Puy de Clinchamps, *La Noblesse* (Paris, 1959), 84–6.
57. See also above, p. 190.   58. Charter, Art. 71.
59. Alain Texier, *Qu'est-ce que la noblesse?* (Paris, 1988), 126–7.
60. David Higgs, *Nobles in Nineteenth Century France: The Practice of Inegalitarianism* (Baltimore, MD 1987), 13.

ennoblements generated by venality over the previous century.[61] Nor did any of these new titles go to men of no means: like Napoleon, the restored Bourbons recognized that poor nobles were a liability. Yet none of the new titles were simply conferred for a payment, as ennoblement largely had been for three centuries before 1789. This was an ignominy that nobody wished to restore. So much so, that when men whose venally acquired nobility had been incomplete[62] in June 1790 applied to complete it, they were consistently refused.

Just as, therefore, the state ruled over by Louis XVIII bore more resemblance to the empire of Napoleon than to the kingdom of his martyred brother, so the nobility of the restoration was scarcely a resurrection of its pre-revolutionary namesake. If old titles again received legal recognition, and marquisates and viscountcies were once more bestowed, they shared legitimacy with imperial titles. If the Order of the Holy Spirit reappeared, the Legion of Honour remained the iconic national decoration. And if these accretions added new layers to the traditional cascades of disdain within noble ranks, the fact remains that the restored Bourbons succeeded far better than Napoleon in fusing the two hierarchies together.[63] New titles, meanwhile, continued to be conferred on Napoleonic terms: no heredity without a *majorat*. Imperial *majorats*, unless they had lain outside the historic boundaries of France and disappeared with the empire itself, remained valid at law, and any person of title was free to apply to create a new one.[64] From 1817 all peers were required to have a *majorat*, and although in 1819 this requirement was waived when the king needed to create a large new batch of sixty peerages, a *majorat* remained essential for a peerage to be hereditary. Seventy-eight peers instituted *majorats* under the restoration, along with 228 other titled nobles. The total, once again, was higher than the 212 created under the Empire.

Majorats looked very much like the recreation of a certain sort of noble privilege. They were certainly glaring exceptions to the egalitarian spirit of the Civil Code, which gave all children claims on parental property. Whatever its advantages for younger siblings, as Napoleon had

61. Doyle, *Venality*, 164 concludes that 8,334 ennoblements can be presumed to have occurred 1725–1789, i.e. an annualized rate of around 130, compared with 134 per year 1814–1830.
62. See above, p. 11.
63. See Natalie Petiteau, *Elites et mobilités: la noblesse d'Empire au xixᵉ siècle, (1808–1914)* (Paris, 1997).
64. Félix Ponteil, *Les institutions de la France de 1814 à 1870* (Paris, 1966), 96–8.

foreseen,[65] the effect was to break up family fortunes even more relentlessly than the diverse pre-revolutionary inheritance customs.[66] Accordingly many nobles now dreamed of holding their estates together down the generations by some form of primogeniture, as in Great Britain. In the atmosphere of reactionary euphoria following the accession of Charles X, the Villèle ministry in 1826 reintroduced entails (*substitutions*), which had been abolished in 1792.[67] The effect was to allow anyone who could afford the legal fees to create an untitled *majorat*. But a further proposal to introduce automatic primogeniture for all higher taxpayers ran into widespread opposition. The caste of landed gentry which it would have created, monopolizing the electoral franchise by fiscal qualification, would have been quite unlike anything that had existed before, but it was denounced as a return to the privileged society of the old regime. In the Chamber of Peers a string of impeccably aristocratic speakers warned of a counter-revolution aimed at enshrining civic inequality. When they voted it down there were popular celebrations on the streets of Paris. As in 1789 or 1790, great aristocrats showed themselves indifferent or hostile to the interests of lesser nobles. It was perhaps the last triumph of aristocratic populism in French history.[68]

There was nothing ostensibly populist about Villèle's other attempt to pander to noble interests. The Charter had repeated Napoleon's fundamental guarantee that national lands sold would never be restored to their pre-revolutionary owners; but émigrés who had refused to return until the legitimate monarch resumed the throne lobbied constantly for their loyalty to be rewarded with some compensation for their losses. Large stretches of forest land, retained by the state for naval use, were given back to their former owners under Louis XVIII[69]—a process which left acquirers of other émigré lands constantly worried that the legitimacy of their ownership might ultimately be challenged. Villèle hoped to reassure them by granting former owners a once and for all indemnity for their losses. But the so-called Émigrés' Billion (*Milliard des Émigrés*) voted in 1825 satisfied nobody.[70] Many acquirers, and other partisans of the Revolution's achievements, saw no reason to compensate anybody who had lost property

65. See above, p. 319.   66. See above, p. 15.
67. Godechot, *Les institutions*, 437.
68. G. de Bertier de Sauvigny, *La Restauration* (Paris, 1955), 384–5.
69. Forster, 'Survival of the Nobility', 138–9.
70. Gain, *La Restauration et les biens des émigrés*.

for fighting alongside foreign enemies of their native land. The money was found from a range of expedients all more or less costly to the public purse or to government stockholders. An initial attempt to make the latter carry the whole burden was thrown out as penalizing the middle class to benefit the new king's noble cronies. Nor were the beneficiaries themselves much better pleased. The compensation they received seldom measured up to the scale of their losses, and was paid in interest, not capital. The process of claiming was complex and costly. So although the recipients of the largest compensations were almost invariably nobles, they were seldom able to use it to reconstitute the equivalent of what they had lost. Yet by accepting it they acknowledged that the issue was definitively settled, and that their lost lands were gone for ever. The indemnity at first sight looked like a monumental act of reactionary propitiation, a challenge to the legitimacy of revolutionary policies. But its effect was to make the resultant losses permanent.

The restoration of the legitimate dynasty, therefore, brought nothing like the return of nobility as it had once been. Even the Bourbons, lamented one returned émigré, who saw his life as proceeding from one disappointment to another, seemed determined to govern 'like revolutionaries'.[71] All Louis XVIII's favours were 'going only to those who murdered us or his brother'. The accession of Charles X scarcely brought the improvements that they expected, but at least it renewed their hopes. The prince who had first raised the standard of counter-revolution in 1789 by the gesture of emigration seemed increasingly determined as king to resume the struggle. He packed his administration with old nobles,[72] and his preferred prime minister was a Polignac, bearer of a name which evoked all the excesses and abuses of the Court of Versailles under Louis XVI and Marie Antoinette, a prince who had spent most of his adult life in Napoleonic prisons, or abroad. None of these things precipitated the crisis which brought down the throne of Charles X in 1830, but they were part of its essential background. And although noblemen were among the leaders of the movement that produced the July monarchy, its anti-aristocratic thrust was clear. Only with regret were proposals abandoned to include abolition of both old and new nobilities in a revised Charter,[73] and under the new order hereditary

71. Vidalenc, *Emigrés français*, 438: 'régner révolutionnairement'.
72. Nicholas Richardson, *The French Prefectoral Corps, 1814–1830* (Cambridge, 1966), 179.
73. Rosanvallon, *Monarchie impossible*, 108–9 and 309–10, Bérard's draft Charter, 4 August 1830.

peerages were abolished, and further creations of *majorats* suspended.[74] Never again would French governments introduce legislation to protect or promote the interests of any sort of nobility.

The midwife of the Revolution of 1830, the man who bestowed the support of the National Guard on the Duke of Orléans and thrust the tricolour into his hands, was Lafayette. Appropriately, his last effective intervention in public affairs was to argue in October 1831 against hereditary peerages; for nobody had done more, over a long career, to discredit the principle of nobility. This Marquis of old stock had made his name in a republican revolution which spurned hereditary distinctions. He had supported their abolition in his own country in 1790. He had consistently refused honours and distinctions from the man whose military power had secured his release from Austrian prisons in 1797. The restored Bourbons offered him none, and their supporters regarded him as little more than a class traitor who out of egotism had consistently flouted or undermined legitimate authority.

Alexandre de Lameth, with whom Lafayette had vied in June 1790 in denouncing nobility,[75] but who had surrendered to the Austrians with him in August 1792, had also been a vocal opponent of Charles X in the Chamber of Deputies. But he had been happy to serve Napoleon, had accepted an imperial barony, and even a peerage during the Hundred Days. He died in 1829, but was replaced in the Chamber by his elder brother Charles, who proved a close ally of Lafayette in July of the next year. But this man, who had bent the rules to achieve the eagle of the Cincinnati, who had derided nobility and titles as puerilities in 1790,[76] although never elevated by Napoleon, had accepted the style of Count from Louis XVIII, and argued in 1831 for peerages to remain hereditary. There was thus no more sustained solidarity or consistency among the trio of old noblemen who had led the original onslaught on their own order, than among the various elements who had welcomed the restoration of titles and hereditary hierarchies since 1808.

1830 also brought the return to France of an even older and more ferociously determined opponent of nobility, the Revolution's original ideological mentor—Sieyès. As a regicide, he had spent the restoration years in prudent exile in Brussels. But the scourge of the noble order in

---

74. Two entirely new *majorats* were created, however, before the suspension was passed in 1835.
75. See above, p. 234.   76. See above, p. 4.

1789,[77] or of royalist *ci-devants* in 1797,[78] had lost his radical fervour long before he paid for it with fifteen years of ostracism. Senator for life, grand officer of the Legion of Honour from 1804, in 1808 he became an imperial Count and took on a coat of arms.[79] Like Lameth, he accepted a peerage during the Hundred Days. But the amnesty to regicides of 1830 was contested, and nowhere more vigorously than in the Chamber of Peers. It was never likely that King Louis-Philippe, though himself the son of a regicide, would appoint a man like Sieyès to his upper chamber. And so Sieyès's nobility remained entirely Napoleonic, but he had the satisfaction of returning to a France where the pretensions of the class he had made his name by opposing had been finally thwarted.

* * *

All the survivors of the original onslaught against nobility disappeared in the course of the 1830s. Increasingly, those who now struggled to curtail or extend the role of hereditary elites in national life were the sons or even grandsons of men who had clashed over these principles in the 1790s. This was in itself a measure of how far the original project had failed. As Landenberg-Wagenbourg, Ferrières, and innumerable others had predicted in June 1790,[80] nobility could not be abolished, and children would be proud and determined to inherit it. Napoleon was right: the French loved distinctions. There is scarcely any record under the Restoration, naturally enough perhaps under kings who once again saw themselves as the first gentlemen of their realms, of children failing to use, much less renouncing, the nobility of their parents. But these reflexes did not disappear under the royal Duke transformed into a citizen king who succeeded them. Louis-Philippe ennobled nobody, and created few titles. He abolished the commission for the seal of titles which had survived since its creation by Napoleon, and abrogated all laws prescribing penalties for their usurpation. The paradoxical result was that titles were flaunted more than ever, and authentication became once more the major industry that it had been before 1789. Those who regarded themselves as authentic nobles now took additional care to avoid misalliance, and the age-old preference for endogamy was reinforced,

77. See above, pp. 178–180.   78. See above, pp. 304–5.
79. Bastid, *Sieyès et sa pensée*, 279.   80. See above, pp. 5, 237.

particularly in the provinces. Until well on into the century the largest landowners and highest taxpayers in many districts were nobles, and they continued to set the tone for polite behaviour everywhere. No doubt the perceived persistence of an exclusive social hegemony lay behind renewed attacks by the republican revolutionaries of 1848. They abolished the peerage, placed terminal restrictions on *majorats,* outlawed nobility afresh and forbade the public use of titles. But these severities proved as transient as the Second Republic itself; and even before the prince-president turned himself into the Emperor Napoleon III he had abrogated the prohibition of titles. He dreamed of a return to his uncle's titled aristocracy, and in 1858 fines were prescribed for anyone assuming an 'honorific distinction' without authorization. But this decree remained a dead letter, and in the end the emperor created only thirty-nine new titles, twenty-seven fewer than Louis-Philippe.[81] The Third Republic, as seemed only appropriate, created none. But it continued to accord legal standing to titles created in due form by previous regimes, and repeated attempts by radical deputies to prohibit or penalize their use never won legislative support. These were battles which triumphant republicans no longer thought worth fighting.

One reason they thought so was that Legitimism had collapsed. The pre-revolutionary noble monopoly of government, administration, and the armed forces was never restored, but under the last Bourbons noblemen once more dominated every major branch of the state. Among them, the largest group enjoyed pre-revolutionary ancestry, overwhelmingly proud to serve the restored legitimate dynasty. These loyalties were challenged by the 1830 revolution. Faced with an obligatory oath of loyalty to the new order, like military officers in July 1791,[82] many noble officials felt unable to renounce a legitimate monarch. Charles X had abdicated in favour of his grandson, the Duke de Bordeaux, later Count de Chambord, a child whom purists now called Henry V, a legitimate king in exile. Large numbers who did take the oath did so with inner reservations, hoping that he would soon be restored. But anybody, swearing or not, who had too zealous a record in restored Bourbon service was deemed unreliable after 1830, and there were wholesale purges of the administration, the magistracy, and the upper ranks of the forces. Nobles were the main victims, and thereafter formed the core of a Legitimist movement which haunted all successive regimes down to the early 1870s. Yet it was never a serious threat until the aftermath of

81. Texier, *Qu'est-ce que la noblesse?,* 126–7.   82. See above, p. 255.

another Napoleonic defeat. Politically active Legitimists were always a small
if eloquent group in the chambers, and they exercised this role in defiance
of the pretender's clear instructions to boycott public life. Most Legitimist
nobles were more than ready to obey, and the years after 1830 were ones of
'internal emigration', when nobles withdrew to their estates and disdained
to soil their hands in the service of usurper regimes. Legitimism reinforced
their sense of social exclusivity and pious altruism. It left them free to shun
those they considered less pure than themselves, to mingle only with people
of shared beliefs—including belief in their own social and genetic superiority.[83] The downfall of Napoleon III, and the bloody anarchy of the Paris
Commune, presented Legitimists with an unexpected opportunity, and more
nobles were returned in the elections of 1871 than in any since 1824. If Legitimists were still outnumbered by Orleanists, the latter knew that Chambord
had no children, and that a son of Louis-Philippe might be expected one
day to reunite the rival monarchist parties. Dukes dominated the politics of
the mid-1870s, and the throne was probably Chambord's for the asking. But
twice he made acceptance dependent on the abandonment of the tricolour as
the national flag. Most Legitimists no doubt supported this stance, but their
fidelity was never put to the test. Orleanists could no more accept the white
flag than republicans, and Legitimist prospects faded away. As in America,
the triumph of a republic spelt the end for aristocracy in public life.

It coincided, too, with the onset of a Europe-wide agricultural depression
which pulverized the fortunes of landowners.[84] Many nobles, particularly
Napoleonic ones, had now diversified their investments into finance and
industry; but, as elsewhere, land was seen as so integral to a noble lifestyle
that it could not be entirely abandoned even though its value was plum-
meting. Nobility was therefore tied to a shrinking asset; eroding, too, every
generation by the effect of the Civil Code and the disappearance of *majorats*.
The long-term decline in the number of nobles also continued. If Terror
and the vicissitudes of emigration accelerated the fall in numbers already so
well established in 1789,[85] the accretion of families ennobled by Napoleon
or Louis XVIII in the early days of the restoration no doubt slowed the

83. See Higgs, *Nobles in Nineteenth Century France*, 148–50; Theodore Zeldin, *France 1848–1945*,
    2 vols. (Oxford, 1973–77), i, 393–402.
84. Arno J. Mayer, *The Persistence of the Old Regime: Europe to the Great War* (New York, 1981),
    31–4; Dominic Lieven, *The Aristocracy in Europe, 1815–1915* (Basingstoke, 1992), 92–100;
    David Cannadine, *The Decline and Fall of the British Aristocracy* (London, 1990), ch. 3.
85. See above, p. 16.

trend for a time. But after 1830 authentic recruitment virtually came to an end. Nobility was now a caste unable to replace itself unless by a high birth rate—and like the French nation at large in the nineteenth century it proved unable or unwilling to achieve this. The only way into the nobility now was usurpation—always in practice an important channel of recruitment.[86] Its continuing appeal in the nineteenth century is paradoxically attested by repeated efforts to restrict it. Their failure is also eloquent, both of continued demand and perhaps of a certain willingness among established nobles to turn a blind eye. All this, however, makes meaningful calculation of noble numbers extremely problematic.[87] If an estimate of around 60,000 individuals in 1884 seems plausible, then noble numbers had fallen by almost 60 per cent since the eve of the Revolution.[88] Almost a century later, in 1977, the total had fallen to just over 25,000.[89] The French nobility—authentic or usurped, pre- or post-revolutionary—constituted an ever-shrinking proportion of an expanding nation. Since the foundation in 1932 of the *Association d'entr'aide de la noblesse française*, it has policed itself with a genealogical rigour not seen since the days of Chérin.[90] But only half of eligible families have joined the Association and the rules of eligibility are not ones that either Chérin or the commission for the seal of titles would have found satisfactory.[91] 'Internal emigration', however, has long disappeared, and nobles are disproportionately well represented still in the armed forces and (at last) business. Two of the Fifth Republic's six presidents, including its founder, have been noblemen. But it was Valéry Giscard d'Estaing who finally, in 1974,[92] decreed that the Elysée Palace would no longer accord recognition to titles, however well authenticated.

✳ ✳ ✳

So nobility survived the attempts of the French to abolish it. But the virtually undisputed dominance which nobles had enjoyed in public and social life before the Revolution could never be restored, and no recovery of anything resembling it was ever more than partial. A spell had been broken, and it

---

86. See above, p. 10.
87. See the bewildering range of estimates brought together in Higgs, *Nobles in Nineteenth Century France*, 28–9.
88. Antoine Bachelin-Deflorenne, *Etat présent de la noblesse française*, 5th edn, quoted ibid.
89. Texier, *Qu'est-ce que la noblesse?*, 135.   90. See above, p. 10.
91. Texier, *Qu'est-ce que la noblesse?*, 144–7.   92. *The Times*, 28 January 1974.

never worked properly again. And the manner in which it had been broken left permanent scars. Abolition had been swiftly followed by persecution, expropriation, humiliation, and massacre. Few noble families remained entirely untouched by emigration, terror, and imprisonment. None could have felt unthreatened. Stories of these traumas and tribulations became as much part of family traditions in the nineteenth century as older tales of the exploits of illustrious ancestors and the distinguished marriage alliances they had made. How more recent ancestors had borne martyrdom or misfortune offered new grounds for comparison with others, fresh fuel for the cascade of disdain. But most nobles shared a profound distaste for the world which had emerged from what they loved to call 'the revolutionary torment'. Even Alexis de Tocqueville, who thought there was no turning back the democratic tide, who sat as a deputy under the July monarchy, and served the Second Republic as a minister, remained a sentimental Legitimist even as he analysed the fatal and unavoidable weaknesses of the old regime.[93] For generations afterwards, the precariousness of whatever nobles had recovered from the revolutionary wreck was never far from their minds; and indeed every new upheaval brought a resurfacing of anti-noble rhetoric from the political left. For the lesson that egalitarians, democrats, and republicans had learnt was that the power of aristocrats was not invulnerable, and that noble claims to natural authority were as fragile as they were unjustifiable. To protect themselves from these forces, willy-nilly surviving nobles found themselves making common cause with the very middle classes who had driven the onslaught against them in the Revolution. Napoleon's dream of a landed elite of *Notables,* bound together by their commitment to order and property, so far from crumbling with the return of Bourbons beholden to their faithful nobility, became ever more of a reality over the three generations following his downfall. The embrace of the *Notables* protected nobles as people of property. It even defined them, in contrast to the old regime, as payers of more tax rather than less. But inevitably it eroded most of what was distinctive about them beyond their sense of genetic exclusivity.

The fate of the French nobility in the 1790s also sounded a warning to the other nobilities of Europe. There but for the Grace of God went they. If the continent's most glittering and self-assured elite, the role model in so many ways for others, could be overthrown and trampled upon

---

93. In his celebrated *L'Ancien Régime et la Révolution française* (1856). See Hugh Brogan, *Alexis de Tocqueville: Prophet of Democracy in the Age of Revolution* (London, 2006), 25–6.

by lower orders, then perhaps it might happen anywhere. Accordingly nobles everywhere rallied behind their rulers, and the armed forces which fought and ultimately vanquished the French were directed and largely officered by men of aristocratic extraction. Despite the fact that by this time nobles had been extensively reintegrated into the machinery of Napoleon's empire, its defeat was initially seen as vindicating traditional hierarchies, securing wider European society against further levelling. It was a victory forged, as the Duke of Wellington reputedly put it, on the playing fields of Eton. Yet the scale of the struggle had torn old Europe apart, destroyed age-old states and institutions, dissipated long-standing loyalties. It proved no more possible outside France than in it for nobilities to resume their old ways and powers as if nothing had happened. Nothing like the French Revolution's attack on aristocratic power and those who wielded it had ever occurred before in history, and with that horrific example always in memory, 'never again would aristocratic politics be quite so carefree'.[94] By determined efforts, extraordinary adaptability, and some good fortune, hereditary landed elites were able to maintain their grip on the societies and power structures of the monarchies under which they dwelt until far into the century, if not indeed until 1914.[95] But when they were overtaken by the same economic forces that hollowed out the fortunes of French nobles, and when, even in monarchies, political representation was inexorably widened, then anti-noble arguments first legitimized in the revolutions of the previous century achieved new resonance. Denunciations of the British House of Lords heard in 1884 or 1910[96] would not have sounded out of place in revolutionary France. And when, in the twentieth century, Communists, the self-proclaimed heirs of the French revolutionaries, seized power in eastern and central Europe, nobles and their property were always among the first targets for destruction. Arguments, however, were now no longer needed. The iniquity of aristocracy seemed perfectly self-evident.

* * *

Two centuries beforehand, the right and destiny of nobilities to govern had seemed equally self-evident. There appeared to be no conceivable

94. Lieven, *Aristocracy in Europe*, 2.
95. Mayer, *Persistence of the Old Regime, passim.*
96. Cannadine, *Decline and Fall of the British Aristocracy*, 41–3, 49.

alternative. It was true that there had always been debates about how well or badly nobles exercised their hegemony. In the course of them the flaws, abuses, and essential irrationality and injustice of rule by hereditary elites were fully exposed. But discussion had never gone beyond reforming rather than removing a group seemingly established for ever in the nature of things. A world without nobles could be nothing more than a utopian dream.

The American Revolution suggested that more was possible. Aristocratic tendencies within the new republic were rapidly stifled, and Europeans were shown that the authority of nobles was not universally preordained by God or nature, that a viable society could exist without it. Yet even then, in Europe, the legacy of centuries seemed far too deeply rooted to be challenged. The Americans had avoided aristocracy, but they scarcely had one to destroy. In the old continent, noble numbers might be shrinking, and in retrospect the elements of a full-blown anti-noble ideology can be seen coming together. But there was no sign in the 1780s that Europe's aristocratic ascendancies were on the wane. This made the shock of the French Revolution all the greater.

Even when the Revolution began, hardly anybody yet thought that nobility could or should be destroyed. Even after noble political aspirations had emerged as the central issue in public debate during the preparations for the Estates-General, the *cahiers* of 1789 suggest that few of the French harboured such mutinously ambitious thoughts. But the persistent intransigence of most noblemen, often led by the denizens of a discredited Court, rapidly eroded goodwill among commoners. The creation, in the teeth of the second estate's resistance, of a National Assembly wielding sovereign power then unlocked undreamed-of possibilities. Suddenly the whole apparatus and acceptance of noble authority began to crumble, and within three months of the meeting of the Estates-General most of the nobility's privileges and powers had been abolished. A complete anti-aristocratic discourse justifying the onslaught took shape simultaneously. Much of it was built on myths—about history, about the Court, about feudalism, about social mobility—which often only dimly reflected what nobles in general were or had been like. They were lurid, but no less powerful for that. And they posed challenges that noblemen characteristically found themselves quite incapable of uniting to refute or resist. A noble minority, in fact, played a leading part in mounting the attacks. It was the same when, less than a year later, the very quality of nobility and its outward signs were outlawed. The revolutionary experience had shown, in the famous words of Tom Paine, that 'nothing of reform in the political world ought to be held improbable. It is an age of Revolutions, in which everything may be looked for'.[97]

With its power broken, and so easily when the moment came, the rapid eradication of nobility understandably looked unproblematic. It was anything but. The levers of power could be torn from their hands, their social and institutional privileges suppressed, recognition of their titles and outward display withdrawn, but nobles stubbornly clung to their family identities. Those who resisted the Revolution's course—by rebelling, by emigrating, by conspiracy—could be further penalized by loss of their properties or even their lives. Thousands of them suffered, but none surrendered their identity. Nor did ever-suspicious revolutionaries allow them to, as repeated measures taken against *ci-devants* show. The attempt to destroy nobility simply proved that it was indestructible.

But not immutable. Whereas nobles liked to see themselves as bastions of continuity and timeless values, the experience of the French Revolution changed almost everything about them except heredity.[98] The network of privilege had gone for ever. Never again could any entitlement be taken for granted. Never would it prove possible (and not all *ci-devants* even thought it desirable) to re-create the nobility as it had functioned and recruited before 1789. Napoleon would court the old nobility, but merely to give tone to a new one whose legitimacy was recognized after only six years of existence by the restored Bourbons. Nor did rational justifications elaborated in the previous century to demonstrate the utility of nobility any longer seem relevant. To appeal to reason, indeed, seemed like conferring legitimacy on the very forces believed to have brought about the revolutionary catastrophe. Burke had taught nobles everywhere that prejudice and habit were the only safeguards not open to argument. After 1830, the French state and nobles of all sorts progressively disengaged from one another. Most turned their backs on the public service which had been the making of their order under the Bourbons; and they were largely left, for the first time since the middle ages, in control of their own definition. There was no further legitimate recruitment. The attack on French nobles

97. *Rights of Man*, Part I, last page.
98. For a provincial example, see J. C. Brelot, *La Noblesse réinventée: Nobles de Franche-Comté de 1814 à 1870* (Paris, 1992).

launched by the Revolution had destroyed the ground-rules and habits which had governed the order over three centuries of absolute monarchy. And if it failed to destroy nobility itself, it began a process of turning nobles into a shrivelling caste. There was no resisting it. All this dwindling band of martyrs to exclusivism could do, amid ever-advancing equality, democracy, and meritocracy, was to embrace their own inexorable decline and fall with proud stoicism, if not patrician disdain.

Select Bibliography

A truly exhaustive list of sources would unbalance this whole volume. Nobles so dominated every aspect of French and indeed European society over most of the period covered by this book that almost any work of history provides something of value or relevance. The argument also distils the fruits of many years of reading, teaching, and research which would be quite impossible to tabulate. Accordingly this is a select bibliography, listing the main sources of information or interpretation, but making no pretension to comprehensive coverage of the subject. Nor have I thought it worthwhile to list standard authors or classic texts which are readily available in many editions.

I have made little use of unpublished sources. The book is largely about attacks on the principles and practices of nobility in the public sphere, and most sooner or later found their way into print. It seems unlikely, indeed, that the hegemony of nobles could ever have been threatened until hostile opinions could be widely disseminated to a literate reading public.

ARCHIVES AND LIBRARIES

Anderson House Library, Washington, DC
Comte d'Estaing, 'Idées sur l'Association des Cincinnati', 13 July 1784
Archives des Affaires étrangères, Paris
Correspondance politique, Etats-Unis, 27
Bibliothèque Nationale, Paris
MSS fr. 6684, 6685, 'Mes Loisirs' of Siméon-Prosper Hardy
British Library, London
French Revolution Collections: F87–93; FR 127–9, 530; R 45–7

PRINTED PRIMARY SOURCES

Newspapers, Journals, Proceedings
Actes des Apôtres, June–July 1790
Archives Parlementaires de 1787 à 1860: Série I, ed. J. Madival and E. Laurent, 90 vols.
   (Paris, 1879–)

[Bachaumont, Louis Petit de] *Mémoires secrètes pour servir à l'histoire de la république des lettres en France depuis MDCCLXII jusqu'à nos jours*, 36 vols. (London, 1780–9)

La Feuille Villageoise, no. 18, 26 Jan. 1792

La Gazette de Paris, June 1790

Journal de la Société de 1789, vi, 10 July 1790

Recueil de Documents relatifs aux séances des Etats-Généraux, ii, (I), ed. Olga Ilovaïsky, (Paris, 1974)

Réimpression de l'Ancien Moniteur, ed. Léon Gallois, 29 vols. (Paris, 1840–5)

La Révolution française vue par ses journaux, ed. Gérard Walter, (Paris, 1948)

Révolutions de France et de Brabant, Apr.-June 1790

Les Révolutions de Paris, Apr.-June 1790

[Métra] *Correspondance secrète, politique et littéraire*, 17 vols. (London, 1788–9)

La Société des Jacobins. Recueil de documents, ed. F. A. Aulard, 6 vols. (Paris, 1889–97)

Memoirs, Diaries, Letters

The Adams Papers: Diary and Autobiography of John Adams, ed. Lyman H. Butterfield, 4 vols. (Cambridge, MA, 1961–2)

Arthur Young: Travels in France during the Years 1787, 1788, and 1789, ed. Constantia Maxwell, (Cambridge, 1929)

Barnave: Introduction à la Révolution française, ed. Fernand Rude, (Paris, 1960)

Benjamin Constant: Oeuvres, ed. Alfred Roulin, (Paris, 1957)

Benjamin Franklin: Writings, ed. J. A. Leo Lemay, (New York, 1987)

Cambacerès: Mémoires inédits, ed. Laurence Chatel de Brancion, 2 vols. (Paris, 1999)

Campan, Mme, *Mémoires sur la vie de Marie-Antoinette, Reine de France et de Navarre* (Paris and Edinburgh, undated)

Le Comte de Las Cases: Mémorial de Sainte-Hélène, ed. Gérard Walter, 2 vols. (Paris, 1956)

Comte de Saint-Priest. Mémoires, ed. Baron de Barante, 2 vols. (Paris, 1929)

Correspondance entre le Comte de Mirabeau et le Comte de La Marck pendant les années 1789,1790 et 1791, ed. A. de Bacourt, 3 vols. (Paris, 1851)

Correspondance secrète inédite sur Louis XVI, Marie-Antoinette, la cour et la ville de 1777 à 1792, ed. M. de Lescure, 2 vols. (Paris, 1866)

The Correspondence and Public Papers of John Jay, ed. Harry P. Johnson, 4 vols. (New York, 1991)

The Correspondence of Edmund Burke vi, *July 1789–December 1791*, eds. Alfred Cobban and Robert A. Smith (Cambridge, 1967)

Crèvecoeur, Hector St. John, *Letters from an American Farmer*, ed. Susan Manning, (Oxford, 1997)

Da Ponte, Lorenzo, *Memorie* Garanzi edn. (Milan, 1976)

Despatches from Paris, 1784–1790, ed. Oscar Browning, 2 vols. (*Camden Third Series*, xvi and xix, London, 1909–10)

The Despatches of Earl Gower, English Ambassador at Paris from June 1790 to August 1792, ed. Oscar Browning (Cambridge, 1885)

A Diary of the French Revolution by Gouverneur Morris 1752–1816, Minister to France during the Terror, ed. Beatrice Cary Davenport, 2 vols. (London, 1939)

Edward Gibbon: Memoirs of my Life, ed. Georges A. Bonnard (London, 1966)

English Witnesses of the French Revolution, ed. J. M. Thompson (Oxford, 1938)

Etienne Dumont: Souvenirs sur Mirabeau et les deux premières assemblées législatives, ed. J. Bénétruy (Paris, 1951)

Général Bertrand: Cahiers de Saint-Hélène, janvier 1816–1821, ed. Paul Fleuriot de l'Angle, 3 vols. (Paris, 1949–1959)

General Washington's Correspondence concerning the Society of the Cincinnati, ed. Edgar Erskine Hume (Baltimore, MD, 1941)

Jacques-André Creuzé-Latouche: Journal des Etats-Généraux et du début de l'Assemblée Nationale, 18 mai -29 juillet 1789, ed. Jean Marchand (Paris, 1946)

Journal d'Emigration du comte d'Espinchal, ed. Ernest d'Hauterive (Paris, 1912)

Journal de l'Abbé de Véri, ed. Jehan de Witte, 2 vols. (Paris, 1933)

Journal de l'Assemblée des Notables de 1787, ed. Pierre Chevallier (Paris, 1960)

'Journal of the General Meeting of the Cincinnati in 1784', ed. Winthrop Sargent, *Memoirs of the Historical Society of Pennsylvania*, vi (Philadelphia, PA, 1858), 71–5

Lafayette in the Age of Revolution: Selected Letters and Papers, 1776–1790, ed. Stanley J. Idzerda, 5 vols. (Ithaca, NY, 1977–83)

Lameth, Alexandre de, *Histoire de l'Assemblée constituante*, 2 vols. (Paris, 1828)

Latocnaye, Jacques Louis de, *A Frenchman's Walk through Ireland, 1796–7*, ed. John A. Gamble (Belfast, 1984)

Letters and Documents of Napoleon, ed. John Eldred Howard (London, 1961)

The Letters of Lafayette to Washington, ed. Louis Gottschalk (Philadelphia, PA, 1976)

Letters of Napoleon, ed. J. M. Thompson (Oxford, 1934)

Lettres d'André Morellet, eds. Dorothy Medlin, Jean-Claude David, and Paul Leclerc, 3 vols. (Oxford, 1991)

Lettres d' 'Aristocrates': La Révolution racontée par des correspondances privées 1789–1794, ed. Pierre de Vaissière (Paris, 1907)

Madame de Staël: Considérations sur la Révolution française, ed. Jacques Godechot (Paris, 1983)

Malesherbes et son temps: Nouveaux documents inédits, ed. Pierre Grosclaude (Paris, 1964)

Marquis de Bombelles: Journal, ed. G. Clam-Martinic, 4 vols. (Geneva, 1978–)

Marquis de Ferrières:Correspondance inédite, 1789, 1790, 1791, ed. Henri Carré (Paris, 1932)

Memoirs of the Life of Sir Samuel Romilly written by himself, with a selection of his correspondence, edited by his sons, 3 vols. (London, 1840)

Mémoires de Armand Louis de Gontaut Duc de Lauzun, Général Biron, ed. Edmond Pilon (Paris, 1928)

Mémoires de la Baronne d'Oberkirch sur la cour de Louis XVI et la société française avant 1789, ed. Suzanne Burkard (Paris, 1982)

Mémoires de Madame la Duchesse de Tourzel, ed. Jean Chalon (Paris, 1969)

Mémoires de l'Abbé Morellet, ed. Jean-Pierre Gucciardini (Paris, 1988)

Mémoires de la Marquise de La Tour du Pin: Journal d'une femme de cinquante ans (1778–1815), ed. Christian de Liedekerke Beaufort (Paris, 1979)

Mémoires du Comte Alexandre de Tilly, ed. Christian Melchior-Bonnet (Paris, 1986)

Mémoires du Comte Dufort de Cheverny, ed. Robert de Crèvecoeur, 2 vols. (Paris, 1909)

Mémoires du Général de Caulaincourt, duc de Vicence, grand Ecuyer de l'Empereur, ed. Jean Hanoteau, 3 vols. (Paris, 1933)

Mémoires du Marquis de Ferrières, ed. M. F. Barrière, 3 vols. (Paris, 1822)

Mémoires de Weber, frère de lait de Marie-Antoinette, reine de France, ed. M. F. Barrière (Paris, 1885)

Mémoires secrets de J. M. Augeard, ed. Evariste Bavoux (Paris, 1866)

Nicolas Ruault: Gazette d'un Parisien sous la Révolution, ed. Anne Vassal and Christine Rambaud (Paris, 1976)

Œuvres complètes de Chamfort, ed. P. R. Auguis, 5 vols. (Paris, 1825)

Oevres complètes de Saint-Just, ed. Charles Vellay, 2 vols. (Paris, 1908)

Oeuvres de Turgot et documents le concernant, ed. G. Schelle, 5 vols. (Paris, 1913–23)

The Papers of Thomas Jefferson, ed. Julian P. Boyd, 34 vols. (Princeton, NJ, 1953–)

Philip Mazzei: Researches on the United States, ed. Constance D. Sherman (Charlottesville, VA, 1976)

Proschwitz, Gunnar and Proschwitz, Mavis von, *Beaumarchais et* Le Courier de l'Europe: *Documents inédits ou peu connus, Studies on Voltaire and the Eighteenth Century* 273–4 (Oxford, 1990)

Ségur, Comte de, *Mémoires ou souvenirs et anecdotes*, 3 vols. (Paris, 1826)

Souvenirs de jeunesse de Mathieu Molé, ed. Marquise de Noailles (Paris, 1991)

Swinburne, Henry, *The Courts of Europe at the Close of the Last Century*, 2 vols. (London, 1895)

Tableaux de la Révolution française, ed. Adolphe Schmidt, 3 vols. (Leipzig, 1867)

Le Testament de Jean Meslier, ed. Rudolf Charles, 3 vols. (Amsterdam, 1864)

Venise et la Révolution française: Les 470 dépêches des ambassadeurs de Venise au Doge, 1786–1795, eds. Allesandro Fontana, Francesco Furlan, and Georges Saro (Paris, 1997)

Voltaire's Correspondence and Related Documents, Definitive Edition, ed. Theodore Besterman, 50 vols., being vols. 85–135 of *Complete Works of Voltaire* (Geneva, Banbury, and Oxford, 1968–)

The Works of John Adams, ed. Charles Francis Adams, 10 vols. (Boston, MA, 1850–6)

The Writings of Benjamin Franklin, ed. Albert Henry Smyth, 10 vols. (New York, 1907)

The Writings of Theobald Wolfe Tone, eds. T. W. Moody, R. B. MacDowell and C. J. Woods, 3 vols. (Oxford, 1983–2007)

The Writings of Thomas Jefferson, eds. Andrew E. Lipscombe and Albert Ellery Bergh, 20 vols. (Washington, DC, 1903)

The Wynne Diaries, ed. Anne Fremantle, 3 vols. (Oxford, 1935–40)

Tracts and Pamphlets

Arc, Chevalier d', *La Noblesse militaire, ou le patriote françois* (Paris, 1756)

Argens, Marquis d', *Lettres juives, ou correspondance philosophique, historique et critique*, 6 vols. (The Hague, 1738)

Barlow, Joel, *Advice to the Privileged Orders in the Several States of Europe resulting from the Necessity and Propriety of a General Revolution in the Principles of Government*, ed. David Brion Davis (Ithaca, NY, 1958)

Boulainvilliers, Henri de, *Essais sur la Noblesse de France, contenans une dissertation sur son origine et abaissement* (Amsterdam, 1732)

Calonne, Charles Alexandre de, *De l'Etat de la France* (London, 1790)

[Burke, Aedanus] *Considerations on the Society or Order of the Cincinnati* (Charleston, SC, 1783)

[Romilly, Samuel] *Considerations on the Order of Cincinnatus, translated from the French of the Count de Mirabeau* (London, 1785)

Chérin, L. N. H., *Abrégé chronologique d'édits … concernant la Noblesse* (Paris, 1788, reprinted 1974)

Coyer, Gabriel François, *La Noblesse commerçante* (London, 1756)

[Holbach, Paul Thiry, Baron] *Ethocratie ou le gouvernement fondé sur la morale* (Amsterdam, 1776)

De la Croix, M., *Hommage à ma patrie: Considérations sur la noblesse de France* (Paris, 1790)

Dulaure, Jacques-Antoine, *Histoire critique de la noblesse, depuis le commencement de la monarchie, jusqu'à nos jours* (Paris, 1790)

Jaubert, Pierre, *Eloge de la roture* (Paris, 1766)

Mackintosh, James, *Vindiciae Gallicae: Defence of the French Revolution and its English Admirers against the Accusations of the Rt. Honourable Edmund Burke* (London, 1791)

Maugard, Antoine, *Remarques sur la noblesse* (2nd edn, Paris, 1788)

Mercier, Louis Sébastien, *L'An 2440, rêve s'il en fut jamais* (Paris, 1771)

—— *Le Nouveau Paris*, ed. Jean-Claude Bonnet (Paris, 1994)

—— *Tableau de Paris*, ed. Jean-Claude Bonnet, 2 vols. (Paris 1994)

Mirabeau, Comte de, *Considérations sur l'Ordre de Cincinnatus* (London, 1784)

Mirabeau, Marquis de, *L'Ami des Hommes ou traité de la population*, 2 vols. (Hamburg, 1758)

Mounier, Jean-Joseph, *Considérations sur les gouvernemens et principalement sur celui qui convient à la France* (Paris, 1789)

—— *Réflexions politiques sur les circonstances actuelles* (Geneva, undated [1790])

Necker, Jacques, *De l'Administration des Finances*, 3 vols. (Lausanne, 1784)
Price, Richard, *Observations on the Importance of the American Revolution, and the Means of Making It a Benefit to the World* (London, 1785)

SECONDARY SOURCES

Unpublished
Greenlaw, Ralph W., 'The French Nobility on the Eve of the Revolution: A Study of its Aims and Attitudes, 1787–9' (Ph.D. dissertation, Princeton University, 1952)

Works of Reference
Bodinier, Gilbert, *Dictionnaire des officiers de l'armée royale qui ont combattu aux Etats-Unis pendant la Guerre d'Indépendance, 1776–1783* (Vincennes, 1983)
Defauconpret, Benoît, *Les Preuves de Noblesse au xviiie siècle* (Paris, 1999)
Hyslop, Beatrice F., *A Guide to the General Cahiers of 1789* (New York, 1936)
Jonquière, Christian de, *Officiers de Marine aux Cincinnati: Annuaire* (Toulouse, 1988)
Lemay, Edna Hindie (ed.), *Dictionnaire des Constituants, 1789–91*, 2 vols. (Paris, 1991)
Marion, Marcel, *Dictionnaire des institutions de la France aux xviie et xviiie siècles* (Paris, 1923)
Soboul, Albert (ed.), *Dictionnaire Historique de la Révolution française* (Paris, 1989)
Tulard, Jean, *Dictionnaire Napoléon* (Paris, 1989)

Studies and Monographs
Adams, Leonard, *Coyer and the Enlightenment, Studies on Voltaire and the Eighteenth Century*, 123 (Oxford, 1974)
Aldridge, Alfred Owen, *Franklin and his French Contemporaries* (New York, 1938)
Anderson, Gordon K., 'Old Nobles and *Noblesse d'Empire*, 1814–1830: In search of a Conservative Interest in Post-Revolutionary France', *French History*, 8 (1994), 149–166
Anglo, Sydney, *Machiavelli—The First Century: Studies in Enthusiasm, Hostility and Irrelevance* (Oxford, 2006)
Arasse, Daniel, *The Guillotine and the Terror* (London, 1989)
Austin, James T., *The Life of Elbridge Gerry, with Contemporary Letters* (Boston, MA, 1828)
Baczko, Bronislaw, *Comment sortir de la terreur? Thermidor et la Révolution* (Paris, 1989)
Baker, Keith Michael, *Inventing the French Revolution* (Cambridge, 1990)
Bardon, Maurice, *'Don Quichotte' en France, 1605–1815*, 2 vols. (Paris, 1931)
Barton, H. Arnold, *Count Hans Axel von Fersen: Aristocrat in an Age of Revolution* (Boston, MA, 1975)
—— *Scandinavia in the Revolutionary Era, 1760–1815* (Minneapolis, MN, 1986)
Bastid, Paul, *Sieyès et sa pensée* (2nd edn, Paris, 1970)

Bastier, Jean, *La Féodalité au siècle des lumières dans la région de Toulouse (1730–1790)* (Paris, 1975)

Beales, Derek, *Joseph II*, i, *In the Shadow of Maria Theresa, 1741–1780* (Cambridge, 1985)

—— *Mozart and the Habsburgs* (Reading, 1993)

Bertier de Sauvigny, G. de, *La Restauration* (Paris, 1955)

Bien, David. D., 'La reaction aristocratique avant 1789: l'exemple de l'armée', *Annales, E.S.C.*, 29 (1974), 23–48, 505–34

—— 'The Army and the French Enlightenment: Reform, Reaction and Revolution', *Past and Present*, 85 (1979), 68–98

Blackman, Robert H., 'What's in a Name? Possible Names for a Legislative Body and the Birth of National Sovereignty during the French Revolution, 15–16 June 1789', *French History*, 21 (2007), 22–43

Blanning, T. C. W., *The Origins of the French Revolutionary Wars* (London, 1986)

—— *The Culture of Power and the Power of Culture: Old Regime Europe, 1660–1789* (Oxford, 2002)

Blaufarb, Rafe, *The French Army, 1750–1820: Careers, Talent, Merit* (Manchester, 2002)

Blondy, Alain, *L'Ordre de Malte au xviiie siècle: Des dernières splendeurs à la ruine* (Paris, 2002)

Bodinier, Bernard and Teyssier, Eric, *L'Événement le plus important de la Révolution: La vente des biens nationaux* (Paris, 2000)

Bosher, J. F., *French Finances, 1770–1795: From Business to Bureaucracy* (Cambridge, 1970)

—— (ed.) *French Government and Society, 1500–1850: Essays in Memory of Alfred Cobban* (London, 1973)

Bouchary, Jean, *Les compagnies financières à Paris à la fin du xviiie siècle*, 3 vols. (Paris, 1943)

Boyle, Nicholas, *Goethe: The Poet and the Age*, i, *The Poetry of Desire* (Oxford, 1992)

Braunbehrens, Volkmar, *Mozart in Vienna, 1781–1791* (London, 1990)

Bredin, Jean-Denis, *Sieyès, la clé de la Révolution française* (Paris, 1988)

Brelot, Jean-Claude, *La Noblesse réinventée: nobles de Franche-Comté de 1814 à 1870* (Paris, 1992)

Brogan, Hugh, *Alexis de Tocqueville: Prophet of Democracy in the Age of Revolution* (London, 2006)

Callahan, North, *Henry Knox: General Washington's General* (New York, 1958)

Cannadine, David, *The Decline and Fall of the British Aristocracy* (London, 1990)

Carcassonne, Elie, *Montesquieu et le problème de la constitution française au xviiie siècle* (Paris, 1927)

Carpenter, Kirsty and Mansel, Philip (eds.), *The French Emigrés in Europe and the Struggle against the Revolution, 1789–1814* (London, 1999)

Carré, Henri, *La fin des parlements, 1788–90* (Paris, 1912)

—— *La Noblesse de France et l'opinion publique au xviiie siècle* (Paris, 1920)

Castries, Duc de, *Maréchal de Castries, serviteur de trois rois* (Paris, 1979)

Cave, Terence (ed.), *Thomas More's Utopia in Early Modern Europe: Paratexts and Contexts* (Manchester, 2008)

Censer, Jack R., *Prelude to Power: The Parisian Radical Press, 1789–1791* (Baltimore, MD, 1976)

—— *The French Press in the Age of Enlightenment* (London and New York, 1994)

Chaussinand-Nogaret, Guy, *La Noblesse au xviiie siècle: de la féodalité aux lumières* (Paris, 1976)

—— 'Un aspect de la pensée nobiliaire au xviiie siècle: l'antinobilisme', *Revue d'Histoire moderne et contemporaine*, xxix (1982), 443–9

Champion, Edmé, *La France d'après les cahiers de 1789* (Paris, 1897)

Childs, Nick, *A Political Academy in Paris, 1724–1731: The Entresol and its Members. Studies on Voltaire and the Eighteenth Century* 10 (Oxford, 2000)

Church, William F., *Constitutional Thought in Sixteenth Century France* (Cambridge, MA, 1941)

Clapham, J. H., *The Causes of the War of 1792* (Cambridge, 1899)

Collins, Irene, *Napoleon and his Parliaments* (London, 1979)

Conchon, Anne, *Le Péage en France au xviiie siècle: les privilèges à l'épreuve de la réforme* (Paris, 2002)

Contenson, Ludovic de, *La Société des Cincinnati de France et la Guerre d'Amérique, 1778–1783* (Paris, 1934)

Crook, Malcolm, *Toulon in War and Revolution: From the ancien régime to the Restoration, 1750–1820* (Manchester, 1991)

Crow, Thomas E., *Painters and Public Life in Eighteenth Century Paris* (New Haven, CT, and London, 1985)

Crubaugh, Anthony, *Balancing the Scales of Justice: Local Courts and Rural Society in France, 1750–1800* (University Park, PA, 2001)

Cubells, Monique, *Les Horizons de la liberté: naissance de la Révolution en Provence, 1787–1789* (Aix-en-Provence, 1987)

Dakin, Douglas, *Turgot and the Ancien Regime in France* (London, 1939)

Darnton, Robert, *Mesmerism and the End of the Enlightenment in France* (Cambridge, MA, 1968)

—— *The Business of Enlightenment: A Publishing History of the* Encyclopédie, *1775–1800* (Cambridge, MA, 1979)

—— *Edition et sédition: L'univers de la littérature clandestine au xviiie siècle* (Paris, 1991)

—— *The Forbidden Best Sellers of Eighteenth Century France* (London, 1996)

Davies, Wallace Evan, 'The Society of the Cincinnati in New England, 1783–1800', *William and Mary Quarterly*, 3rd series, v (1948), 5–12

Davis, Curtis Carroll, *Revolution's Godchild: The Birth, Death and Regeneration of the Society of the Cincinnati in North Carolina* (Chapel Hill, NC, 1976)

Devyver, André, *Le Sang épuré: les préjugés de race chez les gentilshommes français de l'Ancien Régime (1560–1700)* (Brussels, 1973)

Deyon, Pierre, 'A propos des rapports entre la noblesse française et la monarchie absolue pendant la première moitié du xviie siècle', *Revue Historique*, cccxxi (1964), 341–56

Dommanget, Maurice, *Le Curé Meslier: athée, communiste et révolutionnaire sous Louis XIV* (Paris, 1956)

Doyle, William, *The Parlement of Bordeaux and the End of the Old Regime, 1771–1790* (London, 1974)

—— 'Dupaty (1744–1788): A Career in the Late Enlightenment', *Studies on Voltaire and the Eighteenth Century*, 230 (1985), 1–125

—— *Officers, Nobles, and Revolutionaries* (London, 1995)

—— *Venality: The Sale of Offices in Eighteenth-Century France* (Oxford, 1996)

Dousset, Emile, *Chamfort et son temps* (Clermont-Ferrand, 1974)

Drake, Francis S., *Memorials of the Society of the Cincinnati of Massachusetts* (Boston, MA, 1873)

Duby, Georges, *The Three Orders: Feudal Society Imagined* (Chicago, IL, 1980)

Duindam, Joen, *Vienna and Versailles: The Courts of Europe's Dynastic Rivals, 1550–1780* (Cambridge, 2003)

Dukes, Paul, *Catherine the Great and the Russian Nobility* (Cambridge, 1967)

Dull, Jonathan R., *The French Navy and American Independence: A Study of Arms and Diplomacy, 1774–1787* (Princeton, NJ, 1975)

Dumanowski, Jaroslaw and Figeac, Michel (eds.), *Noblesse française et noblesse polonaise. mémoire, identité, culture. xvie–xxe siècles* (Bordeaux, 2006)

Du Puy de Clinchamps, Philippe, *La Noblesse* (Paris, 1959)

Echeverria, Durand, 'Franklin's Lost Letter on the Cincinnati', *Bulletin de l'Institut français de Washington*, iii (1953), 119–26

—— *Mirage in the West: A History of the French Image of American Society to 1815* (Princeton, NJ, 1957)

—— *The Maupeou Revolution: A Study in the History of Libertarianism, France, 1770–1774* (Baton Rouge, LA, 1985)

Edelstein, Melvin, '*La Feuille Villageoise*, the Revolutionary Press, and the Question of Rural Political Participation', *French Historical Studies*, 7 (1971), 175–203

Edmonds, Bill, *Jacobinism and the Revolt of Lyon, 1789–1793* (Oxford, 1990)

Egret, Jean, *Le Parlement de Grenoble et les affaires publiques dans la deuxième moitié du xviiie siècle*, 2 vols. (Grenoble, 1942)

—— *La Révolution des Notables. Mounier et les Monarchiens, 1789* (Paris, 1950)

—— *La Pré-Révolution française, 1787–1788* (Paris, 1962)

—— *Necker, ministre de Louis XVI* (Paris, 1975)

Ellis, Harold A., *Boulainvilliers and the French Monarchy: Aristocratic Politics in Early Eighteenth Century France* (Ithaca, NY, 1988)

Félix, Joël, *Finances et politique au siècle des lumières: le ministère L'Averdy, 1763–1768* (Paris, 1999)

—— *Louis XVI et Marie-Antoinette. un couple en politique* (Paris, 2006)

Ferrone, Vincenzo, *La Società giusta ed equa: reppublicanesimo e diritti dell'uomo in Gaetano Filangieri* (Rome, 2003)

Fiette, Suzanne, *La Noblesse française des lumières à la belle époque* (Paris, 1997)

Figeac, Michel, *Destins de la noblesse bordelaise (1770–1830)*, 2 vols. (Bordeaux, 1996)

—— *L'Automne des gentilshommes: noblesse d'Aquitaine, noblesse française au siècle des lumières* (Paris, 2002)

Fitzsimmons, Michael P., *The Night the Old Regime Ended: August 4, 1789, and the French Revolution* (University Park, PA, 2003)

Forster, Robert, 'The Survival of the Nobility During the French Revolution', *Past and Present*, 37 (1967), 71–86

Forsyth, Murray, *Reason and Revolution: The Political Thought of the Abbé Sieyès* (Leicester, 1987)

Fox-Genovese, Elizabeth, *The Origins of Physiocracy: Economic Revolution and Social Order in Eighteenth Century France* (Ithaca, NY, 1976)

Fuoc, Renée, *La Réaction thermidorienne à Lyon (1795)* (Lyon, 1957)

Furet, François and Halévi, Ran, *La Monarchie républicaine: La constitution de 1791* (Paris, 1991)

Gain, André, *La Restauration et les biens des émigrés*, 2 vols. (Nancy, 1929)

Galliani, Renato, *Rousseau, le luxe et l'idéologie nobiliaire: etude socio-historique, Studies on Voltaire and the Eighteenth Century* 268 (Oxford, 1989), 268

Garaud, M., *Histoire générale du droit privé français: la révolution et la propriété foncière* (Paris, 1959)

Gardiner, Asa Bird, *The Order of the Cincinnati in France* (Newport, RI, 1905)

Geffroy, A., *Gustav III et la Cour de France*, 2 vols. (2nd edn, Paris, 1867)

Gershoy, Leo, *Bertand Barère: A Reluctant Terrorist* (Princeton, NJ, 1962)

Godechot, Jacques, *Les Institutions de la France sous la Révolution et l'Empire* (2nd edn, Paris, 1968)

—— *The Taking of the Bastille, July 14th 1789* (London, 1970)

—— *The Counter-Revolution: Doctrine and Action, 1789–1804* (1961, English trans., London, 1972)

Goodrich, Amanda, *Debating England's Aristocracy in the 1790s: Pamphlets, Polemics and Political Ideas* (Woodbridge, 2005)

Gossman, Lionel, *Medievalism and the Ideologies of the Enlightenment: The World of La Curne de Sainte-Palaye* (Baltimore, MD, 1968)

Gottschalk, Louis, *Jean-Paul Marat: A Study in Radicalism* (New York, 1927)

—— *Lafayette Joins the American Army* (Chicago, IL, 1937)

—— *Lafayette and the Close of the American Revolution* (Chicago, IL, 1942)

—— *Lafayette between the American and French Revolution (1783–1789)* (Chicago, IL, 1950)

—— and Maddox, Margaret, *Lafayette in the French Revolution: Through the October Days* (Chicago, IL, 1969)

———— *Lafayette in the French Revolution: From the October Days through the Federation* (Chicago, IL, 1973)

Grange, Henri, *Les Idées de Necker* (Paris, 1974)

Greer, Donald, *The Incidence of the Terror during the French Revolution* (Cambridge, MA, 1935)

—— *The Incidence of the Emigration in the French Revolution* (Cambridge, MA, 1951)

Groethuysen, Bernard, *The Bourgeois: Catholicism vs. Capitalism in Eighteenth Century France* (1927; English translation, New York, 1968)

Grosclaude, Pierre, *Malesherbes, témoin et interprètre de son temps* (Paris, 1961)

Gruder, Vivian R., *The Notables and the Nation: The Public Schooling of the French, 1787–88* (Cambridge, MA, 2007)

Habbakuk, H. J., *Marriage, Debt, and the Estate System: English Landownership, 1650–1950* (Oxford, 1994)

Hale, E. E. and Hale, E. E. Jr, *Franklin in France*, 2 vols. (Boston, MA, 1887)

Hampson, Norman, 'The "Recueil des pièces intéressantes pour servir à l'histoire de la Révolution en France" and the Origins of the French Revolution', *Bulletin of the John Rylands Library*, 46, (1964) 385–40

—— *Will and Circumstance: Montesquieu, Rousseau, and the French Revolution* (London, 1983)

Hardman, John, *Louis XVI* (London, 1993)

—— *French Politics, 1774–1789: From the Accession of Louis XVI to the Fall of the Bastille* (London, 1995)

Harris, Robert D., *Necker and the Revolution of 1789* (Lanham, MD, 1986)

Hayden, J. Michael, *France and the Estates-General of 1614* (Cambridge, 1974)

Higgs, David, *Nobles in Nineteenth Century France: The Practice of Inegalitarianism* (Baltimore, MD, 1987)

Higonnet, Patrice, *Class, Ideology, and the Rights of Nobles during the French Revolution* (Oxford, 1981)

Hill, Christopher, *Puritanism and Revolution: Studies in the Interpretation of the English Revolution of the Seventeenth Century* (London, 1958)

Hirsch, Jean-Pierre, *La nuit du 4 août* (Paris, 1978)

Hume, Edgar Erskine, 'Early Opposition to the Cincinnati', *Americana*, xxx (1936), 597–638

Hünemörder, Markus, *The Society of the Cincinnati: Conspiracy and Distrust in Early America* (New York and Oxford, 2006)

Hutt, Maurice, *Chouannerie and Counter-Revolution: Puisaye, the Princes and the British Government in the 1790s*, 2 vols. (Cambridge, 1983)

Israel, Jonathan I., *Radical Enlightenment: Philosophy and the Making of Modernity, 1650–1750* (Oxford, 2001)

Jameson, J. Franklin, *The American Revolution Considered as a Social Movement* (2nd edn, Princeton, NJ, 1967)

Jensen, Merrill, *The Articles of Confederation* (Madison, WI, 1940)

—— *The New Nation: A History of the United States during the Confederation, 1781–1789* (New York, 1950)

Jones, P. M., *The Peasantry in the French Revolution* (Cambridge, 1989)

—— *Reform and Revolution in France: The Politics of Transition, 1774–1791* (Cambridge, 1995)

Jouanna, Arlette, *Le Devoir de révolte: la noblesse française et la gestation de l'Etat moderne, 1559–1661* (Paris, 1989)

Kaplan, Herbert H., *The First Partition of Poland* (New York, 1962)

Kapp, Friedrich, *The Life of Frederick William von Steuben* (New York, 1859)

Keane, John, *Tom Paine: A Political Life* (London, 1995)

Kennett, Lee, *The French Army in the Seven Years' War: A Study in Military Organisation and Administration* (Durham, NC, 1967)

Kessel, Patrick, *La nuit du 4 août 1789* (Paris, 1969)

Kohn, Richard H., 'The Inside History of the Newburgh Conspiracy: America and the *coup d'Etat*', *William and Mary Quarterly*, 3rd series, 27 (1970), 187–220

Kors, Alan Charles, *D'Holbach's Coterie: An Enlightenment in Paris* (Princeton, NJ, 1976)

Kramer, Lloyd, *Lafayette in Two Worlds* (Chapel Hill, NC, 1996)

Kwass, Michael, *Privilege and the Politics of Taxation in Eighteenth Century France* (Cambridge, 2000)

Laugier, Lucien, *Duc d'Aiguillon: commandant en Bretagne, Ministre d'Etat* (Paris, 1984)

Lefebvre, Georges, *The Great Fear of 1789* (Paris, 1932; London trans., 1973)

Lemay, Edna Hindie, *La vie quotidienne des députés aux Etats-Généraux de 1789* (Paris, 1987)

Lenôtre, G., *Le Jardin de Picpus* (Paris, reprinted, 1989)

Léonard, Emile G., *L'Armée et ses problèmes au xviiie siècle* (Paris, 1958)

Lieven, Dominic, *The Aristocracy in Europe, 1815–1915* (Basingstoke, 1992)

Linton, Marisa, *The Politics of Virtue in Enlightenment France* (Basingstoke, 2001)

Loft, Leonore, *Passion, Politics and Philosophie: Rediscovering J.-P. Brissot* (Westport, CT, 2002)

Lough, John, *Paris Theatre Audiences in the Seventeenth and Eighteenth Centuries* (London, 1957)

—— *The* Philosophes *and Post-Revolutionary France* (Oxford, 1982)

Mackrell, J. Q. C., *The Attack on 'Feudalism' in Eighteenth Century France* (London, 1973)

Madariaga, Isabel de, *Russia under Catherine the Great* (London, 1981)

Madelin, Louis, *Histoire du Consulat et de l'Empire*, iv, *Le Consulat*; vi, *L'Avènement de l'Empire* (Paris, 1939)

Main, Jackson Turner, *The Sovereign States, 1775–83* (New York, 1973)

Malone, Dumas, *Jefferson the Virginian* (Boston, MA, 1948)

—— *Jefferson and the Rights of Man* (Boston, MA, 1951)

Mansel, Philip, *Louis XVIII* (London, 1981)

—— *The Court of France, 1789–1830* (Cambridge, 1988)

Margerison, Kenneth W., *Pamphlets and Public Opinion: The Campaign for a Union of Orders in the Early French Revolution* (West Lafayette, IN, 1998)

Markoff, John, *The Abolition of Feudalism: Peasants, Lords and Legislators in the French Revolution* (University Park, PA, 1996)

Marraud, Mathieu, *La Noblesse de Paris au xviiie siècle* (Paris, 2000)

Maury, Fernand, *Etude sur la vie et les oeuvres de Bernardin de Saint-Pierre* (Paris, 1892)

Maxwell, Constantia, *The English Traveller in France, 1698–1815* (London, 1932)

Mayer, Arno J., *The Persistence of the Old Regime: Europe to the Great War* (New York, 1981)

Maza, Sarah, *Private Lives and Public Affairs: The Causes Célèbres of Pre-Revolutionary France* (Berkeley and Los Angeles, CA, 1993)

Meleney, John C., *The Public Life of Aedanus Burke: Revolutionary Republican in Post-Revolutionary South Carolina* (Columbia, SC, 1989)

Meyer, Jean, *La Noblesse bretonne au xviiie siècle*, 2 vols. (Paris, 1972)

Miquel, Pierre, *Les Aristos* (Paris, 2000)

Morris, Richard B., *The Forging of the Union, 1781–1789* (New York, 1987)

Mortier, Roland, *Anacharsis Cloots, ou l'utopie foudroyée* (Paris, 1995)

Murphy, James and Higonnet, Patrice, 'Les députés de la noblesse aux états-généraux de 1789', *Revue d'Histoire moderne et contemporaine*, xx (1973), 230–47

Murray, William J., *The Right-Wing Press in the French Revolution, 1789–92* (Woodbridge, 1986)

Myers, Minor, Jr., *Liberty without Anarchy: A history of the Society of the Cincinnati* (Charlottesville, VA, 1883)

Nicolas, Jean, *La Rébellion française: mouvements populaires et conscience sociale, 1661–1789* (Paris, 2002)

Olsen, Mark, 'A Failure of Enlightened Politics in the French Revolution: The Société de 1789', *French History*, 6 (1992), 303–34

Palmer, J. M., *General von Steuben* (New Haven, CT, 1937)

Palmer, R. R. *The Age of the Democratic Revolution: A Political History of Europe and America, 1760–1800*, i, *The Challenge* (Princeton, NJ, 1959)

Pelenski, Jaroslaw (ed.), *The American and European Revolutions, 1776–1848* (Iowa City, IA, 1980)

Petiteau, Natalie, *Elites et mobilités: la Noblesse d'Empire au xixe siècle (1808–1914)* (Paris, 1997)

Pole, J. R., *Political Representation in England and the Origins of the American Republic* (London, 1966)

Ponteil, Félix, *Napoléon 1er et l'organisation autoritaire de la France* (Paris, 1956)

—— *Les Institutions de la France de 1814 à 1870* (Paris, 1966)

Popkin, Jeremy D., *News and Politics in the Age of Revolution: Jean Luzac's* Gazette de Leyde (Ithaca, NY, 1989)

Price, Munro, *The Fall of the French Monarchy: Louis XVI, Marie-Antoinette, and the Baron de Breteuil* (London, 2002)

—— *The Perilous Crown: France between Revolutions, 1814–1848* (London, 2007)

Pritchard, James, *Louis XV's Navy, 1748–1752: A Study in Organisation and Administration, 1748–1762* (Kingston and Montreal, 1987)

Rahe, Paul A., *Republics Ancient and Modern* (Chapel Hill, NC, 1994)

Réau, Louis, *L'Europe française au siècle des lumières* (Paris, 1951)

Reinhard, Marcel, 'Elite et noblesse dans la seconde moitié du xviiie siècle', *Revue d'histoire moderne et contemporaine*, iii (1956), 5–38

Rials, Stéphane, *La Déclaration des Droits de l'Homme et du Citoyen* (Paris, 1989)

Richard, Carl J., *The Founders and the Classics: Greece, Rome, and the American Enlightenment* (Cambridge, MA, 1994)

Richard, Guy, *Noblesse d'affaires au xviiie siècle* (Paris, 1974)

Richardson, Nicholas, *The French Prefectoral Corps, 1814–1830* (Cambridge, 1966)

Roberts, Michael, *Essays in Swedish History* (London, 1967)

Roberts, Warren, *Morality and Social Class in Eighteenth Century French Literature and Painting* (Toronto, 1974)

Root, Hilton L, *Peasant and King in Burgundy: Agrarian Foundations of Absolutism* (Berkeley, CA, 1987)

Rosanvallon, Pierre, *La Monarchie impossible: les Chartes de 1814 et 1830* (Paris, 1994)

Rosenthal, Louis, *America and France: The Influence of the United States in France in the xviiith Century* (New York, 1882)

Schalk, Ellery, *From Valor to Pedigree: Ideas of Nobility in France in the Sixteenth and Seventeenth Centuries* (Princeton, NJ, 1986)

Schama, Simon, *Patriots and Liberators: Revolution in the Netherlands, 1780–1813* (London and New York, 1977)

Shapiro, Gilbert and Markoff, John, *Revolutionary Demands: A Content Analysis of the Cahiers de Doléances of 1789* (Stanford, CA, 1998)

Schwarz, Robert M. and Schneider, Robert A., *Tocqueville and Beyond: Essays on the Old Regime in Honor of David D. Bien* (Newark, DE, 2003)

Scott, Samuel F., *The Response of the French Royal Army to the French Revolution: The Role and Development of the Line Army, 1789–1793* (Oxford, 1978)

Scott, William, *Terror and Repression in Revolutionary Marseilles* (London, 1973)

Serna, Pierre, *Antonelle, aristocrate révolutionnaire, 1747–1817* (Paris, 1997)

Sewell, William H., *A Rhetoric of Bourgeois Revolution: The Abbé Sieyès and* What is the Third Estate? (Durham, NC, 1994)

Shapiro, Barry M., *Revolutionary Justice in Paris, 1789–90* (Cambridge, 1993)

Shovlin, John, 'Towards a Reinterpretation of Revolutionary Antinobilism: The Political Economy of Honor in the Old Regime', *Journal of Modern History*, 72, (2000), 33–6

—— *The Political Economy of Virtue: Luxury, Patriotism, and the Origins of the French Revolution* (Ithaca, NY, 2006)

Skinner, Quentin, *The Foundations of Modern Political Thought*, 2 vols. (Cambridge, 1978)

Smith, Jay M., *The Culture of Merit: Nobility, Royal Service, and the Making of Absolute Monarchy in France, 1600–1789* (Ann Arbor, MI, 1996)

—— 'Social Categories, the Language of Patriotism, and the Origins of the French Revolution: The Debate Over *noblesse commerçante*', *Journal of Modern History*, 72 (2000), 339–74

—— *Nobility Reimagined: The Patriotic Nation in Eighteenth Century France* (Ithaca, NY, 2005)

—— (ed.) *The French Nobility in the Eighteenth Century: Reassessments and New Approaches* (University Park, PA, 2006)

Soboul, Albert, *Problèmes paysans de la Révolution* (Paris, 1956)

Solnon, Jean-François, *La Cour de France* (Paris, 1987)

Stone, Bailey, *The Parlement of Paris, 1774–1789* (Chapel Hill, NC, 1981)

Sutherland, D. M. G. (ed.), *Violence and the French Revolution (Historical Reflections/Réflexions historiques)*, 29, no. 3 (2003), 289–582

Tackett, Timothy, *Becoming a Revolutionary: The Deputies of the French National Assembly and the Emergence of a Revolutionary Culture (1789–1790)* (Princeton, NJ, 1996)

—— *When the King took Flight* (Cambridge, MA, 2003)

Taylor, George V., 'Revolutionary and Nonrevolutionary Content in the Cahiers of 1789: An Interim Report', *French Historical Studies*, viii (1972), 479–502

Texier, Alain, *Qu'est-ce que la noblesse?* (Paris, 1988)

Tillyard, Stella, *Citizen Lord: Edward Fitzgerald, 1763–1798* (London, 1997)

Touzery, Mireille, *L'Invention de l'impôt sur le revenu: la Taille tarifée 1715–1789* (Paris, 1994)

Tulard, Jean, *Napoléon et la noblesse d'Empire* (3rd edn, Paris, 2001)

Van Doren, Carl, *Benjamin Franklin* (New York, 1938)

Vidalenc, Jean, *Les Emigrés français, 1789–1825* (Caen, 1963)

Walmich, Sophie, *L'impossible Citoyen: l'étranger dans le discours de la Révolution française* (Paris, 1997)

Westrich, Sal Alexander, *The Ormée of Bordeaux: A Revolution during the Fronde* (Baltimore, MD, 1972)

Whatmore, Richard, *Republicanism and the French Revolution: An Intellectual History of Jean-Baptiste Say's Political Economy* (Oxford, 2000)

Wick, Daniel, *A Conspiracy of Well-Intentioned Men: The Society of Thirty and the French Revolution* (New York, 1987)

Wills, Garry, *Cincinnatus: George Washington and the Enlightenment* (Garden City, NY, 1984)

Woloch, Isser, *Napoleon and his Collaborators: The Making of a Dictatorship* (New York, 2001)

Wood, Gordon S., *The Creation of the American Republic, 1776–1783* (Chapel Hill, NC, 1969)

—— *The Radicalism of the American Revolution* (New York, 1991)

Wright, Johnson Kent, *A Classical Republican in Eighteenth Century France: The Political Thought of Mably* (Stanford, CA, 1997)

Zeldin, Theodore, *France, 1848–1945*, 2 vols. (Oxford, 1973–77)

Index